The End Th

Millennialism and Society
Series Editor: Brenda E. Brasher
Senior Advisor: Frederic J. Baumgartner (Virginia Polytechnic Institute)

Millennialism and Society had its genesis in the 1996–2002 annual meetings of the Center for Millennial Studies at Boston University. Those meetings brought together an international array of scholars to discuss the texts and traditions of religious revelation or apocalypses concerning the end of the world as we know it, whether in a tumultuous final judgment or a utopian eternal paradise. As apocalyptic texts advance an argument that massive change on earth is possible, even desirable, because it is part of a divine plan, the scholars' goal was to attain a richer, more nuanced understanding of our most ancient ideas of social change, including their influence on societies today.

The series consists of three volumes. Taken together, *Millennialism and Society* as a series represents a sustained effort on the part of this scholarly network to advance our understanding of what is a frequently unruly element of our cultural heritage.

Other volumes in the series:

War in Heaven/Heaven on Earth:
Theories of the Apocalyptic
Edited by: Glen S. McGhee and Stephen D. O'Leary

Gender and Apocalyptic Desire
Edited by: Brenda E. Brasher and Lee Quinby

The End That Does

Art, Science and Millennial Accomplishment

Edited by
Cathy Gutierrez and Hillel Schwartz

Senior Advisors
Jeffrey Stanley and Matt K. Matsuda

Millennialism and Society, Volume 3

LONDON   OAKVILLE

Published by

Equinox Publishing Ltd

UK: Unit 6, The Village, 101 Amies St., London SW11 2JW

US: 28 Main Street, Oakville, CT 06779

www.equinoxpub.com

First published 2006 by Equinox Publishing Ltd.

British Library Cataloguing-in-Publication Data
A catalogue record for this book is available from the British Library.

Library of Congress Cataloging-in-Publication Data
The end that does : art, science, and millennial accomplishment / edited
   by Cathy Gutierrez and Hillel Schwartz.
      p. cm. -- (Millennialism and society ; v. 3)
   Includes bibliographical references and index.
   ISBN 1-904768-89-X (hb) -- ISBN 1-904768-90-3 (pb)
   1. Millennialism--Congresses. 2. Religion and culture--Congresses.
   I. Gutierrez, Cathy, 1967-   . II. Schwartz, Hillel, 1948-   . III. Series.
   BL503.2.E53 2005
   202'.3--dc22
                       2005015985

ISBN 1-90476-889-X (hardback)
        1-90476-890-3 (paperback)

Typeset by CA Typesetting, www.sheffieldtypesetting.com
Printed and bound by Lightning Source UK Ltd., Milton Keynes
and Lightning Source Inc., La Vergne, TN

Con/tense

Series Foreword

The *Millennialism and Society* series had its genesis in the 1996–2002 Annual meetings of the Center for Millennial Studies at Boston University. Each year, those meetings brought together an international array of scholars to discuss the texts and traditions of religious revelation or apocalypses concerning the end of the world as we know it, whether in a tumultuous final judgment or a utopian eternal paradise. As apocalyptic texts advance an argument that massive change on earth is possible and even desirable, the over-arching scholarly goal of those gatherings was to attain a richer, more nuanced understanding of what some argue are the most ancient ideas of social change.

The series consists of three volumes. *Gender and Apocalyptic Desire* focuses on the significance of sex and sexuality for the apocalyptic traditions, and on gender as a critical framing element within apocalyptic narratives as well as for how apocalyptic narratives have been appropriated. *The End That Does* recounts the myriad cultural contributions that apocalyptic concepts and energies have spawned, from atomic films to rap. The other volume, *War in Heaven/Heaven on Earth*, critically evaluates the variety of theories employed to analyze the persistence of apocalyptic beliefs and activity into the present day. Taken together, *Millennialism and Society* represents a sustained effort on the part of an established scholarly network to advance our understanding of what frequently has been a rather unruly element in our cultural heritage.

None of this would have been possible without the contributions and support of numerous key people and organizations. Richard Landes along with Stephen O'Leary founded the Center. The two provided intellectual depth and rigour to each gathering that challenged the scholars who came to push their critical abilities to maximum effectiveness. Lilly Endowment provided the funds that underwrote most of the costs of each meeting. Boston University provided space, administrative support, and a professional and student population that served as a willing and engaging audience for the various sessions.

The editors for each volume put in long, hard hours, for little reward. Without them, the series would not have made it into the public domain. Thanks go to Glen McGhee, Stephen O'Leary, Hillel Schwartz, Cathy Gutierrez, and Lee Quinby for months of patient work in assembling these volumes. Finally, thanks go to Janet Joyce and the publishing team at Equinox Publishing Limited for their belief in and support of the series.

The *Millennialism and Society* series is dedicated to Richard Landes, the founder of our intellectual feast.

Brenda E. Brasher
Editor in Chief
University of Aberdeen
Scotland

List of Contributors:

In Reverse Alphabetical Order, as Befits an End That Does

Working in cultural history, history of religions, and the history of science and technology, **Hillel Schwartz** is a poet, historian, and dancer. He has published six books, taught in six university departments, and was founding director of the curriculum for Sixth College (Culture, Art, Technology) at UC San Diego. He has consulted on public arts, sustainability, and interfaith projects in Europe, North America, South Korea, and South Africa.

Hai Ren teaches in the Department of Popular Culture at Bowling Green State University. His research focuses on everyday life and politics. He is the guest editor of 'Neo-liberal Governmentality: Technologies of the Self & Governmental Conduct' (a special issue of the on-line journal *Rhizomes*). He is working on his first book, *The Countdown of Time*, and has begun a second book tentatively entitled *Everyday Life Under Neo-Liberalism: Themed Environments, Consumption, and the Middle Class*.

Fred Nadis writes about American cultural history, the popular arts, and science and technology. His most recent book is *Wonder Shows: Performing Science, Magic and Religion in America* (Rutgers, 2005). In addition to scholarly work, he has published fiction and humor in journals such as the *Atlantic Monthly*. He is a lecturer in the Department of History at California State University, Channel Islands.

Geoffrey McVey teaches religious studies at Mount Royal College, Calgary. His research and writing focus on Renaissance magic, the works of the Italian philosopher Giordano Bruno, and the theological problems surrounding imagination in early modern texts. In his spare time, he writes, and has been known to build small worlds of his own – complete with imaginary apocalypses.

Trained in theology, European history, and the history of science, **Steven Matthews** is an assistant professor of history at the University of Minnesota, Duluth. His research focuses on the interaction of Christian theology and science with a specific focus on Francis Bacon and those in Bacon's literary circle.

Poet and actor **Thomas MacKay** was a one-time doctoral student in the study of religion at the University of Toronto. His poetry has appeared in such venues as *Acta Victoriana*, *The Hart House Review*, and *The Apostle's Bar*. He has also presented papers on film, religion, and sacrifice, including one on a sacrificial filmic tableau in 'The Sweet Hereafter' and another on the gooey, wound-driven ecstasies in David Cronenberg's film, 'Crash'.

Cathy Gutierrez is an Associate Professor of Religion at Sweet Briar College in Virginia, USA. She works broadly in the history of religions and specializes in nineteenth-century America. She primarily explores millennialism and esotericism and has published on the Spiritualists, Freemasons, and the Free Love movement as well as the Theosphists.

Professor at the University of East London, **Patrick Fuery** has published nine books in the fields of film studies, philosophy, psychoanalysis, and cultural theory. His most recent volumes include *Madness and Cinema* and *New Developments in Film Theory* (both from Palgrave). He is currently at work on a study of psychoanalysis and Kantian philosophy, and another on cinema and the body.

Kelli Fuery is a lecturer in Contemporary and Post 1960s Visual Cultures at Birbeck College, University of London. She is the co-author of *Visual Cultures and Critical Theory* (Hodder Press) and is currently completing a book on *New Media, Digitality, and the Image* (Palgrave). Her research interests also include psychoanalysis and art. As a practicing photographer, she is working on a collection of images on the Digital Sublime.

A writer of science fiction and fantasy, **Tom Doyle** has published more academic papers on Christian apocalyptic fiction and science fiction in the *Journal of Millennial Studies*, and he has given presentations on apocalyptic fiction at several international conferences. He lives in Washington, DC. See also http://ourworld.compuserve.com/homepages/tmdoyle2, or e-mail him at tmdoyle2@yahoo.com.

In addition to her dissertation, 'Rehearsing the End: Millennium 2000, World's Fairs, and the Future Tense', **Michelle Dent**'s recent work examines utopianism in dance and urban planning. Publications include 'Checking the Time: Bill T. Jones's American Utopia'; 'Staging Disaster: Reporting

Live (sort of) from Seattle', in *The Drama Review*, and 'The Fallen Body: Butoh and the Crisis of Meaning in Sankai Juku's "Jomon Sho" ', in *Women and Performance*. She teaches undergraduates at New York University.

Eric Casey is an Assistant Professor of Classical Studies at Sweet Briar College in Virginia. He has published on the voice of the dead in Greek epitaphs as well as on ancient mystery cults and their influence on modern secret societies. His current research projects include Ovidian intertextuality in the *Metamorphoses* and a cultural history of the Greek philosophical schools.

A medieval art historian, **Amelia Carr** teaches a course on The End of the World at Allegheny College, where she is Associate Professor of Art History. Her current project is a performance history of liturgical drama at Klosterneuburg with musicologist Michael Norton. Her publications include studies of Klosterneuburg's patrons Saint Leopold and Elisabeth of Austria. A devotee of SheRa, Princess of Power, she is also collecting materials for a study on feminine cultural authority entitled 'The Sword and the Comb'.

Charles Cameron is the designer of the HipBone analytic tools and games, www.beadgaming.com. He was Senior Analyst with The Arlington Institute and Principal Researcher with the Center for Millennial Studies during the run-up to Y2K. He continues to monitor religious violence globally, believing religious devotion to be among the most powerful and underrated of human drives. Another special interest is conflict resolution, particularly in the Middle East.

Will

Thomas MacKay

God bless the fat kids
and the wide vibrating way they make things
things, all meaty and rosy. Them and the wading pool.
Them and the fat-kid parents.

God bless that woman with the tinted eyewear
who brings herself out of the summer shrug
to scratch the neck of some dog, to, oh,
read and let her words range
as if the sky were storied and strange.
Her and her book-chapter tan.
Bless.

And so I meet this guy, God bless him,
God bless his stoop, bent like the ash end,
left to smoke; he's got a cigarette from me
and he's out with a story.
His eyes have a flipping-page glare, but soon,
his words stick and mess like cut paper, piles of corners;
what starts with a faraway, lakeside place, untangled by sidewalks,
becomes a room of
related anger. She's a whore. She got abused.
She. He. And, as some story
weeps and shudders on a summer's day,
he's at the tree branches now, tearing down leaves
as if gestures can stagger and fall.

We're history, we're place, and we're
imperfect in either case.
I don't know
what will encircle my world to bless it, or give it grace.
You see apocalypse sometimes as the last breakdown,
but maybe it's a glue, some hurried move to pick up the fragments,
slip them back into the mirror-frame,
that make a shining wholing scheme of the true.

In/tensions

Cathy Gutierrez

This third and final volume of the *Millennialism and Society* series brings us not to the end but to a new beginning. While the study of millennialism has traditionally taken place within the confines of departments of religion, anthropology, sociology, or history, the editors of this series hope to widen the parameters of discussion beyond departmental entrenchments and beyond the academy itself. The theoretical structures and sociocultural responses of millennialism exceed the confines of any strict definition even as they expand across time and space as a means toward ordering the cosmos and reassuring believers in the essential trustworthiness of an unfolding history.

Millennialism has conventionally been understood as a sense-making position: people focus on the approaching end of time as a means to make sense of their immediate situation. Time itself may be linear or cyclical or helical, but the nearness of its end, however plotted, convinces believers that meaning must be created in relation to endings, a situation that infuses the present with a sense of urgency. Millennialism is unstuck in time, and despite its semantic similarities to millennial years such as 1000 or 2000, its uses exceed calendrical events. Unmoored from specific dates, millennialism appears in history whenever an approaching end is the governing idea behind a social, intellectual, or artistic movement.

Millennialism is most narrowly defined by its strictest sense in Christian religious texts and imagery as the imminent return of Jesus and his reign on earth for a period of 1000 years. The advent of Biblical literalism that came with Reformation insistence upon direct access to Scripture mandated that Protestants in particular attend to the canonical apocalypses in the books of Daniel and Revelation. The most narrow use of millennialism, then, would be the interpretative schema used by Christians as they anticipate the end of time and the return of their savior – with Daniel, an historical chronology of fallen empires and prophetic intervals, and with St John, a more particular indexical sequence following the breaking open of each of seven seals. With the infinite flexibility of religious symbolism, Daniel's chronology and John's seals have unslipped their moorings in antiquity and have been variously applied to many subsequent times of perceived crisis; the end of Charlemagne's line, the fall of the Ottoman

Empire, constellations of war and epidemic, the creation of the state of Israel, and innumerable astronomical anomalies have all been 'read' as signs of the end times.

By taking potentially devastating events and plugging them into a plan for history, believers render time itself trustworthy, defusing the random or the absurd by calming it within an always-already chaos always-already anticipated. Working actively in history to lift believers beyond the griefs of the historical, God assures that any suffering is at once necessary and redemptive. Because of this, believers may adopt the counter-intuitive posture of not only expecting the end of time but actively soliciting it. No futile or permanent state to be endured, suffering is rather a warrantable stage in the unfolding of the divine plan. Believers will not only be vindicated, they will often be on hand to watch as their oppressors are punished in the final cosmic drama. The ultimate justice provides the ultimate meaning, as the end of time inaugurates perfection.

These deeply imbedded structures of reading history, however, expand past the strict definition of millennialism and recur outside of Christian or Indo-European worlds, often stripped of explicitly religious content and context, as in preparations for a nuclear apocalypse, worldwide economic collapse, global climate change, or systemic technological disasters like Y2K. Both apocalyptic and utopian movements may be millennial; most at least are shot through with the language of millennialism. Even utopian visions that rely on structures defiantly non-theological – Marx's economic utopia, for instance – use familiar millennial frameworks to make creative sense of history. The end of the world as it is portrayed in movies or novels often arouses and exploits a sense of apocalyptic urgency without any of the sense-making components essential to religion.

This particular volume focuses on the creative and generative acts that millennialism inspires. While much excellent scholarly work has been done on social transformations that millennial movements often engender, no other joint work to our knowledge specifically addresses the culturally productive aspects of millennialism. By highlighting the end of time as immanent or imminent, the individual refocuses both history and her place in it toward new and potentially productive arenas. Whether as the unwilling subject of history or as a catalyst bringing about its end, the believer reorients herself to ideas of hope, justice, and time itself. Time is reordered and space is transformed at the threshold of the millennial moment – the future is pure possibility and the range of creative responses to that is endless.

We have divided the book up into seven seals or sections, each marked by a play on words. While tension is the commonality running throughout, in each section a particular kind of tension is transformed into something greater than itself, reflecting the creative process that can result from millennial anticipations. The studies range across diverse times and worlds, revealing an array of millennial accomplishments, ends that do amount to something, cultural creations that are more than exequies or excuses for what has not come to pass. Even in eras when millennialism was *avant la lettre* or in places where apocalypticism was not on native soil, expectations of endtimes are shot through with millennial invention. With Hillel Schwartz joining these pieces one with another, we hope to juxtapose inquiries and disciplines not usually found in conversation, demonstrating not just the intentions but the tensions inherent in the production of culture from the vantage point of

The End

Part I
At/tension

Tension: from the Greek *teinein*, stretching. *Attention*: from the Greek through the Latin, the mind stretching in one direction. These are mutually catalytic: heightened tension prompts heightened attention; heightened attention prompts heightened tension. Apocalyptic imagery – and without imagery there could be no appeal to or from apocalypse – calls attention to the tension between the daily and the decisive, flow and finale, for the apocalypse enjoins a revelation, a lifting of the veil on the ordinary, that becomes a resolution, an irrevocable decision about guilt and damages. Millennial imagery – which may be overrun by the sheerness of number – calls attention to that which lies beyond apocalypse, states of being no longer in jeopardy of time. Both the apocalyptic and the millennial attend upon people in motion, people seeking and beseeching, but apocalyptic thought concerns the springform moment, millennial anticipations concern the last stretch.

Here in Part I, Patrick Fuery and Kelli Fuery take the Greek notion of the *pharmakon* as diagnostic of Western apocalypse, demonstrating how immensely – even monstrously – creative are the powers of unfulfilled cataclysm; as poison and cure, the *pharmakon* forbids foreclosure even as it feeds upon fears of mortal seizure. By way of contrast, Hai Ren crosses from Western to Chinese senses of a countdown, demonstrating how the Western options of count-up to millennial launch (into timeless space) or countdown to apocalyptic disaster (on earth under the aegis of the clock of the cover of the Bulletin of the Atomic Scientists) become far more sinous in Taoist and Chinese bureaucratic contexts where time itself is so differently compounded. All three scholars turn the discussion of apocalypse away from the blank wall of an End toward processes of ending, so bringing to light a wildly productive if uncanny tension (a 'fissure-splendour', writes poet Thomas MacKay) between the time of the other (the state, the clone) and the time of the self.

In this double regard, one would do well to add into the mix the work of François Jullien on efficacy (*The Propensity of Things: Toward a History of Efficacy in China* [trans. Janet Lloyd; New York: Zone, 1995]), for questions of disposition, potential, and tendency – in short, questions of timeliness – surround both *pharmakon* and countdown/up. Not finality but At/tension drives millennial accomplishment.

H.S.

The Pharmakon of the Apocalypse*

Kelli Fuery and Patrick Fuery

Cast into the Abyss with Pharmacia's Friend

As Socrates and Phaedrus walk to the cool place under the trees so that they can begin their now famous dialogue, the topic of Pharmacia and Oreithyia is evoked. Phaedrus asks Socrates if they are near the spot where the two girls played before the north wind – Boreas – blew Oreithyia to her death on the rocks below. Socrates isn't so sure and even goes on to doubt the entire story. All of this seems to be a sort of detached preface to what is to follow, and much of *Phaedrus* deals with other matters. And yet Pharmacia continues to haunt the dialogues and speeches that ensue, for in her name we find the recurring motif of the *pharmakon*.

Throughout *Phaedrus* the word *pharmakon* slides with all its polysemic qualities. It denotes in Greek both poison and cure, as well as drug, recipe, and remedy. As such, *pharmakon* is that which inflicts addiction and yet also promises release. As Jacques Derrida puts it: 'This type of painful pleasure, linked as much to the malady as to its treatment, is a *pharmakon* in itself. It partakes of both good and of ill, of the agreeable and the disagreeable. Or rather it is within its mass that these oppositions are able to sketch themselves out.'[1] This, we argue here, is the quality of the *pharmakon* that allows the sense of apocalypse to exist. Not all versions of apocalypse, it must be noted, but specifically in this sense of the unveiling, and within a context of Western thought.

Our central idea is that humanity copes with, and delights in, the sense of endings not simply because of a death drive, but because contained within many versions of the apocalypse is this weight, this core, of the *pharmakon*. In this way the apocalypse is both a poison and cure, destruction and remedy. We need the apocalypse not for its sense of finality, but because it possesses within itself a cure for finality and closure; it presents the remedy for all necessary poisons. We suggest here then that Pharmacia, who watches her companion being swept onto the rocks, represents the quality of death and rebirth through her role as the originary *pharmakon*.

We are suggesting that the sense of apocalypse holds a certain fascination because it contains within itself the possibility of a panacea. It is as if the poison carries its own cure as well as all other potential remedies. This remediation also operates at the hermeneutic and epistemological levels – the *pharmakon* of the apocalypse promises an interpretative gesture that is only possible when it is encountered within its complexities of opposites, including madness, misreadings, and misgivings. This is perhaps why versions of the apocalypse so often contain confusion and revelation at the same time. It is also why any apocalyptic disappointment is immediately subsumed into its opposite, celebration, and why any sense of success is subject to a succeeding despair. It could in addition be part of the reason that the apocalypse is often positioned within the space of the carnivalesque. A great many eschatological narratives and images are infused with this sense of the carnival and festival.

Of particular interest to us here is how apocalyptic phenomena have been inflected in recent years with the celebration of the coming of a new calendrical millennium. In the following essay, we read these millennial anticipations in light of the *pharmakon,* the apocalypse, and their related cultural textualities: the clone and the double, temporality and the double bind, processes of transference. These textualities come into play as means of overcoming the curious disappointment attached to millennial anticipation. Our underlying premise is that it is precisely the *eidos* of the apocalyptic process that allows opposites to co-exist, especially the sense that non-arrival is no failure, because the *pharmakon* imbedded in apocalypse extends the gift of immunization, the likelihood that people and things may carry on even after the final moment.

One last epigraphical note about the *pharmakon:* In a footnote to his section on Plato's Pharmacy, Derrida suggests that the *pharmakon* is to Plato what the *supplément* is to Rousseau. Derrida's line is ultimately about writing, speech, and the privileging by Plato and Rousseau of speech over writing.[2] Our take on this must be somewhat different, though we retain the idea that the *pharmakon* may indeed act like the *supplément*. (This is a key term for Derrida's analysis of Rousseau, initially, and Western philosophy since the Enlightenment, in the formation of the other and of origins. We shall offer definitional gestures as we proceed.) For here the supplement is nothing less than the apocalyptic imagination, or even apocalypse itself serving as an Other to customary versions of the world and time. Still, we build upon Derrida's use of the supplement in his attempt to deconstruct the notion of origins, so that every supplement becomes a supplement of another supplement, rather than a supplement of the origin. We thus find that there is never a single apocalypse, but instead a series of supplementary apocalypses, each one legitimate in its own fashion, but none fulfilling the apocalyptic brief for which it supposedly stands. Not only are these apocalypses supplements to each other;

they also establish a relationship of supplementarity to all non-apocalyptic temporality. This reminds us of the courtroom scene in the Marx Brothers' film *Duck Soup,* where Groucho defends his client by arguing: 'This man may look like an idiot and act like an idiot, but don't be fooled, because this man *is* an idiot'. The apocalyptic moment as supplement also looks and acts like the apocalypse, but don't be fooled, it *is* an apocalypse. And the reason why the supplementary apocalypse is an apocalypse without actually delivering the end of the world (or even the end of the world order) is because it carries with it the *pharmakon* of cure and remedy, delivering up the end as well as the renewal. Because these are never the true ends, disappoint ensues, but at precisely this moment the *pharmakon* is at its most effective – for this is the bittersweet moment. One of the primary ways in which the *pharmakon* carries forward the supplementarity of apocalypse is through this doubling effect.

Our next task is to note some connections between the doubleness of the *pharmakon* and the cultural configuration of the clone, with particular reference to how the clone, and other versions of the double, act as a type of insurance against the endings as well as a bulwark against millennial disappointments.

Spalanzani's Daughters and the *Pharmacoppola*

One of the ways in which millennial disappointments are overcome is through the creation of a double. Doubling in effect allows apocalypse without anyone having to experience the consequences; it enables apocalypse to take place without disappointment because there is always the continuity that doubling affords. In order to illustrate this, we have chosen the example of cloning, or rather, the cultural textuality produced by notions of cloning. We read clones and cloning less as a narrowly specific biological technique than as a broader cultural concept incorporating a variety of discourses, including that of the double. To work through this idea, we commence not with Dolly the sheep or the recently cloned kitten and mule, but with an altogether earlier engagement with the double in the guise of Freud's *unheimlich.*

Freud used E.T.A. Hoffmann's early-nineteenth-century story, 'The Sandman', as the backdrop for analyzing experiences of the uncanny, especially experiences of something that seems human, all too human in fact, yet is really a mechanism, an automaton. The initial scene in this regard finds the young hero, Nathaniel (= 'Gift of the Lord') in his room peering through a telescope into a room across the street and seeing Olympia for the first time. Freud's summary of the story from this point on is concise and accurate, with just the right inflection:

With its aid he looks across into Professor Spalanzani's house opposite and there spies Spalanzani's beautiful, but strangely silent and motionless daughter, Olympia. He soon falls in love with her so violently that, because of her, he quite forgets the clever and sensible girl to whom he is betrothed. But Olympia is an automaton whose clockwork has been made by Spalanzani, and whose eyes have been put in by Coppola, the Sand-man. The student surprises the two masters quarrelling over their handiwork. The optician carries off the wooden eyeless doll; and the mechanician, Spalanzani, picks up Olympia's bleeding eyes from the ground and throws them at Nathaniel's breast, saying that Coppola has stolen them from the student.[3]

Though Freud's own interests lie more with the madness of Nathaniel and less with the mechanisms of Olympia, even his discussions are dominated by the problem of the double, of the automaton as at once lifeless and beloved. She fulfils Freud's definition of the uncanny in that she is both the familiar and the unfamiliar. Uncanny because so life-like, Olympia is never just an object – never just a beautifully crafted doll: her eyes, it would seem, are real. Her features are thus those of an originary cyborg or, more in keeping with the theme of this paper, a kind of clone.

Clone-like because she doubles mothers, lovers, and daughters, Olympia repeats the women in Nathaniel's life. If she is hardly a literal clone, her uncanny presence problematizes many of the issues that cloning itself puts in question: the status of subjectivity, the line between original and copy, and the relationship between clones and others. With or for Nathaniel, she also embodies the supposed circularity and madness of cloning – the self revisiting the self – and concurrent ethical dilemmas of ownership and self-determination.

Even more significantly, read as a clone, Olympia prompts repetitions of time. Nathaniel loops back into madness after each encounter with her, so Olympia becomes his recurrent apocalypse. This temporal return is significant, because it makes the rendering of time itself uncanny. Olympia destabilizes the process by which we all (in a Western version at least) go about ordering our lives, making sense of the world, and positing all events as part of a teleological sequence. Time is out of joint and all of its uncanny attributes come to the fore when we encounter the apocalyptic sensibility. In this unstable mutation of time we will find some of the cinematic daughters of Spalanzani – in *Bladerunner*, in *Invasion of the Body Snatchers*, in *Gattaca*. Each film moves along the edge of an apocalyptic moment where time is out of joint and bodies are uncannily doubled.

In 'The Sandman', it is Coppola, the itinerant optician, who gives readers a version of apocalypse by virtue of his gift of eyes – the eyes of Olympia returning the gaze of Nathaniel. Olympia becomes more human through his gift of eyesight, while Nathaniel loses his humanity to love-madness because of what he sees. (Significantly, Nathaniel also mis-sees Coppola as Coppelius and believes that Coppola had killed his father.) Gift and poison. Eyes reappear at the center of many of the cloning narratives in recent films: *Bladerunner* tests the humanity of the clones/replicants through their eyes; the security systems in *Gattaca* and *Minority Report* depend on the eyes – and are tricked through their retinal falsification. Through such a *pharmacoppola* of gift and poison, versions of truth regarding the human and the cloned are decided. And, to return to our opening scene: the discussion between Socrates and Phaedrus commences precisely with what may be seen and what is hidden from view; indeed, they spend their time looking for a spot in which dialogue can be had and truths deciphered. The *pharmacoppola* dispenses truth and revelation as well as disguise and misreadings.

Freud the psychoanalyst argues that the uncanny enters our lives when distinctions between reality and the imaginary are effaced and when a symbol 'takes over the full functions of the thing it symbolizes'.[4] The full uncanniness of apocalypse arrives when the symbol of time overtakes time itself, which is far more substantial than what literary analyst Frank Kermode describes as apocalypse's movement from *nunc stans* to *nunc movens*, for that is simply the translation of quotidian time into time pregnant with meaning and force. Such a reading fits within the configuration of time as modern science describes it in terms of the singularity – that is, not to explain the passing of time, but time within the schema of interpreting the birth of the universe, and developing the idea of parallel universes. In such contexts time becomes part of the hermeneutic process – something to make interpretations with rather than to be interpreted.

And it is within such a context of thwarted interpretations that bitter disappointment lies. Apocalypse promises time with meaning, and meaning through time. This promise is the moment when time stops being something that slides away and becomes a central part of the interpretive gesture. The disappointment in this sense has nothing to do with calendrical miscalculations or the investment of faith in an event that fails to transpire. The disappointment is pendent upon the hope that a veil will be lifted (the Greek meaning of 'apocalypse') and at last we might make sense of things. As in moments of the uncanny, a symbol transcends what it represents; the language of time rises above itself to become something other than measurement and process.

The Double Bind of the Apocalypse

With the effacement of the distinction between the real and the imaginary, the uncanny disturbs demarcations between the conscious and unconscious, the known and the unknowable. It taps into a volatile relationship predicated on repression and foreclosure. Where repression and foreclosure are problematized or unhinged, the very sense-making and rule-governing processes employed to distinguish between what is and what cannot be (or should not be) are themselves put at risk. In other words, the uncanny is so disruptive precisely because it upsets all the psychic techniques designed not only to maintain the measure of time but also to maintain order and meaning.

The clone's existence in the world, whether cultural or biotechnological, problematizes the notion of, and distinction between, the real and the imaginary as it is played out in the body and in formations of subjectivity. The body of the clone violates the primacy of the subject; like the Derridean supplement it brings into question origin and supplement, the original and its doubles. Challenging the status of origins and authenticity, the clone declares itself as much an original as the organism from which it was derived, and so it is consistently if differently disruptive, from the carnivalesque in *Multiplicity* to the foreboding in *Star Wars*, from the dehumanized in *Alien Resurrection* to the seemingly inhuman in *Twins* and the Austin Powers films. These examples share the other attribute nominated by Derrida contra Rousseau. For Rousseau the dangerous supplement: 'adds itself from the outside as evil and lack to happy and innocent plenitude'.[5] Rousseau's examples – which include writing as a supplement to speech and masturbation as a supplement to sexual intercourse – introduce this evil other to the 'natural' world order. And in many ways this is how the clone has come to be represented – as the supplement to the originary subject. This is the case from the cinematic representations to the clones that actually exist (such as the sheep and the kitten). However, as Derrida shows us, such a version of the supplement by Rousseau is filled with difficulties, not the least being the issue of the original (the plenitude) to its supplements. The two versions that have come to dominate our textual order (at least in terms of the popular imagination directed through cinema) is the clone that is more human than human, the superhuman, and the clone that is the waste product – a failure of left-overs. Either way subjectivity comes to be questioned and disruption always follows. To return, now, to the apocalypse we see another version of the *pharmakon*.

As superhuman or as left-over, the clone circumvents apocalypse where apocalypse conflates the end of the world with the end of the individual. In the clone we double ourselves so that we can continue to live on after apocalyptic catastrophe. Our supplemental self is the cure for death, for individual mortality and collective ends. Yet each time the remedy of the clone is introduced, it comes with a complementary poison. Even when the form of the clone seems to be purer than the original, there is always poison – if not the poison of despair in a post-apocalyptic 'left-over' world, then the poison of a master race in *Star Wars* and *The Boys From Brazil*. Every attempt to avert apocalypse through cloning results in a different version of apocalypse, which is the classic double bind.

As initially formulated by Gregory Bateson in his analysis of schizophrenia, double binds are premised on conformity and contradiction.[6] They are put in place through a threefold sequence: a primary negative injunction, a secondary injunction that conflicts with the first, and a tertiary negative injunction that prohibits escape. The first injunction normally takes the form of threat and punishment ('Don't do this or I will punish you'); the second injunction conflicts with this, often at a non-verbal level ('If you do this, I will punish you'). And because there is no escape even when the subject recognizes the 'damned if you do, damned if you don't' situation, he/she is still trapped within it. Apocalyptic thought has a remarkably similar quality, for it brings with it the double bind of entrapment and disappointment. Whether it arrives or not, the apocalypse disappoints (because it either fulfils its promise or postpones it yet again), and there can be no escaping the idea of such eschatological events.

Similarly, the clone operates within a discourse of the double bind. It must be more authentic than the original in order to seem clone-like, yet the closer it approaches the original, the more uncanny it becomes, and so the more it puts in question origins and supplements. So every attempt at escaping the apocalypse through the clone immediately sets another apocalyptic scenario in motion. For just as the clone represents a sort of technological version of escape and renewal, it is also, equally, a figure of the apocalypse, challenging the original and signalling its demise. The clone is thus that element that can contain within itself the oppositional tensions of compulsion and repulsion. The clone is a reminder of the fallibility of the original for it brings into question the very status of what it is to be, to exist, by allowing the question of authenticity. This can be seen in all the examples we have encountered so far. The uncanny double forces the original subject into the position of seeing the self as a position of the

familiar and the unknown. This brings us to the third part of this paper –
which is the neurotic phantasies of the apocalypse.

'In you more than you – I love you, therefore I mutilate you'

In all the films about clones that we have cited, there has been a compelling sense of love that underpins the existence of the clone. It is as if the
clone must, at some point, come to the question of love in order for us to
confront the deep challenge to our own subjectivity. The clone's existence, and its subsequent movement toward human subjectivity, more
often than not demands an encounter in the domain of love. However,
it is a particular type of love, a sort of meta-discourse on love, which
emphasizes just how much the capacity to show love and to be 'in love'
has come to define human subjectivity in recent times.

We may best appreciate the intimate connection between expressions
of love and subjectivity by recalling the analytic scene as described by
French psychoanalyst Jacques Lacan. The analysand, searching for answers,
sees in the analyst the one who is supposed to know and who has the
capacity to interpret truly. However, this quest inevitably relies upon a
process of transference in which the analysand sees the analyst not only as
knower but as lover or, at the very least, love-object. Lacan sums this up
in the unspoken words of every analysand's relationship to every analyst:
'I love you, but, because inexplicably I love in you something more than
you – the *objet petit a* – I mutilate you'.[7] When the subject encounters
the clone, and all its attendant attributes, they are placed in this position
of transference, desire, mutilation, and love. The clone in this sense is
bound up with the subject in this curious relationship of distorted love.

Now in the moments of apocalypse – from expectation, experience,
belief, and disappointment – we see a similar discourse taking place.
Apocalyptic believers operate in a situation premised on love and mutilation; or, to return to our central motif, of cure and poison. In order to
make sense of the world – and this is precisely what any apocalyptic
system says that it is doing – there must be an attachment to the world.
That attachment is love, but it demands mutilation.

A great deal of apocalyptic thought belongs to what psychoanalysis
often designates as obsessional neurosis, a fixation on a single idea that
overrides all other processes, so much so that all sense-making processes
are drawn into reframing the world to fit this one idea. Such neuroses can
only engage and make sense of the world by bringing everything into the
context of the obsession; every act and event is a potential sign confirm-

ing the belief. The deep-seated need for incessant, massive confirmation of belief, to the extent that disconfirmation is always nearly impossible, derives from an initial *Angst* whose source puzzled Freud for years. Where did this essential tension come from, and why were obsessional neurotics so in love with it as to resist any abandonment of the associated obsession? Any answer had serious consequences for psychoanalytic theory in general, since obsessional neurosis was so difficult a nut to crack. If the source of the *Angst* were in the ego, psychoanalytic theory would be constrained to privilege the sense of the self; if in the id, analysts would have to acknowledge the primacy of libidinal urges. Freud at last resolved the dilemma by arguing that *Angst* is ego-based and therefore inextricably tied to the preservation of the self, while at the same time involving a certain repression of libidinal urges. This would seem to fit perfectly with the apocalyptic believer who falls in love with the apocalyptic moment yet fears it at the same time.

Like apocalypse, the clone is simultaneously an object of love and fear: a way of escaping the End, it also comes to stand for that End. Doubling our selves through the clone, we find our own egos threatened, our own sense of purpose and authenticity under siege. The clone is at once the initiator and subject of difference – a state of subjectivity that continually defers beingness and offers difference through sameness. As we can observe in a great many cultural narratives of the apocalypse and the clone, the more the double resembles the origin, the more the politics of difference come into play. Such politics embroil the subject and clone in a ritual of playing out the differences between the two, whilst at the same time declaring their sameness. Such complex relations are eventually tracked back to the idea of what it is to be, to have certainty, to be allowed to interpret and even to speak. And within these relationships lies the root of finitude, for the double of the clone and the apocalypse resonates with the sense of an ending.

In as much as the apocalypse is the end, part of the response to it must be a type of negotiation through repression. If we take the cultural idea of cloning to represent that larger order of repressions and denials of the end, then part of the clone's function is to ward off the fear of the ending through complete denial. That is, the end cannot take place because there will be a double to continue on, at our behest. On the other hand, the intervention of the clone spells the end of the subject by bringing into question the authenticity of what is intrinsically human. This is the double bind, the poison and the cure, the neurotic denial and acceptance, success and disappointment. It is, in short, the perpetual state of being and non-being that shadows every millennial moment and every apocalyptic belief.

Bibliography

Bateson, Gregory, *Steps to an Ecology of Mind* (London: Granada, 1985).
Derrida, Jacques, *Of Grammatology* (trans. G.C. Spivak; Baltimore: The Johns Hopkins University Press, 1976).
Freud, Sigmund, 'The Uncanny', in *Standard Edition Vol. XVII* and *Art and Literature* (trans. J. Strachey; Middlesex: Penguin Books, 1985 [1919]).
Lacan, Jacques, *The Four Fundamental Concepts of Psychoanalysis* (trans. A. Sheridan; Middlesex: Penguin Books, 1986).

Notes

*   The authors would like to offer their thanks to Hillel Schwartz whose editorial suggestions and comments went far beyond the mechanical. His depth of knowledge and astute observations are gratefully acknowledged.

1.   Jacques Derrida, *Of Grammatology* (trans. G.C. Spivak; Baltimore: The Johns Hopkins University Press, 1976), 99.

2.   It is important to recognise, as Derrida does, that the closing part of *Phaedrus* is as much about acknowledging that this distinction is a preference rather than a point of better or worse, good or bad.

3.   Sigmund Freud, 'The Uncanny', in *Standard Edition Vol. XVII* and *Art and Literature* (trans. J. Strachey; Middlesex: Penguin Books, 1985 [1919]), 350.

4.   Freud, 'The Uncanny', 367.

5.   Derrida, *Of Grammatology*, 215.

6.   See Gregory Bateson, *Steps to an Ecology of Mind* (London: Granada, 1985).

7.   Jacques Lacan, *The Four Fundamental Concepts of Psychoanalysis* (trans. A. Sheridan; Middlesex: Penguin Books, 1986), 268.

The Merit of Time:
A Genealogy of the Countdown*

Hai Ren

How do we construct a genealogy or effective history of the countdown of time? Such countdowns involve both *telling* time and *counting* time, marked off in pre-determined increments to a pre-determined end. Countdowns both spectacular and mundane have become a routine part of contemporary life in the United States. At New York City's Times Square, for example, hundreds of thousands (recently, millions) of people gather in front of a giant countdown clock every 31 December to count off the final ten seconds of the old year and welcome a new year. In sports such as football and basketball, a countdown clock is used not merely to tell the amount of time remaining until the end of the game but also to divide the game into timed segments, between which a television commercial may be inserted or an instant replay staged to settle a dispute over a particular referee ruling. The music industry also commonly uses a countdown in its Top Forty playlists and rankings of popular songs or music videos. In downtown Columbus, Ohio, in the year 2000, I saw a countdown clock used at a construction site to tell the public the remaining seconds before the completion of the building.[1]

Public countdowns also take place in other countries, as in China, where a giant multimedia countdown clock was set up at Beijing's Tiananmen Square to count down to Hong Kong's 'return' to China on 1 July, 1997. The clock, mounted on a 16 meter high, 9.6 meter wide metal panel overhung with Chinese national flags, was placed between two pillars in front of the building jointly occupied by the National Museum of Chinese History and the National Museum of the Chinese Revolution. The top of the panel carried the five gold stars of the Chinese flag. Below the stars were four lines of Chinese characters: 'The Chinese Government' (*Zhongguo zhengfu*) / 'Resumes the exercise of sovereignty over Hong Kong' (*dui Xianggang huifu xingshi zhuquan*) / 'Counting-down time' (*daojishi*) / 'to 1 July, 1997' (*ju 1997 nian 7 yue 1 ri*). Beneath were the days (*tian*) and seconds (*miao*) remaining before the British release of Hong Kong. Near the bottom, in small characters, appeared the names of the sign's sponsors, including the magazine *China Top Brands*, China's Southern Aviation Engineering Company, Linghua Food-Flavoring Group, Ji'ning, Shangdong, and the National Museum of the Chinese Revolution. Finally, below the sponsors, the panel memorialized the date on which the clock began its countdown: 19 December, 1994.

From 11:10 on 19 December, 1994, to 0:00 on 1 July, 1997, the countdown clock counted 925 days or 79.8798 million seconds. A week later, on 8 July, 1997, the clock was removed from Tiananmen Square and put on display at the Cultural Square under the Badaling section of the Great Wall. Meanwhile, a miniature at 1:16 scale was displayed at the National Museum of the Chinese Revolution (*Beijing Evening News*, 10 July, 1997, 19). The clock was significant enough for the government to display in two different venues because it was a temporal structure through which the public had been made aware of the imminent 'return' of Hong Kong and because, at the same time, it embodied a distinctive mode of cultural, historical, and economic production/consumption.

The Tiananmen Square countdown clock cannot therefore be understood by reference exclusively to countdowns in the modern Western world, in good measure because the notion of time operating in the Chinese countdown differs substantially from countdowns in the Christian West, infused as these are with expectations of an endtime or 'apocalypse'.[2] The notion of apocalypse, which is both subjective in nature and subjectively administered (independently of objective or clock time), has underwritten the construction of a series of Christian eschatological dates ever since the time of Hippolytus (200 CE).[3] As tracked by historian Richard Landes, each of the dates for the end-time, ever-revised and revamped, was nonetheless said to be fixed and final, though none was ever actualized. In the long run, the notion of apocalypse has given rise to a Western discourse of modernity transfused by a familiar mode of counting down toward 'the end of time'. Landes calls this 'apocalypticism', which he characterizes as 'the most explosive of forms that hope takes… Despite its innumerable disappointments, it has always arisen anew, energized and momentarily mighty, in every generation.'[4]

Moreover, the use of apocalypse as the rationale for subjectively 'measuring' the end of time has been made possible by the active management of subjective time independently of clock time. Historical inquiry into the intellectual genealogy of time shows that the separation of subjective time from objective time was actively maintained.[5] One of the key figures who greatly influenced this division was Augustine of Hippo, who not only formulated the schema of a threefold historical time in terms of past, present, and future,[6] but also was one of the earliest advocates for an apocalyptic counting toward the end of time.[7] When such counting down is projected onto the horizon of the future, it has to take the form of continuous disappointments, recalculations, and reconciliations. Thus, each apocalyptic countdown, initially defended as an objective arithmetic of time, really entails a subjective process.

In contrast to the subjective, apocalyptic time inherent in Christian traditions, the Chinese countdown clock engaged both objective and subjective qualities of time. As a device for public time-telling of Hong Kong's 'return' to China, the clock incorporated mechanical, electric, and digital forms of media, integrating the linearity of the traditional mechanical clock, the precision and calculating powers of the computer, and the allure of visual representation of change. That is, this kind of timekeeping maintained both the *precision-orientation* of clock time (as refined by the development of the mechanical clock in Western Europe and North America since the fifteenth century)[8] and an *objective* quality of time that is measurable and thus accountable in social organization.[9]

In addition, however, the Hong Kong countdown clock implicated a distinctively Taoist notion about the subjective accumulation of time in dealing with the relation of the self to the other. I call this element in the countdown 'the merit of time' (*gongfu* or kung fu), which has no immediate counterpart in the eschatological traditions of premodern Christianity or Judaism. 'The merit of time' refers to the accumulation of the transcendent force in completing a movement in which the self interacts with the other (more discussion later in this essay).

What other historical and cultural contexts might be relevant to my construction of a genealogy of the countdown of time as merit? I suggest two very different contexts: an international culture of fear during the Cold War era (1945-1989) and Taoist (or Daoist) practices of time management. In brief: the nuclear arms race during the Cold War promoted the development of an integrated notion of time (both objective and subjective) as an important tactic for time management, and Taoist time management entails a practice of incorporating the external time of the other into the inner time of the self.

'Hot Count' in the Cold War

In the context of the Cold War, 'countdown' reflected popular fears of nuclear war as a result of the arms race between the United States and the Soviet Union. One of the most prominent forms taken by the countdown was the 'Doomsday Clock' created in the late 1940s by a Chicago artist, Martyl Langsdorf, the wife of physicist Alexander Langsdorf, a founder of the *Bulletin of the Atomic Scientists*. The Doomsday Clock first appeared on the cover of the June 1947 issue of the *Bulletin,* set at seven minutes to fateful midnight. Since then, the hands of the Clock have been moved 16 times – sometimes back away from midnight, sometimes closer – based on decisions made by the Board of the magazine as it reviews general 'trends'. Each move was tied to the further development or proliferation of nuclear weapons or to restraints in their development and deployment.[10] As such, the Clock has been a surprisingly neutral mechanism. Mike Moore, in his 'Midnight Never Came: The History of the Doomsday Clock' (see http://www.bullatomsci.org/clock/nd95moore1.html), tells us:

> 'For hawks, the clock was a handy reminder of how dangerous the world was, thus justifying yet another multi-billion-dollar arms buildup. For doves, the clock also said the world was dangerous, but that called for conciliatory gestures and arms control treaties. Senator Tom Harkin, an Iowa Democrat and member in good standing of the olive branch school of international relations, titled his 1990 book on the perils of Cold War thinking, *Five Minutes to Midnight.*'[11]

Not long after the publication of the Doomsday Clock, countdowns became an integral part of the process of launching a rocket. Inspired by the launch countdown scene in Fritz Lang's 1929 film *Frau im Mond (The Woman in the Moon)*, the German (and later American) scientist Wernher von Braun (1912–1977) had counted down to his successful launch of a V-2 in 1942, the world's first launch of a ballistic missile and the first rocket to go into the fringes of space.[12] The countdown as he instituted it in post-war America was a technical procedure for the last moments of launch, standardized during the US program to develop reliable nuclear weapons and missile delivery systems. By 1957, National Aeronautics and Space Administration (NASA) technicians had established a procedure called 'hot count', referring to a countdown preceding a static firing on the pad, followed a few days later by the actual launch. The count took 400 minutes and featured 1,000 separate events, checks of equipment on the ground as well as aboard the missile. If any problem showed up, the count would be put on hold until the problem was fixed, which could take hours.[13]

Several points must be made about the use of countdowns by NASA. First, the countdown was primarily designed to *slow down* the actual launch. Second, the countdown was a procedure rather than a measurement; countdown time was not constrained by the actual passage of clock time. (Although 400 minutes might be allocated to the period of the countdown, technicians were not bound by a 400-minute clock time.) Third, the countdown could be stopped the moment a problem was found, even in the last few seconds prior to a launch; that is, the period allocated to the countdown was subjectively controlled and actively managed, so that time in effect could be frozen and, as a result, the countdown might never reach its end or zero-point. Major General John B. Medaris, who led the Army Ballistic Missile Agency in the late 1950s, wrote:

> 'In the countdown to the launching of a big missile, the transition from success to failure – from glistening beauty to flaming disaster – can be sudden and complete. But the clock *can* be stopped – disaster *can* be avoided. Hundreds of instruments are monitoring everything related to the missile to catch the slightest indication that all is not perfect.'[14]

Unlike the Doomsday Clock, then, the NASA countdown was cautious, not cautionary. Inseparable from the possibility of delay, it was in a strong sense a mechanism for deferring the time of launch.[15] What is most interesting about this deferral was that it was used to manage time for making decisions, not simply to delay some absolute race against time. 'The key to success', wrote Medaris,

> 'is still in the hands of people – constantly watchful, instantly ready to make a *decision*. If a small red light or a single wavering needle on a dial goes undetected, or if the first sign of trouble is not followed immediately by firm decision and instant action, the work of months can be destroyed in seconds.'[16]

So the countdown could be adopted as a trope by Cold War politicians regardless of where they stood on the peace-and-security continuum. Major General Medaris regarded the countdown process as a matter of 'the survival or destruction of our way of life, and quite possibly toward the survival or destruction of the human race'.[17]

While the *Bulletin of the Atomic Scientists* was irregularly recalibrating its Doomsday Clock and the American military was counting slowly down toward missile launches, Hollywood swiftly translated the idea of countdown into cinematic language, capturing and escalating a Cold War culture of fear. Many film plots did this by way of the 'time-bomb', beginning perhaps with Alfred Hitchcock's *Four O'Clock* (1957), where the final 'clocktime' minute before the explosion lasts 72 seconds of narrative time – the real time it took for the film to ratchet through the projector.[18] As both a technology of representation and a form of media, cinema can be used to manipulate the experience of time; in *Four O'Clock*, Hitchcock manipulated the temporality of the countdown itself, creating a complex, continually transforming set of relations between the 'clocktime' of the bomb, the narrative time it takes to reach the zero-moment of explosion, and the passage of time as experienced by movie audiences in suspense.[19]

Like the NASA countdown, cinematic countdowns are as much procedures as they are arithmetic, objective but also subjective.

The Doomsday Clock's contribution to Cold War filmmaking was different: it inspired filmmakers to conceptualize the atomic bomb as what Paul Virilio in his book *Popular Defense & Ecological Struggles* (1990 [1978]) calls 'the weapon of the apocalypse'.[20] A series of nuclear arms race events – such as the first Soviet atomic bomb on 29 August, 1949, the first US thermonuclear device (H-Bomb) on 1 November, 1952, and the first Soviet H-Bomb on 12 August, 1953 – had resulted in widespread fears about a nuclear war.[21] To express and transform the culture of fear, Stanley Kubrick released *Dr. Strangelove, Or: How I Learned to Stop Worrying and Love the Bomb* and Sidney Lumet gave audiences *Fail Safe* in 1964. Both films explore scenarios in which US bombers erroneously attack the Soviet Union with nuclear weapons. In *Fail Safe*, Moscow is destroyed, whereupon the US President orders the destruction of New York; in *Dr. Strangelove*, the planet is fatally irradiated by a secret Soviet 'Doomsday Machine'.[22] Both Kubrick and Lumet were optimists. Although things don't turn out so well for a few million people in *Fail Safe* and a few billion in *Dr. Strangelove*, in each case a fictional president has hours to correct the original attack-the-Soviets mistake. Thus, though representing the fatal power of nuclear weapons, Kubrick and Lumet each used a series of cinematic images to transform fear into a countdown opportunity for survival.

Hollywood's use of the time-bomb and the countdown clock continued after the Cold War, although the sociopolitical context has shifted from the nuclear arms race to terrorism, as in the 1994 film *Speed* (Jan De Bont). What remains unchanged about the Hollywood countdown is its expression of time that is at once objective and subjective, coordinated to a standard clock but measured from start to end, as with NASA technicians, by filmmakers and their audiences. This raises an important question: In what ways does the public countdown establish and condition a relationship between the self and the other?

The Merit of Time

To address this question, I turn to a discussion of the accumulation of 'time as merit' through the incorporation of the external time of the other into the inner time of the self.[23] I focus here on 'the practice of Tao' (*xingdao*) as an important context for understanding how a countdown may be an opening to innovative ways of managing the time of social interaction.

In Taoism, the countdown is an active measure for compressing an external form of time (the time of the other) into a sense of inner time. This form of time management results in 'merit' (*gong, gongfu*, or kung fu), a key concept referring to the accomplishment or achievement of a cyclical movement. To achieve something without failing, to accomplish a full cycle, by giving and taking, by fulfilling a task, by following difficult rules, or, more generally, by living one's span of allotted life, all these accomplishments add to one's merit. Completing a cyclical action or movement, human beings accumulate energy that 'transform and purifies' (*hua*) us.[24] The larger the scale of a cyclical movement, the greater its achievement and its upgrading power. Moreover, the completion of a cyclical action and the accumulation of transforming and purifying energy take place as part of the same ritual process of examining and measuring the relation of inner time to outer time or, more precisely, resolving outer time into inner time.

'Inner time' and 'outer time' have quite specific meanings for the Taoist. Inner time refers to a period of transformation before the diversification (*fen*) of the energies that make up the universe. In the inner time, what Lao Zi (or Lao Tsu) calls 'something chaotically structured' (*youwu huncheng*) (*Daodejing*, chapter 25) evolves into 'that which has a name and thus gives birth to all beings' (*youming wanwu zhi mu*) (*Daodejing*, chapter 1).[25] Taoism explains the length of the inner time in terms of human gestation.[26] During the period of pregnancy, the embryo passes through a ninefold transforming process, corresponding to the time cycle and the process of the shaping of the universe inside chaos. Because the Chinese count and value the entire period of inner time, they allot to a newborn child the age of one year, the approximate length of gestation. Extraordinary people – those who accumulate high merits – are believed to have a longer gestation than common mortals. Divine heroes are born after 12 months, great sages after 18 months. Lao Zi, for example, is believed to have remained in the womb for 81 years. The term '*lao*' (old) is often used as an honorific, regardless of the calendar age of the person, since the person's inner time is always counted in association with certain intrinsic merits.

Outer time exists after the diversification (*fen*) of the energies that make up the universe; it is the time of the world, which is governed by the interaction of yin-yang and by the cycles (or situations) that develop from their alternation. Outer time is hierarchical and objectified, comparable with Hegelian dialectical historical time.[27] *Yijing* (*The Book of Changes*), a key text of Taoism, offers a theory about outer time (*shi*) and its worldly situations (*wei*)[28] that has been variously interpreted by Chinese scholars over the centuries. The most influential interpreters included Meng Xi (c.90–40 BCE) of the Han Dynasty, who paired the 'four directions' with the 'four seasons' to explain the 'breaths of the hexagrams'; Wang Bi (226–249 CE) of the Wei-Jin period, who argued that time determined situations; and Zhu Xi (1130–1200) of the Song Dynasty, who focused on 'hitting the right time,' 'correct situation', and 'appropriate situation' in elaborating practical Confucian principles.[29] The neo-Confucianist appropriation of *Yijing* by Zhu Xi and his successors had political repercussions, maintaining outer time (in the sense of change) as ceaseless production and reproduction,[30] a view used by the Chinese state as an important rationale for developing the economy of the country.

Mathematically, however, *Yijing* is related to number theory, particularly set theory. It is a guide for addressing changes, or measuring a number of situations rather than chances.[31] Archaeological evidence has shown that oracle bones were first used as media to give interpretations to decisions of needed actions (including the action of not-acting) in the Shang period (c.1650 – c.1050 BCE).[32] It is in the process of burning that two kinds of cracking lines (broken or continuous) appear on the bone. The *Yijing* considers the interaction between the two types of lines, '—' (positive, continuous, yang) and '– –' (negative, discontinuous, yin), as the first and primary situation. Both the number of situations and their degree of complexity increase when the number of lines increases. The two-line structure, that is, adding one more line above or below the first line, includes a total of four situations. The three-line structure, adding two more lines above or below the first line, includes a total of eight situations. These eight situations are the most commonly used; they are called 'Eight Trigrams' (*bagua*). When the line number increases to four, there are a total of 16 situations; when five, a total of 32 situations; when six, a total of 64, called 'sixty-four hexagrams'. Thus, when the line number increases to n, the total number of situations increases to 2^n. The *Yijing* usually interprets the 64 situations, each of which also includes a subset of six situations. Among the 64 situations, for example, the situation of *qian* consists of six parallel '—' (unbroken) lines. When the force of change – assuming it begins at the top line – moves from the top line to the bottom line, the situation also changes. Thus, the situation *qian* includes a subset of six situations.[33] When considering that each of the 'sixty-four hexagrams' includes a subset of six situations, the whole book in fact takes into account a total of 384 situations (64 × 6).

The acquisition of merit is based on the development of a relation of the self to the other. Another important Taoist text, *Lao-Tzu Chung-Ching* (*Lao Zi Zhongjing*) (*The Middle Book of Lao Zi*) or *Zhugong Yulu* (*Jade*

Calendar of the Pearly Palace) (dated c.1125 or earlier), delineates a notion of the self on the basis of constructing a relation of the inner world to the external world. The external world, according to the book, is associated with a progression from crisis to crisis toward the inexorable end, from the distinct (all beings or the 10,000 beings) to the indistinct (chaos).[34] The inner world follows the opposite impetus, moving from the incipient to more distinct creatures, from an invisible and undifferentiated state to the existence of form. The construction of the self's identity – whether as the transcendental 'I' of the 'True Person' (*zhenren*), the 'Great One' (*taiyi*), or as the Tao ('I am the Tao') – takes places in the process of 'returning' (*gui*) to the inner world.[35]

The return to the inner world as an active regressive process, which is called '*ke*' (measure, scale, classify, grade, or examine), involves the measuring or examining of the relation of inner time to outer time. The process is developed to address a paradigm in ancient Chinese calendar theory, according to which the 60-year cycle (a traditional Chinese calendar notion) shows a certain irregularity that results in an imbalance between inner and outer time.[36] The appearing of the irregularity, called an 'irrational opening' (*qimen*), allows the development of the notion of the 'hidden period' (*dunjia*), referring to a hidden regressive cycle that aims at counterbalancing the irregularity of outer time.

Taoist ritual enacts the passage from outer to inner time in an enclosed space called 'altar' (*tan*) where a human person interacts with both the celestial and the earthly forces. The space of 'altar' is built as an environment representing a multilevel mountain where the sky and the earth meet.[37] In the ritual process, a specialist moves within the environment from the outer to the inner sphere.[38] The 'outer altar' (*waitan*) is a sphere in which 24 pickets are used to form 24 territories that represent '24 energy nodes' (*ershi si jieqi*), 24 periods of 15 days in a year. Beyond this demarcation line of the outer altar are installed 28 groups of oil lamps representing constellations. The sphere of the 'middle altar' (*zhongtan*) is symbolically marked by the 12 'earthly branches' (*dizhi*) arranged in a square, the 'eight trigrams,' and the four gates (the Door of the Earth, the Road of Ghosts, the Gate of Man, and the Gate of Heaven) at the four corners. The spatial arrangement of the 'eight trigrams' forms a spatial structure known as the 'nine palaces' (*jiugong*) where the 'inner altar' (*neitan*) is enacted during the period from midnight to dawn.[39] The 'inner altar' includes five cardinal points, each marked by a bushel of uncooked white rice grains, symbolizing a measure of life (metal, wood, water, fire, or earth).[40] Inside each of these five bushels is placed a sacred 'true writ' (*zhenwen*) in the form of a wooden tablet or a sheet of paper inscribed with so-called cosmic writing or archetypal characters that express the fundamental configuration of cosmic energies as they emerge from chaos and coagulate to form all beings.[41] Moreover, the five 'true writs' also symbolize the five directions (east, south, west, north, and center).

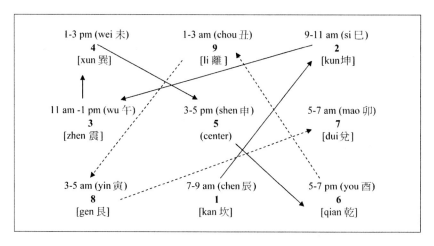

Figure 1: *The ninefold transformation of inner life shown by the nine steps of movement in a Taoist ritual.*[42]

After entering into the inner altar, a ritual master begins to 'practice the Tao', a ninefold ritual of circulation that symbolizes the ninefold transformation of inner life (shown by the numbers from 1 to 9 in Figure 1). In the ninefold ritual, the master performs dance steps called 'the paces of Yu' (*Yubu*), enacting a return to the womb that symbolizes a compression of outer time into inner time, which itself involves two different trajectories. After moving successively in the first six phases (from the number 1 to 6, shown in Figure 1), the ritual master goes regressively by walking backward from the number 9 to 7. This change is called 'the irrational or uneven opening'; it reenacts the appearance of an irregularity of the outer time (according to traditional Chinese calendar theory). The regressive movement or return to inner time is called 'the hidden period', in which the ritual master disappears from the outer world and enters into the 'other world' (*bieyou tiandi*), where nature exists in its original, spontaneous state, which is often expressed by the image of the mountain and the unspoiled landscape. Therefore, in 'practicing the Tao', the progressive process annihilates the form of outer time and its associated outer world through different stages, and the regressive process constructs a form of inner time and its inner world out of a primal formlessness.

As expressed in ritual, not only does inner time precede outer time; it also determines outer time. The ritualistic return to inner time is a construction of a specific relation of inner time to outer time. Outer time is telescoped to the extent that creation and destruction, the beginning and the end, take place during the span of the ritual. Outer time is reduced to a single moment that corresponds to the duration of inner time – the ninefold transformation. This moment of time is 'the instant of chaos, of total communication, one and undifferentiated, yet perceived as an endless multiple'.[43] The experiential length of the moment, or the duration of the ninefold transformation, is flexible.

This flexibility makes possible that the active management of the duration of inner time enhances agency in a social interaction. The merit acquired through a social interaction is determined by one's ability to stretch the duration of the internal 'transformation' (*hua*). The further or longer the duration, the greater the speed at which the stretching takes place, and the more effective the control of the external world (including time), as depicted in such martial arts films as *The Matrix* (1999, Andy Wachowski and Larry Wachowski) and *Crouching Tiger, Hidden Dragon* (2000, Ang Lee). The agency of the body in the transformation may include physical exercises, but its intellectual capacity is developed through a cultural process, which first acquires the time of the other in a progressive movement and then develops the time of the self through turning in upon oneself.

Conclusion

I have shown that in order to appreciate the social value of the countdown of time, we must understand both objective and subjective time. In the Cold War context of rocket and missile launches, the countdown ostensibly established the objective end-time for a launch, but it also allowed for a flexible, subjective management of that time toward a successful launch. With respect to Hollywood films, the countdown establishes an objective end-time for (usually) explosion or apocalyptic destruction, but the duration of the narrative is determined less by clock-time than by the imperatives of cinematic storytelling and the *felt* duration is determined by the audience's subjective experience of suspense or anxiety. If my discussion of NASA missile launches and Hollywood films raises the issues of the flexibility and multiplicity of time, my analysis of the Taoist countdown draws attention to the problematic of the accountability of time in a culturally determined relationship. If time in a countdown establishes a relationship between the self and the other, the time must have what is called, in Taoist terms, 'merit'. The accumulation of time's merit lies precisely in the multiplicity of the countdown.

The traditional Taoist countdown of time, integrating progressive and regressive forms of time, has implications for understanding recent count-downs, such as that of Hong Kong's 'return' to China, where we can find two parallel practices of stretching the duration of inner time. In Tianan-men Square, the movement from the external world to internal world was a journey from the external time 'contaminated' by British colonization of Hong Kong since 1840 to the inner experience of Chinese national time – whether economic, social, or cultural. For Hong Kong itself, the stretching of the duration was revealed in Hong Kong cinema, especially martial arts films such as the series *Once upon a Time in China* (1991–1993, Tsui Hark), and *Ashes of Time* (1994, Wong Kar-wai). This stretching was aimed at freeing Hong Kong from the influence of China's national time, as well as refining and maintaining Hong Kong's own cultural time. For both China and Hong Kong, the management of relation of an external time to an inner time during this historic period entailed the construction of a qualitatively different time, that is, a time about modernity.[44]

In addition, the traditional Taoist countdown may help us understand an important shift in recent Western notions of historical time: the shift from Hegelian dialectical time to Nietzschean genealogical time – that is, from an objective, progressive, and teleological notion of historical time to a notion of historical time as discontinuous and interruptive, as pointed out by Michel Foucault's discussion of genealogical or effective history.[45] Such a change in the understanding of historical time has also been re-flected in the history of communication media. Gilles Deleuze's work on cinema[46] has revealed a shift from a classic focus on continuous move-ment ('the movement-image') to a neo-cinematic focus on discontinuity, contingency, and interruption ('the time-image').[47] Some regard this change in the understanding of historical time as radical or 'postmodern'[48] because the shift declares the end of the Hegelian dialectical historical time, often expressed in terms of the phrase 'the end of history'.[49]

The postmodern sense of historical time does not permit the time of the other to become a source of accumulation in social action. As a result, with respect to its role in establishing a relationship between the self and the other, time has no merit. In contrast, the Taoist countdown does not surrender objective, continuous time (that is, the time of the other) even as it develops a personal and communal sense of the multiplicity of time. In Taoism, therefore, time may become a source of innovation in social organization – that is, it not only establishes a link between the self and the other but also allows for changes in that relationship during the countdown process. For the Taoist, the development of a genealogical historical time incorporates rather than rejects dialectical historical time, toward more compatible ends.

Bibliography

Armitage, John, 'From Modernism to Hypermodernism and Beyond: An Interview with Paul Virilio', in *idem* (ed.), *Paul Virilio: From Modernism to Hypermodernism and Beyond* (London: SAGE, 2000), 25-55.

Bogue, Ronald, *Deleuze on Cinema* (New York: Routledge, 2003).

Boltz, William G., *The Origin and Early Development of the Chinese Writing System* (New Haven: American Oriental Society, 1994).

Castoriadis, Cornelius, 'Time and Creation', in John Bender and David E. Wellbery (eds.), *Chronotypes: The Construction of Time* (Stanford, CA: Stanford University Press, 1991), 38-64, 231-32.

Deleuze, Gilles, *Cinema 1: The Movement-Image* (trans. Hugh Tomlinson and Barbara Habberjam; Minneapolis: University of Minnesota Press, 1986 [1983]).

—*Cinema 2: The Time-Image* (trans. Hugh Tomlinson and Robert Galeta; Minneapolis: University of Minnesota Press, 1989 [1985]).

Foucault, 'Nietzsche, Genealogy, History', in Paul Rabinow (ed.), *The Foucault Reader* (New York: Pantheon Books, 1984), 76-100.

Fraser, J.T., *Of Time, Passion, and Knowledge: Reflections on the Strategy of Existence* (New York: George Braziller, 1975).

Graham, John F., *Space Exploration: From Talisman of the Past to Gateway for the Future* (1995) (http://www.space.edu/projects/book/index.html), ch. 8.

Henriksen, Margot A., *Dr. Strangelove's America: Society and Culture in the Atomic Age* (Berkeley, CA: University of California Press, 1997).

Heppenheimer, T.A., *Countdown: A History of Space Flight* (New York: John Wiley and Sons, 1997).

Jameson, Fredric, *Postmodernism, or the Cultural Logic of Late Capitalism* (Durham, NC: Duke University Press, 1991).

Jung, C.G., 'Foreword', in Wilhelm, *The I Ching or Book of Changes*, xxi-xxxix.

Kristeva, Julia, 'Women's Time', in *idem*, *New Maladies of the Soul* (trans. Ross Guberman; New York: Columbia University Press, 1995), 201-24.

Kubrick, Stanley, Peter George, and Terry Southern, *Dr. Strangelove or: How I Learned to Stop Worrying and Love the Bomb* (New York: Bantam Books, 1963).

Landes, David L., *Revolution in Time: Clocks and the Making of the Modern World* (rev. enlarged edn; Cambridge, MA: Harvard University Press, 2000).

Landes, Richard, 'Lest the Millennium Be Fulfilled: Apocalyptic Expectations and the Pattern of Western Chronography 100–800 CE', in Werner Verbeke, Daniel Verhelst and Andries Welkenhuysen (eds.), *The Use and Abuse of Eschatology in the Middle Ages* (Leuven: Leuven University Press, 1988), 137-211.

—'The Apocalyptic Year 1000: Millennial Fever and the Origins of the Modern West', in Strozier and Flynn, *The Year 2000: Essays on the End*, 13-29.

Ledderose, Lothar, *Ten Thousand Things: Module and Mass Production in Chinese Art* (Princeton, NJ: Princeton University Press, 2000).

Li-Chen Lin, 'The Concepts of Time and Position in the *Book of Change* and their Development', in Chun-Chieh Huang and Erick Zürcher (eds.), *Time and Space in Chinese Culture*, 89-113.

Mattelart, Armand, and Michele Mattelart, *Rethinking Media Theory: Signposts and New Directions* (trans. James A. Cohen and Marina Urquidi; Minneapolis: University of Minnesota Press, 1992).

Medaris, John B., *Countdown for Decision* (New York: G.P. Putnam's Sons, 1960).

Mullarkey, John, *Bergson and Philosophy* (Notre Dame: University of Notre Dame Press, 2000).

O'Leary, Stephen D., *Arguing the Apocalypse* (New York: Oxford University Press, 1994).

Ren, Hai, *The Countdown of Time: Public Displays and Symbolic Economy in China and Hong Kong* (forthcoming).

Ricoeur, Paul, *Time and Narrative, III* (trans. Kathleen Blamey and David Pellauer; Chicago: University of Chicago Press, 1988 [1985]).

Rodowick, D.N., *Gilles Deleuze's Time Machine* (Durham, NC: Duke University Press, 1997).

—*Reading the Figural, or, Philosophy after the New Media* (Durham, NC: Duke University Press, 2001).

Schipper, Kristofer, *The Taoist Body* (trans. Karen C. Duval; Berkeley, CA: University of California Press, 1993[1982]).

—'Vernacular and Classical Ritual in Taoism', *Journal of Asian Studies*, 45.1 (1985), 21-57.

—'The Inner World of the *Lao-Tzu Chung-Ching*', in Chun-Chieh Huang and Erick Zürcher (eds.), *Time and Space in Chinese Culture* (Leiden: E.J. Brill, 1995), 114-31.

—'Daoist Ecology: The Inner Transformation: A Study of the Precepts of the Early Daoist Ecclesia', in N.J. Girardot, James Miller and Liu Xiaogan (eds.), *Daoism and Ecology: Ways within a Cosmic Landscape* (Cambridge, MA: The Center for the Study of World Religions, Harvard Divinity School, 2001), 79-93.

Schipper, Kristofer, and Wang Hsiu-huei, 'Progressive and Regressive Time Cycles in Taoist Ritual', in T.J. Fraser, N. Lawrence, and F.C. Haber (eds.), *Time, Science, and Society in China and the West* (Amherst: University of Massachusetts Press, 1986), 185-205.

Shapiro, Jerome F., *Atomic Bomb Cinema: The Apocalyptic Imagination on Film* (New York: Routledge, 2002).

Stearns, Peter N., *Millennium III, Century XXI* (Boulder, CO: Westview, 1996).

Stiegler, Bernard, 'The Time of Cinema/On the "New World" and "Cultural Exception" ', *Tekhnema* 4 (Spring 1998), 84-90.

Strozier, Charles B., and Michael Flynn (eds.), *The Year 2000: Essays on the End* (New York: New York University Press, 1997).

Thompson, E.P., 'Time, Work-Discipline and Industrial Capitalism', in *idem*, *Customs in Common* (New York: The New Press, 1991).

Weber, Max, *The Theory of Social and Economic Organization* (trans. A.M. Henderson and Talcott Parsons; New York: The Free Press, 1964 [1947]).

—*The Protestant Ethic and the Spirit of Capitalism* (trans. Talcott Parsons; New York: Charles Scribner's Sons, 1958).

Wilhelm, Richard, *The I Ching or Book of Changes* (trans. Cary F. Bayness; Princeton, NJ: Princeton University Press, 3rd edn, 1997 [1950]).

Wise, M. Norton (ed.), *The Values of Precision* (Princeton, NJ: Princeton University Press, 1995).

http://liftoff.msfc.nasa.gov/Academy/History/vonBraun.html
http://www.mille.org/people/rlpages/cchat.html
http://www.pbs.org/wgbh/amex/bomb/timeline/indextxt.html
http://www.space.edu/projects/book/index.html
http://www.thebulletin.org/index.html

Notes

*   The initial fieldwork in 1995–96 was funded by a grant from the Wenner-Gren Foundation for Anthropological Research; follow-up research in 2000 was supported by the Institute for Collaborative Research and Public Humanities at the Ohio State University; and drafting of the paper in 2002 was made possible by a fellowship from the Institute for the Study of Culture and Society at Bowling Green State University. An earlier version of this essay was presented at the conference 'Sweet in the Mouth, Bitter in the Stomach: Apocalyptic Disappointment and its Millennial Mutations', hosted by the Center for Millennial Studies at Boston University in November 2002. I deeply appreciate the support of these institutions in the research and writing processes. I would like to thank Chris Zacher and Vicki Patraka for their encouragement. Many thanks to Hillel Schwartz for his editorial assistance. Finally, special thanks to Eithne Luibheid for helping me refine the main argument of the essay.

1.   In addition to their uses in public settings, countdown timers and clocks are sold as gifts or tools for managing time in individual uses. For example, skymall.com has advertised the countdown clock as 'a new way to look at time': 'experience the anticipation of watching the days, hours, minutes and seconds tick away until that important date, whether it's 10 months or 10 years away!' The online store tells its consumers to use a countdown clock both to prepare for such an event as wedding, pregnancy, retirement, or 'the big day'; and to do such things as 'reach your goal', and 'complete the project'.

2.   The Christian context of the countdown has been well documented in the scholarly literature on apocalypse. See, for example, Charles B. Strozier and Michael Flynn (eds.), *The Year 2000: Essays on the End* (New York: New York University Press, 1997); Stephen D. O'Leary, *Arguing the Apocalypse* (New York: Oxford University Press, 1994); Peter N. Stearns, *Millennium III, Century XXI* (Boulder, CO: Westview, 1996); and Richard Landes, 'Lest the Millennium Be Fulfilled: Apocalyptic Expectations and the Pattern of Western Chronography 100–800 CE', in Werner Verbeke, Daniel Verhelst and Andries Welkenhuysen (eds.), *The Use and Abuse of Eschatology in the Middle Ages* (Leuven: Leuven University Press, 1988), 137-211.

3.   For a detailed discussion of some of the dates, see Richard Landes, 'The Apocalyptic Year 1000: Millennial Fever and the Origins of the Modern West', in Strozier and Flynn, *The Year 2000: Essays on the End*, 13-29 (22-23).

4.   Landes, 'The Apocalyptic Year 1000', 24.

5.   In Europe and North America, philosophical understanding of time tends to be divided along objective and subjective lines. See J.T. Fraser, *Of Time, Passion, and Knowledge: Reflections on the Strategy of Existence* (New York: George Braziller, 1975), 11-71; Paul Ricoeur, *Time and Narrative, III* (trans. Kathleen Blamey and David Pellauer; Chicago: University of Chicago Press, 1988 [1985]).

6.   See Cornelius Castoriadis, 'Time and Creation', in John Bender and David E. Wellbery (eds.), *Chronotypes: The Construction of Time* (Stanford, CA: Stanford University Press, 1991), 38-64, 231-32.

7.   See Richard Landes, 'Lest the Millennium Be Fulfilled', 156-60.

8.   David L. Landes, *Revolution in Time: Clocks and the Making of the Modern World* (rev. enlarged edn; Cambridge, MA: Harvard University Press, 2000). For a discussion of the wide influence of precision in Europe since the Enlightenment, see M. Norton Wise (ed.), *The Values of Precision* (Princeton, NJ: Princeton University Press, 1995).

9.   See Max Weber's *The Protestant Ethic and the Spirit of Capitalism* (trans. Talcott Parsons; New York: Charles Scribner's Sons, 1958) and *The Theory of Social and Economic Organization* (trans. A.M. Henderson and Talcott Parsons; New York: The Free Press, 1964 [1947]); D. Landes, *Revolution in Time*; and E.P. Thompson, 'Time, Work-Discipline and Industrial Capitalism', in his *Customs in Common* (New York: The New Press, 1991).

10.   For more information, see http://www.thebulletin.org/index.html.

11.   This peace-security continuum may be compared with the Christian apocalyptic discourse based on what Richard Landes calls the rooster-owl continuum – 'Roosters crow that the dawn is imminent and hope to rouse the barnyard to action; owls hush that it is still the middle of the night, the foxes are about, and the master yet sleeps' (http://www.mille.org/people/rlpages/cchat.html).

12.   See John F. Graham, *Space Exploration: From Talisman of the Past to Gateway for the Future* (1995) (http://www.space.edu/projects/book/index.html), ch. 8.

13.   T.A. Heppenheimer, *Countdown: A History of Space Flight* (New York: John Wiley and Sons, 1997), 118.

14.   John B. Medaris, *Countdown for Decision* (New York: G.P. Putnam's Sons, 1960), vii.

15.   This sense of deferral in the countdown to the launching of a rocket is different from the Christian countdown. Delay in launching a rocket is temporary whereas delaying in the Christian discourse of the countdown is an incessant deferral, as shown by the work of Richard Landes, 'The Apocalyptic Year 1000', 13-29.

16.   Medaris, *Countdown for Decision*, vii.

17.   Medaris, *Countdown for Decision*, viii.

18.   Bernard Stiegler, 'The Time of Cinema/On the "New World" and "Cultural Exception" ', *Tekhnema* 4 (Spring 1998), 84-90.

19.   My reading of this film benefits from D.N. Rodowick's discussion of Gilles Deleuze's work on cinema. See D.N. Rodowick, *Gilles Deleuze's Time Machine* (Durham, NC: Duke University Press, 1997) and *Reading the Figural, or, Philosophy after the New Media* (Durham, NC: Duke University Press, 2001).

20.   John Armitage, 'From Modernism to Hypermodernism and Beyond: An Interview with Paul Virilio', in John Armitage (ed.), *Paul Virilio: From Modernism to Hypermodernism and Beyond* (London: SAGE, 2000), 25-55 (36). For a general historical discussion of filmmaking influenced by the nuclear arms race, see Jerome F. Shapiro, *Atomic Bomb Cinema: The Apocalyptic Imagination on Film* (New York: Routledge, 2002).

21.   For a detailed chronology of nuclear arms race between the United States and the Soviet Union between 1941 and 1963, see: http://www.pbs.org/wgbh/amex/bomb/timeline/indextxt.html

22.   Doctor Strangelove apparently represented a German scientist, most likely Wernher von Braun, the German-born rocket scientist who developed the V-2 rocket

for Germany and then defected to the United States, where he helped John F. Kennedy's race to the moon by supervising the development of Saturn rockets. The published screenplay gives more detail: 'Though he was known personally to few people in this room, he had long exerted an influence on United States defense policy. He was a recluse and perhaps had been made so by the effects of the British bombing of Peenemünde, where he was working on the German V-2 rocket. His black-gloved right hand was a memento of this.' See Stanley Kubrick, Peter George, and Terry Southern, *Dr. Strangelove or: How I Learned to Stop Worrying and Love the Bomb* (New York: Bantam Books, 1963), 34-35. Also see Margot A. Henriksen, *Dr. Strangelove's America: Society and Culture in the Atomic Age* (Berkeley, CA: University of California Press, 1997), 323. For a brief biography of Wernher von Braun, see http://liftoff.msfc.nasa.gov/Academy/History/vonBraun.html

23. While the Christian idea of a countdown may be traced to Hippolytus (see Richard Landes, 'Lest the Millennium Be Fulfilled', 144-49, 210-11, Chart II), the Taoist idea may be traced to Zhang Daoling in 142 CE, if not earlier. There is no reason to presume that the Christian tradition is the only relevant context for a genealogical understanding of the countdown of time as an international (if not global) cultural phenomenon. My discussion of Taoism primarily draws upon the work of Kristofer Schipper, *The Taoist Body* (trans. Karen C. Duval; Berkeley, CA: University of California Press, 1993[1982]); *idem*, 'Vernacular and Classical Ritual in Taoism', *Journal of Asian Studies*, 45.1 (1985), 21-57; *idem*, 'The Inner World of the *Lao-Tzu Chung-Ching*', in Chun-Chieh Huang and Erick Zürcher (eds.), *Time and Space in Chinese Culture* (Leiden: E.J. Brill, 1995), 114-31; and *idem*, 'Daoist Ecology: The Inner Transformation: A Study of the Precepts of the Early Daoist Ecclesia', in N.J. Girardot, James Miller and Liu Xiaogan (eds.), *Daoism and Ecology: Ways within a Cosmic Landscape* (Cambridge, MA: The Center for the Study of World Religions, Harvard Divinity School, 2001), 79-93. Also see Kristofer Schipper and Wang Hsiu-huei, 'Progressive and Regressive Time Cycles in Taoist Ritual', in T.J. Fraser, N. Lawrence, and F.C. Haber (eds.), *Time, Science, and Society in China and the West* (Amherst: University of Massachusetts Press, 1986), 185-205.

24. For a detailed discussion, see Schipper and Wang, 'Progressive and Regressive Time Cycles in Taoist Ritual'.

25. Schipper and Wang, 'Progressive and Regressive Time Cycles in Taoist Ritual', 196.

26. The link of inner time to the pregnant body suggests a relationship between the experience of subjective time and feminine temporality. How may we incorporate this Taoist insight into the understanding of women's time? Perhaps not merely in terms of women's struggles against being inserted into men's linear time, as Julia Kristeva points out (in 'Women's Time', *New Maladies of the Soul* [trans. Ross Guberman; New York: Columbia University Press, 1995], 201-24), but also in terms of feminine temporality, its relations to innovative uses of time in capitalism, and change of modes of communication from the mechanical to the fluid, as seen by scholars such as Armand Mattelart and Michele Mattelart in their *Rethinking Media Theory: Signposts and New Directions* (trans. James A. Cohen and Marina Urquidi; Minneapolis: University of Minnesota Press, 1992), esp. chapters 5 and 10.

27. Compared with the Hegelian dialectical historical time that refers to an objective, continuous, progressive, teleological notion of time (see D.N. Rodowick, *Reading the Figural*, 190-93), the outer time in Taoism is not only hierarchical and objectified but also multiple (that is, as a series or a set of temporal elements).

28. For a good English translation, see Richard Wilhelm, *The I Ching or Book of Changes* (trans. Cary F. Bayness; Princeton, NJ: Princeton University Press, 3rd edn, 1997 [1950]).

29. For a detailed discussion, see Li-Chen Lin, 'The Concepts of Time and Position in the *Book of Change* and their Development', in Chun-Chieh Huang and Erick Zürcher (eds.), *Time and Space in Chinese Culture*, 89-113. It would be more appropriate to translate the term *wei* as 'situation' rather than 'position' (the translation used by Lin).

30. Li-Chen Lin, 'The Concepts of Time and Position in the *Book of Change* and their Development'.

31. Scholars often confuse the difference. For example, C.G. Jung, 'Foreword', in *The I Ching or Book of Changes*, xxii.

32. One of the earliest forms of Chinese script, 'oracle bone inscriptions' (*jiaguwen*) that appeared around 1200 BCE, originated in the process of explaining the meaning of the cracks shown on burned bones. The inscriptions, incised on the scapulae of oxen (or occasionally sheep) and on turtle plastrons, recorded questions that diviners in the service of the ruler posed to his deceased ancestors. The diviners recorded the answers as well, and the collected bones served as historical archives. See Lothar Ledderose, *Ten Thousand Things: Module and Mass Production in Chinese Art* (Princeton, NJ: Princeton University Press, 2000), 18; and William G. Boltz, *The Origin and Early Development of the Chinese Writing System* (New Haven: American Oriental Society, 1994).

33. See Wilhelm, *The I Ching or Book of Changes*, 3-10.

34. Examples of harmful events include floods, draughts, wars, and famines. See Schipper, 'The Inner World of the *Lao-Tzu Chung-Ching*', 128-29.

35. Schipper, 'The Inner World of the *Lao-Tzu Chung-Ching*', 129-30.

36. Schipper and Wang, 'Progressive and Regressive Time Cycles in Taoist Ritual', 185. Each traditional Chinese calendar cycle includes 60 years, each of which is formed through the interaction between the celestial and the earthly forces. The celestial force includes ten elements called the 'celestial stems' (*tian'gan*); the latter includes 12 elements called the 'earthly branches' (*dizhi*). See *idem*, 204, Appendix.

37. Schipper, *The Taoist Body*, 91.

38. Schipper and Wang, 'Progressive and Regressive Time Cycles in Taoist Ritual', 188-94.

39. Schipper and Wang, 'Progressive and Regressive Time Cycles in Taoist Ritual', 192.

40. The five measures of life are called the 'five elements' (*wuxing*).

41. The five 'true writs' are considered as basic Taoist text, the first holy book from which all others, including *Daodejing* and *Yijing*, have derived in successive stages of degeneration. See Schipper and Wang, 'Progressive and Regressive Time Cycles in Taoist Ritual', 193.

42. The diagram illustrates a one-day period. It is adapted from Schipper and Wang, 'Progressive and Regressive Time Cycles in Taoist Ritual', 202, figures 6-7.

43. See Schipper and Wang, 'Progressive and Regressive Time Cycles in Taoist Ritual', 197. This sense of inner time is similar to Henri Bergson's concept of 'durée' (duration), the inner experience of 'real time' and psychologically qualitative, hetero-geneous and dynamic with no hint of predictability or linear determinism. See John Mullarkey, *Bergson and Philosophy* (Notre Dame: University of Notre Dame Press, 2000), 2, 9. Bergson's notion of *durée* allows Gilles Deleuze to develop his theory on cinematic 'time-image' which, according to D.N. Rodowick, was a kind of genealogi-cal historical time used in Foucault's discussion of 'effective history'. See Rodowick, *Reading the Figural*. It is important to note that Foucault's notion of 'effective history' is similar to the notion of time in the Taoist countdown. See 'Nietzsche, Genealogy, History', in Paul Rabinow (ed.), *The Foucault Reader* (New York: Pantheon Books, 1984), where Foucault argues that effective history rejects the Hegelian history as 'a teleological movement or a natural process', 76-100 (88). This rejection may be viewed as the affirmation of the end of time associated with 'History' (with a capital-ized 'H'), as shown in Foucault's description of a historical *event* as 'the reversal of a relationship of forces, the usurpation of power, the appropriation of a vocabulary turned against those who had once used it, of a masked "other"' (88). This rejection of the Hegelian historical time involves an irrational turning, just like the Taoist notion of 'the irrational opening', which allows the unfolding of the effective history. Moreover, the construction of this kind of history for Foucault takes place at the site of the body (89), just where Taoism locates the meaning of inner time.

44. For a detailed discussion, see Hai Ren, *The Countdown of Time: Public Displays and Symbolic Economy in China and Hong Kong* (forthcoming).

45. Foucault, 'Nietzsche, Genealogy, History'.

46. Gilles Deleuze, *Cinema 1: The Movement-Image* (trans. Hugh Tomlinson and Barbara Habberjam; Minneapolis: University of Minnesota Press, 1986 [1983]), and *Cinema 2: The Time-Image* (trans. Hugh Tomlinson and Robert Galeta; Minneapolis: University of Minnesota Press, 1989 [1985]).

47. See Rodowick, *Gilleuze's Time Machine*; idem, *Reading the Figural*; Ronald Bogue, *Deleuze on Cinema* (New York: Routledge, 2003).

48. For example, Fredric Jameson, *Postmodernism, or the Cultural Logic of Late Capitalism* (Durham, NC: Duke University Press, 1991).

49. Although Rodowick uses the term 'digital culture' instead of 'postmodernism' to refer to the change, he still regards the change as radical – that is, he maintains that the development of a genealogical historical time is based on a break from the dialec-tical historical time, as shown by his argument that non-linearity or multiplicity com-pletely rejects linearity. See his *Reading the Figural*.

Postcard I

Thomas MacKay

what makes it –
this generous spray of branches –

so ecstatic?

fissure-splendour, up, wood, widening brown
into a shudder of blue

and the part bitten away:
the clutch of sky, the hole
of imagined ramification

bursting
like glee, spilled;

my long sentences end
cut, at breath,

a shearing

song-wounds, song-words
made while passing the leaves
a trembling wake

my votive rounded mouth,
my lexic eye:

what makes it so
plaintive?

hagiographies make martyrs
medieval flat
worded by egg-paint

the pulse beneath the day
meant
by the returning hours
the grudge of rooftops

my time here will be
a map of anecdote

roads of compromise
roads of compromise

the scuttle-sigh of boots over gravel
history paginated by senseless travel

Part II
Re/tension

Holding back, or holding in? Keepsake or imperial reach? What does it mean to take stock of the world, and what are the repercussions of such attempts when absolute? To the degree that a millennial faith underlies ambitions to take full stock of an entire world (by collecting all known writings, for example, or by mapping all realms of knowledge, or by systematizing all aspects of Nature), is apocalypse equally and necessarily incumbent? Are such grand efforts made under the impress of desires to save the world from itself or to open the world to itself?

Here in Part II, Eric Casey explores the curiously longstanding oscillation between the millennial impulse of bibliographers to collect/protect every last scrap and the apocalyptic image of great libraries in ashes, paying particular attention to the sources supporting and legends crowding the ancient libraries of Alexandria and Pergamum. Does such a millennial enterprise as completed collection of the world's wisdom entail catastrophe as requisite punishment for a scholarly hubris, or is it a preemptive strike against the growing likelihood of failure across time, as gaps in a collection become more glaring and irremediable? Is apocalypse in this context an apt but cruel remedy, a *pharmakon,* to millennial illusions of comprehensiveness and the utopian ideal of universal comprehension?

Geoffrey McVey, examining a 1584 text, *The Expulsion of the Triumphant Beast,* finds the Italian philosopher and self-professed magus Giordano Bruno looking back to a fantastic, mystical, elemental Ancient Egypt to find the tools for a total reimagination of the heavens as a means of effecting total transformation of the earth. Bruno's millennium engaged a world of self-magicians who use their incredible arts of memory to reconstruct and conceptually retain the entire, infinite universe; his mission was as much political as philosophical; his end was apocalyptic, a revelation of the world as it could be re-called in great circular graphs, and a flaming disaster, burnt at the stake by the Italian Inquisition. How much would we remember him had he not been put to the torch in the centurial year 1600? How much would he have acted to put the world to rights had he not disputed those astrological and Calvinist schemes of predestination that were being imposed upon a world for which he had been protective, poetic, and passionate?

Francis Bacon meant his 'Great Instauration' of learning and the sciences, described at length in the 1620s, to set in motion a new age as promised by the God of the Old Testament, who gave Adam a mastery of Nature that humankind could eventually resume in the lands beyond Eden, given a labor-intensive method of cultivating evidence and reasoning through the world. Steven Matthews shows that Lord Bacon's own fall from worldly authority (impeached as Chancellor of the Exchequer) led to a shift in his sense of the imminence of the new age, for if he himself had no longer the stately authority to guide the Instauration, the progress of science would be slower, and the new age would have to be more gradual. The restoration, or re-tension, of right religion would come from a proper reading of Scripture in tandem with a perspicacious and cumulative reading of Nature; both kinds of readings would, after all, lift the veil on – and fulfill the promise of – the root of Christianity, not the crucifixion but the incarnation.

H.S.

Collecting the Cosmos:
The Apocalypse of the Ancient Library*

Eric Casey

The Egyptian priests of Thoth reportedly described the *Book of Mankind* as being comprised of 36,525 separate books.[1] A certain Hermes Trismegistus is named as the editor of this massive compilation of texts. The surviving number of hermetic texts is, of course, much smaller and modern scholarship is in general agreement that Hermes Trismegistus is a figure of legend. The extant hermetic texts were composed between 100 and 300 CE, but the magus' existence was so culturally desirable that the myth of this wise Egyptian priest grew up quickly and covered its tracks effectively. Early Church Fathers such as Lactantius and Augustine accepted without question the historicity and productivity of Hermes Trismegistus. Lactantius lived at the time when these texts were being produced, and his belief that one sage man could be the source of so much knowledge evinces a readiness to entertain fantastic notions of textual totality. Hermes embodies classical learning and his purported Egyptian lineage is fitting in that Egypt has often been conceived as one of the most ancient cultures and as a repository for all important knowledge.

The quest for textual totality can be expressed either as producing or as absorbing vast amounts of texts. While Hermes Trismegistus was declared to be the inspiration for most of the favored ancient authors, there are examples of the converse activity of obsessively gathering and collecting to be found in the worlds of history and fiction. In *Nausea*, Jean Paul Sartre created a memorable character in the autodidact who goes to the local library and attempts to read all of the books in alphabetical order. In the nineteenth century, Sir Thomas Phillipps amassed over a lifetime one of the largest private collections of books and manuscripts ever known. Sir Thomas preferred that his collection be called the *Bibliotheca Philippica*, and by the time of his death, he had acquired somewhere near 50,000 books and 60,000 manuscripts. In a letter a few years before his death, Phillips wrote the following to a fellow collector: 'I am buying Printed Books because I wish to have ONE COPY OF EVERY BOOK IN THE WORLD!!!'[2] The impulse to produce, compile, and absorb the totality of texts is taken to the ultimate degree in Borges' short story, 'The Library of Babel', in which the utterly complete library exceeds the bounds of sense-making and contains all possible combinations of letters. By holding absolutely every imaginable text, this library represents an image of infinity itself, and within the walls of this necessarily fictional place, order and chaos merge in a textual totality which cannot begin to be fully ordered or catalogued.

The modalities of collecting, compiling, and consuming enormous amounts of information are epitomized in the greatest of ancient textual experiments, the library constructed by the Ptolemies in Alexandria. In this library and that at Pergamum, we witness an apocalyptic project in the etymological sense of a revealing or unveiling (from the Greek *apokalyptein*, to unveil). In seeking to obtain a universal collection of texts, the Alexandrian leaders and librarians in effect attempted to replicate the contents of the larger cosmos itself, creating what might be termed a textual apocalypse that mirrored the universe while containing it in miniature. While there were libraries and collections of documents for more than 2,000 years before the rise of Alexandria, the Greek librarians in this city did more than merely gather and shelve texts. In attempting to provide the first critical editions, these scholar-librarians altered the texts and by presuming to establish 'correct' readings, they became authors themselves to the extent that they rewrote and thus revealed or unveiled the great works of the past. In this way, Hellenistic editors changed the textual cosmos and textual criticism thereby became merged with cosmological speculation. The libraries at Alexandria and Pergamum are instructive for their differences on this count, as there were at least two distinct strands of ancient editing which relied on different first principles in their common goal of trying to order the collected knowledge of the time. When Alexandrian leaders became involved in sponsoring the translation of the Septuagint and other major cultural and religious texts into Greek, the library became more than a repository for Greek thought: it was nothing less than an effort to encompass the collected knowledge of the known world. This process of gathering texts from across the world paralleled the imperial territorial ambitions of the Ptolemies, a connection strengthened by the fact that the first Ptolemies were serious scholars as well as generals.[3]

We shall examine the prevalent myths surrounding the destruction of libraries and in so doing we shall have recourse to another sense of apocalypse, that of catastrophe and destruction. These two major types of apocalypse (i.e., revelation and destruction) are bound together in narratives about the process of collecting the entire textual cosmos. Collecting itself can function as a kind of defense against fears of systemic cultural collapse, acting to contain a culture in just so many volumes and thereby defending against a disordered society run amok.

Librarians and the Gathering of Information before Alexandria

From their humble beginnings in Mesopotamia, textual collections were dominated by lists and catalogues, and so writing appears to have begun as a way to monitor economic transactions as well as to take inventory of the physical world and its activities. Interestingly, the majority of the first written documents were what Assyriologists call 'receipts' of external expenditures, that is, what had been taken out and disbursed in the world outside the archive.[4] These are more records, then, of what left the archive, not a static notation of things in permanent storage.[5] Many of the documents found in these early archives are records of external matters such as land plans and surveys, agricultural holdings, estimates, and projections.[6] From the beginning, writing was used to create a picture of the larger world and to maintain as an ideal a stable record of ephemeral actions and objects, even if this ambition was unattainable in practice. The earliest archives were often divided into spaces for economic record-keeping and scriptoria where scribes learned to write by copying and recopying all kinds of texts, including long lists of titles, professions, and even sundries found in the world.[7] These word lists include names of plants, trees, cities, birds, fish, and many other categories of creatures and creations.[8] While scribal education was clearly an important factor in the construction and repetition of these lists (many of which were bilingual in Sumerian and Akkadian), their existence constitutes early evidence of the desire to bring order to all parts of the world through writing. Even before kings gathered both territory and texts, scribes amassed lists of kings. The famous Sumerian King List, a lengthy inscription dating back to at least the eighteenth century BCE, purports to list all of the kings of the land dating back to the original descent of kingship from heaven. The list includes brief descriptions of kingly accomplishments and is remarkable for its inclusion of clearly mythical kings such as Enmenluanna who is said to have ruled for 43,200 years. By attributing such fantastic spans of time to the earliest royals, the King List essentially represents a creation story as told and ordered by scribes.[9]

Lists found in archives not only are organized by subject matter but also by the very shape of the tablets which could be circular (e.g., agricultural texts at Tello dating to the Ur III period, 2100–2000 BCE), or oblong (often used for lists of words divided into many columns).[10] The tablets themselves were often grouped by subject matter in baskets or boxes.

Already by the end of the third millennium in Mesopotamia, tablets were well organized and laid out in comprehensible systems. While these archives were generally used for the temporary preservation of daily economic transactions, there is evidence that some texts such as those from Uruk were preserved for several generations, longer than would be strictly necessary for purposes of mundane record-keeping. This suggests a nascent interest in curating archival collections of documents,[11] and it is this tendency along with an expanded range of preserved texts which will transform the archive into a library.

The development of catalogues from bare lists of names and things into detailed bibliographical guides certainly played a role in the further rise of the library. There is a series of tablets from Hattusas dating to the thirteenth century BCE which detail the length of works (by number of tablets), occasionally the authors, and even brief summaries of the contents and notations of missing sections of works. The title of the work is sometimes indicated by listing the first line of the text.[12]

The Assyrian king Ashurbanipal (reigned from 668 to 627 BCE) did not have the first royal library,[13] but he certainly amassed one of the most extensive collections of texts in that early era. Due to the presence of multiple copies and other factors, scholars are divided as to the number of texts, but the estimates range between 1,500 and 5,000 works (most of which took up many tablets each). For our purposes, it is instructive to focus on the content of the extant tablets. By the 1950s, an astonishing 25,357 tablets from this library had been published,[14] divided by the historian Oppenheim into genres according to order of frequency.[15] Omen texts make up the largest group and the next largest concerns magical rituals, prayers, and incantation. After this, we find scholarly lists of names and words as well as bilingual lexical lists to aid translations from Sumerian into Akkadian. Literary texts are by far the smallest group in this eclectic catalogue. This kind of variety makes it clear that Ashurbanipal was engaging in something more wide-ranging and comprehensive than the earlier archives in which agricultural records were the most common type of text. There is an extant Assyrian inscription in the form of a letter which may record the words of Ashurbanipal on the topic of his book collecting and scholarly abilities: 'the hidden treasure, the complete art of the written tablet, have I examined in the houses of heaven and earth, it has been delivered up to me among all experts'.[16]

Priding himself on being the first Assyrian ruler to be so highly trained in scribal matters, Ashurbanipal ordered that tablets be confiscated from public and private collections all across his land. While he mentioned specific desirable ritual and literary texts, Ashurbanipal also issued a general call for any rare tablets and for all the tablets in certain houses, temples, and libraries.[17] While there are some doubts as to the authenticity of the following text, it is fascinating for the sheer scale of its demand to collect almost any available text in the kingdom at large and it would seem to prefigure the Alexandrian impulse to create a universal library:

> You shall collect the tablets (which are recited on) the royal shores of the rivers during the days of the month of Nisan, the stone amulet (which is worn) on the river during the month of Tishri, (the tablet) of the ordeal by water, the stone amulet (which is worn) by the river for reckoning the day (?) 'the four stone amulets (which are placed) at the head and foot of the royal bed', 'the weapon of *eru* wood at the head of the royal bed' (and the tablet bearing) the incantation, 'May Ea and Marduk complete wisdom'. You shall search for and send me (the tablets of) the series 'Battle', as many as are available, together with the tablet 'Their blood' (and) the remaining ones, all that are available; (also the tablets): 'In the battle the spear (?) shall not come near a man', 'To rest in the wilderness (and) again to sleep in the palace', (as well as) rituals, prayers, stone inscriptions and whatever is useful to royalty (such as) expiation (texts) for (the use of) cities, to ward off the (evil) eye at a time of panic, and whatever (else) is required in the palace, all that is available, and (also) rare tablets of which no copies (?) exist in Assyria. I have (already) written to the temple overseer (?) and to the chief magistrate (that) no one shall withhold any tablet from you. And in case you should see some tablet or ritual which I have not mentioned to you (and) which is suitable for the palace, take possession of it, and send it to me.[18]

The sheer length of this request speaks volumes, as it were, about the king's desire to gather texts of all sorts. Amulets in the ancient world often had written on them magical incantations and apotropaic spells, and they were thus worn for the sake of protection. Ashurbanipal seems to have been seeking these amulets in the hopes of finding not only protection but texts.[19] The other texts identified here in all likelihood by reference to their first lines sound as if they might be epic narratives; they may not be related to omens at all.

The above inscription may be the first solid evidence for the concept of a universal library. It can at least be said that Ashurbanipal sought books as plunder in war. We learn from a fragmentary library acquisition catalogue that after conquering his half-brother, who in 648 BCE was ruling Babylon, Ashurbanipal took many tablets from temples and private collections as well as from libraries and brought them all back to the capital Nineveh. The total of this new acquisition appears to be about 2,000 tablets and 300 wooden boards;[20] already at this period the collecting of texts and territory were considered parallel processes.

The prominence of omen texts is also significant in that the collection of such documents suggests another way in which libraries aim to create a textual cosmos that can protect important people from the world outside the library or the land in which it is set. Whereas the early archives sought to capture records of economic transactions and also to create orderly lists of creatures and professions, the library of Ashurbanipal seems also to have been seeking a complete collection of prophetic utterances that could then presumably protect the king and all those close to him in the palace. The impulse to collect as many such texts as possible suggests that this library functioned partly as a repository of divine utterances related to the fate of the king and his country. The types of omen texts are worthy of note as well. The three most popular types of omens described are terrestrial, astrological, and haruspical.[21] Such omens are to be found on the earth, in the sky, and inside the bodies of animals, and so would seem to cover large sectors of the cosmos outside the library. Dream omens are another common type of text mentioned in the acquisition catalogue and thus the individual mental space of humans was also taken into consideration.

Ashurbanipal also collected oracular texts which took the form of re-quests to the sun-god Shamash for information about the present and future health and fortune of the king. In a further effort to divine and catalog the future, the king gathered prophecies about his court delivered not to priests but to ordinary individuals, often women.[22] Note the shift in temporal frames as the first archives recorded transactions from the pre-sent and recent past while the library of Ashurbanipal is full of predictions of the future as well as magical incantations designed to alter the present and future. By collecting all the omen texts and prophecies and keeping them at the library, Ashurbanipal was in a way creating his own apocalyp-tic shrine – a shrine which could reveal the future of his own country.

Literacy and libraries often play a role in the display of royal wealth and cultural status but in the case of Ashurbanipal they also act to protect his very life. The existence of clay tablets with annalistic accounts of kingly exploits has been interpreted to mean that Assyrian kings often used his-torical and literary texts as a form of propaganda to broadcast royal power and prestige to the people at large. There may even have been public read-ings as the royal inscriptions were written in a rarified literary dialect which presumably only the highly trained scribes could read with any ease.[23] While he may have overseen such attempts at textual outreach, Ashur-banipal seems also to have gathered many texts for his own delectation and protection as he states quite clearly in the following inscription:

> The wisdom of Nabu, the signs of writing, as many as have been devised, I wrote on tablets, I arranged [the tablets] in series, I collated [them], and for my royal contemplation and recital I placed them in my palace.[24]

By gathering these tablets for his own private contemplation, Ashurbanipal acknowledged the importance of libraries and consequently the convergence of power and knowledge. He learned the scribal arts himself and effectively became the prime user in his own library, thereby acquiring unmediated access to the pronouncements of the gods. By hoarding texts for his library and circumscribing other people's access to them,[25] Ashurbanipal established his library as an epicenter for the confluence of the royal and the religious and created the image of a bookish conqueror, a veritable librarian king.

Alexandrian Book Collecting and the Creation of a Universal Library

For an institution as well known as the great library at Alexandria, it is remarkable how little reliable information exists about its every aspect: Whose idea was it originally? Who was the first chief librarian?[26] How many books did it hold at its height?[27] When and in what manner were those books lost? Even the physical location of the library itself is not certain. The sources for this kind of information are often late and they offer differing answers to these questions. Aristonicus, a native Alexandrian and noted Homeric scholar who lived at the end of the first century BCE, reportedly wrote a text titled 'On the Museum' but unfortunately it did not survive.[28] In one of the most tantalizing ancient mentions of Alexandria, the second-century CE antiquarian author Athenaeus begins to discuss the origins of the library but stops short: 'And concerning the number of books, the establishing of libraries, and the collection in the Hall of the Muses (Mouseion), why need I even speak, since they are in all men's memories?'[29] In the absence of any new sources, much of this will probably remain shrouded in secrecy,[30] yet our uncertainty has not diminished the status of this institution as a cornerstone of Western culture and history. To the contrary, the disappearance and destruction of the library seem to hold our fascination just as much as – likely even more than – its creation and cultural significance. The library at Alexandria did not emerge out of a cultural vacuum, of course, and some of its notable features recall Aristotle's own book collection[31] as well as the Near Eastern libraries such as that of Ashurbanipal, although the Alexandrians clearly conducted the collection and ordering of texts on an unprecedented scale. The librarians extended the range and sophistication of the earlier lexical lists, created the first comprehensive catalogue of all Greek literature, and, most importantly for our purposes, produced the first critical editions of literary texts. They did not merely gather the texts but actually edited them in an effort to retain the original integrity and authenticity of the works. All of these scholarly activities contributed to an overall project both to preserve and reveal the totality of Greek literature within the confines of a single great library. These activities can be seen as apocalyptic insofar as they aimed at an ultimate revealing or unveiling of a textual cosmos whose stability and uniformity could provide an orderly solution to the chaotic politics outside the library.

Callimachus and the Creation of a Universal Catalogue

While perhaps not one of the chief librarians at Alexandria,[32] Callimachus of Cyrene was a vital contributor to the development of the library and the rise of scholarship. He created one of the most important scholarly works whose influence is still felt indirectly today in the world of bibliography in institutions such as the Library of Congress. Commonly referred to as the *Pinakes* ('Tables'), the complete title of this work is 'Tables of Persons Eminent in Every Branch of Learning together with a List of their Writings' and it was a massive compilation of lists filling 120 books. The *Pinakes* represent the first attempt at a comprehensive catalogue, going well beyond selective lists of titles and professions.[33] The ancient historian P.M. Fraser describes it as 'a sort of universal biography and bibliography',[34] and as such, it combined brief sketches of authors along with titles (or first lines) of their works. Callimachus divided up all these works into genres such as lyric poetry, epic, oratory, philosophy, and so on. This work spawned many imitations such as the anonymous *Pinakes* produced at the rival library in Pergamum and Hesychios' *Onomatologos*.[35] Unfortunately now lost, the *Pinakes* were not merely a collective catalogue of the current library holdings but rather an attempt to describe all known works written in Greek.[36] The *Pinakes* represent the height of the Alexandrian scholarly impulse to order and classify. It is tempting to think that Callimachus compiled the *Pinakes* as a hopeful prediction of the future holdings of the library, when the Alexandrian library catalogue and a master list of all known works would be one and the same. It was intended to be a universal catalogue.

Callimachus also wrote many prose works that sought to describe unexpected and unfamiliar parts of the natural world.[37] Callimachus gathered all of these works into a larger text titled 'Collection of Wonders of the World, Arranged Geographically', but we also have some titles of the individual treatises: On Games; On Winds; On Birds; On Rivers in the Inhabited World; On the Rivers of Europe; On the Wonders and Marvels in the Peloponnese; and On the Changes of Names in Fish.[38] Unlike the researches of Aristotle, these texts were apparently compiled entirely on the basis of earlier written accounts and so Callimachus was creating a prose map of the known world,[39] all while remaining in the confines of the textual universe of the library itself.

About 50 years later, the wide-ranging Alexandrian scholar and chief librarian Eratosthenes composed a similarly comprehensive chronological world history in his work titled *Chronographiai* ('Chronological Tables') which took human history from the Trojan war down to his own time. In so doing, Eratosthenes created possibly the first 'complete' Western chronological table of human history.[40] Eratosthenes was also the first systematic geographer, writing treatises[41] such as 'On the Measurement of the Earth', and *Geographica*, in which he discussed mathematical and descriptive geography, and he famously came up with a surprisingly accurate estimate of the circumference of the earth.[42] These attempts to capture large parts of the known world in the confines of texts could be seen as logical extensions of the lexical lists and vocabularies which were found in the Near Eastern archives of Mesopotamia. It is believed that Eratosthenes constructed and presented to the royal Egyptian court a map of the known world which was by far the most scientific and accurate one of its day. Interestingly, Eratosthenes in his *Geographica* divided the continents geometrically into what he called 'seals' (*sphragides*), a term which can indicate plots of land as well as numbered areas on a map, but which can also refer to the identifying seal on the outside of a papyrus roll. This sort of overlapping terminology between texts, maps, and the physical world suggests an awareness on the part of the Greeks that the earth was a kind of mappable text which could be 'plotted' and closely analyzed. Indeed, the very word *pinax* meant 'board' or 'writing-tablet' but could also be used to describe maps or even astronomical tables.[43] The title of Callimachus' massive bibliographical work (*Pinakes*) could then be metaphorical in that this work indeed mapped out the textual terrain of Greek literature.[44]

There is virtually no direct testimony from the Alexandrian scholars about the project to create a universal library in which all knowledge can reside.[45] However, the unprecedented scope of texts such as Callimachus' *Pinakes* and the mapping projects of Eratosthenes testify to an urge to capture and order the world through scholarship and writing. In fact, there are a number of ancient sources that explicitly state that the plan was to collect all the texts in the known world for the great library. The famed

Letter of Aristeas declares that 'Demetrius of Phalerum, as keeper of the king's library, received large grants of public money with a view to his collecting, if possible, all the books in the world'.[46] Another source describes Ptolemy I as 'being very anxious to adorn (*kosmesai*)[47] the library, which he had founded in Alexandria, with all the best extant writings of all men...'[48] In yet another source we hear that Ptolemy II (Philadelphus) 'brought together every book from everywhere in the inhabited world, so to speak, at the instigation of Demetrius of Phalerum'.[49] Finally, consider the testimony of the fourth-century CE writer Epiphanius who says that Ptolemy Philadelphus ordered Demetrius of Phalerum to 'collect the books in existence in every quarter of the world, and he wrote letters importuning every king and governor on earth to send ungrudgingly the books (that were within his realm or government)'. Epiphanius goes on to say that Ptolemy wanted 'the works of poets and prose writers, orators and sophists, physicians, professors of medicine, historians, and so on'.[50]

It is disputed how many non-Greek works were translated and then stored in the library,[51] but there were certainly a fair number of them, including most notably the Septuagint (Greek translation of the Hebrew Bible), which was probably commissioned in 280 BCE as a way to enlarge the library and to celebrate the beginning of the reign of Ptolemy II.[52] During the reign of Ptolemy Philadelphus, the library benefited from the scholarly work of Manetho, the earliest known Egyptian to write in Greek. In addition to composing a history of Egypt in three books, Manetho translated and added commentary to an Egyptian King list.[53] Perhaps most incredibly, we hear that Hermippus, a scholar and student of Callimachus, set out to write a comprehensive index to a Greek translation of over 2,000,000 Persian verses attributed to Zoroaster.[54] Relying on these anecdotes and a Byzantine treatise claiming that scholars were recruited from around the world, Luciano Canfora argues that the Alexandrians (both the Ptolemies and their librarians) were seeking 'not only to collect every book in the world, but to translate them all into Greek'.[55] As such a translation of Zoroastrian verses would have filled at least 800 volumes, Fraser may be right to be suspicious of this feat of translation as well as the scope of Hermippus' index, but the preponderance of all of these anecdotes does suggest a distinct interest on the part of the Alexandrian librarians to go beyond the confines of Greek literature.

The Alexandrian acquisition methods recall those of Ashurbanipal[56] in that books are procured through sale,[57] donations, and pure thievery. Galen reports that Ptolemy was so concerned about the reputation of his library[58] that he ordered all books found on ships in Alexandria to be confiscated, copied, and the copies handed back to the owners. These books were labelled as having come 'from the ships' (ek *ploion*) so as to distinguish them from books bought or taken elsewhere. In one of the most famous episodes of such bibliomaniacal plunder, Ptolemy (Euergetes I) borrowed from Athens the official copies of the plays of the three great tragedians, had the library staff copy them carefully, and then kept the originals, handing the new copies back to the Athenians. As a result of this, Ptolemy forfeited the enormous sum of 15 talents which he had paid as a deposit for their safe return.[59] This concern for keeping the 'original' text can be seen much earlier in Assyrian libraries and archives,[60] but it is not entirely clear why Ptolemy did not simply keep the lavish copies made by his own library staff. In these cases, the texts sought were valued both for their contribution to the completeness of the library and also for their status as valuable objects themselves.

The Ptolemies and their agents undoubtedly amassed a large number of texts although the sources are frustratingly unclear on this count. In one of the only sources to give a specific number, the twelfth-century Byzantine scholar John Tzetzes claims that the great library within the palace had 490,000 volumes, of which 400,000 were 'mixed' scrolls and 90,000 were 'unmixed' scrolls, and that the smaller, so-called 'daughter' library in the temple of Serapis had 42,800 texts.[61] The 'mixed' (*symmigeis*) scrolls contained more than one work per scroll, either by the same author or by more than one writer, while the 'unmixed' (*amigeis*) scrolls presumably had only one work per scroll, or even parts of a larger work. This rather large number of rolls in the great library has been interpreted to mean that there were many multiple copies of certain authors, although it remains unclear whether such duplicates would be counted in the grand total.

From Word to World: Editors as Authors at Alexandria and Pergamum

The creation and organization of a textual cosmos entails an attempt to interpret and re-organize the order of the larger cosmos. Callimachus was not the only scholar engaged in more than a mundane activitiy of organizing large piles of papyri. Selected by Ptolemy II to be the first librarian at Alexandria, Zenodotus was also the first scholar to produce something like a critical edition of Homer.[62] We have enough evidence to suggest that Zenodotus did more than gather and arrange the Homeric epics, although the exact nature of Zenodotus' critical work is murky in many spots.[63] Tzetzes tells us that Zenodotus was the first to revise and emend the text of Homer,[64] but there is unfortunately very little direct evidence concerning the motivations for his editorial choices.[65]

While there are similarities in the way that both libraries tried to gather as many books as possible, there were important differences in the editorial strategies of scholars at Alexandria and Pergamum. The center of the Attalid kingdom, Pergamum quickly became a scholarly competitor to Alexandria although to some extent, this rivalry has been exaggerated and it appears that the two places had different areas of expertise. The Alexandrian librarians prided themselves on creating careful critical editions of literary texts while the Pergamene scholars were more philosophically motivated and tended to approach the editing of literary texts from a Stoic perspective. For instance, in accordance with the Stoic belief in the primacy of reason (*logos*) everywhere, the Pergamene scholar Crates sought to find grand philosophical allegories in Homer. The Stoics often used allegory to show that Homer and other early Greek poets were important precursors for Stoic ideas.[66] For his part, Crates used the Stoic methods not so much to prove the existence of Stoic ideas in Homer, but rather to discern the true meaning of Homer's poetry. Crates was engaged in a process of unveiling the true meanings of a text whereas Zenodotus and the Alexandrians were more concerned to recover the exact words of the original text. Crates' enthusiasm for all things Stoic led him to criticize Hesiod's depiction of Earth and Sky in the *Theogony* and we hear that he may have even rewritten a line of Hesiod about the Cyclopes so as to better fit Stoic ideas. The scholia preserve traces of many disputes between Crates and the Alexandrian librarian-scholar Aristarchus, and it is not difficult to see why these scholars would tend to disagree. While Aristarchus might have suggested a different word or phrase in a given line of Homer, he always tried to be consistent with the rest of the Homeric corpus, and he probably would not have taken out a line he didn't like and composed a new one.[67]

In order to get a better sense of the competing strategies of textual editing and interpretation at both libraries, let us consider the evidence for how Crates and Zenodotus handled a single Homeric passage. Crates insisted that the lengthy description of Achilles' shield in book 18 of the *Iliad* should be interpreted allegorically. By way of contrast, Zenodotus simply banished the entire 125-line description of the shield presumably for being atypical in the text of Homer and thus inauthentic. Crates interpreted the shield of Agamemnon (11.32-40) in much the same way, suggesting that the ten parts of this shield represented nothing less than the ten celestial circles. Crates indeed seems to have described one or both shields as 'an imitation of the cosmos' (*kosmou mimema*).[68]

The Alexandrian editors beginning with Zenodotus have generally been criticized for their tendency to question the authenticity of literary passages solely because they depict the gods in unseemly and unflattering lights. For instance, Zenodotus is said to have rejected three lines in the *Iliad* where Aphrodite is depicted as carrying a chair for Helen.[69] In another instance, an ancient commentator or scholiast claimed that Zenodotus altered a line of the *Iliad* 'because he believed it is out of character for a goddess to *endeavour* to find the object of her search'.[70]

Despite their differing interpretive stances, Crates and Zenodotus were both doing something revolutionary in that they were turning the scribe into an author and, more importantly, inverting the usual relationship between the author and the world. While the earlier Near Eastern curators and scribes were using lists of words and names to organize and describe the world, Crates relied on Stoic philosophical ideas about the universe in order to create the best possible text of Homer and Zenodotus did the same in imposing a certain moral framework on the epic poem. [71] They were using their conceptions of the cosmos so as to create a better text whereas earlier scribes typically used texts to order the cosmos.

There are anecdotes about a certain spirit of rivalry between the two libraries. This extended even to differing preferences in what to call themselves. Eratosthenes was the first scholar to call himself a philologist (*philologos*) and many Alexandrians followed suit or chose the term *grammatikos*. The Pergamenes preferred the term *kritikos*. On a more serious note, the ancient sources claim that Ptolemy V banned the export of papyrus to Pergamum so as to frustrate Eumenes II in his attempt to build up the library at Pergamum. In response, Crates is supposed to have invented the art of writing on parchment. While this is technically false since writing on animal skins had been done for centuries already, it is possible that Crates and his fellow Pergamenes did advance the method of treating and preparing the animal skins and thus produced a higher quality of writing material.[72]

The competition between the libraries to procure ever more books led to the purchase of forgeries, and in at least one case, Alexandrian scholars gleefully pointed out the presence of a forged speech in a Pergamene edition of the works of the great orator Demosthenes.[73] This apparently did not stop the Alexandrians from buying the same edition for their own library. Scholars at both libraries even occasionally created their own forgeries as a pastime. We hear that a certain Cratippus composed a work titled *Everything Thucydides Left Unsaid*, and wrote it in the voice of an Athenian contemporary of Thucydides. Evidently not everyone realized it was a fabrication and both Dionysius of Halicarnassus and Plutarch treat it as a legitimate source. Despite the rivalry and the different foci at each library, there was some overlap between the two groups of scholars in terms of methodologies and interpretive first principles.[74] Alexandrians did apparently make some textual decisions on philosophical and even ethical grounds. Conversely, there is evidence of some Pergamene interest in, and even plagiarism of, Callimachean works.[75] The Alexandrians generally acknowledged the Pergamenes as being superior in their researches into grammar, but the first formal grammar of the Greek language was produced in Alexandria by Dionysius of Thrax, a student of Aristarchus.

Regardless of the range of motivations for their editorial changes, in 'correcting' the texts of Homer and other esteemed authors, Zenodotus, Crates, and the other librarian-scholars[76] were in the position of rewriting or recreating the great works of the past, and they were in a sense secondary creators who decided what would remain and what would be ostracized from their respective textual territories. It is often difficult to tell whether the editors chose a better text from a different manuscript or simply composed what seemed a more appropriate word or phrase, as the Greek word for 'correction' (*diorthosis*) can refer to either process.[77] In any case, either sort of alteration involves a creative intrusion into the textual universe of the authors. Zenodotus and his successors effectively became in the process authors themselves and transformed the job of the librarian-curator from merely gathering, arranging, and storing texts to participating in the creation and re-presentation of these texts. The process of editing texts amounts to a process of unveiling or revealing the literary cosmos and is thus a creative act that produces culture even while purporting merely to be collecting and guarding it.

The Apocalyptic Eschata of Libraries

Eventually, the library becomes the world, as the librarian cannot allow even the smallest hint of life outside the structure to remain. To do so would be to reveal a fatal flaw, to place the entire structure in danger of collapse, of burning down, and it would force him to face his own bodily existence, which is not monumental or likely to become so.[78]

As we turn to the endings of Alexandria and Pergamum, we are confronted with a different sort of apocalypse, that of catastrophe by fire or ruination. Since the ancient sources for the fire in Alexandria are inconsistent and incomplete, we will probably never know with absolute certainty how extensive this fire was and how much of the book collection was destroyed. Most remarkable for our purposes is the fervent desire on the part of many sources to connect cultural catastrophe with this site of knowledge and revelation. While it may seem that apocalypse as catastrophe is primarily a modern concept, the ancient library is consistently associated in the scholarly and popular imagination with both the preservation of information and the fiery destruction of that site of knowledge. In some cases, the sources create fanciful and fiery stories about earlier libraries and their similarly untimely ends. Despite uncertainties about the very location of the royal library and whether in fact the fire may have damaged only the smaller library located in the temple of Sarapis,[79] scholars both ancient and modern spend a great deal of time debating the particulars of the fire and how many books were lost, ignoring other potential reasons for this loss of Greek literature. The truth of the matter about the end of both Alexandria and Pergamum was in all likelihood more mundane but this only makes the longstanding interest in the stories of textual catastrophe all the more intriguing. We will briefly look at the evidence for the fire at Alexandria and then turn to the story of Pergamum and the alleged theft of all its books by Mark Antony. This improbable but interesting story provides perhaps the last point of connection between the fates of these rival libraries.

For part of the story, at least, the sources are all in agreement. Julius Caesar was involved in a brief war against Egyptian forces in 48 BCE and he occupied the Brucheion, that region of Alexandria in which the enormous royal palace was located. According to Plutarch's frustratingly brief description, this is what occurred on that momentous day:

> First, he [Julius Caesar] came very close to being cut off from any sources of water when the enemy dammed up the canals. Second, in order to save his fleet from being cut off he had to repel the danger with fire, which then spread from the docks and destroyed (*diephtheire*) the great library (*megalen bibliotheken*). Third, during a battle off Pharos, he leapt from the breakwater into a dinghy in order to lend his support to his men in the thick of fighting, but Egyptian ships bore down on him from all sides, and he had to hurl himself into the sea and swim to safety – a difficult feat which he only just managed.[80]

This is unfortunately all Plutarch has to say on the matter of the famous fire, and it does not even merit as much textual space as Caesar's unexpected plunge into the sea. It is perhaps significant that he specifies the great library, as if to distinguish it from the lesser library in the Serapeion. There are a multitude of sources for this mysterious fire and many of them expand or combine versions of the story in confusing ways. Luciano Canfora has done an admirable job disentangling the knotted skein of references and I will not attempt to duplicate here his careful and extensive treatment of the sources and the complicated interrelations between them.[81] I will only point to a few major currents that are of interest to us.

Before this, it will be useful to review what is known about the great library and the smaller one in the Serapeion. The great library was inside or attached to the Mouseion, a temple dedicated to the Muses[82] which was located within the king's larger palace complex. Unfortunately, not a single account of the Mouseion survives from the third or second centuries BCE and we are left only with the later (first-century BCE) description of Strabo, who makes no mention of the library in his tour.[83] Strabo's silence and the complete lack of archaeological evidence suggest that there was no separate building for the great library at Alexandria. This famous library may have consisted of little more than storage rooms with bookshelves and perhaps a single large room attached to the back of one of the stoas (i.e., covered colonnades) in the Mouseion.[84] The rival library at Pergamum is the only Hellenistic library whose physical structure can still be traced in any detail and it consists only of a few store-rooms and a large cult-room located near a stoa in the precinct of Athena Polias.[85] The Athenian Lyceum – the school of Aristotle – may also have influenced the layout of Alexandria's library and from what we can tell, this had a similar configuration of storage rooms with an adjoining stoa at the back of the structure.[86] The more familiar modern image of a monumental library with reading rooms derives from the later libraries in Imperial Rome and Athens.[87]

There is no direct evidence from the Ptolemaic period about how many libraries there were in Alexandria, but most scholars have accepted Tzetzes' claim that there were two, which he distinguished by calling one the library outside the palace and the other the library within the palace.[88] The fourth-century CE writer Epiphanius says more specifically that the library in the Broucheion region was the first library and 'still later another library was built in the Serapeion, smaller than the first, which was called the daughter of the first one'.[89] Unlike the situation for the great library, there is some archaeological evidence for the Serapeion and there was a stoa at the south end of the sanctuary which could have housed the smaller library.[90]

This brief discussion of the two libraries and their possible locations is important because of the ways that the fire is described in the sources. Whereas Plutarch straightforwardly suggests that the great library was destroyed, other sources such as Cassius Dio imply that the fire destroyed a great number of rolls but left the great library relatively or even completely unscathed. Cassius Dio describes the fire in the following way: 'Many places were set on fire, with the result that, along with other buildings, the dockyards and the storehouses of grain and books, said to be great in number and of the finest, were burned'.[91] As Canfora demonstrates through a careful comparison of phrases in a variety of sources, Cassius Dio derives his information ultimately from Livy, although unfortunately it is one of the lost books of Livy for which we have only a brief epitome by the later author Florus. In passages apparently also derived from Livy, Seneca the Younger[92] and Orosius claim that 40,000 rolls were lost in the fire, which certainly would suggest that much if not all of the smaller library was lost. This number is close to the figure cited by Tzetzes for the number of rolls in the smaller library in the Serapeion; thus it is tempting to conclude that only the smaller library was affected by the fire. Orosius' description is worth citing as it adds something potentially significant: 'when the flames also invaded part of the city they consumed forty thousand books that chanced to be in the buildings nearby'.[93] If we combine the information from Orosius and Cassius Dio, it would seem that the fire started down by the water in the dockyards and spread to some depots or storehouses which happened to be storing 40,000 rolls. The great library was known to have an accessions department which would carefully take down the basic information about books before they were placed into the general collection. The 40,000 rolls could then reasonably represent either the texts in the smaller library in the Serapeion or a cache of rolls recently acquired and waiting to be catalogued by the accessions department. As we noted above in the story about the standing order to seize texts from ships visiting Alexandria, such rolls were carefully labelled as having come 'from the ships'. Unfortunately, we do not have any idea where the accessions department for the great library was located and to make things worse, we are not certain of the function of the smaller library in the Serapeion. It is conceivable but impossible to confirm that these two places were one and the same.[94]

It was suggested in a nineteenth-century German dissertation that Caesar dragged books out of the great library and brought them down to the harbor, with the intent of sending them all to Rome. This would give another explanation for why a large quantity of books chanced to be down by the dockyards when the unfortunate fire started. This is imaginative but it seems rather unlikely that Caesar would have had the time or presence of mind to move that many books out of the great library when he was surrounded by Egyptian forces and fighting for his life.[95] We do hear, however, that Julius Caesar was sufficiently impressed by the great library at Alexandria that he planned to create a major library in Rome upon his return, one of many projects cut short by his assassination in 44 BCE.[96] In another attempt to connect the great library with the fire, some eighteenth-century scholars tried to push the location of the great library closer and closer to the sea so that it could then plausi-

bly have been destroyed in the fire by the dockyards.[97] It is worth noting
that the fourth-century CE Roman historian Ammianus Marcellinus was
apparently offended by the thought that a Roman could have set such a
disastrous fire, and chose to follow the second-century CE author Aulus
Gellius' suggestion that some auxiliaries fighting alongside Caesar must
have accidentally set the fire.[98] In an amazing irony of history, the auxiliaries in question would probably have been recruited from Pergamum.
Hence it is just possible that Pergamene soldiers set a fire that ultimately
destroyed the great library and thus brought to a seemingly definitive
conclusion the rivalry between Alexandria and Pergamum.

Before turning to the evidence for the end of the library at Pergamum,
I want to examine briefly Aulus Gellius' account of Greek libraries before
Alexandria as it brings up an interesting constellation of ideas surrounding the end of an empire and a corresponding catastrophe. Aulus Gellius
locates the origins of Greek libraries in sixth-century BCE Athens with the
following words:

> Pisistratus, the tyrant, is said to have been the first to make books concern-
> ing the liberal arts available to the public to read. Afterwards, the Athenians
> themselves built up the collection with care and toil. But when Xerxes
> occupied Athens and burned the city apart from the Acropolis, he stole all
> this wealth of books and took them away with him to Persia. Much later
> King Seleucus, known as Nicanor, had all these books restored to Athens.[99]

While this account has little to recommend it by way of historical
accuracy, it is fascinating for the idea of the displacement of public libraries to archaic Athens.[100] Even more significant is the notion that Xerxes
stole all of the rolls from these Athenian libraries and then burned the city.
In this case, an ancient source imaginatively combines the end of an empire with a great theft of books and an accompanying fiery catastrophe.
Aulus Gellius is here taking the historical burning of Athens by Xerxes and
infusing it with elements of the alleged later fire in the Alexandrian library.
There is no evidence to support the claim that Xerxes plundered large
numbers of rolls from Athens, and it is probably anachronistic for Aulus
Gellius to suggest the existence of a public library at Athens in the sixth
century BCE.[101] Aulus Gellius has displaced the end of the library at Alexandria back in time. In so doing, Aulus Gellius provides an attractive but
illusory parallel between the fates of what he thinks to be the first and last
of the great Greek libraries. Already in the second century CE, writers were
so interested in juxtaposing sites of revelation and destruction that they
inserted a fictional library into an anecdote about fiery catastrophe.

There is a similar nexus of revelation, destruction, and theft in the story
about the end of the library at Pergamum. In stark contrast to the numer-

ous extant accounts of the fiery destruction at Alexandria, the end of Pergamum's library is told only once in an ancient source, Plutarch's life of Mark Antony. As was the case with his account of the fire at Alexandria, Plutarch is quite laconic in his description of this momentous event, but I will give a bit of the surrounding text for reasons that will become obvious:

> Besides this, Calvisius, one of Octavian's friends, accused Antony of a number of other excesses in his behavior towards Cleopatra: he had presented her with the libraries at Pergamum which contained two hundred thousand scrolls; at a banquet with a large company present he had risen from his place and anointed her feet, apparently to fulfil some compact or wager...[102]

Even more remarkable than the brevity of the remark and its context as just one of five seemingly slanderous accusations from a certain Calvisius, Plutarch himself virtually discounts this anecdote: 'However, Calvisius was generally believed to have invented most of these accusations'. Despite the fact that this story about Antony appears nowhere else and does not even seem to convince the one author who recounts it, the episode has been accepted by a large number of modern scholars without any questions asked.[103]

The putative gift of books from Antony to Cleopatra is interesting on several counts. Antony was in control of the area that included Pergamum and so in a sense, he represents Pergamum on his visit to Cleopatra who was the last Ptolemaic ruler of Alexandria. The gift, which is often explained as having taken place around 41 BCE, is alleged to have been recompense for the terrible fire which destroyed so much of the library at Alexandria. Once fierce rivals, the libraries were then brought together by amorous representatives of each place. Thus, the gift of the books simultaneously revives one library and destroys another. Here again is the collocation of revelation and catastrophe, the two major senses of apocalypse. In order for Alexandria to revive and reveal more information, Pergamum must be destroyed and its books presented by Antony as an offering to Cleopatra.[104]

The decision of ancient and modern scholars alike to focus on the possible spectacular ends of these libraries surely speaks to a desire to associate the ends of empire with the destruction of centers of learning and revelation. The association between conquering and the theft or destruction of books was operative already in Mesopotamia by the time of Ashurbanipal, and the act of burning books as a dramatic expression of victory and of the triumph of one culture over another can be seen in other times ranging from ancient China to Nazi Germany.[105] In fact, however, the actual historical ends of Alexandria and Pergamum are more accurately termed slow declines than quick catastrophes. In the case of Alexandria, Ptolemy VIII continued the tradition of the first few Ptolemies in that he was interested in learning and scholarship, but he was also apparently psychologically unstable and eventually banished the great librarian and scholar Aristarchus as well as many other top scholars. The library never really recovered its scholarly momentum and by the time of the putative fire in 48 BCE, the only scholars left working in the library at the Mouseion were diligent but drab souls such as Didymus whose incredible lifetime output of about 3,500 commentaries earned him the sobriquet 'the bronze-gutted one', an apparent reference to his productive but plod-ding ways. He was also called *bibliolathas* ('forgetful of books') since it was claimed that he could not even remember all the books he had com-posed.[106] Almost every scrap he wrote has been lost, but Didymus is of special interest in that he was working in the library at the time of the alleged fire and he continued to do so for many years thereafter. It is diffi-cult to explain how he could have written so much without most of the resources of the great library at his disposal.[107]

It is certainly suggestive as well that nowhere in his voluminous writ-ings and frequent paeans to the power and beauty of learning and knowl-edge does Cicero ever mention a fire in the library at Alexandria. Writing in the second century CE, the imperial biographer Suetonius provides two more anecdotes about the continuing existence and functioning of the great library. First, we hear that the emperor Claudius enlarged the Mou-seion at Alexandria and arranged public readings of his own works there, something that would certainly imply the continuing existence of the great library.[108] Second, Suetonius recounts that the emperor Domitian sent scholars and scribes to Alexandria in order to make copies of works previ-ously lost during the reign of Nero in the great fire at Rome in 64 CE.[109] This story is particularly intriguing in that the collection at Alexandria not only seems to have been extant during the reign of Nero (54–68 CE), but to have been a resource used to restore the holdings of Roman libraries after a major fire.[110] This would certainly suggest that Alexandria still had the best collection of Greek literature more than 100 years after the fire that allegedly consumed the bulk of the collection. As a final example of Roman interactions with the Alexandrian library in the Imperial period, the emperor Hadrian, during whose reign (117–138 CE) Suetonius com-posed his biographies, appointed his own teacher to be both the director of libraries in Rome and also the head of the Mouseion in Alexandria.[111]

While its ostensible pillaging by Mark Antony was not as widely broadcast as the purported fire at Alexandria, the Pergamene library also seems to have survived well past the tale of its catastrophic end. Unlike earlier regimes where leaders courted the image of being intellectuals who worked closely with the royal librarians, the oversight of the Pergamene library gradually fell to political appointees and lesser intellectual lights.[112] The death of Attalus II ushered in what had to be a nadir for the library when he was succeeded by his dim nephew who apparently spent his brief time in office (138–133 BCE) poisoning his relatives, tending to a garden, and creating wax models.[113] At the end of the unproductive reign of Attalus III, Pergamum was given over to Rome and it became part of the Roman province of Asia. While it became less of a priority for those now in charge of Pergamum, the library remained an important intellectual center for several hundred more years. The dramatic tale of Pergamum being looted by Mark Antony is belied by the largely reliable reports of the library's later patronage by leading intellects such as the medical writers Galen in the second century CE and Oribasius in the fourth century CE. We also hear that the emperor Julian studied philosophy at Pergamum in his youth.

Why do we not focus on the gradual decline but rather on the dramatic fall of these great libraries – no matter how fanciful the stories seem? The answer may be that vanished libraries are metonymic for disappearing empires of culture and knowledge, and it is perhaps no coincidence that both libraries allegedly met their ends at the hands of culturally ascendant Romans. Just as these great collections of texts stood as monuments to Alexandrian and Pergamene power and prestige, the persistent rumors of their destruction embodied the general decline in the cultural and military hegemony of Greece at the close of the Hellenistic period.

In succeeding centuries, Alexandria continued to be the subject of attacks both real and imagined at the hands of Roman rivals, fellow pagans, Christians, and finally the Arab general Amru.[114] The Roman general Aurelian and the emperor Diocletian reportedly besieged the city of Alexandria near the end of the third century CE and probably caused further damage to the Mouseion and the royal book collections. The smaller library in the Serapeion was reportedly destroyed in 391 CE by the Christian bishop Cyril and a band of fanatical monks as part of sweeping attacks on pagan temples in Alexandria. The story of the seventh-century CE Caliph Omar ordering the burning of all the books in Alexandria is in all likelihood a similar fiction representing another shift of power as exemplified through the possession or destruction of a culture's collected knowledge.[115] According to the story, after kindling the ire of the Caliph for their pagan contents, the books were relegated to be the fodder for heating the several thousand public baths throughout the city. It allegedly took up to six months to burn all the books.

While the library served as a symbolic repository for the successes and failures of competing empires, the actual fate of the grand collections was probably more mundane. The Egyptian preference for fragile papyrus[116] over the more durable clay tablets of the Near East undoubtedly played a larger, if less dramatic, role in the eventual disappearance of the Alexandrian library than any of these imagined fiery conflagrations. The invading forces of mould, worms, and decay provided the unromantic and unstoried denouement for much of the ancient library's holdings.

Making Ends Meet in the Library

In the end, it cannot be denied that the Alexandrians failed at their project of completing the universal library. In a telling exchange between Ptolemy II and Demetrius of Phalerum, the king asks how many works they have collected thus far. Demetrius is said to have responded with the following words:

> There are about 54,800. We hear, however, that there is a great quantity of books among the Ethiopians, the Indians, the Persians, the Elamites, the Babylonians, the Chaldaeans, the Romans, the Phoenicians and the Syrians. At Jerusalem, in Judea, too, there are sacred books that speak of God...[117]

One could argue that they were just beginning the process of creating the collection that would become the great library, but the fact remains that they were never able to procure all the books from all of these countries, and we have evidence as well that they could not ever acquire all of Greek literature as a number of texts had already been lost by the Hellenistic period.[118] The failure of Alexandria to achieve the universal library did not deter others from continuing to try to do so, and there are numerous later attempts at textual totality in the historical record. To facilitate his writing of a complete human history, the tenth-century Emperor Constantine VII Porphyrogennetos put out a call for 'books of all kinds' to be retrieved from all over the known world.[119] The Renaissance humanist Johannes Cuno is reported to have kept a collection of all the proofs from the press of Aldus Manutius, including even bad copies with mistakes. Apparently, he believed that any and every written or printed text could be helpful in the search for philosophical truth.[120] August, the sixteenth-century Duke of Saxony, made it his goal to collect all of the printed works available in Europe; he reportedly spent many years writing by hand the titles and vital information for each book on the spines. The Bodleian library in England was started as an imitation of Alexandria and the Library of Congress for a long time aimed to have a copy of every book printed in the United States. In the age of information and with millions of pages of text posted on the web and constantly changing, this quest seems ever more remote, and it is telling that Matthew Battles begins his history of libraries with the following words: 'When I first went to work in Harvard's Widener Library, I immediately made my first mistake: I tried to read the books'.[121]

Regardless of the ultimate folly in attempting to collect and absorb all of the books, there is enduring value in the collecting impulse. A certain transformation of time occurs in the composition and replication of the textual universe. Even if the universalizing impetus to gather a textual totality in a single space ultimately fails, nevertheless all libraries do succeed in bringing the past into the present. The desireable consequence of collapsing history into an accessible and eternal present has been noted by many. For instance, Socrates hoped that the afterlife could be a continual conversation with great minds of the past,[122] whereas Jonathan Swift envisioned a comical confrontation involving famous authors in his 'Battle of the Books'. Machiavelli provides perhaps the most magisterial description of such an encounter:

> On the threshold I slip off my day's clothes with their mud and dirt, put on my royal and curial robes, and enter, decently accoutred, the ancient courts of men of old, where I am welcomed kindly and fed on that fare which is mine alone, and for which I was born: where I am not ashamed to address them and ask them for the reasons for their action, and they reply considerately; and for two hours I forget all my cares, I know no more trouble, death loses its terrors: I am utterly translated in their company. [123]

Beginning at the End

As sites of revelation and catastrophe in both personal perception and cultural preservation, libraries simultaneously succeed and fail. The Alexandrians found themselves amidst a chaotic world of competing languages and cultures, and their response was to create a single space in which all communication could be contained. Their attempt to make this a true universal library fell short, but they created an indelible ideal of containing the cosmos through collecting. Perhaps the stories of fiery conflagration serve to mask the inevitable failure of this sisyphean struggle to create a universal library. By creating an apocryphal apocalypse in the popular imagination, the great fire of Alexandria preserved the cultural hope for textual totality even while consigning the actual collection to flames. Because knowledge never ceases to be produced, any library is always and

necessarily incomplete.[124] The fruitless attempts to create universal libraries have shown that the apocalyptic revelation of knowledge cannot continue forever in one place, but will necessarily migrate: the textual cosmos
has to be a moveable monument if it is to escape the flames.

In certain circumstances, one culture's catastrophe becomes another
culture's revelation. The over 1,800 papyri at Herculaneum which are
still being unrolled survive only because of the accidental preservation
afforded them through the volcanic eruption of Mount Vesuvius in 79
CE.[125] I conclude with a brief return to the Assyrian clay tablets as a final
image of the coupling of apocalyptic revelation and destruction at the site
of the ancient library. Most of these clay tablets were never intended to
be permanent records; they were kept generally as long as they were
relevant, and then discarded. Not infrequently, hostile forces would burn
down an archive as an act of aggression, but this has proven to be as reve-
latory for us as it was destructive for the owner. The flames reached the
tablets, baking them and thereby transforming them from ephemeral
records into permanent documents. The immediate catastrophe of an
apocalyptic destruction sometimes is the necessary condition for future
apocalyptic revelations where endings are really beginnings.

Bibliography

Archi, Alfonsi, 'Archival Record-Keeping at Ebla 2400–2350 BC', in Brosius (ed.), *Ancient
     Archives and Archival Traditions*, 17-37.
Basbanes, Nicholas A., *A Gentle Madness: Bibliophiles, Bibliomanes, and the Eternal Passion
     for Books* (New York: Henry Holt, 1995).
—*Patience and Fortitude: A Roving Chronicle of Book People, Book Places, and Book
     Culture* (New York: Harper Collins, 2001).
—*A Splendor of Letters: the Permanence of Books in an Impermanent World* (New York:
     Harper Collins, 2003).
Battles, Matthew, *Library: An Unquiet History* (New York: W.W. Norton, 2003).
Blum, Rudolf, *Kallimachos: The Alexandrian Library and the Origins of Bibliography* (trans.
     Hans H. Wellisch; Madison: University of Wisconsin Press, 1991).
Brosius, M. (ed.), *Ancient Archives and Archival Traditions: Concepts of Record-Keeping in
     the Ancient World* (New York: Oxford University Press, 2003).
Canfora, Luciano, *The Vanished Library: A Wonder of the Ancient World* (trans. Martin Ryle;
     Berkeley, CA: University of California Press, 1989).
Casson, Lionel, *Libraries in the Ancient World* (New Haven, CT: Yale University Press,
     2001).
Castillo, Debra, *The Translated World: A Postmodern Tour of Libraries in Literature* (Talla-
     hassee: Florida State University Press, 1984).
Collins, Nina L., *The Library in Alexandria and the Bible in Greek* (VTSup, 82; Leiden: Brill,
     2000).
Copenhaver, Brian, *Hermetica* (New York: Cambridge University Press, 1992).
Dilke, O.A.W., *Greek and Roman Maps* (Baltimore: The Johns Hopkins University Press,
     1985).

Diringer, David, *The Book before Printing: Ancient, Medieval, and Oriental* (New York: Dover Publications, 1982).

P.E. Easterling and B.M.W. Knox, 'Books and Readers in the Greek World', in *idem* (eds.), *The Cambridge History of Greek Literature* (Cambridge: Cambridge University Press, 1985), 1-41.

Fraser, P.M., *Ptolemaic Alexandria*, I and II (3 vols.; New York: Oxford University Press, 1972).

Gigante, Marcello, *Philodemus in Italy: The Books from Herculaneum* (trans. Dirk Obbink; Ann Arbor: University of Michigan Press, 2002).

Grandazzi, Alexandre, *The Foundation of Rome: Myth and History* (trans. J.M. Todd; Ithaca: Cornell University Press, 1997).

Hansen, E.V., *The Attalids of Pergamon* (Ithaca: Cornell University Press, 1971).

Kotansky, Roy, 'Incantations and Prayers for Salvation on Inscribed Greek Amulets', in C.A. Faraone and D. Obbink (eds.), *Magika Hiera: Ancient Greek Magic and Religion* (New York: Oxford University Press, 1991), 107-137.

Kilgour, Frederick G., *The Evolution of the Book* (New York: Oxford University Press, 1998).

Kramer, Samuel N., *The Sumerians: Their History, Culture, and Character* (Chicago: University of Chicago Press, 1963).

Kuhrt, Amélie, *The Ancient Near East c. 3000–330 BC*, I (2 vols.; New York: Routledge, 1995).

Lerberghe, Karel Van, 'Private and Public: The Ur-Utu Archive at Sippar-Amnanum (Tell ed-Der)', in Brosius (ed.), *Ancient Archives and Archival Traditions*, 59-77.

Mahaffy, J.P., *Greek Life and Thought from the Death of Alexander to the Roman Conquest* (London: Macmillan, 1896).

Marcus, Leah, 'Renaissance/Early Modern Studies', in S. Greenblatt and G. Gunn (eds.), *Redrawing the Boundaries: The Transformation of English and American Literary Studies* (New York: MLA, 1992), 41-63.

Millard, Alan, 'Aramaic Documents of the Assyrian and Achaemenid Periods', in Brosius, *Ancient Archives and Archival Traditions*, 230-40.

Mosshammer, A. (ed.), *Georgii Syncelli Ecloga Chronographica* (Leipzig: Teubner, 1984).

Muensterberger, Werner, *Collecting: An Unruly Passion* (Princeton, NJ: Princeton University Press, 1994).

Ogden, Daniel, *Magic, Witchcraft, and Ghosts in the Greek and Roman Worlds* (New York: Oxford University Press, 2002).

Oppenheim, A.L., *Ancient Mesopotamia: Portrait of a Dead Civilization* (Chicago: University of Chicago Press, 2nd edn, 1977).

Parsons, Edward Alexander, *The Alexandrian Library, Glory of the Hellenic World: Its Rise, Antiquities, and Destructions* (New York: Elsevier Press, 1952).

Pearson, Edmund, *The Old Librarian's Almanack* (Woodstock: The Elm Tree Press, 1909).

Pedersén, Olof, *Archives and Libraries in the Ancient Near East 1500–300 B.C.* (Bethesda: CDL Press, 1998).

Pfeiffer, Robert H., *State Letters of Assyria* (New York: Kraus Reprint, 1967 [1935]).

Pfeiffer, Rudolf, *History of Classical Scholarship: From the Beginnings to the End of the Hellenistic Age* (New York: Oxford University Press, 1968).

Potts, D.T., 'Before Alexandria: Libraries in the Ancient Near East', in R. MacLeod (ed.), *The Library of Alexandria: Centre of Learning in the Ancient World* (New York: I.B. Tauris, 2001), 19-33.

Reynolds, L.D., and N.G. Wilson, *Scribes and Scholars: A Guide to the Transmission of Greek and Latin Literature* (New York: Oxford University Press, 2nd edn, 1974).

Steinkeller, P., 'Archival Practices at Babylonia in the Third Millennium', in Brosius (ed.),
    Ancient Archives and Archival Traditions, 37-58.

Stephens, Susan A., *Seeing Double: Intercultural Poetics in Ptolemaic Alexandria* (Berkeley,
    CA: University of California Press, 2003).

Staikos, Konstantinos Sp., *The Great Libraries: From Antiquity to the Renaissance* (trans.
    Timothy Cullen; London: Oak Knoll Press and the British Library, 2000).

Tsuen-Hsuin Tsien, *Written on Bamboo and Silk: The Beginnings of Chinese Books and
    Inscriptions* (Chicago: University of Chicago Press, 1962).

Veenhof, Klaas R., 'Archives of Old Assyrian Traders', in Brosius (ed.), *Ancient Archives and
    Archival Traditions*, 78-123.

Vrettos, Theodore, *Alexandria: City of the Western Mind* (New York: The Free Press, 2001).

Notes

*   Many people were helpful to me in writing this article and I would like to thank all of them, in particular the editors and Edward S. Casey.

1.   Konstantinos Sp. Staikos, *The Great Libraries: From Antiquity to the Renaissance* (trans. Timothy Cullen; London: Oak Knoll Press and the British Library, 2000), vii. For more on Hermes Trismegistus and the extant hermetic writings, see Brian Copenhaver, *Hermetica* (New York: Cambridge University Press, 1992), xl-lix.

2.   This is quoted in Werner Muensterberger's *Collecting: an Unruly Passion* (Princeton, NJ: Princeton University Press, 1994), 74. The capitalization and punctuation are rendered here as they are in the original text. For a very readable survey of the passions and acquisitive impulses of bibliophiles, see Nicholas A. Basbanes, *A Gentle Madness: Bibliophiles, Bibliomanes, and the Eternal Passion for Books* (New York: Henry Holt, 1995). Basbanes followed this with two wider inquiries into the pervasive presence of books in culture: *Patience and Fortitude: A Roving Chronicle of Book People, Book Places, and Book Culture* (New York: Harper Collins, 2001), *A Splendor of Letters: The Permanence of Books in an Impermanent World* (New York: Harper Collins, 2003).

3.   In a striking choice of topic that combines gathering of texts and lands, Ptolemy I wrote a well-regarded history of Alexander's military conquests. Ptolemy II was interested in zoology, while Ptolemy IV was a playwright. See Rudolf Pfeiffer, *History of Classical Scholarship: From the Beginnings to the End of the Hellenistic Age* (New York: Oxford University Press, 1968), 95-96, and for more details, see P.M. Fraser, *Ptolemaic Alexandria* (3 vols.; New York: Oxford University Press, 1972), I, 306-11, 495-96, and the accompanying notes in II, 465-66, 717-18.

4.   In the introduction to his comprehensive catalogue of Near Eastern archives and libraries, Olof Pedersén broadly defines an archive as a collection of documents and a library as a collection of texts. Libraries also typically have multiple copies of at least some of their texts while archives tend only to have one copy of each document. See Pedersén, *Archives and Libraries in the Ancient Near East 1500–300 B.C.* (Bethesda: CDL Press, 1998).

5.   P. Steinkeller, 'Archival Practices at Babylonia in the Third Millennium', in M. Brosius (ed.), *Ancient Archives and Archival Traditions: Concepts of Record-Keeping in the Ancient World* (New York: Oxford University Press, 2003), 37-58 (37). 'When one looks at the assemblages ("archives") of administrative records of the third mil-

lennium in their totality, the most striking fact about them is that the overwhelming majority of documents concern items (generally material objects, but also such ephemera as human labour and the rental period of boats, to offer two examples) that were deployed or expended *outside* of the institution responsible for the preparation of a given record. Conversely, records of the items that were delivered to and subsequently stored in the institution in question are comparatively infrequent'. Italics are in the original.

6.   Steinkeller mentions also plans and surveys of orchards, lists of the labor force, and letter-orders (instructions to disburse items). See Steinkeller, 39, 51.

7.   D.T. Potts, 'Before Alexandria: Libraries in the Ancient Near East', in R. MacLeod (ed.), *The Library of Alexandria: Centre of Learning in the Ancient World* (New York: I.B. Tauris, 2001), 21.

8.   Potts, 'Before Alexandria', 20. For more on the oldest known vocabulary lists (monolingual and bilingual), see Alfonsi Archi, 'Archival Record-Keeping at Ebla 2400–2350 BC', in Brosius (ed.), *Ancient Archives and Archival Traditions*, 17-37 (20-21).

9.   The eight kings before the Flood are said to have ruled for an incredible collective total of about 250,000 years. For a recent discussion of the problematic status of the Sumerian King list as an historical source, see Amélie Kuhrt, *The Ancient Near East c. 3000–330 BC* (2 vols.; New York: Routledge, 1995), I, 29-31. See also Samuel N. Kramer, *The Sumerians: Their History, Culture, and Character* (Chicago: University of Chicago Press, 1963), 36-52. Despite its claims to comprehensiveness, the King List leaves out certain kings and also lists many kings as having succeeded each other when in actuality, these kings were often contemporary with each other. There are later Babylonian and Assyrian King Lists similar to the one from Sumer.

10.   Potts, 'Before Alexandria', 22. For a detailed analysis of the organization (including the shape of the tablets) in a private archive in Iraq dating back to the seventeenth century BCE, see Karel Van Lerberghe, 'Private and Public: The Ur-Utu Archive at Sippar-Amnanum (Tell ed-Der)', in Brosius (ed.), *Ancient Archives and Archival Traditions*, 59-77.

11.   Potts, 'Before Alexandria', 21.

12.   Lionel Casson, *Libraries in the Ancient World* (New Haven, CT: Yale University Press, 2001), 5. Here is an example of one of these classificatory texts (cited in Casson, 6): 'one tablet, the end, on the purification of a murder. When the exorcist-priest treats a city for a murder. Words of Erija.'

13.   Tiglath-Pileser I, who ruled Assyria from 1115 to 1077 BCE, was the earliest known founder of a library. While only some 100 extant texts can currently be connected to this library, it can be assumed that the original holdings were much more extensive. See Casson, *Libraries in the Ancient World*, 9, and Potts, 'Before Alexandria', 27. Potts argues that the collection may go back further to the reign of Tukulti-Ninurta I (1243–1207 BCE).

14.   In the meantime, another 5,000 tablets or fragments thereof have been under analysis and subject to cataloguing by W.G. Lambert. See Potts, 'Before Alexandria', 32, for more information.

15.   A.L. Oppenheim, *Ancient Mesopotamia: Portrait of a Dead Civilization* (Chicago: University of Chicago Press, 2nd edn, 1977). The results are cited in Potts, 'Before Alexandria', 23-24.

16. Cited by Potts, 'Before Alexandria', 27.

17. Ashurbanipal clearly did not gather all of the texts in the larger area associated with the Neo-Assyrian Empire. For instance, if his men had travelled to the Northern town of Assur, they could have plundered a large library of about 800 clay tablets (most dating from the seventh century BCE) belonging to a family of exorcists. In addition to incantations and prescriptions to combat illness and evil, this library contained prayers, lists of medicinal plants and stones, and there was a separate room for archival documents. For more on this library, see Pedersén, *Archives and Libraries*, 135-36.

18. This is translated by Robert H. Pfeiffer in *State Letters of Assyria* (New York: Kraus Reprint, 1967 [1935]), no. 256, cited by Potts, 'Before Alexandria', 25-26.

19. For a selection of translated examples of inscribed amulets from all over the ancient Mediterranean, see Daniel Ogden, *Magic, Witchcraft, and Ghosts in the Greek and Roman Worlds* (New York: Oxford University Press, 2002), 261-74. For a discussion of Greek amulets, see Roy Kotansky, 'Incantations and Prayers for Salvation on Inscribed Greek Amulets', in C.A. Faraone and D. Obbink (eds.), *Magika Hiera: Ancient Greek Magic and Religion* (New York: Oxford University Press, 1991), 107-37.

20. Casson, *Libraries in the Ancient World*, 12. Clay tablets were not the only form of writing material as this mention of wooden boards suggests. In addition to the perishable wooden boards on which there would be a thin layer of wax, there were texts written on leather and papyrus, none of which survive. For more on writing materials in the Near East and Egypt during the period from the tenth century BCE to the eighth century BCE, see Alan Millard, 'Aramaic Documents of the Assyrian and Achaemenid Periods', in Brosius, 230-32. There are eighth-century BCE Assyrian wall sculptures that depict scribes writing on clay tablets, wax-covered boards, and also on sheets of leather or papyrus. See Millard, 231.

21. Cited in Potts, 'Before Alexandria', 24.

22. For discussion and examples of oracle texts and court prophecies, see Kuhrt, *The Ancient Near East*, II, 502-503.

23. There were also inscribed stelae and publicly displayed inscriptions set up in a variety of locations such as along roads, at the edges of kingly territorial expansion, and near conquered cities. For a summary of scholarly arguments along these lines, see Kuhrt, *The Ancient Near East*, II, 476-77.

24. Quoted by Casson, *Libraries in the Ancient World*, 10.

25. Casson reasonably hypothesizes that royal secretaries and other such people probably had access to the texts in the library, but the restricted range of users is suggested by extant colophons (identifying inscriptions on the backs of tablets) warning against theft and the taking of tablets outside the library. See Casson, *Libraries in the Ancient World*, 12. Consider the following excerpt (quoted by Casson, 12): '...Whoever removes [the tablet], writes his name in place of my name, may Ashur and Ninlil, angered and grim, cast him down, erase his name, his seed, in the land'. The problem of theft and mistreatment of tablets seems to have been a widespread problem in Near Eastern archives and libraries. See Casson, 12-13, for further examples of injunctions against rubbing out characters, pouring water on the text, breaking the tablets themselves, etc.

26. Most scholars name Zenodotus as the first librarian hired by Ptolemy II, but some believe that Demetrius of Phalerum (a student of Theophrastus and head of

Athens from 317 to 307 BCE) may have preceded Zenodotus, in which case the library may have been first set up by Ptolemy I (since Demetrius was so much older than Zenodotus). For a defense of Demetrius as the first librarian (and Ptolemy I as the ruler to start up the library), see Nina L. Collins, *The Library in Alexandria and the Bible in Greek* (VTSup, 82; Leiden: Brill, 2000), 82-114. For a detailed look at the sources involved in this controversy and for the conclusion that Demetrius was influential in the formation of the library but was not the first librarian, see R. Pfeiffer, *History of Classical Scholarship*, 87-104. For a survey of what the ancient sources can tell us generally about Demetrius, see Edward Alexander Parsons, *The Alexandrian Library, Glory of the Hellenic World: Its Rise, Antiquities, and Destructions* (New York: Elsevier Press, 1952), 124-38. While his scholarship was uneven, Parsons himself was quite a fervent bibliophile and his personal collection of 50,000 volumes, known as the *Bibliotheca Parsonia*, is now housed at the University of Texas in Austin.

27. Throughout this paper, I will follow scholarly convention and refer to Hellenistic Greek texts as 'books' even though the book as we know it (i.e., the codex, a bound volume of parchment leaves) did not come into use until the second century CE, a technological shift attributed by some scholars to the early Christians. The previous form of the book, used throughout the classical period for all literary texts, was the roll consisting of a long row of papyrus sheets glued together and rolled up. The word 'volume' derives from the Latin equivalent of 'roll' (*volumen*) and originates from the verb *volvere* meaning 'to roll' (hence a volume is something rolled up). The codex was similar in form to writing tablets which were comprised of wax-covered wooden boards tied together with a piece of leather or a clasp. The wax tablet was generally a casual medium for writing, used by the Greeks for schoolwork, letters, and taking notes. The ever practical Romans saw the potential in this technology and replaced the wax-covered boards with parchment leaves. They started using this 'proto-codex' for serious writing such as legal documents and the early Christians used codices for biblical texts from the start. The codex allowed for much longer texts to be grouped together and was much more convenient in many ways. See L.D. Reynolds and N.G. Wilson, *Scribes and Scholars: A Guide to the Transmission of Greek and Latin Literature* (New York: Oxford University Press, 2nd edn, 1974), 30-32. For a history of the book from clay tablet to the age of computers, see Frederick G. Kilgour, *The Evolution of the Book*, (New York: Oxford University Press, 1998). For more detail on the book in the Greek world, see P.E. Easterling and B.M.W. Knox, 'Books and readers in the Greek world', in *idem* (eds.) the *Cambridge History of Greek Literature* (Cambridge: Cambridge University Press, 1985), 1-41. For a comprehensive history of the production of ancient books, see David Diringer, *The Book before Printing: Ancient, Medieval, and Oriental* (New York: Dover Publications, 1982).

28. Parsons, *The Alexandrian Library*, 169, names this as one of the most unfortunate textual losses, second only to the *Pinakes* of Callimachus. According to the *Suda*, a tenth-century CE Greek encyclopedic reference work, Callimachus wrote a monograph on the Museum, but like most of Callimachus' prose works, this has not survived. See Parsons, 208-209.

29. Athenaeus, *Deipnosophistae* ('Dinner of the Sophists'), Book 5, 203e, trans. C.B. Gulick.

30. The comment by J.P. Mahaffy in 1896 (*Greek Life and Thought from the Death of Alexander to the Roman Conquest* [London: Macmillan, 1896], 92, cited by Parsons, *The Alexandrian Library*, 169) is unfortunately still quite true: 'the whole modern literature on the subject is a literature of conjectures'.

31. The scholarly geographer Strabo (first century BCE) claims that Aristotle was 'the first man, of those we know about, to have gathered a collection of books and to have taught the kings in Egypt the arrangement of a library' (*bibliothekes syntaxin* 13.1.54; my own translation). Aristotle is thought to have had the largest Greek book collection of his time and there is much anecdotal evidence to suggest that his collection was one of the inspirations for the creation of the library at Alexandria. Aristotle was one of the first writers to begin his treatises with a survey of written sources. For more on Aristotle's need to accumulate a large collection of sources for his learned treatises, see R. Pfeiffer, *History of Classical Scholarship*, 67-70. For the complicated story of Aristotle's library and what happened to it after his death, see Luciano Canfora, *The Vanished Library: A Wonder of the Ancient World* (trans. Martin Ryle; Berkeley, CA: University of California Press, 1989), 20-25, and Fraser, *Ptolemaic Alexandria*, I, 314-15. Athenaeus (*Deipnosophistae*, 1.3) says that Ptolemy II bought Aristotle's book collection and brought it to Alexandria. This story is not given much credence by modern scholars but it can be taken to indicate a certain amount of Aristotelian influence on the entire project of the Alexandrian library, including some of the scholarly directions pursued there. For instance, Aristotle is credited with writing a book on *Homeric Problems* and this sort of inquiry may have been one of the inspirations for the textual research on Homer produced by the scholar-librarians at Alexandria.

32. Scholars such as Pfeiffer and Fraser think Callimachus to be an important scholar-poet who was closely associated with the library but who never actually served as the head librarian. See R. Pfeiffer, *History of Classical Scholarship*, 128, and Fraser, *Ptolemaic Alexandria*, I, 330-31. For a spirited argument in favor of Callimachus being the second librarian (after Zenodotus), see Rudolf Blum, *Kallimachos: The Alexandrian Library and the Origins of Bibliography* (trans. Hans H. Wellisch; Madison: University of Wisconsin Press, 1991), 124-81. Blum also provides a most extensive discussion of Callimachus' *Pinakes* and how this really transformed the function and purpose of a catalogue.

33. It would be interesting to trace out a history of the catalogue as it retains a steady presence throughout Greek and Roman literature beginning with the Catalogue of Ships in Homer's *Iliad* (2.584-762), Hesiod's fragmentary *Catalogue of Women*, and on through Ovid's mocking catalogues of hunting dogs (3.206-25) and hunters (8.301-17) in the *Metamorphoses*, the astrological catalogues in Senecan tragedy, and so forth. In the post-classical world, there is the extensive inventory of books near the beginning of Cervantes' *Don Quixote* and the parodic universal catalogue in Borges' *Library of Babel*, among many such examples. J.K. Huysman's novel *Against the Grain* takes the conceit of the catalogue to an extreme. In addition to many other catalogues of various objects, almost a third of the entire novel is given over to a presumably comprehensive catalogue of the protagonist's own personal library. See Debra Castillo, *The Translated World: A Postmodern Tour of Libraries in Literature* (Tallahassee: Florida State University Press, 1984), 14-17, 80-113.

34. Fraser, *Ptolemaic Alexandria*, I, 452.

35. Hesychios Illustrios of Miletus was a sixth-century CE historian and official of the Byzantine Empire. The full title of his lost lexicon of authors was *Onomatologos or List of Those Renowned in Branches of Learning*. In this massive work, Hesychios created a list of over 800 predominately Greek authors and gave both biographical and bibliographical information about each one. *Onomatologos* can either mean a collector of words or one who tells people's names. In Imperial Rome, the equivalent word was *nomenclator*, which was the title of a slave whose job it was to inform his master of the name and relevant information about any important person they might happen to meet. In an analogous way, Hesychios' work gave scholars the names of any important writers in a given field. Much of the information in Hesychios' work made its way into later reference works such as the *Suda*. For more on Hesychios and his works, see Blum, *Kallimachos*, 202-204.

36. Pfeiffer says this about the scope of the *Pinakes*: 'the intention was clearly to omit nothing from this inventory of the *pasa paideia* (entire education), not even books on cookery'. See R. Pfeiffer, *History of Classical Scholarship*, 131.

37. As with much scientific prose, these works probably had their origins in ambitious treatises such as Aristotle's *History of Animals* or Theophrastus' *History of Plants*.

38. For more such titles, see the *Suda* entry for Callimachus. The *Suda* is a valuable text as it was compiled from scholarly comments (scholia) contained in ancient critical editions, and from earlier antique reference works that are preserved only through their presence in the *Suda* (e.g., the *Onomatologos* of Hesychios, on which see above n. 36). While there does not yet exist a complete English translation of this lengthy text, there is currently an ongoing collaborative project to do just that and it is known by the acronym SOL (Suda On Line). In a rare example of true international scholarly collaboration, dozens of researchers are currently putting together a collective translation and commentary. The project is run by Raphael Finkel, Ross Scaife, and Huar-En Ng.

39. Aristotle and Hellenistic Greek writers used the word *oikoumene* to refer to the known or inhabited world. In later Greek, *kosmos* appears as a synonym for *oikoumene* and so in a sense the universe was thought to be coextensive with the known or inhabited world.

40. These too are unfortunately lost but parts of them can be reconstructed through examination of later authors who either summarize or criticize them. Cleomedes summarized the conclusions of 'On the Measurement of the Earth' while Strabo criticized the *Geographica*.

41. Pfeiffer suggests that Eratosthenes may have coined the term *geographia*, which means literally 'writing (about) the earth'. See Rudolf Pfeiffer, *History of Classical Scholarship*, 164.

42. For a description of Eratosthenes' methods for determining the circumference of the earth, see O.A.W. Dilke, *Greek and Roman Maps* (Baltimore: The Johns Hopkins University Press, 1985), 32-35.

43. Strabo, for instance, uses *pinakographia* to mean 'drawing of maps' (2.1.11) and elsewhere uses the phrase *pinax geographikos* to mean 'geographical map' (1.1.11). Herodotus also uses *pinax* to mean 'map' (5.49).

44. For a contemporary use of this metaphor, consider the following words in Castillo (57): 'For the librarian, language is viewed conceptually as a map of the universe, a map which at best is only partially comprehensible. But this partially assimilated map is also a labyrinth, the most inhuman simulacrum of a map devised by man, because the labyrinth perverts the cartographer's enterprise of representing a chaotic multiplicity ordered by human intelligence.'

45. In addition to discussing examples of non-Greek works translated for the library, Fraser, *Ptolemaic Alexandria*, I, 329, states that 'it is likely enough that the early organizers aimed at a complete corpus of Greek literature, although they did not succeed'. For a good discussion of the ancient evidence for the idea of Alexandria as a universal library, see Canfora, *The Vanished Library*, 20-25.

46. Aristeas' letter is an important source and as it dates from the second century BCE, it is one of the earliest extant sources to discuss the formation of the library. It is a bit unsettling that the letter is a patent forgery claiming to be written by someone at the court of Alexandria in the third century BCE, but despite this, Aristeas' testimony was taken seriously and was probably the source for all later Christian sources discussing the beginning of the library (e.g., Epiphanius). This translation is by H. Thackeray and cited by Parsons, *The Alexandrian Library*, 94.

47. The word here meaning to 'adorn' is *kosmein*, a verb which is etymologically related to *kosmos* (also spelled *cosmos* as it is throughout this paper), and which can have a variety of meanings including to order, adorn, or to equip. The overlap of order and adornment explains why 'cosmos' and 'cosmetics' share the same etymology.

48. Translation by Collins, *The Library in Alexandria*, 111. This is an excerpt from Irenaeus (*Adv. Haer.* 3.21.2) as preserved in Eusebius (*Hist. Eccl.* 5.8.11) and it represents the only source to claim that Ptolemy I established the library. It is certainly possible that Ptolemy I was thinking about the idea of the library and that Ptolemy II made it a reality. It is also possible that there was some confusion in the sources about the Museion and the library since it is reported that Ptolemy I did bring together the Museion. See Plutarch, *Mor.* 1095D. For more discussion on the establishment of the library, see R. Pfeiffer, *History of Classical Scholarship*, 95-104.

49. George the Synkellos 518 (text from *Georgii Syncelli Ecloga Chronographica* [ed. A. Mosshammer; Leipzig: Teubner, 1984]) translated and cited by Collins, *The Library in Alexandria*, 112. George the Synkellos was a ninth-century monk and historian who wrote a history starting from creation of the world and getting all the way up to Diocletian (284 CE) before illness and ultimately death intervened. In a similar vein, consider the words of the Byzantine scholar John Tzetzes on the activities of Ptolemy II: 'for that king, well acquainted with the philosophers and other famous authors, having had the volumes sought out at the expense of the royal munificence all over the world as far as possible by Demetrius of Phalerum (and other counsellors), made two libraries, one outside the palace, the other within the palace' (from the *Plautine Scholium*, trans. E.H. Wilkins and cited by Parsons, *The Alexandrian Library*, 108).

50. Epiphanius (fourth-century CE Bishop of Salamis), *On Weights and Measures*, 3-5, cited by Parsons, *The Alexandrian Library*, 101.

51. For instance, Fraser dismisses the remarks of George the Synkellos and Tzetzes that there were already Roman works represented in the library of Ptolemy II for the

very good reason that Roman literature barely existed at this time. Fraser goes on to acknowledge the possibility that the library may have acquired Latin literary works by the end of the Ptolemaic period. He bases this on the rare survival of Latin papyri from this period, including a fragment of Cicero's speeches against Verres. See Fraser, *Ptolemaic Alexandria*, I, 330, and for more on this, see also II, 487 n. 185. See also Blum, *Kallimachos*, 103. Staikos finds it likely that there was a large-scale ongoing project to translate works into Greek. See Staikos, *The Great Libraries*, 73.

52. Collins has an elaborate and well-documented discusssion for dating the translation of the *Septuagint* to 280 BCE. In considering why the translation occurred, Collins argues against the influential nineteenth-century scholarly idea that the Jews requested such a translation because of widespread ignorance of Hebrew in Hellenistic Egypt. She notes that two of the most important sources, Aristeas and Josephus, both specifically state that the translation was destined for the library at Alexandria. While the library was part of the Temple of the Muses [Museion] and thus a religious institution for the Greeks, the Jews presumably would have viewed this as a heathen place and not an ideal place to store a sacred religious text. She furthermore argues that a majority of Jews in Egypt at the time of the early Ptolemies would have spoken Aramaic and thus would not necessarily have requested a Greek translation, and may have even been against such a project (*pace* Casson, *Libraries in the Ancient World*, 35-36). Virtually all 70 or so ancient accounts of the translation follow the reasoning given in Aristeas that Demetrius of Phalerum recommended the translation project to Ptolemy II as a way to increase the library and also to attract more scholars to his court. For her complicated argument about the date of 280 BCE, see 6-57, and for the discussion of why the translation occurred, see 115-81.

53. Fraser recounts this anecdote as well as a story that Eratosthenes translated chronological tables from Egyptian records. See Fraser, *Ptolemaic Alexandria*, I, 330. However, there are grave difficulties with the textual evidence for the Eratosthenes episode and consequently that story may be spurious.

54. Pliny the Elder (*Natural History* 30.4) is the only source for this amazing story.

55. Canfora, *The Vanished Library*, 24. Here is the Byzantine excerpt (quoted by Canfora, 24): 'learned men were enlisted from every nation, men who as well as being masters of their own languages were wonderfully well acquainted with Greek. Each group of scholars was allocated the appropriate texts, and so a Greek translation of every text was made.'

56. Similarities between the libraries of Ashurbanipal and Alexandria may not be entirely coincidental. There is a tradition that Alexander the Great visited the site of Ashurbanipal's library in Nineveh and was then inspired to create his own library. For the possibility of direct Near Eastern influence on the storage and labeling of texts in Alexandria, see R. Pfeiffer, *History of Classical Scholarship*, 7, 103, 126.

57. According to Galen, Athens and Rhodes were known as good places to purchase books.

58. Galen literally says that Ptolemy is *philotimos peri biblia* (ambitious or zealous about books). See Fraser, *Ptolemaic Alexandria*, II, 480.

59. Both the general policy of confiscating original texts and the specific story about the Athenian tragedies are to be found in Galen, *Comm. in Hipp. Epidem.* 3.17 and 606-607. The Greek text of this passage as well as almost all of the obscure Greek and

Latin sources that touch upon the Alexandrian library are to be found in volume 2 of Fraser, *Ptolemaic Alexandria* (Galen passages on 480, note 147; cf. 487 n. 184, in which there is a similar description of Ptolemy's acquisitive impulses from George the Synkellos, 516.3).

60. For instance, see the discussion of Assyrian archives in Klaas R. Veenhof, 'Archives of Old Assyrian Traders', in Brosius (ed.), *Ancient Archives and Archival Traditions*, 78-123 (esp. 90 n. 24).

61. Tzetzes gives these figures in an introduction to the plays of the Greek comic playwright Aristophanes. For the text and discussion, see Fraser, *Ptolemaic Alexandria*, I, 328-29, and II, 474, 485, nn. 107 and 170. Eusebius (*Praep. Evang.* 350b) gives the lower number of 200,000 volumes in the main library.

62. Antimachus of Colophon, an early fourth-century BCE poet and scholar, was another important influence on the Alexandrians and he is the only known pre-Hellenistic author to have created some kind of edition of Homer. Plato apparently was one of the few people to like the poetry of Antimachus and we hear that when Antimachus gave a long reading of his poems, Plato was the only person in the audience who did not leave early. For more on Antimachus, see R. Pfeiffer, *History of Classical Scholarship*, 93-95.

63. For a judicious look at the extant evidence for Zenodotus and his efforts to edit Homer, see R. Pfeiffer, *History of Classical Scholarship*, 105-122.

64. This is from Tzetzes' *Prolegomena* to a critical edition of the Greek comic poet Aristophanes, cited by R. Pfeiffer, *History of Classical Scholarship*, 105-106.

65. Unlike later editors such as Aristarchus and Aristophanes of Byzantium, Zenodotus did not create any commentaries to go along with his critical editions of texts, and so we are left with later sources that suggest possible reasons for the method of Zenodotus. It is possible that there was an oral tradition passed down from one librarian-editor to the next and that the comments in part derive from this tradition.

66. The relationship between the Stoics and the Pergamene scholars was mutually beneficial. The later Stoic philosopher Posidonius reconstructed Crates' allegorical interpretation of Achilles' shield and used it to find in Homer ideas about the tide of the Ocean which happened to confirm his (i.e. Posidonius') own theories. See R. Pfeiffer, *History of Classical Scholarship*, 240-41.

67. The line in question is Hesiod, *Theogony* 142, and for this episode, see R. Pfeiffer, *History of Classical Scholarship*, 241.

68. The famous Iliadic *ekphrasis* of Achilles' shield can be found at 18.483-608. We can be fairly certain that Crates used this phrase because two different scholia attribute it to him. While one reference to Achilles' shield appears in a commentary on Aratus' *Phaenomena*, the other is a scholium to the passage about Agamemnon's shield: 'Crates says that this is an imitation of the universe (*kosmou mimema*)'. For more information on these passages, see Pfeiffer, 240-41.

69. The lines in question are *Iliad* 3.423-26, and for discussion of this practice of Zenodotus and others to reject lines because of Homer's portrait of the gods and humans as unethical, see Reynolds and Wilson, *Scribes and Scholars*, 12-15. In case the modern reader is concerned that such heavy-handed editing may have damaged the transmitted text of Homer, most such emendations were mentioned only in

commentaries or in marginal notations, and the controversial lines were generally left in the critical editions. The alternative readings suggested by Zenodotus do not seem to have been very influential on later editors of the text. Out of 413 emendations suggested by Zenodotus, a mere six of these readings went on to appear in all the extant papyri and manuscripts and only 34 such proposed changes show up with great frequency. 240 of Zenodotus' emendations never appear at all in our textual tradition for Homer. See Reynolds and Wilson, *Scribes and Scholars*, 12, for these and similar figures for the effect of Alexandrian editorial decisions on subsequent manuscript traditions.

70. See R. Pfeiffer, *History of Classical Scholarship*, 108, for this excerpt from an ancient commentary (*hypomnema*).

71. There is some evidence that many Alexandrian editors used philosophical doctrines as a basis for textual alterations. For the influence of Aristotle and Peripatetic doctrines on Alexandrian editors, see R. Pfeiffer, *History of Classical Scholarship*, 111-13.

72. The writing-skins were originally known as *diphtherai* and their name changed to *pergamenai* probably in the second century BCE when Pergamum did become the center of production for the highest quality animal skins for writing. The word 'Pergamum' is the ultimate etymological origin of our word 'parchment' while 'paper' derives from the word 'papyrus'. See R. Pfeiffer, *History of Classical Scholarship*, 236.

73. For this episode in which Alexandrian scholars figured out the original source for the pseudo-Demosthenic speech, see Canfora, *The Vanished Library*, 45-47. For the work of Cratippus, see Canfora, 47-48. This practice of librarians creating forgeries has continued to the present day and for a particularly charming example of this genre, see *The Old Librarian's Almanack*, which purports to have been written in 1773 by a certain Philobiblos (also known as Jared Bean), but which in fact was written in the twentieth century by a librarian named Edmund Pearson (Woodstock: The Elm Tree Press, 1909). This book also fooled quite a few people with its seemingly serious preface by Pearson and its claim to be the first issue of a yearly Librarian's Almanack, complete with pithy sayings about books and astrological matters. Critics, columnists, and librarians all quoted it approvingly. The inclusion of Philobiblos' alleged epitaph in the preface should have made more people suspicious, the last two lines of which are as follows: Ye page is turn'd & I'm at rest /Ye last word said, Finitum est. For a discussion of this book, see Matthew Battles, *Library: An Unquiet History* (New York: W.W. Norton, 2003), 8, 216.

74. It is clear that Crates and other Pergamene scholars were heavily influenced by the Stoic Chrysippus' theory of anomaly in language, while the Alexandrians seem to have taken a different path, emphasizing the presence and importance of analogy in language. This Alexandrian interest in analogy could be one of the reasons why Zenodotus seemed to question the authenticity of unusual words or lines in Homer. There was a longstanding dispute between rival grammarians who favored either analogy or anomaly but this debate survives only in later Latin sources and so we cannot be sure how important a guiding principle these concepts were for the scholars at Alexandria and Pergamum. See R. Pfeiffer, *History of Classical Scholarship*, 203, 243. These sorts of disputes about the relationship of words and things can be traced

back to the work of the fifth-century BCE sophists in Athens and the extended responses of Plato and Aristotle. For a good survey of this complicated terrain, see Pfeiffer, 16-86.

75. The Pergamene king Attalus I (241–197 BCE) summoned Antigonus of Carystus to his court and Antigonus produced first-hand accounts of his travels to Athens and other parts of the Greek world. While he reportedly diverged in some ways stylistically from Callimachus and his student Hermippus (particularly in how they wrote literary biographies), Antigonus apparently copied some of Callimachus' paradoxographical passages word for word and today scholars sometimes use Antigonus to reconstruct Callimachean paradoxography (a genre apparently started by Callimachus in which strange and marvelous things in the natural world were collected and recounted). See R. Pfeiffer, *History of Classical Scholarship*, 247.

76. While we only know by name one Pergamene libararian, the first-century BCE Stoic Athenodorus, there is some evidence that Crates may have helped to set up the library at Pergamum. See R. Pfeiffer, *History of Classical Scholarship*, 235.

77. See R. Pfeiffer, *History of Classical Scholarship*, 110-12.

78. Castillo, *The Translated World*, ix.

79. Sarapis (later spelled in the Roman period as 'Serapis') was a newer god introduced into Alexandria by Ptolemy I (see Fraser, Ptolemaic Alexandria, I, 246-50). In his essay titled 'On Isis and Osiris', Plutarch says the following about the name of the god: 'But Serapis is the name of him who sets the universe in order, and it is derived from "sweep" (*sairein*), which some say means "to beautify" and "to put in order" ' (*Moralia* 362c, trans. F.C. Babbitt). While Plutarch and his sources are undoubtedly incorrect from the perspective of modern historical linguistics, this play on words may not have gone unnoticed by the Hellenistic residents of Alexandria. It certainly makes an interesting choice of location for the smaller library, i.e., in a temple dedicated to a god whose very name suggests the process of ordering. Sarapis was occasionally called the 'Lord of the Universe' and even identified with the Sun in the Imperial period.

80. Plutarch, *Life of Caesar*, section 49, trans. Robin Waterfield. In an interesting detail given Caesar's alleged role in the fire and the ensuing destruction of texts, Plutarch then recounts that Caesar 'stubbornly held on to a sheaf of papers, even though he was under attack from the boats and was being swamped by the waves, using one arm for swimming and holding the papers above the water with the other'.

81. The entire second half of Canfora, *The Vanished Library* is a detailed analysis which devotes a chapter to each one of the major sources.

82. Fraser discusses the evidence for other shrines of the Muses in an effort to speculate what the Mouseion may have looked like structurally. See Fraser, *Ptolemaic Alexandria*, I, 312-14. Most shrines to the Muses consisted of open porticoes and included an altar, and some included an actual shrine. These Mouseia had a priest of the Muses assigned to them and they combined attention to religious and cult matters as well as to literary activities. Only in the Roman period do the Mouseia become altogether secular places of learning. The Muses were for the Greeks long associated with learning and philosophy and such connections can be traced back through the schools of Plato and Aristotle and even all the way back to Pythagoras and his school in the sixth century BCE.

83. In his massive work on geography in 17 books, Strabo has this to say about the Mouseion: 'The Mouseion is part of the royal quarter and it has a cloister (*peripaton*, i.e., a public walkway) and an arcade and a large house in which is provided the common meal of the men of learning who share the Mouseion. And this community has common funds, and a priest in charge of the Mouseion, who was appointed previously by the kings, but now by Caesar (Strabo, 17.1.8, cited and translated by Fraser [*Ptolemaic Alexandria*, I, 315; cf. II, 470 n. 74]).

84. Fraser (*Ptolemaic Alexandria*, I, 324) notes that the word *bibliotheke* may refer simply to a storage room where books are stored. Fraser also acknowledges, however, the uncertainty of his interpretation of *bibliotheke* as the word is usually not given any detailed explanation (II, 479).

85. Given the influence of Alexandria, it is generally assumed that Pergamum modeled its library on the already well-established Alexandrian library. See, for instance, Casson, *Libraries in the Ancient World*, 49-52.

86. For information on the layout of the Athenian Lyceum, see Fraser, *Ptolemaic Alexandria*, II, 468. The third-century CE writer Diogenes Laertius (*Lives of the Philosophers* in ten books) preserves the wills of Aristotle and Theophrastus and these describe the Lyceum (5.11-16 and 5.51-57 respectively).

87. While there are many reports of extensive private libraries in Rome dating as far back as the second century BCE, the first major Roman public library was completed in 39 BCE under the direction of Gaius Asinius Pollio, a wealthy supporter of Julius Caesar and a respected author himself in Rome. In 28 BCE, Augustus created the famed Palatine library in Rome, modeled on Pollio's earlier building. All future Roman libraries were built on this model of two large adjoining reading rooms, one for Greek literature and the other for works in Latin. For the development of Roman libraries, see Casson, *Libraries in the Ancient World*, 80-92. For the fall of Roman public libraries and possible connections to the rise of Christianity, see Staikos, *The Great Libraries*, 131-40.

88. For more information on this, see Fraser, *Ptolemaic Alexandria*, I, 323.

89. Epiphanius, *On Weights and Measures*, 11 (translated and cited by Fraser, *Ptolemaic Alexandria*, I, 323). Aristeas is apparently the ultimate source for this passage as well as another from Tertullian (*Apol.*18), but Aristeas does not mention the Serapeion specifically as do these later sources, and when Aristeas is discussing the project of translating the Pentateuch, he mentions only 'the library', or 'the library of the king'. See Fraser for more on this and other puzzling disparities in references to the two libraries (*Ptolemaic Alexandria*, II, 478 nn. 131 and 132).

90. The building dates to the time of Ptolemy III (Euergetes), fitting with Epiphanius' comment that the second library was built later than the great library which was realized under the guidance of Ptolemy II (Philadelphus).

91. Cassius Dio was a third-century CE Greek historian who wrote a history of Rome in 80 books. This passage appears at 42.38.2. See Canfora, *The Vanished Library*, 69, 133-35.

92. The second-century CE writer Florus wrote a massive *Abridgement of all the Wars over 1200 Years*, which used as a major source the now missing books of Livy and which may have preserved some of his original wording. Because some phrases

appearing in Florus also occur in Seneca and Orosius, Canfora deduces that Livy was the ultimate common source for both Seneca and Orosius.

93. The fifth-century CE writer Orosius says this in his seven-book *Histories against the Pagans*, 6.15.31. See Canfora, *The Vanished Library*, 133.

94. It has been argued that the great library was restricted to the court scholars and librarians in the Mouseion while the smaller library in the temple of Sarapis was intended for patronage by a wider Alexandrian readership. This sounds reasonable but there is no direct evidence to support this theory and Fraser argues against this strand of scholarship, calling the theory 'entirely conjectural'. Despite the apparent physical distance between the two libraries, Fraser suspects that the smaller library operated in conjunction with the larger library, citing the fact that in the Roman period, the smaller library was referred to as the 'daughter' library. See Fraser, *Ptolemaic Alexandria*, II, 486 n. 178. Casson states several times that the great library at Alexandria was open to the public but does not support this with any evidence. See Casson, *Libraries in the Ancient World*, 28, 31.

95. For this complicated set of sources radiating out from the lost book of Livy and information about the dissertation, see Canfora, *The Vanished Library*, 132-36.

96. According to Suetonius (*Life of the Deified Julius Caesar*, trans. C. Edwards, section 44), Caesar 'planned to open libraries of works in Greek and Latin to the most extensive possible public, putting Marcus Varro in charge of equipping and managing them'. Varro was a prolific scholar who wrote, among many other things, the only known ancient work on libraries (*de bibliothecis*). Like most of Varro's works, this text sadly did not survive.

97. For this story, see Canfora, *The Vanished Library*, 138-39.

98. Ammianus Marcellinus is a troublesome source as he seems to confuse the two libraries at Alexandria and even speaks of more than one library in the Serapeion (*bybliothecae inaestimabiles* 22.16.13).

99. Aulus Gellius, *Attic Nights* (*Noctes Atticae* 7.17), translated from the Latin and discussed by Canfora, *The Vanished Library*,123-25. This fascinating antiquarian work in twenty books (all of which is extant except for a preface and book 8) was published in 180 CE. Aulus Gellius' account of the rise and fall of the library at Alexandria was influential and followed in large part by later authors such as Ammianus Marcellinus and Isidore of Seville, among others.

100. The desire to tie cultural developments back to ancient Athens is also evident in the works of the Alexandrians. For instance, Callimachus clearly read the Atthidographers (local historians of Athens whose books survive only in fragments) and often sprinkled his poetry with detailed references to the geography and culture of Athens, as if he is trying to pass himself off as a native resident. The geographical catalogues in Callimachus' *Hymns* are also incredibly detailed and seem the work of a native Greek writer and not someone who was born in Cyrene and worked in Alexandria. For an interesting meditation on ways in which the Alexandrians were poised between the literature and cultures of Egypt and Greece, see Susan A. Stephens, *Seeing Double: Intercultural Poetics in Ptolemaic Alexandria* (Berkeley, CA: University of California Press, 2003), 20-73.

101. Casson does not even mention this story about Pisistratus and argues for Alexandria as the first Greek public library, suggesting that the necessary conditions (a

certain number of texts in circulation, levels of literacy, etc.) for a public library in Greece were not present until at least the fourth century BCE. See Casson, *Libraries in the Ancient World*, 28. Staikos places the advent of public libraries later, saying that 'the first person in the ancient world to conceive the idea of founding a public library (in the modern sense) was Julius Caesar'. See Staikos, *The Great Libraries*, 110. Staikos accepts the story of Pisistratus creating the first public library in Athens and the subsequent story of Xerxes burning it down, but he does not specify in what way this is different from Julius Caesar's idea of a public library. See Staikos, 30. The story of Pisistratus starting a library may very well derive from the equally suspicious anecdote that he was the first person to commission a standardized text for Homer for the purpose of recitation at the annual Panathenaic festival.

102. Plutarch, *Life of Mark Antony*, section 58. The passage goes on for some time detailing the five separate occasions on which Mark Antony allegedly acted inappropriately with Cleopatra.

103. Fraser (*Ptolemaic Alexandria*, II, 494 n. 229) has the following to say about the episode: '[I]t is striking that no other reference to the alleged gift survives. The statement has, however, been generally accepted.' For an example of a source which accepts the story, see Parsons, *The Alexandrian Library*, 30-31, where he immediately in one paragraph accepts this as fact and yet spends over one hundred pages trying to argue that the fire never destroyed the great library at Alexandria, carefully sifting the evidence from many sources. He even has a three-page annotated list at the end of his book comprising nine Greek, Roman, and Arabic sources which do not mention the burning of the books. See also Battles, *Library*, 24, who notes that Plutarch 'doubts the truth of this tale' but fails to mention that Plutarch is also the only source for this story. Battles simply cites the story of Antony's gift to Cleopatra as a legend.

104. Julius Caesar had stopped in Alexandria in 48 BCE out of an apparent desire to support Cleopatra in a dispute between Cleopatra and her brother who was the current ruling Ptolemy. Plutarch tells us that Cleopatra was out of the country when Caesar arrived but that she smuggled herself into his room at the palace by rolling herself up in a sleeping bag and then springing out before a surprised Caesar. Given that Cleopatra is a motivating factor in the stories about both the destruction of books at Alexandria and the theft of books at Pergamum, it is quite striking that she makes her first appearance to Caesar by unrolling herself out of a sleeping bag as if she were hiding in an oversized papyrus roll. See Plutarch, *Life of Caesar*, section 49.

105. In the third century BCE, the Qin emperor Shi Huangdi ordered what may indeed be the most comprehensive book burning in human history. He desired that all Chinese texts written before the beginning of his dynasty be burned. There is another story that he ordered Confucian scholars to be buried alive at the time when their books were burned. The historian Sima Qian claimed that 460 scholars were killed in this way and he even coined a phrase for this terrible practice which was invoked by generations of Confucian scholars: *fengshu kengru* (literally meaning 'the burning of books and the burial of scholars'). For these stories and more information about Chinese book burnings and their connection with the beginnings and ends of empires, see Battles, *Library*, 32-36. For an extensive discussion of the evolution of writing methods and materials in ancient China, see Tsuen-Hsuin Tsien, *Written on Bamboo*

and Silk: The Beginnings of Chinese Books and Inscriptions (Chicago: University of Chicago Press, 1962). The title refers to the fact that the Chinese used bamboo and silk as writing materials from antiquity through the sixth century CE. For information specifically on book burning in ancient China, see Tsuen-Hsuin, 11-13.

106. For more on Didymus and other first-century BCE Alexandrian scholars such as Theon, see R. Pfeiffer, *History of Classical Scholarship*, 274-79.

107. As Fraser puts it, 'the decline in the importance of the Library as a centre of learning and research belongs to a considerably earlier period, and is in no way connected with the fire. It would then probably be wrong to attribute to the fire any decisive importance in the history of Alexandrian scholarship', I, 335. Staikos similarly focuses on the slow decline of Alexandria as a process of 'progressive decay leading to extinction'. See Staikos, *The Great Libraries*, 89.

108. See Suetonius, *Life of Claudius*, section 42. Claudius, whose reign extended from 41 to 54 CE, seems to have been quite the scholar, writing histories of Carthage and Etruria, and he may have been one of the last Romans to know well the now mostly lost Etruscan language. It is unclear whether Claudius' efforts to expand the Mouseion would have entailed any changes to the actual collection of texts in the great library housed therein.

109. See Suetonius, *Life of Domitian*, section 20. Domitian ruled Rome from 81 to 96 CE.

110. The famed Palatine library in Rome was the victim of fire several times: first under Nero or Titus, and then again in 191 CE, and finally, in 363 CE. The Romans seem to have had a particularly unlucky relationship to fire. When the Gauls sacked Rome in 390 BCE, they may have set a massive fire that destroyed important early Roman records. The evidence for this event is slight and Alexandre Grandazzi believes that this fiery apocalypse is probably a fantasy of both ancient and modern scholars. See Grandazzi, *The Foundation of Rome: Myth and History* (trans. J.M. Todd; Ithaca: Cornell University Press, 1997), 177-85. This is an interesting fiction in that the Gallic sack is often cited as one of the earliest verifiable historical events at Rome, and yet it is notable in part for the alleged destruction of records by fire. History is then ushered in with an event which erases traces of a more remote past.

111. Hadrian was known for his love of Greek literature and scholarship. This information about his teacher (Lucius Iulius Vestinus) is preserved in an inscription (*Inscriptiones Graecae*, 14.1085). See Staikos, *The Great Libraries*, 88 n. 101.

112. There may have been a similar shift in leadership of the library at Alexandria during the Roman period in that membership to the Mouseion was apparently extended to military and government officials, as well as athletes. We do not know much about librarians at Alexandria once Egypt becomes a Roman province in 30 BCE, but the one head librarian whose name we know in the first century CE, Tiberius Claudius Balbillus, was known not as a scholar but rather as an administrator and military official. See Casson, *Libraries in the Ancient World*, 46-47.

113. For more on the changing fortunes of the Attalid family, see E.V. Hansen, *The Attalids of Pergamon* (Ithaca: Cornell University Press, 1971).

114. See Theodore Vrettos, *Alexandria: City of the Western Mind* (New York: The Free Press, 2001), 207-11.

115. Staikos describes the story of Caliph Omar's destruction of books as 'probably a figment of the imagination of late chroniclers'. See Staikos, *The Great Libraries*, 89. There is no evidence whether these late antique sieges damaged the Mouseion and the great library's collection. For this story and the general decline of the city of Alexandria, see Vrettos, *Alexandria*, 211-17, and Canfora, *The Vanished Library*, 97-99. It is more than likely that by the time of any of these assaults, the collection had fallen into total disrepair through neglect. By the time of the Arabic conquest of Alexandria in the seventh century CE, the city had become associated with corruption and temptation and was avoided by Arabs who abandoned Alexandria for a site near Cairo.

116. The Egyptians were not alone, of course, in their use of papyrus as the Greeks used papyrus as the dominant material for book production from the seventh century BCE to about the fourth century CE. See Diringer, *The Book before Printing*, 141-61.

117. Epiphanius, *On Weights and Measures*, 1-2, translated and cited by Canfora, *The Vanished Library*, 120. Epiphanius briefly interjects after the list of peoples that the Romans were not yet known by that name.

118. For a brief discussion of Hellenistic Greek methods of referring to texts as either preserved or lost, see Fraser, *Ptolemaic Alexandria*, II, 486 n. 179.

119. For more on the vast library and writings of Constantine VII and the emperor's influence on Byzantine encyclopedic reference works such as the *Suda*, see Staikos, *The Great Libraries*, 164-67.

120. Staikos, *The Great Libraries*, ix.

121. Battles, *Library*, 3.

122. Plato, *Apology* 35C-D.

123. This quotation from Machiavelli's letters (xxix) is quoted in Leah Marcus, 'Renaissance/Early Modern Studies', in S. Greenblatt and G. Gunn (eds.), *Redrawing the Boundaries: The Transformation of English and American Literary Studies* (New York: MLA, 1992), 41-63, 45.

124. As Castillo says, 'inside the walls of the archive, or library, the human nostalgia for a cosmic unity finds its most perfect expression; inside the library the fascination with plurality also manifests itself'. See Castillo, *The Translated World*, 13.

125. For more on this amazing library of philosophical papyri preserved in Herculaneum, see Staikos, *The Great Libraries*,116-17. Among other treasures, there are numerous treatises by the first-century BCE Epicurean philosopher Philodemus. These texts are now in the process of being published for the first time ever in scholarly editions and it will be many years before the riches of the Herculaneum library are fully revealed. For a survey of what we know about this library and the recovered works of Philodemus, see Marcello Gigante, *Philodemus in Italy: The Books from Herculaneum* (trans. Dirk Obbink; Ann Arbor: University of Michigan Press, 2002).

Giordano Bruno and the Rewriting of the Heavens

Geoffrey McVey

In 1584, the Italian philosopher Giordano Bruno published a dialogue entitled *Lo spaccio de la bestia trionfante (The Expulsion of the Triumphant Beast)*. In a period of religious conflict and scientific revolution, it was only one millennialist work among many; had its author not later been imprisoned and executed for heresy in Rome, it might have been ignored entirely. In comparison to his other philosophical writings, for which he was best remembered until the early-twentieth century, or his essays on magic and especially the art of memory, the *Expulsion* has achieved relatively little attention until now. English-language scholarship on Bruno has, since Frances Yates' pioneering *Giordano Bruno and the Hermetic Tradition*, focused strongly on his role in the lengthier history of the Hermetic revival – that movement of expansive religious reform based on Renaissance translations of the Late Antique *Corpus Hermeticum*. While Yates' interpretation of Bruno has come under increasing criticism, she rightly recognizes his desire to bring about a global transformation through his unique ideas.[1]

That Bruno had utopian aspirations is evident from several of his Italian works: the scope of his interests encompassed both science and religion, and while he has been more frequently remembered for his outspoken defense of the Copernican model of the solar system or his interest in the tradition of the Hermetic *magus*, his focus on religious reform should not be overlooked. The *Expulsion* is one manifestation of this focus, offering its reader a blueprint for an unusual kind of earthly reformation: the rewriting of the constellations, under the belief that they would then radiate a transformative power onto the world. The method by which this transformation was to take place is characteristically Brunian, bound up in principles of astrology, talismanic magic, and the power of imagination.

Bruno's biography is a colorful one,[2] beginning with his decision to flee, at the age of 28, the Dominican monastery in which he had spent his adult life. Although he had attained some distinction for his intelligence already – earning an audience with Pope Pius V five years before – he began to develop an increasingly tense relationship with his superiors for his iconoclastic beliefs and humanistic tendencies; the end came when he was caught after smuggling a text by Erasmus into the monastery. In 1576, rather than face an indictment, he fled Naples and began his wandering of Europe.

After a brief stint in Geneva and three years in France, Bruno crossed the Channel to spend the next three in England, in the household of the French ambassador, Michel de Castelnau. Bruno's actions in England are somewhat better-documented than those of his time in France, but are also of less bearing on the present subject.[3] The works he published in this period were nearly all dialogues, written in Italian rather than Latin, on the subject of cosmology. It is at this time that he produced his best-known philosophical works, *La cena de la ceneri* (*The Ash-Wednesday Supper*); *De la causa, principio et uno* (*Cause, Principle, and Unity*); *De l'infinito universo et mundo* (*The Infinite Universe and World*); and also the *Expulsion*. The latter stands out among Bruno's works for being one of the few that were specifically named in the proceedings of his trial (under the shortened title *La bestia trionfante* – a form that made it even less appealing to the Inquisition), but also for the eclecticism of its subject.

The Expulsion is arranged as a collection of three dialogues in which the earthly embodiment of wisdom, Sophia, relates to a philosopher the reaction of the Olympian gods to the momentous discovery that they have grown old. Working in and around the dialogues are conversations on such diverse subjects as predestination, natural law, the making of idols, historiography, and the legitimate uses of magic, among others (Bruno was not one to dwell for long on a single topic in any of his works). At their heart, however, is a striking plot: looking back at 36,000 years of divine rule, the god Jove is embarrassed and ashamed by the deeds that he and the other Olympians have performed. Most troubling to him is the fact that many of the gods' most compromising moments have been captured eternally in the stars, memorialized as images and constellations.

Sophia recites to the philosopher Saulino some of Jove's complaints about the allocation of stars:

> Who could give me any reason, other than the simple and irrational decree of the gods, why Serpentarius, called Ophiuchus by us Greeks, receives, with his mate, an area occupied by thirty-six stars? What grave and opportune reason causes Sagittarius to usurp thirty-one stars? It is because he was the son of Euschemo, who was nurse or wet nurse to the Muses. Why was not rather his mother put there? It is because he also knew how to dance and to perform sleight of hand.[4]

Other constellations in Jove's exhaustive catalogue of the stars receive a similar treatment: one by one, they are revealed as a succession of past lovers, accidental victims, and convenient accessories to one or another divine whim. The structure of the rest of the dialogue is established when Jove gives the gods three days to devise a plan to completely rework the stars into patterns which will better reflect the dignity of their advancing years: old constellations are to be removed and new, more virtuous ones, are to be set in their place.

On the one hand, the *Expulsion* is a relatively gentle jab at both Classical mythology and the process of growing old. On the other, it is an imaginative and clever reworking of the assumptions of astrology and the power of celestial images over humanity, put towards the purpose of ushering in a millennial age of peace that relies as much on human as on divine intervention. Three aspects of the dialogue make its millennial aims clear: Bruno's use of Renaissance theories of astrology and Neoplatonic magic; his dispute with the Calvinist doctrine of predestination; and his appropriation of passages from the *Corpus Hermeticum*, a collection of Greek philosophical texts.

The Power of the Stars

The astrological component of the *Expulsion* is the most significant, but to understand the basis of Bruno's belief that renaming constellations could effect a change in the world of human societies, one must understand the principles of astrology as they were understood in the Renaissance. Those principles were rooted in a controversy in Christian thought with a lengthy history: St Augustine's dismissal of the power of the stars to control the unfolding of one's life directly shaped the opinions of later theologians and perhaps best represents the predominant view on astrology in the Church even in Bruno's day. According to Augustine's well-known arguments in Book 5 of *The City of God,* stars could neither be said to influence or even signify the events of individuals' lives, since one could readily observe that the lives of a pair of twins could be nothing alike.[5]

Despite his statements, other views arose, using Arabic philosophers as their source. Translations of the work of al-Kindi's *De radiis* gave medieval and Renaissance astrologers a philosophical and scientific grounding for their theories by proposing that all bodies in the universe radiated their qualities outwards to influence other things.[6] These theories were later supported with the translation, in the late-fifteenth century, of Hermetic and Neoplatonic texts, reintroducing to philosophical conversation ideas of cosmic sympathy and natural magic. For Bruno, the primary sources of the idea that a rewriting of the heavens could lead to a transformation of the world below appears in Marsilio Ficino's *Book of Life* (*Liber de Vita*).

Marsilio Ficino was one of the more colorful figures of the Florentine Renaissance, the translator of Plato, the *Hermetica*, and several Neoplatonic authors into Latin as well as a proponent of a union between the Christianity of his day with principles of natural magic and astrology. His own interest in magic was in the generally 'safe' realm of medicine, combining dietary advice based on astrological principles with the use of talismanic images. If he were living in the twenty-first century, he would not be out of place in the culture of the New Age; his vision of the magus was, as Ioan Couliano observes, 'an innocuous individual whose habits are neither reprehensible nor shocking in the eyes of a good Christian'.[7] Clean living, a healthy diet, tranquil music, and the cultivation of a garden – these were the traits of Ficino's magus. Nevertheless, Ficino trod very close to the boundaries of orthodox Christian doctrine in his work on the power of images (especially astrological images) to influence human life. It was this feature of his thought that had the greatest impact on Bruno's own.

It was accepted in Ficino's time, on the authorities of Augustine and Thomas Aquinas, that the stars had the capacity to affect material bodies.[8] Through the creation of talismans – specific materials inscribed with images that corresponded to constellations – a magus could, in a sense, reverse that relationship. Working from principles of universal sympathy, whereby all things were attracted to those like them, Renaissance devotees of astrology and natural magic like Ficino believed that the proper use of materials and images could act as a lure for the power of certain stars and planets. If a person needed the influence of Venus in his life, for love or good health, he could surround himself with those things for which the planet had a sympathy – the colors white and green, swans, rabbits, pomegranates, ambergris – while wearing a talisman engraved with the planet's sign.

So long as the power of the stars was restricted to the physical level, it did not conflict with theological or ecclesiastical authority, but Ficino crossed the line from bodies to minds; not only did he argue that human health was under the influence of the stars, but that certain aspects of life that fell clearly within the bounds of the intellectual did as well:

> [P]ay attention every day to the location and aspects of the stars, and under these explore which speeches, songs, movements, dances, customs, and actions usually excite people, so that you might be able to imitate such things for the sake of the powers that are in these songs, which please some similar heavenly object.

> Very often, then, in human affairs we are subject to Saturn, through idleness, solitude, or strength, through Theology, and more secret philosophy, through superstition, Magic, agriculture, and through sadness. We are subject to Jove through civil and ambitious business, through natural and common philosophy, and through civil religion and laws.[9]

Ficino's assertions concerning the relationship between the planets and culture (in the form of religion, philosophy, and law) suggest that there is also a talismanic mode of existence beyond that derived from the simple use of talismans themselves. Through actions, individuals may be 'inscribed' in such a way as to become subject to invisible powers. Ficino does not wish to claim that the planets or stars actually control one's actions (and thereby remove the possibility for free will), since to do so would put him in conflict with the traditions of Augustine and Aquinas. Instead, he simply extends the metaphysical logic he has applied to objects, described above, to people.

It is here that Bruno finds the intellectual basis for the plan of the *Expulsion*: by reinscribing the images of the stars, he will impress their power on individuals across the world. His later works on the subject of magic outline a theory of universal correspondences in which every part of the cosmos is interconnected in a complex web of sympathies and antipathies. But Bruno has become better known for his ideas on imagination and memory, on the power of images to shape the soul, and it is in the idea of the talismanic power of the constellations that one finds the union of his own theories with those on astrology.

The power of the stars in the *Expulsion* has nothing to do with the heavenly bodies themselves: Jove, after all, is not proposing that the stars themselves be moved, only that the constellations, their images, be changed. What Bruno describes in his dialogue is a comprehensive reimagining of the heavens. When Jove explains his project to the gods of Olympus, he gives this command:

> Let there be expelled from the heavens these ghosts, statues, figures, images, portraits, recitations, and histories of our avarice, lusts, thefts, disdains, spites, and shames... Let us prepare ourselves, I say, first in the heaven which intellectually is within us, and then in this sensible one which corporeally presents itself before our eyes. Let us drive away from the heaven of our mind the Bear of Deformity, the Arrow of Detraction, the Foal of Levity, the Canis Major of Murmuring, the Canis Minor of Adulation.[10]

Once this has been done among the gods, the passage goes on, the rest of the world will change.

The Power of Fate

In the corpus of Bruno's writings, the *Expulsion* falls between his early mnemotechnic treatises and his better-known Italian philosophical dialogues. On his way to England, he became acquainted with, and quickly developed a dislike of, Genevan Calvinism as he had encountered it.[11] In the *Expulsion*, a work so concerned with the role of Fate and the stars, he reserves a lengthy passage for his criticisms of the Calvinist doctrine of predestination. The god Momus describes Calvinists as

> that idle sect of pedants, who, without doing good, according to divine and natural law, consider themselves and want to be considered religious men pleasing to the gods, and say that to do good is good, and to do ill is wicked. But they say it is not by the good that is done, or by the evil that is not done, that one becomes worthy and pleasing to the gods, but rather it is by hoping and believing, according to their catechism.[12]

Elsewhere, they are referred to as maggots, locusts, harpies, wolves, bears, serpents, 'this stinking filth of the world', and 'this plague'.[13] The degree of invective that Bruno employs in his description of Calvinists is not unusual for his writing – if there is one feature that typifies his rhetorical style, it is the passion with which he pursues his opponents – but the cause of his intense abhorrence for the sect is only apparent in light of the purpose of the *Expulsion* as a whole.

What troubles Bruno so much about the Calvinist view of salvation by grace alone is that there is no place in such a doctrine for his vision of the transformation of the world through acts of imaginative reform: Jove's plan, and thus Bruno's own, has no place for a religion in which good works have no effect. This is a simplified reading of the doctrine, perhaps, but the language of the anti-Calvinist passages of the *Expulsion* makes it apparent that it is the reading to which Bruno holds. Calvinists are repeatedly referred to as hostile to other Christians, but also as parasitic: while performing no good deeds themselves ('their only labor is to speak ill of others'), they benefit from the work of others.[14] In short, their view of the world is utterly incompatible with that of the magus, for whom the capacity for self-transformation is vital.

There is a tension in these passages between the arguments against predestination and a recognition on the part of the Olympians of the power of Fate. The urgency in Jove's command to the gods is brought about by an awareness that they are not immortal, that they, like everything else, are subject to mutability even while they act outside of the boundaries of time. In order to understand Bruno's argument for reform in the *Expulsion*, it is vital first to understand his interpretation of Fate. Fate, in this dialogue, is not the fixing of a specific or even general destiny. Rather, it is a more vague (but no less inexorable) flux to which every part of the universe is subject. Everything is constantly in the process of becoming everything else. It is this perpetual metamorphosis, combined with a belief in the sympathy and interconnection of the elements of the cosmos that make reformation possible. As the god Mercury explains,

> Everything, then, no matter how minimal, is under infinitely great Providence; all minutiae, no matter how very lowly, in the order of the whole and of the universe, are most important; for great things are composed of little ones, and little things of the smallest, and the latter, of individuals and of minima.[15]

This passage has been taken as a statement of Bruno's belief in atomism, but it also applies on a societal level: since each individual has the potential for infinite self-transformation, each one has the power for great reform. Whoever understands enough of the workings of Fate to manipulate the process of change can, by this theory, change the world. This step provides the second element of Bruno's method for global transformation, and also brings the subject back to the question of magic and the *Expulsion*.

The Power of Images

After the work of Francis Yates, and later Ioan Couliano, the figure of Bruno as magus has begun to overshadow his previous image as martyr for science and philosopher of the infinite. Whether any of these images are more accurate or complete than any other is not at issue here, except insofar as they relate to Bruno's views in this particular work. The principles of sympathy and universal correspondence described above were already well-established in the esoteric literature of Bruno's day; it is not an unreasonable leap to connect his ideas on the significant interconnectivity of every element of the cosmos and those which had previously appeared in the works of al-Kindi, Ficino, Cornelius Agrippa, and others. Particularly useful for Bruno's argument for the importance of images is a passage on Egyptian religion that borrows directly from the *Corpus Hermeticum*, which gained popularity in Renaissance intellectual circles after their translation by Ficino in the mid-1400s.

The section in question begins with an argument for the superiority of Egyptian religion on the basis of its acknowledgement of the correspondence between material things (animals) and spiritual ones (gods). It moves on to a defense of the making of idols and statues on the same grounds, and finishes with a lament for the passing of Egypt quoted directly from the Hermetic text known as the *Asclepius*. Why is this here? While the passage was well known in Bruno's day by virtue of having been mentioned in *The City of God*,[16] it still stands out in the context of the *Expulsion* as an apparent tangent spoken by goddess Isis – already something of an outsider in the company of Olympians. In order to understand the connection between Bruno's aims and this otherwise anomalous passage, one must first consider the status of its source.

'Egypt', in Bruno as in the Hermetica, acts as a cipher for the ideally spiritual nation, the one closest to divinity and most understanding of the principles of magic. It is a fantasy of Egypt, but in this case a fantasy that serves a very specific purpose: the *Asclepius* explains how statues can be animated in order to provide help for those that make them. Remember Jove's command to the gods: 'Let there be expelled these ghosts, *statues*, figures'. Bruno translates the Hermetic language of magical statues into the imaginal realm, with the argument that those statues that the gods (and humanity) have created in their minds must be torn down and re-placed by better ones. The fantasy of Egypt, of the nation whose devotion to images could not keep it from falling into ruin, serves as both an ideal to be matched and a caution against becoming complacent with one's images.

This association of mental images and statues is already well established in Bruno's work by the writing of the *Expulsion*. As mentioned above, his earliest works were on mnemotechnics, notably the art of memory. This system, which began as a rhetorical device and later developed esoteric overtones, was based on the imagining of spaces and the placement of images in them as tokens of those things that one wished to remember. The best images, according to the Classical guides to the art of memory, were essentially statues fixed in active and striking poses, jarring in their strangeness. In order to remember a detail, one only had to recall the image and reconstruct its meaning. Whole arguments or speeches could be recalled by walking an imaginary path through the memory space – a house, a temple, a theatre – and observing the statues one by one.[17]

What separates Bruno's use of the art of memory from the rhetorical use is his implication that these images do, in fact, act as a kind of idol. That is, they act as simulacra of and links to divine or celestial powers. Here, Bruno is using a combination of his own theories of images and the philosophical arguments of his day about the role of imagination as the locus of the individual and the spiritual. The details of this connection are not worked out until later in Bruno's career, in his treatises specifically on magic, but already in the *Expulsion*, one can see the assumption that a disciplined and carefully restructured imagination can have substantial effects on society and the world.

Bruno's millennial aims with the *Expulsion*, then, rely on two basic prin-ciples: first, on an interpretation of Fate which grants every element and individual in the world equal significance and potential for change. This is demonstrated by his arguments against predestination, and his use of the theories of magical correspondence and sympathy. Bruno's view of the universe is that of an infinite and infinitely complex web of relationships, any one of which has the potential to influence the entire system. In such a view, the freedom to act becomes vitally important, and raises the status of the individual immensely. Second, Bruno relies on ideas drawn from the esoteric branches of art of memory by which *imaginata* have the potential to effect changes in the individual. The statues and images of the 'heavens within us', as Jove puts it, may be changed according to the rules of the art of memory. Once one has changed one's interior world, the exterior world will change to match.

But what, exactly, is he trying to accomplish? Despite what one may think, it is not a Hermetic utopia like that which Yates sees in Campanella's *City of the Sun*, where magical images instruct and enrich the citizens. For all of Bruno's fascination with images and their power, the reimagined cosmos is remarkably empty of them. Consider this example from the *Expulsion*, on the banishing of one sign from the zodiac:

> Leo drags [away] with himself Tyrannical Terror, Fear, Formidibility, Perilous and Hateful Authority, the Glory of the Presumption, and Pleasure of being feared rather than loved. [To his place] ascend Magnanimity, Generosity, Splendor, Nobility, Pre-eminence, which administer within the area of Justice, Mercy, Just Conquest, and Worth Condoning...[18]

To each sign is attached a host of qualities, most of them negative, which are to be expelled along with the constellation. In their place arise a new set of qualities, but no new image. When Leo is removed from the heavens, no lion takes its place; only words: magnanimity, generosity, splendor... Bruno, Yates' Hermetic reformer, is slowly emptying the heavens of their images.

Couliano divides the Renaissance from modernity by marking the former as the age of the imaginary, and the latter as the age of imagination's death.[19] While Bruno's affinity for images and the art of memory have generally served to establish him as a late-Renaissance thinker, the *Expulsion* is a work that troubles and complicates his place in that world. Writing in England after seeing the religious wars of France and debating the Calvinism of Geneva, Bruno's position in this work is balanced – perhaps more delicately than in any other of his writings – between the Renaissance and the modern. Later in his career, he would turn back to the art of memory, to magic, and to theories of cosmic sympathy; he would also return to Catholicism and Italy, even though it would cost him his life at the hands of the Inquisition. But here, in the *Expulsion*, his writing bears the strong imprint of the Protestant iconoclasm that he has encountered.

What to make of this work, then – a dialogue that grounds social and moral reform in esoteric theories of correspondences and the stars, that champions the power of imagination even while moving away from the traditional uses of images as instruments of transformation? The *Expulsion* offers us a framework for understanding those movements which privilege imaginative reform as a precursor to or vehicle of social, political, or religious reform. There is a political purpose to Bruno's writing in the *Expulsion* as well as a philosophical one. One of the few constellations left intact in the heavens after the gods enact their changes is the Tiara, or Crown, which is to remain among the stars but be promised to the earthly ruler most deserving of it: in this case Henry III of France, whose patronage of the arts and interest in Bruno's work on memory earned him a place in the author's mind (if not in history) as the ideal just monarch.

The awarding of the Crown to King Henry is left until the very end of the dialogues, as if to say, 'This is what these reforms will produce: enlightened rulership given authority by heaven and supported by celestial virtues'. But while the right of rulership is given to Henry, the process by which the world will recognize that right – namely, the reordering of the heavens – is put in the hands those individuals who are dedicated to applying Bruno's imaginative plan. In his essay simply entitled *On Magic*, Bruno would define a magus as 'the wise man with the power to act'.[20] The *Expulsion*, then, is a call for people to become magi – to take control of, and responsibility for, the images they create.

Bibliography

Bruno, Giordano , *The Expulsion of the Triumphant Beast* (ed. and trans. Arthur D. Imerti; New Brunswick: Rutgers, 1964).
—*Cause, Principle, and Unity and Essays on Magic* (ed. Richard J. Blackwell and Alfonso de Lucca; Cambridge: Cambridge University Press, 1998).
—*Opere Italiane*, III (4 vols.; ed. Eugenio Canone; Firenze: Leo S. Olschki, 1999).
Carruthers, Mary, *The Book of Memory* (Cambridge: Cambridge University Press, 1990).
Copenhaver, Brian, 'Scholastic Philosophy and Renaissance Magic in the *De vita* of Marsilio Ficino', *Renaissance Quarterly* 17 (1984): 523-54.
Couliano, Ioan P., *Eros and Magic in the Renaissance* (Chicago: University of Chicago Press, 1987).
Firpo, Luigi, *Il processo di Giordano Bruno* (Rome: Salerno Editrice, 1993).
Gatti, Hilary, 'The State of Giordano Bruno Studies at the End of the Four-hundredth Centenary of the Philosopher's Death', *Renaissance Quarterly* 54.1 (2001): 252-61.
Schaff, Philip (ed.), *Nicene and Post-Nicene Fathers*, II (14 vols.; Peabody, MA: Hendrickson, 1995).
Singer, Dorothea, *Giordano Bruno, his Life and Thought* (New York: Greenwood, 1968).
Yates, Frances, *The Art of Memory* (London: Routledge & Keegan Paul, 1966).

Notes

1.   For a recent overview of scholarship on Bruno, see Hilary Gatti, 'The State of Giordano Bruno Studies at the End of the Four-hundredth Centenary of the Philosopher's Death', *Renaissance Quarterly* 54.1 (2001): 252-61.

2.   Dorothea Singer, *Giordano Bruno, his Life and Thought* (New York: Greenwood, 1968), 12-13, and Luigi Firpo, *Il processo di Giordano Bruno* (Rome: Salerno Editrice, 1993), 157. Bruno's biography is known almost entirely through the records of his trial, combined with very sparse mention of him in the writings of his contemporaries and a handful of autobiographical details that may be gleaned from his own work.

3.   The biographical facts of this part of his life – most notably his erratic friendship with Sir Philip Sydney and his arguments with scholars at Oxford – are summarized in Singer, *Giordano Bruno*, 26-45.

4.   Giordano Bruno, *The Expulsion of the Triumphant Beast* (ed. and trans. Arthur D. Imerti; New Brunswick: Rutgers, 1964), 107. Imerti's translation has been the standard in English since its publication; for a recent facsimile edition of the original Italian of the text, see Giordano Bruno, *Opere Italiane*, III (4 vols.; ed. Eugenio Canone; Firenze: Leo S. Olschki, 1999).

5.   Philip Schaff (ed.), *Nicene and Post-Nicene Fathers* (14 vols.; Peabody, MA: Hendrickson, 1995), II, 86.

6.   Ioan P. Couliano, *Eros and Magic in the Renaissance* (Chicago: University of Chicago 1987), 119-23.

7.   Couliano, *Eros and Magic*, 136.

8.   For an overview of Ficino's use of Aquinas and Augustine, see Brian Copenhaver, 'Scholastic Philosophy and Renaissance Magic in the *De vita* of Marsilio Ficino', *Renaissance Quarterly* 17 (1984): 523-54.

9.   Couliano, *Eros and Magic*, 161, 93.

10.   Bruno, *Expulsion*, 115.

11.   Singer, *Giordano Bruno*, 14-15. While Singer writes that 'Bruno was in his incurable mental detachment in fact completely indifferent to the quarrels between Catholic and Protestant', his attitude to Calvinism suggests that there was at least one branch of Protestantism to which he was far from indifferent.

12.   Singer, *Giordano Bruno*, 124.

13.   Singer, *Giordano Bruno*, 126.

14.   Singer, *Giordano Bruno*, 125.

15.   Singer, *Giordano Bruno*, 137.

16.   Schaff, *Nicene and Post-Nicene Fathers*, II, 160.

17.   For Frances Yates' interpretation of Bruno's mnemotechnics, see her *The Art of Memory* (London: Routledge & Keegan Paul 1966). More recently, Mary Carruthers has written a much-needed re-examination of the same subject in *The Book of Memory* (Cambridge: Cambridge University Press 1990).

18.   Bruno, *Expulsion*, 84.

19.   Couliano, 193-95.

20.   Giordano Bruno, *Cause, Principle, and Unity and Essays on Magic* (ed. Richard J. Blackwell and Alfonso de Lucca; Cambridge: Cambridge University Press, 1998), 107.

Francis Bacon's Scientific Apocalypse

Steven Matthews

The events of 1621 brought tremendous change to the life of Francis Bacon. For in this year his meteoric rise to political power, which had landed him in the office of Lord Chancellor, abruptly ended. Accused and convicted of accepting bribes (though not an uncommon practice even among his accusers), he was impeached, removed from office, and exiled from the King's Court and the vicinity of London. These events had a profound effect upon what Bacon regarded as his life's work, his program for the restoration of learning and the sciences which he called the 'Instauratio Magna'. This 'Great Instauration' was to have been the beginning of a new apocalyptic age, ordained by Divine Providence and foretold in the Scriptures, in which mankind's original mastery over nature would be restored through proper scientific method. It was also to have been ushered in by Francis Bacon himself, for God, in Bacon's way of thinking, had given him political power, in addition to his own special insight, in order to accomplish this task. The loss of this power was more than a blow to his personal fortunes. It brought a crisis in his apocalyptic expectations and forced a serious shift in his interpretation of what he called 'the history of providence', by which he meant the unfolding of God's plan for the world.

Although the influence of Bacon on the early development of the Royal Society was significant, most of Francis Bacon's ideas about the natural world and the proper method for studying it had been abandoned or superseded by the end of the seventeenth century.[1] But if his contribution to actual scientific method was not enduring, his writings have had a lasting impact upon the way science is perceived in our culture. Much of the motivation for continued research and technological development is the firm belief that if we keep our method right and our motives pure, science and technology hold the keys to our deliverance from the cares and troubles of life, even those troubles which are the result of past technology and industrialization. While the threat posed by technology gone wrong has become abundantly clear in recent generations, contemporary Western culture still shares Bacon's faith in the ability of science and technology to *ultimately* usher in a new and better age.

It was clear to Francis Bacon, prior to 1621, that the world had recently crossed the threshold of just such an age. It was an *apocalyptic* age, in the original sense of the word 'apocalypse' as a 'divine revelation'. For God, according to Bacon, had revealed both in his Scriptures and in world events that this age was imminent. Bacon drew this idea principally from his reading of Daniel 12.4, which is *'multi pertransibunt et augebitur scientia'* in the Vulgate, or, as he interpreted it in English, 'many shall pass to and fro, and science shall be increased'.[2] This is the celebrated scripture verse on the cover of his *Instauratio Magna* of 1620, but it is found throughout his writing as a theological support for his program of the reform of natural philosophy. The clearest expression of the meaning of this verse, as Bacon understood it, is found in his early unpublished work, *Valerius Terminus*:

> This is a thing which I cannot tell whether I may so plainly speak as truly conceive, that as all knowledge appeareth to be a plant of God's own planting, so it may seem the spreading and flourishing or at least the bearing and fructifying of this plant, by a providence of God, nay not only by a general providence, but by a special prophecy, was appointed to this autumn of the world: for to my understanding it is not violent to the letter, and safe now after the event, so to interpret that place in the prophecy of Daniel where speaking of the latter times it is said, *Many shall pass to and fro, and science shall be increased;* as if the opening of the world by navigation and commerce and the further discovery of knowledge should meet in one time or age.[3]

In later works, Bacon's explanation of this verse may seem less explicit, but nowhere does he suggest that he ever significantly modified his understanding of the apocalyptic implications here. In fact, if anything his later discussion of this verse as he published it in the *Novum Organum* of 1620, is less cautious about his interpretation:

> The beginning is from God: for the business which is in hand, having the character of good so strongly impressed upon it, appears manifestly to proceed from God, who is the author of good and the Father of Lights. Now in divine operations even the smallest of beginnings lead of a certainty to their end. And as it was said of spiritual things, 'The kingdom of God cometh not with observation', so is it in all the greater works of Divine Providence; everything glides on smoothly and noiselessly, and the work is fairly going on before men are aware that it has begun. Nor should the prophecy of Daniel be forgotten, touching the last ages of the world – 'Many shall go to and fro, and knowledge shall be increased'; clearly intimating that the thorough passage of the world (which now by so many distant voyages seems to be accomplished or in course of accomplishment), and the advancement of the sciences, are destined by fate, that is by Divine Providence, to meet in the same age.[4]

It is important to note that Bacon's certainty of his reading of Daniel became stronger after his rise to power. Just prior to his fall Bacon's conviction that he was living in an apocalyptic age was at its height, or, alternately, he was now so confident in his reading of this verse that he was willing to publish it without qualification.[5] He knew that he was living in this age of the increase of knowledge. It was not a matter of personal opinion, to his way of thinking, for it was empirically proven by developments such as the discovery of America and the proliferation of trade routes. The 'advancement of the sciences' was also coming to pass, for Bacon himself was accomplishing it in the publication of the very work in which this passage is found. The hand of Providence could not have acted more clearly.

The 'further discovery of knowledge' to which Bacon referred was nothing other than man learning to read God's revelation in the Book of Nature properly. This was the hallmark of Bacon's apocalyptic age. Bacon drew heavily upon the idea stemming from Christian antiquity that God had revealed himself in two separate books, the Book of Nature (or 'Book of Creation') and the Book of Scripture.[6] In Bacon, the common Christian idea of God's 'two books' took a unique turn and provided an apocalyptic context for his reform of natural philosophy. Bacon drew a clean line between the subject matter of the two books, and insisted that they not be confused, though they were complementary and must be read together. He also claimed that it was precisely in reading the Book of Nature that previous generations of Christians had failed. Thus mankind had been subject to pain and suffering until his own age, in which the Book of Nature, containing the secrets of the Power of God, and the key to the functioning of the cosmos would come to be properly understood. Now, in his own age, the Book of Nature would become clear to those who would, in proper piety, devote themselves to studying it, and from thence forward human suffering would be gradually curtailed and Edenic mastery over nature would be restored.

In his *Advancement of Learning* of 1605 Bacon wrote to the new king, James concerning the two books:

> For our Saviour saith, *You err, not knowing the Scriptures nor the power of God;* laying before us two books or volumes to study, if we will be secured from error; first the Scriptures, revealing the will of God, and then the creatures expressing his power; whereof the latter is a key unto the former; not only opening our understanding to conceive the true sense of the Scriptures, by the general notions of reason and rules of speech; but chiefly opening our belief, in drawing us into a due meditation of the omnipotency of God, which is chiefly signed and engraven upon his works.[7]

This particular doctrine of the two books runs throughout the writings of Bacon. The first book (in order of prominence, not chronological order), the Scriptures, revealed the will of God, while the second book, Creation, revealed his power, to those who were learned in God's ways and read it properly. Both books function for Bacon as a single interactive theological system. While we note from the above passage that the book of Creation supports and gives insight into the proper understanding of the Scriptures, we must also note that the Scriptures, as the repository of God's will, both set the limits of, and prescribe the proper motivation for, the study of Creation:

> Wherefore seeing that knowledge is of the number of those things which are to be accepted of with caution and distinction; being now to open a fountain, such as it is not easy to discern where the issues and streams thereof will take and fall; I thought it good and necessary in the first place to make a strong and sound head or bank to rule and guide the course of the waters; by setting down this position or firmament, namely, *That all knowledge is to be limited by religion and to be referred to use and action.*[8]

Elsewhere, and often, Bacon explains that the original sin of man, which caused the Fall, was nothing more than a rejection of the normative role of God's revealed will (after the Fall to be recorded as the Scriptures).[9] In order to properly read the book of Creation, the limits of reason prescribed by the Scriptures must be firmly in place. Thus divinity remains normative for natural philosophy, and natural philosophy is necessary to have a properly informed divinity.

What was most important for Bacon however, was that the substance of these two books should not confounded, for when that occurs the proper limits and motivation of science are lost, and the good results which it would have produced may never transpire. If the understanding of God's power were sought in the Scriptures, confusion would result, for God does not explain his physical laws there, though they may be read, by those skilled for it, in the Book of Nature. Those who sought to understand the nature and will of God and the way of salvation, on the other hand, by studying nature, would again come up with wrong answers, as God reveals these only in the Scriptures, to the extent that they are revealed at all. Thus in Aphorism 65 of the *Novum Organum* Bacon clearly spells out the danger of confounding the two books which he had warned against already 15 years earlier in *The Advancement of Learning*, cautioning on the one hand against those who would see clear explanations of cosmology in the books of Genesis or Job, and on the other hand against those who would make of the natural world a religious system, as did Pythagoras, particularly. Either is a theological transgression, which constitutes what Bacon calls 'the apotheosis of error'.[10] The common belief that Bacon drew a sharp distinction between matters of faith and matters of science, which is based heavily upon Aphorism 65, must be qualified.[11] He was not distinguishing between what we now would call the 'sacred' and the 'secular' in this aphorism, but between two inherently sacred, and even theological, categories: the revelation of the will of God, and the revelation of his power. Bacon's condemnation of the 'admixture of things divine and things human' is an injunction to keep things in their proper logical order: the Scriptures, as God's Word, are given by divine agency and must set the limits for experiment, which is a matter of human agency – the result of man's choice and action. Experiment cannot be given normative authority over religion, and it cannot reveal something new about God's plan, even as the Scriptures do not provide a shortcut for understanding God's creation. To confuse the order of things is to confuse the roles of God and man. What will result is not only a 'fantastical philosophy', derived from reading things into the revealed will of God, but also an 'heretical religion', resulting from the elevation of human discovery to divine status.[12]

Bacon's vehement insistence that the messages of the two books should not be confounded was an outgrowth of his unique reading of the Genesis Fall narrative. The Fall of man, according to Bacon, was twofold in nature: 'For man by the fall fell at the same time from his state of innocency and from his dominion over creation'.[13] The double nature of the Fall required a double solution for Bacon: as man's fall was twofold, falling from 'innocency' and 'dominion over creation', so the means of recovery was twofold. Thus the recovery of Edenic perfection for Bacon followed two separate yet interrelated paths toward a double solution, spiritual recovery through God's action of the Incarnation, and material recovery, even in this life, through the cooperative effort of God and man in the Instauration.

The twofold fall was followed immediately by curses and promises, Adam and Eve alike were cursed with pain and death as their lot in life, but both were also given promises for the eventual recovery. The woman was indirectly, through the serpent, given the promise which Christian divines had regarded for centuries as a prophecy of the Christ (hence called the 'protoevangelion'): 'And I will put enmity between you and the woman, And between your seed and her seed; He shall bruise your head, and you shall bruise his heel'. But to the man also was given a promise regarding the future Instauration, and here, Bacon has reinterpreted a curse as a blessing, when he understands the words of Genesis 3.19, 'in the sweat of thy brow shalt thou eat bread' as foretelling the apocalyptic age of Daniel 12.4. Bread, of course, in the thought of most Christian theologians of this era, meant 'all things needful for this life'. And Bacon understood it as such. But he has done something unique here, beyond merely changing a curse to a promise: he has interpreted the 'sweat of the brow' not as physical labor, but mental labor, the labor of observation, experiment, and scientific activity. As he explained it in *Valerius Terminus* this is:

> ...that the consent of the creature now being turned into reluctation, this power cannot otherwise be exercised and administered but with labor as well as in inventing and executing; yet nevertheless chiefly that labour and travel which is described by the sweat of the brows more than of the body; this is such travel as is joined with the working and discursion of the spirits in the brain.[14]

The fulfillment of the promise made to the woman comes, in the fullness of time, when God himself becomes man, in the person of Jesus the Christ, and restores the lost spiritual relationship of Eden through his life, ministry, death, and resurrection. This is the spiritual answer to the spiritual problem. The fulfillment of the promise made to the man comes later in the event of the Instauration, when God would 'renew the face of the earth' as Bacon understood Psalm 104.30.[15]

It is worth noting that Bacon thought this age of material restoration would come only after the restoration of the right religion. 'Right religion' encompassed far more than merely the Incarnation restoring a right relationship with God to believers. In order to finally get the pure and true religion, the fullness of the meaning of the Incarnation would have to be unpacked by the gradual process of coming to read the Scriptures correctly. This task was addressed in the early centuries of Christianity by the best minds of the era, Bacon says in the *Novum Organum,* because there could be no work more important than the careful reading of the text which told of salvation.[16] The Bible, again, takes priority over the book of Nature, even as the spiritual outranks the material. The project of reading the book of Nature was understandably shelved until the weightier issues were handled. Under medieval scholasticism, however, the interpretation of Scripture became, for a time, derailed, as theologians like Thomas Aquinas and Peter Lombard took 'liberty to coin and frame new terms of art to express their own sense' rather than the literal sense of the Scriptures.[17] Significantly for Bacon, the scholastics also managed to derail the material recovery which would result from the proper reading of the Book of Nature, by approaching natural phenomena with bare logic, rather than experiment.[18]

The age in which the true Religion would come into its own was the age of the Reformation, especially the Reformation in England. In the *Advancement of Learning* Bacon wrote:

> And we see before our eyes, that in the age of ourselves and our fathers,
> when it pleased God to call the church of Rome to account for their
> degenerate manners and ceremonies, and sundry doctrines obnoxious
> and framed to uphold the same abuses; at one and the same time it was
> ordained by the Divine Providence that there should attend withal a
> renovation and new spring of all other knowledges.[19]

Martin Luther had begun a process that would liberate the proper reading of the Bible from the scholastics, restoring its authority as a spiritual text, and ending, by proper interpretation, the errors which resulted from scholastic misreading. The next stage of the work, establishing the proper reading of the Book of Nature, was up to Francis Bacon.

We may note an interesting system of correspondences between the Incarnation and the Instauration: each had its particular fall, and each had its particular promise. As the Incarnation was the solution for the spiritual fall, the Instauration was the solution for the material. Each had its particular scripture which in the fullness of time would be read correctly, and a proper understanding of both God's will and his power would result. Finally, the culmination of each should be noted: The ultimate result of the Incarnation would be reunion with God in the 'Kingdom of God' of the New Heaven and the New Earth after the old had passed away. The culmination of the Instauration would be the 'Kingdom of Man' when the mastery of nature would be completely restored and human suffering, other than the toil of labor itself, would be overcome. This would give way, at the end of all things, to the New Heaven and the New Earth. We may note from *Valerius Terminus* again, that, when he was being most candid, Bacon regarded this material recovery as complete control of the universe. For God had placed this potential in the mind of man, and man could, through labor, live up to it if he chose:

> Let no man presume to check the liberality of God's gifts, who as was said,
> *hath set the world in man's heart.* So was whatsoever is not God but parcel
> of the world, he hath fitted it to the comprehension of man's mind, if man
> will open and dilate the powers of his understanding as he may.[20]

Even if not completed in his own lifetime, for in 1620, at the venerable age of 59 he could see the measure of his days, it would still be a matter of only a few years before mastery over nature would be accomplished and the fullness of this golden age would begin.

From the quotation of *Valerius Terminus* above it follows that the Book of Nature, properly read and guided by right religion, would lead to the complete recovery of mastery over nature which man enjoyed in Eden. However, there are sections in Bacon's later, and less candid, writing, particularly at the end of the second book of the *Novum Organum*, where it seems that the edenic mastery, even as the spiritual innocence, may only be recovered 'in part' in this sinful life, or 'to some degree'.[21] While this cautious language may be attributed to Bacon's well-known political circumspection after he has just suggested what is undeniably a radical rereading of the Scriptural narrative, a much simpler interpretation of this passage may be derived from observing another point in *Valerius Terminus,* which we have already noted in part elsewhere, in the context of the Genesis curse in which it occurs:

> It is true, that in two points the curse is peremptory and not to be removed; the one that vanity must be the end in all human effects, eternity being resumed, though the revolutions and periods may be delayed. The other, that the consent of the creature being now turned into reluctation, this power cannot otherwise be exercised and administered but with labour, as well in inventing as in executing...[22]

The work of the 'sweat of the brows' will result in the complete recovery of edenic mastery, but with the notable difference that this mastery may not be enjoyed, on this side of heaven, without continual labor. Thus, Bacon's qualification of recovery in the second book of the *Novum Organum* is in keeping with the concluding ideas of the first book of the same work, where Bacon writes that edenic mastery remains, even in the fallen world a 'divine bequest' to man, and Bacon's own method is then the key to 'extending the power and dominion of the human race over the universe'.[23] At the end of the earthly age of man's mastery over nature, even humanity's good works would be rendered vain, when the New Heaven and the New Earth would be established, where man's knowledge of God would be unmitigated by the Scriptures, and man's mastery over the New Earth would again be without the need for sweaty labor.[24] For now, the age of human labor was at hand, and Bacon was offering a methodological beginning to this divinely ordained enterprise.

This was the optimistic state of Bacon's understanding of providential history in 1620. Then, through the turmoil of an ill-starred parliamentary session in which Bacon's adversaries rallied against him, he emerged a disillusioned man. He had gotten something wrong. But which of his convictions did he then discard as being illusory? Bacon optimistically chose the path of least epistemic resistance. God's Word was above reproach, as was God himself, thus the clear prophecy of an apocalyptic technological age remained. Neither did Bacon find it reasonable to question his own method or his own identity as God's chosen instrument to guide others in reading the Book of Nature. No, if he had been wrong about anything, he had obviously been wrong about the people of his own generation.

Although nothing had changed but his own fortunes, Bacon came to view his own age as one still lost in darkness rather than at the dawn. The tone of the Forerunner was displaced in his later philosophical writings by that of the Old Testament prophet. After 1621 Bacon denounced his own age for repeating the original sin by refusing to accept true knowledge and lusting after power and false knowledge. In one of his most extensive post-1621 theological passages Bacon elaborates on the continuing error of his own age:

> And now of late by the regulation of some learned and (as things now are) excellent men (the former variety and license having I suppose become wearisome), the sciences are confined to certain and prescribed authors, and thus restrained are imposed upon the old and instilled into the young ...and authority is taken for truth, not truth for authority. Which kind of institution and discipline is excellent for present use, but precludes all prospect of improvement. For we copy the sin of our first parents while we suffer for it. They wished to be like God, but their posterity wish to be even greater. For we create worlds, we direct and domineer over nature, we will have it that all things are as in our folly we think they should be, not as seems fittest to the Divine wisdom, or as they are found to be in fact; and I know not whether we more distort the facts of nature or our own wits, but we clearly impress the stamp of our own image on the creatures and works of God, instead of carefully examining and recognizing in them the stamp of the Creator himself. Wherefore our dominion over creatures is a second time forfeited, not undeservedly; and whereas after the fall of man some power over the resistance of creatures was still left to him...yet this too through our insolence, and because we desire to be like God and to follow the dictates of our own reason, we in great part lose.[25]

Bacon's vision of the dawning golden age, which had been his hope for the present, became a hope for future generations. Mankind, according to Bacon, had never lost the faculty of free will, as Calvin had insisted.[26] This was essential to Bacon's understanding of the Instauration. The experimental method which Bacon proposed required a free range of choice. The recovery of Edenic mastery over nature, with all the blessings that would ensue, was to be the result of human effort and will as well as divine preparation. God had prepared the way, and given to man the power to comprehend the universe, if man would but approach the task in humility and faith. But Bacon's generation re-enacted the hubris of the Fall itself, putting greater faith in past accomplishments than in Divine Wisdom, and they again forfeited the opportunity for mastery over creation. As with the wandering tribes at Kadesh Barnea, God's chosen people had refused to trust His promise and follow their leader into the promised land.[27] Hope remained, but not for his generation.

Thus, although Bacon was still on good terms personally, though not politically, with King James, he dedicated the *Historia Naturalis et Experimentalis* in which the above passage is found, to the future king, then Prince Charles: 'The first-fruits of my Natural History I most humbly offer to your Highness; a thing like a grain of mustard seed, very small in itself, yet a pledge of those things which by the grace of God will come hereafter'.[28]

While the pledge applies primarily to a promise that Bacon will produce more himself, the dedicatory epistle continues to include others who 'will be stirred by my example to a like industry; especially when they shall fully understand what it is we are about'.[29] We may note in passing the metaphor of planting a seed, and specifically a mustard seed. The language of harvest from *Valerius Terminus* has for the most part given way to the metaphor of planting something, which, as Jesus said about the Kingdom of God itself, would grow to be great and fruitful, but not among those to whom he was sent.[30] The seed had also been scattered abroad, and Bacon took hope where it might be found. Bacon's friend, Father Tobie Matthew, had ensured that Bacon's works were circulated among the Roman Catholic scholars on the Continent, where his ideas were received with interest. Father Redemptus Baranzano, a young professor of natural philosophy and mathematics at Anneci, sent Bacon a letter lauding his work and asking questions of clarification. In his response, written in 1622, Bacon solicited the professor's help in writing a natural history of the stars and planets.[31] Unfortunately, Baranzano died shortly thereafter. Later, in 1625, Bacon wrote to Father Fulgentino in Venice, carefully outlining his entire scheme but confiding at the end that when it came to the natural history, or the discovery of the secrets of nature, 'of this I have given up all hope, but that perhaps the ages and posterity will make it sprout forth'.[32] In the same letter Bacon made it clear that his faith in God and his understanding of his own divine calling remained intact:

> But my hope is in this – that these things appear to proceed from the providence and infinite goodness of God. First, because of the ardour and constancy of my own mind, which in this pursuit has not grown old or cooled in so great a space of time: it being now forty years, as I remember, since I composed a juvenile work on this subject, which with great confidence and a magnificent title I named 'The Greatest Birth of Time'. Secondly, because it seems, by reason of its infinite utility, to enjoy the sanction and favor of God, the all-good and all-mighty.[33]

In the face of disappointment hope was transferred, by Bacon, from the present to an indeterminate future age, and from his own people to a people yet unknown. In this spirit, Bacon left his 'name and memory', in his last will and testament, 'to men's charitable speeches, and to foreign nations, and the next ages'.[34]

What foreign nations and the next ages have done with this bequest is significant for understanding the endurance of Bacon's vision. It is also significant that Bacon's theological support for the Instauration did not remain intact. This is hardly surprising when we consider that Bacon's theological justification for the Instauration was unique, and conflicted on any number of points with the common theological systems of his day. The understanding of man's total depravity after the Fall which was held by the Calvinist majority in Bacon's England cannot be reconciled with Bacon's insistence upon human free will and the power, inhering in man even after the Fall, to understand and control the universe. Catholics would have had particular difficulty with Bacon's view of the Reformation preparing the way for a better age. Even a theologian from his own literary circle, Lancelot Andrewes, who shared Bacon's interest in natural philosophy and did not conform to the Calvinist norm in England, did not share Bacon's optimistic outlook for material recovery this side of heaven.[35] Yet Bacon's theological position was complex enough to allow subsequent generations of 'Baconians' to adapt his writings to their own views, and adopt those elements of his philosophy which corresponded to their own, while de-emphasizing others.

Charles Webster has examined the first generation of Baconians after Bacon and shown that his writings were taken in hand by Reformed millennialists, who saw their millennium in Bacon's apocalyptic age, and took to heart his message that science was divinely sanctioned.[36] Webster was careful to present millennialism and Bacon's philosophy as two separate trends, for Bacon himself was not a millennialist, in the proper sense of the word.[37] His age of technology and knowledge was not the millennium of the Revelation of St John. It came quietly, without cataclysm or warfare. It was a period of the relief of human suffering, but it was not a period of rest for the faithful. It required intense and continual labor. It was not an age of the 'reign of Christ on earth', and it was not even directly connected to the second coming of Christ at all. It would come some time in the 'last days' and before the end of all things, but beyond this there was nothing inevitable about the time frame. The Instauration proceeded along a separate salvific path from the Incarnation. It would come when mankind heeded the words of its chosen prophet, and cooperated with God for the recovery of human dominion over the cosmos. Thus, when the cataclysm and warfare in which the English millennialists had placed their hope ended in the disappointment of the restoration of the monar-

chy, it by no means meant that Bacon had been wrong. The next generation of Baconians simply read him differently.

The Royal Society, founded after the restoration, was self-consciously
Baconian.[38] Thomas Sprat, in his *History of the Royal Society*, written in
1667, five years after the Society's founding, proclaims the greatness of
Bacon while acknowledging that Bacon's method and observations were
never properly done, by the standards of the Royal Society itself.[39] Bacon's
greatness was due to his vision. Bacon had recognized the need for proper
method in natural philosophy, and he had recognized what it would produce in benefits for mankind. Sprat's history is prefaced by an extensive
poem of Abraham Cowley, celebrating Bacon as the 'Moses' who led
mankind out of the desert of ignorance to the promised land of science,
though Bacon himself could not enter. As Sprat presented it, one prominent feature of this promised land was the separation of natural philosophy, and the activities of the Royal Society generally, from the religious
questions dividing Europe at the time.[40] Religion was not unimportant, but
to the founders of the Royal Society it had been seriously implicated in
the recent warfare and turmoil which had divided England, while natural
philosophy had not.[41] The result was a much more 'secularized' science.
Natural philosophy was not an a-theological activity, but it was no longer
bound to the theological structure which Bacon had erected.

The Royal Society contributed significantly to the spread of Bacon's
vision for a technological age, and Bacon's own writings were reprinted
and republished numerous times throughout the latter-seventeenth century. In the Enlightenment, natural philosophy had changed beyond anything Bacon himself would have recognized, due to mechanical philosophy
as well as the not entirely mechanical contributions of Isaac Newton. The
universe came to appear as a magnificent, but self-sufficient, clockwork,
without the need for the constant concern of its Creator. God would be
dismissed from the cosmos and an irrelevant hypothesis by LaPlace and
his colleagues, and the authority of the first scripture was discarded, while
the second scripture, Nature, developed into the self-sufficient locus of
truth which would be the hallmark of the scientific perspective of modern
western culture. Among the emerging atheists and deists of the Enlightenment, Bacon's theological justification for science was as obsolete as his
method. Yet Bacon was, if anything, more widely read than ever. Among
the English, Bacon had an established place as the forerunner of Newton,
while Diderot and the French Encyclopaedists paid him open tribute as
the founder of their own work, and modeled the plan of the *Encyclopedie*
off of Bacon's *Instauratio Magna*.[42] Bacon's writings had crossed the Atlantic, and were also influential on the new breed of philosophers in the New

World. Benjamin Franklin hailed Bacon as 'justly esteem'd the father of modern experimental philosophy'.[43] In Monticello, Thomas Jefferson grouped Bacon's portrait along with those of Newton and Locke as one of the three 'greatest men that have ever lived', the founders of the modern age.[44]

Bacon provided impetus for the development of the empirical method of the Royal Society, and he was an icon of modernity to the architects of the Enlightenment, but the original contours and purpose of Bacon's apocalyptic understanding of history have become obscured by his later interpreters. Nevertheless, an important element of his belief persisted, and was celebrated by his admirers in every generation: his firm faith in the sufficiency of science and technology to overcome suffering and hardship and create a better world. Today, Bacon's contribution to the ethos of a scientific culture lies in the persistence of this spirit of eschatological hope, along with a mechanism by which the disappointments of the present, when they come, may be overcome by transferring hope to a more distant and more glorious technological utopia.

The very activity of the scientific endeavor remains attached to a Baconian structure of belief. It is a cultural commonplace in the developed West that what is called 'the progress of science' is normal, even if setbacks or technological catastrophes occur. This is so in spite of the fact that 'progress' as a value judgment of positive change, is not demonstrable, and is inherently 'unscientific'. When oil tankers spill their cargo or weapons proliferate, when we realize that diseases have become immune to our vaccines, or when we are faced with the need for alternative energy sources, we do not hesitate to look to science and the advanced solutions of the future, where we believe all solutions must lie. If we have become skeptical, in the shadow of the mushroom cloud and in light of the prospect of a silent spring, there are still but few Luddites among us. Our generation may get it wrong, but one day, we believe, there will be a more humane, less polluted, and healthier world, if our motives are pure, and our knowledge of the universe more complete. We continue to believe, for 'scientific progress' and 'technological advance' has assumed a status of epistemological and moral authority in the West, even though it is divorced from the scriptural and prophetic context which first legitimized it for Bacon.

We retain Bacon's belief in progress, but we also retain his belief that scientific advance must come through labor. Thus, the words of a common television commercial on the noncommercial Public Broadcasting System exhorts us to: 'Imagine a world where no child begs for food. While some may look on this as a dream, others will look long and hard and get to work. ADM – the nature of what's to come.'

If the prospect of global warming threatens to render the verdant fields of this utopia a blasted waste, we are not without hope. On the internet, at this very moment, electronic signals are passing to and fro, and our knowledge of the problem increases, and with this knowledge, passes the message that we must get to work, for the necessary solutions are at hand.

Our belief in the promise of a new age yet to be revealed are also expressed by the introduction to the most recent installment of the popular Star Trek space series, the television show, 'Enterprise'. As images of scientific advance flash before our eyes presenting a visual march from the era of the scientific revolution into a computer-generated utopian future of space travel and scientific victories, the words of the theme song repeat the epistemological fulcrum by which such a future will become possible: 'You gotta have faith, faith in the heart'.

Bibliography

Andrewes, Lancelot, *Apospasmatia Sacra* (London, 1653).

Briggs, John Channing, 'Bacon's Science and Religion', in Markku Peltonen (ed.), *The Cambridge Companion to Bacon* (Cambridge: Cambridge University Press, 1996), 172-99.

Campbell, James, *Recovering Benjamin Franklin: An Exploration of a Life of Science and Service* (Chicago: Open Court, 1999).

Cohen, I. Bernard, *Science and the Founding Fathers* (New York, W.W. Norton, 1995).

Cru, R. Loyalty, *Diderot as a Disciple of English Thought* (New York: AMS Press, 1966).

Gaukroger, Stephen, *Francis Bacon and the Transformation of Early Modern Philosophy* (Cambridge University Press, 2001).

Harrison, Peter, *The Bible, Protestantism and the Rise of Natural Science* (Cambridge: Cambridge University Press, 1998).

Henry, John, *The Scientific Revolution and the Origins of Modern Science* (New York, Palgrave, 2nd edn, 2002).

Jefferson, Thomas, *Writings* (Merill D. Peterson edition; The Library of America, 1984).

Lynch, William T., *Solomon's Child: Method in the Early Royal Society of London* (Stanford, CA: Stanford University Press, 2001).

de Maistre, Josef, *An Examination of the Philosophy of Bacon, Wherein Different Questions of Rational Philosophy Are Treated* [trans. and ed. Richard A. LeBrun; Montreal and Kingston: McGill-Queen's University Press, 1998).

Milner, Benjamin, 'Francis Bacon: The Theological Foundations of *Valerius Terminus*', in *Journal of the History of Ideas* 58.2 (1997): 245-64.

Perez-Ramos, Antonio, 'Bacon's Legacy', in Markku Peltonen (ed.), *The Cambridge Companion to Bacon* (Cambridge: Cambridge University Press, 1996), 311-34.

Sprat, Thomas, *History of the Royal Society for the Improving of Natural Knowledge* (London, 1667).

Voltaire, *Letters on England (Lettres philosophiques)* (trans. Leonard Tancock; New York: Penguin Books, 1980).

Webster, Charles, *The Great Instauration: Science, Medicine, and Reform 1626–1660* (New York: Holmes & Meier, 1975).

White, R.J., *The Anti-Philosophers: A Study of the Philosophes in Eighteenth Century France* (New York: MacMillan, 1970).

Whitney, Charles, 'Francis Bacon's Instauratio: Dominion of and over Humanity', in *Journal of the History of Ideas* (July-September 1989), 371-90.

Notes

NB: In these endnotes, citations of 'WFB' refer to the collection of Bacon's works, *The Works of Francis Bacon* (ed. James Spedding, Robert Leslie Ellis and Douglas Denon Heath; 14 vols.; London: Longman, 1857-1874). Until the current production of the Oxford Editions of Bacon's works is completed, this collection remains the authoritative critical edition.

1.   On Bacon's influence on the development of the Royal Society see Thomas Sprat, *History of the Royal Society for the Improving of Natural Knowledge* (London, 1667). The more recent studies of Charles Webster (*The Great Instauration: Science, Medicine, and Reform 1626–1660* [New York: Holmes & Meier, 1975), and William T. Lynch (*Solomon's Child: Method in the Early Royal Society of London* [Stanford, CA: Stanford University Press, 2001]) offer a more critical analysis. By the end of the seventeenth century Bacon's geocentrism and doctrine of spirits had been abandoned (cf. Stephen Gaukroger, *Francis Bacon and the Transformation of Early Modern Philosophy* [Cambridge: Cambridge University Press, 2001], 222), and the mathematicized method of Newton held the field in England, (cf. Lynch, *Solomon's Child*, 239-46), and the true mechanistic systems were ruling the Continent where Newton was not. (Cf. John Henry, *The Scientific Revolution and the Origins of Modern Science* [New York: Palgrave, 2nd edn, 2002], ch. 3).

2.   See *Valerius Terminus*, WFB, III, 221, for Bacon's translation. Elsewhere, including on the title page of his *Instauratio Magna*, Bacon usually uses the Vulgate directly.

3.   WFB, III, 220-21.

4.   WFB, IV, 91-92. This is the Spedding translation which is much closer to the Latin in this section than some others, particularly that found in Basil Montagu's collection of Bacon's works.

5.   This should also serve to qualify the recent claim of Benjamin Milner that between *Valerius Terminus* and the publication of the *Great Instauration* Bacon's desire to ground his work theologically had waned after he (supposedly) recognized it to be untenable. (Cf. Benjamin Milner, 'Francis Bacon: The Theological Foundations of *Valerius Terminus*', in *Journal of the History of Ideas* 58.2 [1997]: 245-64.)

6.   The pervasiveness of this doctrine and it's development from the patristic era onward is well outlined by Peter Harrison in his book, *The Bible, Protestantism and the Rise of Natural Science* (Cambridge: Cambridge University Press, 1998), see esp. 1-63.

7.   WFB, III, 301.

8.   Emphasis mine. *Valerius Terminus*, here, concisely states a principle which *The Advancement of Learning* elaborates. [cf. WFB, III, 218. and WFB, III, 265-68 respectively.]

9.   Note, the early example of this interpretation of the Fall in *Valerius Terminus* (WFB, III, 217-18), the later example found in the preface to the *Instauratio Magna* (WFB, I, 209), and the very late example from Bacon's preface to the *Natural and Experimental History*, of 1623 (WFB, V, 131-33).

10. See Aphorism 65, (WFB, I, 175). The Latin must be read carefully here to recognize that the phrase of condemnation with *errores Apotheosis* at its center applies equally to that which goes before (the error of Pythagoras) and that which comes after (the error of those Christians who sought physical answers in the Biblical books). Note especially the carefully worded parallel structures beginning with *Huic…* in each case. Re: the *Advancement of Learning*, see WFB, III, 268.

11. As John Channing Briggs has observed, it remains a commonplace among scholars of Francis Bacon and his writings to insist that Bacon drew a sharp line between matters of faith and matters of science, and that his program for the reformation of learning was concerned solely with the latter. Briggs noted that a serious problem with this assumption, given Bacon's practice of discussing matters of 'science' in the loftiest religious language, as well as his habit of providing biblical proof texts for his project of the reform of learning (cf. 'Bacon's Science and Religion', in Markku Peltonen [ed.], *The Cambridge Companion to Bacon* [Cambridge: Cambridge University Press, 1996], 172-99).

12. *'quia ex divinorum et humanorum malesana admistione non solum educitur philosophia phantastica sed etiam religio heretica'* (WFB, I, 175-76.)

13. Conclusion of the second book of the *Novum Organum*, Spedding translation, WFB, IV, 247-48.

14. WFB, III, 223.

15. Note the use of the word *instaurabis* in the Latin. Charles Whitney has suggested that this is a possible source for Bacon's own adoption of *Instauratio*. (Cf. Charles Whitney, 'Francis Bacon's Instauratio: Dominion of and over Humanity', in *Journal of the History of Ideas* [July-September 1989], vol. 50, 371 n. 3). Cf. Bacon's *Translation of Certaine Psalmes*, WFB, VII, 294.

16. Cf. *Novum Organum*, Book 1, Aphorism 79: '…*At manifestum est, postquam Christiana fides recepta fuisset et adolevisset, longe maximam ingeniorum praestantissimorum partum ad Theologiam se contulisse; atque huic rei et amplissima praema proposita, et omnis generis adjumenta copliosissime subministrata fuisse…'* (WFB, I, 187).

17. The clearest statement of the errors of the scholastics is found in the extended account in the *Advancement of Learning* of 1605, Book 1 (WFB, III, 282-83).

18. Cf. *Novum Organum*, Book 1, Aphorism 82 where the Scholastics are implied in the condemnation of misapplied logic (WFB, I, 189-90).

19. WFB, III, 300.

20. WFB, III, 221.

21. Note: *'ex parte reparari potest'* and *'ex parte'* in the final paragraph of the second book (WFB, I, 365).

22. WFB, III, 223.

23. Consider the last paragraph of Book 1, Aphorism 129: *'Recuperet modo genus humanum jus suum in naturam quod ei ex dotatione divina competit, et detur ei copia; usum vero recta ratio et religio gubernabit'*. WFB, I, 223. (The last phrase is particularly significant in light of this present discussion.)

24. Thus the reading of *Valerius Terminus* places Bacon's qualification of recovery in the Scriptural context of the commonplace doctrine of Christian eschatology/apocalyptic that at the end of all things the old order will pass away to be replaced by a new

heaven and a new earth. While possibly obscure to us, Bacon's audience would have had no difficulty recognizing this allusion in the words 'vanity must be the end in all human effects, eternity being resumed...'. Cf. Revelation 21, Matthew 24.33-36, etc.

25. Spedding's translation of Bacon's introduction to *Historia Naturalis et Experimentalis* of 1622. (WFB, V, 132.) Cf. Latin in WFB, II, 14.

26. Cf. *Institutes*, I, 15, 8.

27. Cf. Deuteronomy chapters 1-2.

28. Spedding's translation, WFB, V, 127. Original Latin: WFB, II, 9.

29. Spedding's translation, WFB, V, 127. Original Latin: WFB, II, 9.

30. It is instructive for understanding what Bacon is saying about the Instauration to consider the varying accounts of the parable of the Mustard seed in Matthew 13.31-32; Mark 4.31-32; and Luke 13.19. Note especially that in the Lukan account the tree is planted by a specific man in his garden. As this was encouragement for Jesus' disciples to internalize the Gospel, Bacon is also encouraging Charles to be the one to nurture the seed of Instauration which was planted in his 'garden'.

31. WFB, XIV, 375-77.

32. WFB, XIV, 530-32. In Latin this passage reads: *'de quam spem omnio abjecimus: sed a saeculis et posteritate fortasse pullulabit'*. In light of the fashion in which Bacon tended to describe the Instauration as a plant, the generative sense of *pullulabit* is significant. Others would make what he had planted 'germinate' or 'sprout'.

33. WFB, XIV, 533. Speddding's translation. The juvenile work to which Bacon here refers has not survived.

34. WFB, XIV, 539.

35. Andrewes, like Bacon, did not accept the doctrine of total depravity, but believed, from his own observation, that although 'the knowledge of the faith' in this time of Reformation, was 'as the morning light which groweth lighter; the knowledge of reason [wa]s as the evening which groweth darker and darker'. cf. Andrewes, *Sacra*, 83.

36. Webster, *The Great Instauration*, see n. 1.

37. Webster, *The Great Instauration*, 1. Although some have read the millennialism of later Baconians into Bacon, this has not been regarded as legitimate by scholars in the field, as there are significant differences between Bacon's use of 'millennial language' and the millennial movements of the sixteenth and seventeenth centuries.

38. The Baconian foundations of the Royal Society, as well as the ongoing influence of Bacon's perspective, if not his conclusions, are the subject of Lynch's recent study, *Solomon's Child*. Lynch examines how Bacon influenced the Society extensively in spite of the fact that his method itself was already outdated.

39. Sprat, *The History of the Royal Society of London*. Sprat makes reference to Bacon throughout his work, and has modeled the history itself on Bacon's writings on the history of proper method. On pages 35-36 Sprat has his most extensive discussion of Bacon's significance for the Royal Society, and for the development of experimental science generally. The Royal Society itself was the fulfillment of Bacon's vision for a college of the learned which he had only been able to realize in fictional form as Solomon's House in the *New Atlantis* (cf. Sprat, 151-52).

40. Cf. Sprat, *The History of the Royal Society of London*, 63, 73-76, 82-83, 100.

41. See Sprat, *The History of the Royal Society of London*, 55-56.

42. R. Loyalty Cru, *Diderot as a Disciple of English Thought* (New York: AMS Press, 1966), *passim*, and 244 for crediting Bacon with the idea and plan of the *Encyclopedie*; R.J. White, *The Anti-Philosophers: A Study of the Philosophes in Eighteenth Century France* (New York: MacMillan, 1970); on England: Cf. Antonio Perez-Ramos, 'Bacon's Legacy', in Markku Peltonen (ed.), *The Cambridge Companion to Bacon* (Cambridge: Cambridge University Press, 1996), 319. While there are problems with imposing Bacon's method on Newton's work, there was a popular conception of linear development from Bacon to Newton among the English. Voltaire's Judgment on Bacon reflects the English environment in which he imbibed it, cf. *Letters on England [Lettres philosophiques]* (trans. Leonard Tancock; New York, Penguin Books, 1980), 57-61. The pervasiveness of the image of Bacon as the forerunner of the Enlightenment, both scientifically and politically, in France is attested also by his leading detractor of the later Enlightenment, Josef deMaistre, who, in defense of altar and crown, condemned Bacon for producing the atheism and turmoil which led to the French Revolution. (Josef de Maistre, *An Examination of the Philosophy of Bacon, Wherein Different Questions of Rational Philosophy Are Treated* [trans. and ed. Richard A. LeBrun; Montreal and Kingston: McGill-Queen's University Press, 1998).

43. In James Campbell, *Recovering Benjamin Franklin: An Exploration of a Life of Science and Service* (Chicago: Open Court, 1999), 43.

44. I. Bernard Cohen, *Science and the Founding Fathers* (New York: W.W. Norton, 1995), 97. Jefferson's direction for the construction of a large oval with all three pictures can be found in his letter to John Trumbull, who was then in Paris. (Thomas Jefferson, *Writings* [Merill D. Peterson edition; The Library of America, 1984], 939-40.) Jefferson wrote to Trumbull: 'I consider them as the three greatest men that have ever lived, without any exception, and as having laid the foundation of those superstructures which have been raised in the Physical and Moral sciences'. Notably, Bacon's portrait is placed at the top of this oval.

Promise

Thomas MacKay

When the coax of a cloudy day finally
claims the hills wholly, and we are all
but creatures of cold gray awaiting
incarnation as dew

When the cushion of trees, closed-eye green,
accepts the last concerns of birds
and the chittering that seems the work of spaces
becomes fingerless

When the intermittent roar of machines
settles into a flat hum, and their wheels
press all animals into the roads, into gray paper,
into flakes of road

When you are less than your eyes, your manner,
and your smoke I could never finish drinking,
when you melt into ghost waters, jungle tales,
occasions of inkling

Then
I will

Part III
De/tension

If 'millennial accomplishment' be more than a play on words, it is about playing profoundly and delightedly with time. Here in Part III our authors find their millennial subjects caught up in a French proverb: *Réculer pour mieux sauter.* Backing up so as to leap farther ahead, Western theosophists of the late-nineteenth century reversed the Brunonian and Baconian arrows of time so as to ground in ancient Egyptian and Vedic secrets a reincarnational future that was millennial in its vision of universal perfectibility and the infinite range of human communication. Backing up so as to leap farther ahead, the Free Energy Movement has been, like its patent applications, in perpetual motion, reversing entropy and installing the millennium by way of what lies imbedded in the universe itself, free for the asking, had we only known how to ask. Active in Theosophy and Free Energy is De-tension in two forms: reducing the tension between apocalypse and millennium through a set of heartwarming and astonishing revelations; de-taining the hidden energies of esoteric bodies in the interest of undoing exhaustion, death, and decay. Cathy Gutierrez puts American Theosophy in the context of a waxing disenchantment with liberal or mechanistic notions of progress; Fred Nadis puts the Free Energizers in the context of a technological revivalism and revivalist technologies that hearken back as often to the initial purities of first atoms and Adams as to the most current articles in *Popular Mechanics*. In both instances, a democracy of aspiration is matched by a democracy of inspiration heralded by a small number of adepts able to interpret esoteric languages; in both instances, equal access to renewal comes with a guarantee of living off the grid, in a free-wheeling but responsive environment replete with invisible, metamorphic powers. Theosophy, however, turned away from the trusted run of a Spiritualist millennium toward a perpetual seeking of truths ever more arcane; Free Energizers have joined the prospect of perpetual energy with a technological sublime that breathes best in the air of an assured millennium. Neither can sustain, or even recognize, irony, which relies upon inherent or inherited tensions, for both look beyond the catch for the release.

H.S.

The Elusive Isis:
Theosophy and the Mirror of Millennialism

Cathy Gutierrez

Millennialism is usually characterized in scholarly literature as a relent-lessly linear understanding of time; history has a clear beginning, middle, and end, and may be read much like a plot in narrative.[1] Unlike many plots, though, the beginning and the end resemble an idea of perfection, and the end that is approaching must recapitulate the particular benefits of the beginning. The choice of origins, however, is unstable, and different groups – even within varying forms of Christianity – will locate the original state of purity at different times. Eden is an obvious choice for many, as is the era of the apostolic church. Other candidates for a good beginning have been the Israelite patriarchs and even the American founding fathers, from whose state of purity the United States has fallen morally and politi-cally according to some paramilitary groups. No matter what beginning is chosen, the end of time will simultaneously put an end to profane time and usher in a new instantiation of sacred time that echoes the origin and confirms its promises. The trajectory of history is thus firmly within the plan of the divine, and time itself is understood to unravel like a novel with God as the author. Time becomes trustworthy, and all subsequent events – including suffering and 'tribulations' – are understood to be the necessary, if tumultuous, preludes to the final days.

American Theosophy conforms to nearly none of this. Born in 1875, Theosophy was the invention of the enigmatic and extremely colorful Helena Petrovna Blavatsky, self-christened both 'countess' and 'madame'. A Russian immigrant with a talent for languages and a flair for secrecy, Madame Blavatsky had long been running in esoteric circles. Widely trav-eled throughout Europe, the Middle East and later India and Tibet, Blavat-sky had already been consorting with Masons and magicians, sufis and Spiritualists, by the time she teamed up with American lawyer Henry Steel Olcott. Together they formed a society devoted to the study of the occult, specifically designed to resurrect the forgotten knowledge of the ancients.

Scholars have remarked that she went through two distinct periods, the first oriented toward Egypt and classically occult in the western sense, and the second oriented toward India and deeply influenced by Buddhist doctrine. Blavatsky's major works, *Isis Unveiled* and *The Secret Doctrine*, demonstrate Blavatsky's shift in emphasis over time and remain the best known records of the American search for occult wisdom during the nineteenth century. America was ripe for new forms of esoteric knowledge, and the culture had already been seeded with curiosity by the time of Blavatsky's arrival.

Theosophy was indebted to American Spiritualism for many of its adherents and, less tangibly, for having created a cultural ambience in which questions of hidden knowledge and occult practices could find a receptive audience. Spiritualism, as I will show, was the epoch's most prolific and inclusive form of millennialist hope, assuring all that humans were steadily achieving perfection both on earth and in heaven. Time itself marched slowly toward perfection in Spiritualism, carrying all of humanity toward the same goal with the help of the benign spirits and the success of liberal reforms.

The relationship between Spiritualism and Theosophy is emblematic of a shift in ideas about time and history, and indicates a growing discontentment in America with the liberal concept of evolutionary progress. Focusing on Blavatsky's Egyptian period, I shall argue that early Theosophy was the mirror of millennialism: when the idea of time-as-progress became increasingly untenable, time in Theosophy became a reversal, a steady and deluded march away from the roots of truth and the secrets of the ancient adepts. The search for religious meaning reached backward in time toward those points of esoteric origins that would be the lodestone for the future. The cultural milieu that fostered so many millennialist articulations thus led to its own antithesis, as dependent on the ideas of millennialism as a shadow is on the body that casts it. Truth lay not in the future but in the past, and time flowed backwards for the Theosophists. The search for origins replaced the anticipation of the future, and, in Madame Blavatsky's hands, Christians were not the population that could expect to be saved at the end of days but rather the obfuscating force that purposefully separated people from the truth.

America the Holy

The landscape of America had been charged with being salvific from the outset; from the Puritan apocalypticism of the City on a Hill to the civic millennialism of the Revolution, the impulse to create a utopia on new and sacred ground pervaded American religious and political thought. The young republic, however, provided both the impetus and the material conditions for many to proclaim that the millennium was indeed at hand. The first decades of the nineteenth century suggested that progress was being made on every front: politically, a new form of government was succeeding, one that posited in theory, if not always in practice, that everybody had a voice in shaping society. Westward expansion, particularly along the Erie Canal, brought youth and vitality to new territories, uprooting traditional religious forms and fostering a space of religious creativity and adaptation. Technological innovations like the telegraph and photography allowed communication across space in unprecedented manners. Successful attempts at proselytizing enslaved peoples and the Native Americans made a universal Christianity seem possible and even inevitable. For many, the concatenation of these exuberant events could only point to one thing – the time was ripe for the reinstatement of perfection, the arrival of the millennium itself.[2]

For many Americans, however, the underbelly of progress was uncontrolled change. Many saw society as becoming unalterably corrupt, as change gave way to apparent chaos, and some of the more anxious called for a return to earlier days. These critiques and calls were also overwhelmingly millennial; the difference, however, had to do with the inclusiveness of salvation. The mainstream of Protestant believers took hope from the pervasive atmosphere of progress and saw society as a whole moving gradually toward perfection. Those who viewed the changes with the most anxiety took solace in a narrower and polarized vision of salvation, a cosmic story of the few who endure suffering and persecution but eventually triumph, to the eternal distress of the many and impious.[3]

Millennialist movements that anticipated the rapid arrival of the end of days (or claimed that it had already arrived) proliferated throughout the United States during the nineteenth century. Those with the longest impact on the religious landscape include the Mormons, the Oneida Community, and the Shakers. The Mormons were the most dramatic and numerically most successful of these new religions. By introducing the Book of Mormon as a scriptural addition to the Christian canon, Mormonism effectively dichotomized true Christians – those who accepted the precepts of the new scripture from those who did not – thereby setting in place a sectarian world-view that was highly conducive to apocalyptic thinking. The social and political atmosphere added to this theological basis for millennialism; under persecution, Mormon rhetoric became increasingly imbued with apocalyptic overtones of a violent end times, as the Mormons were repeatedly run out of states because of local hostility to their tendency toward block-voting and rumors of polygamy.[4]

In contrast, both the Oneida Community and the Shakers posited that the millennium had already arrived and therefore perfection was a matter of perception rather than transformation. The Oneida Community, founded by John Humphrey Noyes in 1848 in upstate New York, believed that Jesus had in fact already returned in 70 CE, so the possibility of living in millennial perfection had all along been available to all. The Shakers had come to America in 1774 with their founder, Mother Ann Lee, whose charisma and rituals drew converts from across New England; a decade later, upon her death, her followers old and new appear to have posthumously deified her, although it is unclear whether she herself ever claimed this position.[5] In so doing, the Shakers lay claim to be the Church of the millennium, as they believed the godhead to be dual in gender and that Mother Ann Lee was the fulfillment of the Second Coming.[6] Throughout the nineteenth century, they continued to attract new believers, celibate and industrious, to communities throughout New England and the Ohio Valley, all come to live in the millennial moment.

The allure of perfection, whether violent or gradual, immediate or eventual, called out to many in this tempestuous era. Cut adrift from tradition and kin, the mobile and literate generations of the middle decades of the century were overwhelmingly open to new forms of revelation and new versions of society, whether those were manifested on earth in experimental communities or in heaven with the spirits of the dead.

Divining Secrets

One of the most influential religious movements of the nineteenth century was Spiritualism. Officially begun in 1848, Spiritualism proposed that the living could remain in contact with the dead, with frequent and easy access to the spheres of heaven achieved through the use of mediums. The spirits of the dead assured grieving relatives that they were thriving in heaven, in the loving company of family and with the wise teachings of angels. The infant mortality rate and the sharp spike in Spiritualist activity after the Civil War attest to its abilities to assuage the pain of loss. Moreover, the vaunted and famous dead were perpetually available to give advice to the living, and the heavens were mined routinely for the superior knowledge held by wise spirits.

Believers understood this process to be utterly scientific and empirical. Much as the telegraph had recently made communication across vast and unknown spaces available in a thrilling new manner, Spiritualists claimed that they had an equivalent technology to reach across the threshold of death.[7] Their earliest communications with those beyond the grave, in fact, relied on a more laborious version of Morse code, with the spirit responding to questions by spelling words with raps, one for a, two for b, and so forth. New methods to improve communications were quickly developed, resulting in a quasi-clerical status granted to those with a talent for communicating with the dead. Mediums would most often be women, preferably young, who would enter a trance state and allow the dead to speak through them in front of a wide range of audiences, from small, intimate gatherings to assemblies of a thousand or more.

Spiritualism deviated from its contemporaneous counterparts on several fronts. Soteriologically, it posited that *all* people went to heaven, not just Christians or a particular denominations. Eschatologically, Spiritualists would have nothing of the traditionally static heaven where the dead instantly became perfect and spent eternity contemplating the divine; instead their heaven was electrified with motion, the locus of constant change and improvement. The dead literally grew up, went to school, met Plato and Shakespeare, got married, and came back to earth via mediums to tell their friends and relatives about their experiences and how much they were learning.

This ethos of progress and education stood as a continuum from earth to heaven, and Spiritualists were at the forefront of nearly every reform movement of their day. Deeply committed to abolition and the equality of the sexes, believers espoused the essential goodness of all humankind and were outspoken critics of religious exclusivity and bigotry.[8] Spiritualist newspapers serialized the latest books on medical progress and joyously recounted the openings of women's colleges. John Murray Spear helped to launch prison reform initiatives, while Amy Post and others provided stops on the Underground Railroad. In its march toward perfection, the politics of Spiritualist piety were hands-on and extremely public.

Despite their tenuous relationship to Christianity on many fronts, Spiritualists furthered the contemporary construction of time and universalized the march of progress. Those who were cruel, criminal, or merely suffered the misfortune of belonging to an 'unadvanced' civilization, would all have the chance to improve after death. However, even while foregrounding progress as the primary cultural concern, Spiritualists looked to the past for answers about the present, calling upon the dead to give advice and solace to the living. The famous dead were routinely consulted for their opinions about politics, literature, and the state of science, with Benjamin Franklin, Emanuel Swedenborg, Francis Bacon, and Shakespeare among the most popular. By increasing the knowledge required to usher in a utopian future, the wisdom of the past contributed not only to premonitions of heaven but also to the inspiration for technological and social advances.

In tandem with the widespread consultation of the dead, secret societies flourished in both Europe and America, many of which claimed occult knowledge as a goal and a product of membership. The Freemasons were the most successful and influential of the secret brotherhoods, initiating men into a fraternity that crossed denominational boundaries and inculcated the mores of the new middle class.[9] These brotherhoods shared a philosophical bond that reflected a Renaissance cosmology in which the world, including humanity, was imbued with the divine rather than commanded by it. Speculative Masonry, as it was called, differentiated the secret society from those organizations for actual stoneworkers, but members nonetheless tended to romanticize the artisans as cultural heroes. Masonic manuals are rife with discussions of architecture and each Masonic Lodge is understood to replicate the building of Solomon's Temple in Jerusalem. The temple functions as the foundation for both ritual and dogma. God is represented as the Grand Architect of the Universe and the basic rituals are designed to reenact a drama that has the master craftsman of Solomon's Temple at its center. The craftsman, Hiram Abiff, is murdered for refusing to disclose a secret key, and the initiate symbolically enters a mystery rite where the past holds the desired knowledge.

These rituals bound members to each other in the shared secrets of initiation; they also bound them to the past, linking contemporary Masons with their cultural forebears. Steven Bullock comments, 'The earliest brothers experienced the Hiram story, not as moral allegory, but as a link to primeval times. Through the rituals and teachings of Masonry, they sought to recover the wisdom of the ancient world, the still-bright divine illumination that shone before corruption and neglect tarnished human perception.'[10] As the nineteenth century progressed, more rituals were added to the available degrees of Masonry, each one of which indicated that the past, rather than the future, was the repository of knowledge.

This reaching backward in time for the locus of lost knowledge is compounded in Masonry by the refutation of ordinary secular time. Each additional school of Masons (e.g., the Royal Arch, Knights Templar, and York Rite) had its own calendrical system, and Masonic manuals often included an appendix correlating the different calendars. For example, an 1865 publication details the origin story of each order and how it dates itself from that time to the present: the Royal Arch Masons begin their calendar at the completion of the Second Temple in Jerusalem and thus add 530 years to the Christian calendar, while the Royal and Select Masters begin theirs at the completion of Solomon's Temple and add 1000 years to the secular calendar, and so forth.[11]

The Masons thus contributed several important habits of thought to the birth of Theosophy and the consequent inversion of millennialism. First,

Masonry pushed for the preeminence of the lost knowledge of the ancients over that of contemporary technological progress. Second, time itself was unstuck from its usual moorings, and the site of originary time was flexible, varying according to an order's choice of a primary historical moment. And third, the Masonic promotion of secrecy itself caught the popular imagination in unprecedented ways.

Some of the fringe movements introduced even more conspicuously occult and exotic aspects to the brotherhood. Attempts to 'orientalize' Masonry took place on several fronts that abutted the life and travels of Madame Blavatsky, including the 'Rite of Memphis', a ninety-five degree order ostensibly brought from Egypt in 1814 and practiced there as well as in America and Britain. The budding interest in Rosicrucianism also influenced Masonry; another secret society, Rosicrucianism was immortalized in the Victorian novels of Edward Bulwer-Lytton and Hargrave Jennings. The Rosicrucians had allegedly begun in the seventeenth century and were devoted to the study of occult lore; however, scholars now believe that there were no actual groups of Rosicrucians until the eighteenth century. Believers espoused a mélange of Neoplatonism, Kabbalah studies, and 'natural magic' stemming from the Renaissance but boasted parentage from Moses and the Egyptian magus, Hermes Trismegistus. In America, Paschal Beverly Randolph, one of the few historical characters both creative and tempestuous enough to rival Madame Blavatsky, began Rosicrucian societies from whose lore Blavatsky borrowed heavily.[12]

Gathering her first adherents from a hodgepodge of Spiritualists and occult enthusiasts, Blavatsky would reposition discussions about the location of utopia and the temporal direction that learning should take. In the mirror of millennialism, time would twist and turn back on itself, heading not for the bright days of the future but for the hidden secrets of the past.

The Brotherhood of Luxor

Blavatsky had been in Egypt in the early 1850s and again in 1871. On her first trip, she met Paulos Metamon, a Coptic magician, as well as a variety of Freemasons and esotericists from Cairo, most notably Albert Rawson, an American with similar occult leanings and with whom Blavatsky (dressed as a man) learned the secrets of snake charmers. From there, she traveled to Paris where she astonished the local Masons with intimate knowledge of their rites. In 1853 she arrived in New York, where she took work as a Spiritualist medium. As historian Joscelyn Godwin points out, she repeated this tripartite itinerary 20 years later with many of the same players involved: 'Everywhere she was involved with Freemasonry, Oriental Secret Societies, occult fraternities, and with the spiritualists who constituted, as it were, the exoteric "church" from which doors opened to the more esoteric circles'. [13] The extent of her involvement in magical and occult practices during this period is a matter of some debate, exacerbated by Blavatsky's public pronouncements on the dangers of magic despite amply suggestive evidence that she and her inner circle were heavily involved in magical practice.

In 1871 she had attempted to form a society in Egypt devoted to the exploration of Spiritualist phenomena; this group resulted in profound failure within two weeks, and charges of fraud ensued. [14] When she returned to New York in 1873, Blavatsky busied herself with local Spiritualists and began gaining notoriety. The decisive turn in her career as a Spiritualist medium took place the following year when her attention was drawn to a series of dispatches about a spirit haunting in Chittenden, Vermont. She traveled to Vermont to see these demonstrations firsthand; there she met Henry Steel Olcott, the man who would become the co-founder of the Theosophical Society and Blavatsky's life-long supporter. Olcott nicknamed the formidable woman 'Jack', and visited her in New York upon his own return to the city.

Theosophy in its mature expression is predicated on the notion that there were a number of adepts (later called 'Mahatmas'), that is, masters who were the bearers of ancient knowledge and who were initiated into a secret society of magicians. The existence of these adepts as living people rather than imaginative projections has been largely upheld in current scholarship, although their status as historically real remains speculative. [15] According to Blavatsky, one society of adepts was based in Egypt and another one in Tibet. The Egyptian sages appear to be what Blavatsky is referring to when she uses the phrase the 'Brotherhood of Luxor'. [16] In 1875, one of the Egyptian adepts contacted Henry Olcott, inviting him to apprentice himself to occult learning and exhorting him thrice, in the manner of Randolph's Rosicrucian societies, to 'Try'. The initial letter was signed by 'Tuitit Bey', and the first correspondence was followed quickly by several more letters from a Serapis Bey. Soon thereafter Blavatsky and Olcott publicly began to encourage Spiritualists to migrate toward more philosophical modes of esoteric thinking and away from what they now characterized as a trivial correspondence with the dead. These missives were signed by the 'Committee of Seven, Brotherhood of Luxor'.

The move toward Egypt as the center of occult teaching begins at the precise moment that the nascent Theosophical Society turned away from classical Spiritualism and its extravagantly millennial beliefs in an imminent perfection for all humankind. Like Spiritualists, Theosophists would continue to cull the past for metaphysical truths, but the answers no longer lay with the genial spirits but rather in more obscure sources that had been purposefully hidden by the Christian church. Many Spiritualists maintained strong enough ties to traditional Christianity for the swiftly arriving perfection to resemble a familiar New Jerusalem. Theosophists, however, refocused the site of originary purity from a renewed Jerusalem of the future to the ever-receding landscape of Egypt.

Beneath the Shell of Spiritualism

The Theosophical Society opened with a lecture on Egypt. In Madame Blavatsky's New York apartment on the seventh of September in 1875, George Felt delivered a lecture on 'The Lost Canon of Proportion of the Egyptians'. His audience included an eclectic array of intellectuals and hermeticists, foremost Henry Olcott, Emma Hardinge Britten, one of the most celebrated Spiritualist mediums of her day and that movement's best historian, and Charles Sotheran, member of numerous fringe-Masonic groups and a ninety-fourth degree member of the Rite of Memphis. Blavatsky had been hosting a salon that featured guest speakers on various occult subjects but it was only on the occasion of this lecture that the group proposed to become a society. It was only after the group rejected the rubrics of 'Egyptological', 'Hermetic', and 'Rosicrucian', that Sotheran's proposal of 'Theosophical' was endorsed. According to historian Bruce Campbell, 'The term *theosophy*, meaning divine wisdom, had become common in the seventeenth century. It was used to refer to the strain of occult, mystical speculation associated with the Kabbalah and the writings of such occultists as Agrippa, Paracelsus, and Fludd... Theosophy was a revival of a late Greek word and, by extension, had been applied to ancient speculative systems, particularly those with a Neoplatonic emphasis.'[17] While Egypt was a literal and metaphorical favorite, Theosophists searched for hidden truth across continents and time. Wisdom was located firmly in the past, and the site of origins was infinitely mobile.

The lecture given that fateful night bore many of the markings that would eventually define Theosophical beliefs. All ancient and Renaissance systems of knowledge contained a kernel of a single, unified divine truth that had become obscured over time, and the rediscovery of that knowledge would lead to the secrets of initiation rites and the ability to invoke 'elementals'. While Blavatsky had begun her career in America as a Spiritualist medium, she had, possibly from the outset, maintained that the supposed spirits of the dead were actually elementals, or impersonal forces that could be harnessed for occult purposes. Godwin summarizes the distinction:

> Her exposure hinged on the revelation that what was communicating in
> spiritualism was not the spirits of the dead but either elementals or 'shells'.
> The former were spirits of earth, water, air, and fire, whose mastery is an
> essential part of ceremonial magic. The shells were psychic detritus left
> behind by human beings who had passed beyond the possibility of com-
> munication. Just as a corpse looks for a while like a living body, so the
> shells could supposedly imitate, up to a point, the individual who had
> sloughed them off.[18]

What is certain about that night is that Felt claimed in his lecture on
Egypt that a particular configuration of geometric forms – a circle with a
square on both the inside and outside – when superimposed on Egyptian
hieroglyphics would reveal the formula for invoking elementals. Access to
this race of invisible beings was necessary for the practice of practical (i.e.,
applied) magic, and Felt claimed to be able to produce these creatures
by means of a mixture of chemicals and herbs. Whether he succeeded
or not, even sufficiently for his audience at the time, is a matter of some
debate.[19] The early Theosophical focus on Egypt, however, had begun.

The same year that the Theosophical Society was founded, one of its
charter members published an important work that would serve, in retrospect, as the hinge between Spiritualism and nascent Theosophy. A prolific author in her own right, Emma Hardinge Britten published two works
by an anonymous friend, one a novel, *Ghost Land*, and the other an in-
struction manual, *Art Magic*.[20] In the latter, the author includes a chapter
devoted to the Egyptian pyramids and the religion they housed. He takes
umbrage with contemporary explanations of the pyramids as merely being
elaborate granaries and criticizes scholars who support such positions for
their lack of imagination and their tendencies toward racism! Far from
being the utilitarian products of a lesser civilization, the pyramids embody
instead the lost knowledge of the ancients that enabled a harmonious and
singular vision of cosmology, history, and geometry. The balance between
the forces of life and death, good and evil, male and female, are all represented in the perfected geometry of the pyramid's base. Given a 'pedestal' by the pyramids, the sun and the moon represent Osiris and Isis at
midnight and noon as they rest in their daily rounds of descent into and
return from the underworld.

In fact, the pyramids' function as a necropolis is given very little play in
the author's discussion; death is not his concern so much as perpetual
resurrection. The pyramids stand for nothing less than a temple of initiation into the mysteries that have been largely lost to modern society. Here
the author overlays the rituals of Freemasonry with the Christian exhortation to be reborn – all truths are unified in the last analysis, and the

coming splendor will be a rediscovery of lost knowledge. He writes, 'The day will come when the magic of the ancients will be the Science of the moderns, and in that morning light of revelation the Great Pyramid of Cheops will be known for what it really is, the alphabet which spells out the signification of the Divine Drama of existence'.[21] This articulation of time encapsulates all of the major trends in Spiritualism at its intersection with millennialism: the coming perfection, made possible by science, will recapitulate the lost knowledge of the ancients; a glowing future perfectly mirrors a brilliant past. All creeds and colors will participate fully in the future perfection, and the antithesis of truth is not evil but rather ignorance.

This cultural inclusivity and the rediscovery of the past represent the most potent changes made by Spiritualists to traditional American millennialism. Instead of transcending history on the way to an ahistorical future, Spiritualism posited that history itself was the most valuable resource for progress. The fact that countless spirits of the dead were consulted about the best way to advance into the future suggests a paradox at the very heart of Spiritualist millennialism, one that Theosophy would exploit and explode. The past would continue to be the locus of wisdom, but rather than being guided by the helpful spirits of the dead, seekers would have to pry knowledge out of history.

The Elusive Isis

In *Isis Unveiled,* Blavatsky takes aim at every potential critic from scientists to the pope. Oscillating between her support of Spiritualism and her wish to unmask it as less substantial than true occultism, she ends up arguing that Spiritualism belatedly proved what the ancients knew all along. She writes, '[T]he Spiritists of France have contracted an everlasting debt of gratitude toward the disputants. The existence of an unseen spiritual universe peopled with invisible beings has now been demonstrated beyond question. Ransacking the oldest libraries, they have distilled from the historical records the quintessence of evidence. All epochs, from the Homeric ages down to the present, have supplied their choicest materials to these indefatigable authors.'[22] While this position is consistent with other Spiritualists' claims about the nature of spirit visitation in the past and the nature of time itself, Blavatsky inverted the millennial inclusivity of Spiritualism and reintroduced an apocalyptic dualism. This time, however, the Christians would be cast as the evildoers.

Blavatsky frames society's unwillingness to embrace the hermetic because of the specter of continuing revelation – mediums and magicians challenged the authority of miracles. Blurring the distinction between a medium and a prophet, a magician and miracle-worker, she confronts both Catholic and Protestant orthodoxy in a manner never before broached by Spiritualists. In one of her innumerable incendiary passages, she writes:

> This great slaughter-house of the Christian church – wherein she butchered, in the name of the Lamb, all sheep arbitrarily declared scurvy – was in ruins, and she found herself left to her own responsibility and resources. So long as the phenomena [resembling Spiritualist contact with the dead] had appeared only sporadically, she had always felt herself powerful enough to repress the consequences... Meanwhile, the enemy had slowly but surely gained ground. All at once it broke out with an unexpected violence. 'Miracles' began to appear in full daylight, and passed from their mystic seclusion into the domain of natural law, where the profane hand of Science was ready to strip off their sacerdotal mask.[23]

Blavatsky's assertions were in the main correct – Spiritualism's appeal had always rested on the prospect of continuing revelation, a continuation of semi-divine communication in addition to, or even in contradiction of, the Christian canon. And many Spiritualists had decried the excesses of priest craft and the heavy-handed authoritarianism of organized religion. However, even at its most critical, Spiritualism remained within a temporal construct of progress; humankind may be hindered along the way, but it was destined to advance toward perfection.[24] In Blavatsky's hands, however, society was certainly not marching forward, but rather festering under the malicious spell of the Christian churches, swathed in lies, programs of disinformation, and an outright conspiracy to keep the truth from the masses. Time had not been a steady march of progress but rather a dark labyrinth designed to keep the people lost and in search of (mis)guidance.

If perfection was no longer to be found in the future, it would now be found in the past, and Theosophy set out to sift through the secrets of all non-Christian cultures. *Isis Unveiled* makes reference to Greek philosophers, the ethnographer Max Mueller, Kabbalists, Hindus, Persians, Chaldeans, Sufis, Zoroastrians, Dionysian mystery religions, Shakers, numerous lineages of European royalty, bishops, popes, and Protestant religious leaders of every stripe. In the project of mining the past for esoteric knowledge, no culture is left unturned. Blavatsky writes, 'During the last fifty years the authentic documents of the most important religions of the world *have been recovered in a most unexpected and miraculous manner.* We now have before us the Canonical books of Buddhism; the *Zend-Avesta* of Zoroaster is no longer a sealed book; and the hymns of the *Rig-Veda* have revealed a state of religions anterior to the first beginnings of that mythology which in Homer and Hesiod stands before us as a mouldering ruin.'[25] Here Blavatsky completed the work that Spiritualism began. Time reached backwards and was omnivorous: secrets of the ages could be extracted from it, but not easily.

With the locus of metaphysical truth now firmly planted in distant history, Blavatsky had nearly polished the mirror of millennialism. However, the location of a geographical site that would be suitable for the original form of purity was more elusive. The single truth that all ancient wisdom was privy to could not be contained in one sacred space; however, some geographies were more appropriate for representing the apex of sacred knowledge than others.

With the cultural fascination for Egypt already firmly established among her immediate followers, Blavatsky leans towards the classic cradle of civilization as most representative of occult prowess. Blavatsky scatters references to Egypt throughout the two volumes that compose *Isis*, citing all manner of proof for the superiority of Egyptian knowledge. The reader learns that ancient Egyptians had not only perfected geometry and architecture, but also the production of maps, beer, and aviary automata, among other things. Blavatsky comments, 'The answers are there. They may be found on the time-worn granite pages of cave-temples, on sphinxes, propylons, and obelisks. They have stood there for untold ages, and neither the assault of time, nor the still ruder assault of Christian hands, have [sic] succeeded in obliterating their records… And so stand these monuments like mute forgotten sentinels on the threshold of that unseen world, whose gates are thrown open but to a few elect.'[26] By reintroducing a polarized vision of the elect, defined by Blavatsky as esoteric adepts rather than the Christian saved, the millennial influence of Spiritualism has come full circle. Held up in the mirror of millennialism, Christians bustle forward when the truth lies behind.[27]

Sadly, almost as soon as Egypt is identified as the prime locus of ancient knowledge, the origin begins to slip its moorings and venture to new lands. The then relatively recent discovery of the Mayan ruins and their pyramids in particular had many people speculating about a possible shared origin between the ancient Egyptians and the Mesoamericans. Blavatsky was no exception, and an architectural excursus to Mexico quickly bleeds into an esoteric cartography that demonstrates similarities ranging from the Hyksos to India, drawing a line for the transmission of secret knowledge from the Indus Valley to Peru. In his magisterial new work, *Claiming Knowledge*, Olav Hammer argues that Blavatsky no sooner established Egypt as an agreed-upon referent for occult practices while in nearly the same breath she began to undermine its position in sacred geography. He writes, 'Blavatsky had already begun to orient her religious creativity further east, towards the Indian subcontinent. The shift is underpinned mythologically by the assumption that the Egyptians were actually the descendants of the Aryans, whose spiritual traditions should thus represent a purer form of the ancient wisdom religion.'[28] Just as time is no longer subject to a trustworthy trajectory, space too begins to recede, with the site of original revelation reaching further back over time.

This shift in the concept of time in Theosophy is indebted to the cultural milieu of millennialism out of which new religious responses sprang. Beginning most urgently with Spiritualism, the metaphysical structure of millennialism suggested the key to its own inversion. By placing the locus of knowledge in the past – the dead – Spiritualism problematized its own millennialist claims to seeing time as coterminous with progress. Heaven, the location of original purity and the destination for all humankind, was itself subject to continual improvement. The gates of inclusion were thrown wide open; no longer would the saved be pitted against the damned in the final days. Progress reigned for all and for everywhere, but did so only with the aid and advice of the spirits of the past.

Theosophy then may be seen as a creative response to a crisis in the idea of progress, a construction of time to counter the prevailing millennialist one. Rather than marking or accounting for improvement, history became a lengthy detour away from truth, the source of which ebbed further back in time with each new search for origins. The Egyptian period of Blavatsky's classical western occultism served as a transitional space between her Spiritualist work and the primarily Buddhist theology of her later decades. I have argued that early Theosophy was deeply indebted to millennialism and its idea of progress, such that its concepts of theological dualism as well as sacred time and space are inverse reflections of its cultural predecessors. By shrouding time itself in occulted forms, Theosophy exchanged the trust in time that millennialism engenders for the mystery and reward of a perpetual seeking – not forward to perfection but back through the taint of history to its tain.

Bibliography

Abzug, R.H., *Cosmos Crumbling: American Reform and the Religious Imagination* (New York: Oxford University Press, 1994).

Barkun, Michael, *Disaster and the Millennium* (New Haven, CT: Yale University Press, 1974).

Blavatsky, H.P., *Isis Unveiled: A Master Key to the Mysteries of Ancient and Modern Science and Technology* (2 vols.; Pasadena, CA: Theosophical University Press, 1972).

Braude, Ann, *Radical Spirits: Spiritualism and Women's Rights in Nineteenth-Century America* (Boston: Beacon Press, 1989).

Britten, Emma Hardinge, *Art Magic, or Mundane, Sub-Mundane, and Super-Mundane Spiritism* (Chicago: Progressive Thinker Publishing House, 1898 [1875]).

Bullock, Steven C., *Revolutionary Brotherhood: Freemasonry and the Transformation of the American Social Order, 1730–1840* (Chapel Hill: University of North Carolina Press, 1996).

Caldwell, Daniel H., (ed.), *The Esoteric World of Madame Blavatsky: Insights into the Life of a Modern Sphinx* (Wheaton, IL: Quest Books, 2000).

Campbell, Bruce F., *Ancient Wisdom Revived: A History of the Theosophical Movement* (Berkeley, CA: University of California Press, 1980).

Carnes, Mark C., *Secret Ritual and Manhood in Victorian America* (New Haven, CT: Yale University Press, 1989).

Crabtree, Adam, *From Mesmer to Freud: Magnetic Sleep and the Roots of Psychological Healing* (New Haven, CT: Yale University Press, 1983).

Deveney, John Patrick, *Paschal Beverly Randolph: A Nineteenth-Century Black American Spiritualist, Rosicrucian, and Sex Magician* (Albany: State University of New York Press, 1997).

Egmond, Daniel van, 'Western Esoteric Schools', in Roelof van der Broek and Wouter J. Hanegraaff (eds.), *Gnosis and Hermeticism from Antiquity to Modern Times* (Albany: State University of New York Press, 1998), 311-46.

Foster, Lawrence, *Religion and Sexuality: The Shakers, the Mormons, and the Oneida Community* (Urbana, IL: University of Illinois Press, 1984).

Givens, Terryl L., *By the Hand of Mormon: The American Scripture That Launched a New World Religion* (New York: Oxford University Press, 2002).

Godwin, Joscelyn, *The Theosophical Enlightenment* (Albany: State University of New York Press, 1984).

Godwin, Joscelyn, Christian Chanel, and John P. Deveney, *The Hermetic Brotherhood of Luxor: Initiatic and Historical Documents of an Order of Practical Occultism* (York Beach, ME: Samuel Weiser, 1995).

Hammer, Olav, *Claiming Knowledge: Strategies of Epistemology from Theosophy to the New Age* (Leiden: Brill, 2001).

Hanegraaff, Wouter J., *New Age Religion and Western Culture: Esotericism in the Mirror of Secular Thought* (Albany: State University of New York Press, 1998).

Hatch, Nathan O., *The Democratization of American Christianity* (New Haven, CT: Yale University Press, 1989).

Jacob, Margaret C., *Living the Enlightenment: Freemasonry and Politics in Eighteenth-Century Europe* (New York: Oxford University Press, 1991).

Johnson, Paul, *The Masters Revealed: Madame Blavatsky and the Myth of the Great White Lodge* (Albany: State University of New York Press, 1994).

Kermode, Frank, *The Sense of an Ending: Studies in the Theory of Fiction* (New York: Oxford University Press, 1967).

Klaw, Spencer, *Without Sin: The Life and Death of the Oneida Community* (New York: Penguin Books, 1993).

Ricoeur, Paul, *Time and Narrative* (3 vols.; trans. Kathleen McLaughlin and David Pellauer; Chicago: University of Chicago Press, 1985).

Shipps, Jan, *Mormonism: The Story of a New Religious Tradition* (Urbana, IL: University of Illinois Press, 1985).

Sickels, Daniel (ed.), *The Freemason's Monitor* (New York: Macoy & Sickels, 1865).

Taves, Ann, *Fits, Trances, and Visions: Experiencing Religion and Explaining Experience from Wesley to James* (Princeton, NJ: Princeton University Press, 1999).

Underwood, Grant, *The Millenarian World of Early Mormonism* (Urbana, IL: University of Illinois, 1993).

Weisbrod, Carol, *The Boundaries of Utopia* (New York: Pantheon Books, 1980).

Notes

1.   The classic work on this analogy is Frank Kermode, *The Sense of an Ending: Studies in the Theory of Fiction* (New York: Oxford University Press, 1967). For more in-depth narrative theory, see Paul Ricoeur, *Time and Narrative* (3 vols.; trans. Kathleen McLaughlin and David Pellauer; Chicago: University of Chicago Press, 1985).

2.   There are numerous excellent works on this period, each tackling a different angle of the Second Great Awakening and post-Revolutionary religion in America. For a sample, see R.H. Abzug, *Cosmos Crumbling: American Reform and the Religious Imagination* (New York: Oxford University Press, 1994); Nathan O. Hatch, *The Democratization of American Christianity* (New Haven, CT: Yale University Press, 1989); Michael Barkun, *Disaster and the Millennium* (New Haven, CT: Yale University Press, 1974).

3.   These distinctions in millennialism, particularly as it tends to be written about in the American context, are frequently referred to as 'postmillennialism', for those who believe in gradual improvement, and 'premillennialism', for those who believe that the world is utterly corrupt and requires God's direct intervention in history. These terms, however, are currently falling out of favor because of the connotations of being hyper- and apolitical respectively. Various scholars have called for replacing these terms with others that do not carry the same associative baggage; for example, Richard Landes has suggested 'transformative' versus 'cataclysmic' millennialism.

4.   In this miasma of oppression, the Mormons quickly adopted what Grant Underwood has called a rhetoric of 'cursing', or a rebirth of the type of prophecy where the God of the Israelites promises to smite their oppressors. For the full dynamics of early Mormon millennialism, see Grant Underwood, *The Millenarian World of Early Mormonism* (Urbana, IL: University of Illinois, 1993), *passim*. For the standard history of Mormonism, see Jan Shipps, *Mormonism: The Story of a New Religious Tradition* (Urbana, IL: University of Illinois Press, 1985). For the reception of new scripture in antebellum America, see Terryl L. Givens, *By the Hand of Mormon: The American Scripture That Launched a New World Religion* (New York: Oxford University Press, 2002).

5.   See Lawrence Foster, *Religion and Sexuality: The Shakers, the Mormons, and the Oneida Community* (Urbana, IL: University of Illinois Press, 1984), first chapter, for this controversy. In addition to Foster, for an excellent history of the Oneida Community, see Spencer Klaw, *Without Sin: The Life and Death of the Oneida Community* (New York: Penguin Books, 1993).

6.   Both communities were relatively small, financially prosperous, and targets for social criticism and even legal action because each deviated from the accepted norms for sexuality. In attempting to adjudicate what Jesus meant when he said that in heaven, 'they neither marry nor are given in marriage' (Matthew 22.30), Noyes concluded that equal love among all community members should be both emotional and physical whereas Ann Lee had banished any form of sexual contact and demanded strict celibacy from her followers. For the legal battles of nineteenth-century millennialist groups, see Carol Weisbrod, *The Boundaries of Utopia* (New York: Pantheon Books, 1980).

7.   I say 'officially' because there is a great deal of question about what specifically designates Spiritualism proper from a host of similar phenomena that predate it both in Europe and America. 1848 stands as the year in which adherents could identify themselves as such by claiming to be Spiritualists, thereby forming for the first time a cohesive group identity for those who agreed with the basic claims, theological structures, and political stances of the movement. For the problems of separating Spiritualism from its precursors, see Adam Crabtree, *From Mesmer to Freud: Magnetic Sleep and the Roots of Psychological Healing* (New Haven, CT: Yale University Press, 1983), ch. 5.

8.   Ann Braude has compellingly argued that Spiritualism had a direct and causal impact on early women's suffrage movements. See her *Radical Spirits: Spiritualism and Women's Rights in Nineteenth-Century America* (Boston: Beacon Press, 1989).

9.   There are many fine works on mainstream Freemasonry from the Revolutionary period to the turn of the twentieth century. For the effect of Masonry on the formation of a republican-minded citizenry in Europe, see Margaret C. Jacob, *Living the Enlightenment: Freemasonry and Politics in Eighteenth-Century Europe* (New York: Oxford University Press, 1991). For its effects specifically in America on the formation of a mobile and cosmopolitan middle class, see Steven C. Bullock, *Revolutionary Brotherhood: Freemasonry and the Transformation of the American Social Order, 1730–1840* (Chapel Hill: University of North Carolina Press, 1996). For a reading of Masonry as indicative of a social discomfort with the preservation of masculine roles and an attempt to cure that situation, see Mark C. Carnes, *Secret Ritual and Manhood in Victorian America* (New Haven, CT: Yale University Press, 1989).

10.   Bullock, *Revolutionary Brotherhood*, 11.

11.   For one example among many, see Daniel Sickels (ed.), *The Freemason's Monitor* (New York: Macoy & Sickels, 1865), 93-94.

12.   The landmark work on both Randolph's life and his interactions with H.P. Blavatsky is John Patrick Deveney, *Paschal Beverly Randolph: A Nineteenth-Century Black American Spiritualist, Rosicrucian, and Sex Magician* (Albany: State University of New York Press, 1997), particularly ch. 12 for the Blavatsky-Randolph interaction.

13.   Joscelyn Godwin, *The Theosophical Enlightenment* (Albany: State University of New York Press, 1984), 281.

14.   For a first-hand account of this episode, see Daniel H. Caldwell (ed.), *The Esoteric World of Madame Blavatsky: Insights into the Life of a Modern Sphinx* (Wheaton, IL: Quest Books, 2000), 32-35. While this work is an invaluable collection of writings about Blavatsky by her contemporaries, one should keep in mind that most of these accounts were written years after the events under discussion.

15.   The primary work delineating which master was most likely which historical person is Paul Johnson, *The Masters Revealed: Madame Blavatsky and the Myth of the Great White Lodge* (Albany: State University of New York Press, 1994). Johnson concedes readily that his thesis requires a leap of speculation in order to work, but many have been happy to make it. Daniel van Egmond, for example, credits Johnson for proving their existence as real human beings 'once and for all'. See his 'Western Esoteric Schools', in Roelof van der Broek and Wouter J. Hanegraaff (eds.), *Gnosis and Hermeticism from Antiquity to Modern Times* (Albany: State University of New York

Press, 1998), 311-46. For an even-handed brief history of the transformation of the Theosophical masters, see Olav Hammer, *Claiming Knowledge: Strategies of Epistemology from Theosophy to the New Age* (Leiden: Brill, 2001), 380-93.

16. The Brotherhood of Luxor should not be confused with the Hermetic Brotherhood of Luxor, the existence of which is not in any doubt. This occult group deviated from Blavatsky's eastern turn by maintaining a classically western esotericism that also, to Blavatsky's great displeasure, espoused sex magic. For the foundational work on this group, see Joscelyn Godwin, Christian Chanel, and John P. Deveney, *The Hermetic Brotherhood of Luxor: Initiatic and Historical Documents of an Order of Practical Occultism* (York Beach, ME: Samuel Weiser, 1995).

17. Bruce F. Campbell, *Ancient Wisdom Revived: A History of the Theosophical Movement* (Berkeley, CA: University of California Press, 1980), 28.

18. Godwin, *The Theosophical Enlightenment*, 282.

19. The study of occult practitioners and members of secret societies is, by its very nature, a morass of conflicting data and purposeful attempts to cover up both facts and failures. In addition, much of the firsthand literature on the topic was written several years after the event discussed, thereby exponentially increasing the odds that – intentionally or not – the witness may have revised his or her original version of the story. One is left with conflicting accounts in both the source and academic literature available. Deveney argues, using Olcott's journals and later claims by Felt, that Felt continued to influence the Theosophical Society for a couple of years after his recorded departure due to his failure to produce elementals. He finds it possible or even probable that Felt's experiments necessitated the secret branch of the Theosophical Society to be formed, devoted to matters of magical practice and requiring degrees of initiation like the Masons. Godwin finds it most likely that Felt 'was referring to some form of scrying, perhaps with chemically treated mirrors such as the French magnetists had been experimenting with', and that the secret branch of Theosophy was indeed begun because of Felt but because of a strongly negative reaction members had to a drawing of a strange animal that Blavatsky pronounced to be an 'Egyptian elemental'. While their arguments are not mutually exclusive, the differences do point to the difficulties of ascertaining cause and effect from this tricky material. See Deveney, *Paschal Beverly Randolph*, 289-95 and Godwin, *The Theosophical Enlightenment*, 286-88.

20. While there is some speculation that Britten herself was the author of these works and that she wished to distance herself or her reputation from them, I find this hypothesis less compelling than her own claims to be merely the editor. She attached her own name to claims much more scandalous than any found in *Art Magic* and in my estimation her character was such that I simply do not see her shying away from a claim she believed in.

21. Emma Hardinge Britten, *Art Magic, or Mundane, Sub-Mundane, and Super-Mundane Spiritism* (Chicago: Progressive Thinker Publishing House, 1898 [1875]), 207.

22. H.P. Blavatsky, *Isis Unveiled: A Master Key to the Mysteries of Ancient and Modern Science and Technology* (2 vols.; Pasadena, CA: Theosophical University Press, 1972), II, 15.

23. Blavatsky, *Isis Unveiled*, II, 22-23, and *passim*.

24. Emma Hardinge Britten's own work is an excellent example of Spiritualist authors who criticized the church while maintaining the essentially millennial endeavor of humanity. For an excellent brief summary of the immediate influences on nineteenth-century occultism, including Britten's, see Wouter J. Hanegraaff, *New Age Religion and Western Culture: Esotericism in the Mirror of Secular Thought* (Albany: State University of New York Press, 1998), 443-48.

25. Blavatsky, *Isis Unveiled*, II, 26. All emphases and italics are in the original.

26. Blavatsky, *Isis Unveiled*, I, 573.

27. It should be noted that while Christianity gets lambasted in Theosophy, Jesus does not. This is also a common trope among the more radical voices of Spiritualism. Jesus is a teacher or an adept, one among many gifted prophets but not singular and divine as Christian doctrine would have him be. For a good treatment of Jesus in various American occult traditions, see Ann Taves, *Fits, Trances, and Visions: Experiencing Religion and Explaining Experience from Wesley to James* (Princeton, NJ: Princeton University Press, 1999), 212-232.

28. Hammer, *Claiming Knowledge*, 112.

Promiseland:
Utopian Technology and the American Millennial Dream*

Fred Nadis

1

As part of a 50-state lecture tour, inventor and entrepreneur Dennis Lee appeared in Austin, Texas, in 2001, in one of the sprawling white buildings of 'Promiseland', a Pentecostal church lit up that night in shades of purple.[1] He came to sell to the public a 'free energy' machine, a miraculous device that would make home energy cost-free. His show combined salesmanship with demonstrations of engines, generators, vacuums, and magnetism. With such apparatus of wonder, he sought to astound his audience, make them appreciate the marvels of the universe, and persuade them that normal science, big business, and government need not have the last word.

Dennis Lee's show, which connects wonder, science, and religion has numerous historical precedents. Historian David F. Noble has argued that the history of science and technology reveals a close affinity between its prime movers and Christian millennial thought. Interest in the redemptive power of the 'mechanical arts', that is, technology, surfaced in twelfth-century abbeys, heavily influenced by the teachings of Joachim of Fiore who had predicted the apocalypse would unveil in the mid-twelfth century. According to such apocalyptic belief, the final confrontation between good and evil would usher in a 1,000-year period of peace on earth. Among others in medieval Europe, the Franciscan monk Roger Bacon argued that developing the mechanical arts and securing humanity's domination of nature would help restore the fallen Adam to his original genius and powers and so prepare humanity for its millennial role.[2] Technological innovation, then, could usher in the apocalypse and its ensuing millennial promises. Four centuries later the prime architect of the modern scientific project, Francis Bacon, likewise linked the advancement of the mechanical arts and science to the restoration of humanity to its original greatness. In the preface to his work *The Great Instauration* Francis Bacon insisted that through the careful study of nature and its wonders the mind of man 'Might be restored to its perfect and original condition'.[3]

If Roger Bacon's technological millennialism was literal, then Francis Bacon's at the very least was rhetorical.[4] This easy rhetorical connection of scientific utopianism with religious millennialism continued until the early-nineteenth century when science textbooks frequently pointed to the fundamental harmony of science and religion, particularly Christianity. By the mid-nineteenth century, though, new theories about geology and evolution, that burst asunder biblical notions about creation, as well as about the age of the earth and humanity, strained the premise that new discoveries in science added to the proof of the intricacy and glories of God's handiwork.[5] Biblical literalism would no longer do. Suddenly the 'nature' of the natural historians and the 'creation' of religious fundamentalists lacked congruence.

Despite this rift, the utopian nature of the scientific project and the sense of awe that scientific and technological breakthroughs inspire continued to offer fertile grounds for populist 'harmonizers' of these spheres. The American public has continuously expressed faith in the redemptive powers of science and technology. Critiques of technology and science, when offered, are generally made in the name of a higher spirituality or ethic – premised on a 'betrayal' of the scientific project's millennial promise.

On the popular level, weddings between the millennial and the scientific are in high demand. Science fiction, for example, is a popular arena in which mythic narratives intertwine apocalyptic premises with futuristic settings; New Age expositions like the Whole Life Exposition are crowded with salespeople for mechanical healing devices based on esoteric energy sources; and showmen and inventors such as Dennis Lee encourage audiences to connect the 'wonders' of science and technology to the spiritual impulse in their sales efforts.

Lee's popular science demonstrations and sales lectures are worthy of examination because they reveal the still-current connection of millennialism, that is, the religiously premised dream of human perfection, with technological and scientific advances. Lee frames his performance in the rhetoric of wonder and conspiracy and so plays both on his audience's desires and its fears of the betrayal of the fundamental Western dream of progress.

2

Inside the Promiseland theater where Lee was to perform, about 150 people filled red-cushioned pews that could seat about 250. Out in the lobby there was a check-in table that included copies of Lee's 1994 book, *The Alternative – A True Story with Solutions to America's Most Pressing Problems*. Its back jacket included the copy: 'Fossil Fuels Are Polluting our

Planet', 'We Are Overrun with Garbage and Toxic Waste', 'The Media Is Manipulating We the People', 'Courts No Longer Uphold our Inalienable Rights', and the litany concluded with 'But, What Is the Alternative?' Like his book, his lecture combined a plea for ecological sanity with right-wing libertarian notions. He promoted the utopian promise of technology and condemned the betrayed dream that issued from the sins of our leaders.

For publicity, Dennis Lee relies on a network that reaches into the free energy community, fundamentalist Christian church culture and rural libertarian circles with his websites and weekly web radio broadcasts. Lee's radio show, which began broadcasting in December, 2000, is titled 'The John Galt Show'. The pseudonym Galt is in homage to the hero of Ayn Rand's novel *The Fountainhead*, a symbol of individualism and of the libertarian ideals that Rand helped originate. Lee's broadcasts from 'down on the farm' would generally appeal to rural, right wing individuals, and to fundamentalist Christians. He notes that his company's president is Jesus Christ, its treasurer is the Holy Spirit, while Dennis Lee is merely the Director of Research. His radio broadcasts have included such titles as: 'God Doesn't Need Us to Make Free Energy'; 'Partial Birth Abortions'; and 'God's Involvement in our Beginning'. His target audience is also indicated by the network he belongs to, the 'Truth Radio Network'; Truth Radio's web page includes the slogan, 'Truth Radio Tells the Truth behind the Dominant Media Propaganda'.[6] Lee's actual broadcasts are rambling and numbing monologues that rely on vernacular humor and reports of conspiracies to stave off the monotony of his pitches for his company's products and promises that listeners that become franchised dealers will soon gain a fortune.

Lee's primary goal on his lecture tour and broadcasts has been to sell audiences his 'free energy' machines, devices that speak precisely to the utopian premises of the scientific project. Here are miraculous devices that may lead the way to a new paradise. Yet 'free energy' is also an old dream, formerly filed under the category of 'perpetual motion'.[7] Since ancient times inventors have explored the possibility of perpetual motion to fulfill all possible energy needs; the posited devices fit two basic variants: devices of the 'first kind' that form a closed circuit and are a self-propelling system, and those of 'the second kind' that rely on a perpetual natural force outside the device.

Perpetual motion machines of the first kind involve a closed circuit that, once started, will somehow overcome forces such as gravity and friction and allow a wheel to turn perpetually and perform work, such as grinding wheat or generating electricity. One such device depicted by Robert Fludd during the Renaissance was a waterwheel that would run a pump that in turn lifted water up to continue the wheel's turning. Other devices, such as 'overbalanced wheels' would, through various ingenious schemes, somehow keep a wheel weighted more heavily on its down turning side than on its up turning side. In the early-eighteenth century several members of the Royal Society of London examined and were beguiled by a mysterious turning wheel seemingly of this sort, engineered by the clockmaker Johann Bessler.[8] Unfolding interests in magnets, mercury, pneumatics, capillary action, and electricity also encouraged more schemes of such closed circuit devices. More promising have been 'perpetual motion machines of the second kind', that is, open-circuit devices that connect the basic clockwork to outside sources such as tides, changes in temperature, or changes in barometric pressure.[9] In this milieu, frauds abounded. For example, from 1873 until his death in 1898, John W. Keeley promoted a mysterious motor that ran on 'etheric force' derived from the 'disintegration of water'. He raised millions from financiers for his company on the strength of his demonstrations and it was not until after his death that it was determined that his devices relied on hidden tubes conveying pressurized air to run.[10]

Lee, founder of Better World Technologies, and the International Tesla Electric Company, fits well into the company of such past dreamers, inventors, and hoaxers.[11] He has attributed the source of his mysterious motor to numerous possibilities including magnets, but he also allies himself with the slightly more respectable contemporary free energy movement. This movement dates to 1989 when University of Utah chemist Stanley Pons and his colleague Martin Fleischmann, a world leader in the field of electrochemistry, reported at a press conference that they had developed an electrical method for achieving nuclear fusion reactions at room temperatures. Pons and Fleischmann announced that with their simple apparatus that involved minimal electrical input enormous heat was released. Their equipment included four electrolysis cells with palladium electrodes immersed in heavy water. With this simple, inexpensive apparatus, they announced they had fused hydrogen nuclei within the interstices of the palladium atoms and generated fusion reactions that emitted heat and nuclear energy.

The scientific and popular reaction was immense. With promised help from the Utah legislature, the University of Utah began plans for a multimillion dollar National Cold Fusion Institute.[12] Thousands of scientists and enthusiasts began to tinker with their own tabletop fusion kits. Early confirmations of anomalous energy emissions eventually led to new studies and retractions of many of the confirmations, as researchers refined methods for measuring the actual output of heat, radioactive particles, and rays. 'Hot' fusion experts insisted that the recorded emissions, if accurate, were far too low for fusion reactions and rejected other attempts to theorize the anomalous results. Cold fusion largely lost legitimacy, as science, in 1990, one year after its 'discovery'. Yet throughout the 1990s interest in free energy of the cold fusion variety remained.

The American Physical Society still allows panels on cold fusion at its annual conferences, but scientists who openly conduct such research are stigmatized. As an alternative, these researchers work on the sly, or have turned to the public realm, allying themselves with the amateurs who are often called 'cold fusioneers'; together, they run their own conferences and have developed popular websites and journals, such as *New Energy News*, *Infinite Energy Magazine* and the *Journal of New Energy*.

In such a way, these researchers have formed their own loose alliance of dedicated amateurs, after-hours scientists, engineers, and futurists. Free energy advocates also are generally welcomed both in New Age circles and in fundamentalist Christian groups, by those whose millennialist assumptions make such miracle devices the expected rather than the unexpected.[13] These assumptions are inscribed haphazardly in the Institute for New Energy website – an encyclopedic mass of links to web postings and articles ranging from the highly-technical to the loosely-metaphysical. Many of the postings dispute ruling paradigms of science and revel, for example, in questioning the principles of thermodynamics, while exploring anti-gravity devices, low-energy nuclear reactions and transmutation (i.e., cold fusion) and perpetual motion. Others insist, with some scientific basis, that the 'ether' of earlier physics tallies with the quantum theory premise that space is not empty but contains quantum-level fluctuations, which, free energy researchers maintain, can be harvested like wind or solar power. The postings also promote a rebellious attitude toward a sinister status quo that encompasses the political, scientific, and business establishments. A scattering of reports of espionage and sabotaged projects also links this website to a strong current of gossip and folklore about such possibilities. The cold fusioneers suspect that they, having neared a new scientific secret that will allow for miraculous technology, have been stopped and oppressed by economic interests.

Borrowing from the free energy community's quasi-scientific status, Dennis Lee also argues that 'free energy' and the transmutation of radioactive materials to inert materials occur. Like many of the cold fusioneers, he sees himself as a modern alchemist, bringing spirituality to technological research. Lee also relies on a conspiracy argument of the 'if authorities are calling me a fraud and out to get me then I must be onto something' variety to boost his appeal. His lectures and web broadcasts also point to the obvious truth that the passion or cognitive pathways opened by wonder have long been a part of American commercial and sales culture. Lee, like the Wizard of Oz, is a pitchman whose enthusiasms and impostures metaphorically reveal the operations of consumerism.

3

Lee is a far better performer live on stage than he is on radio. The stage for the Dennis Lee show at the church in Austin was filled with apparatus such as engines, a boiler rigged to run off of gas from a septic tank, a welding machine, a kitchen stove, a generator beneath a row of light bulbs, and posters for products such as Fire Shaker and Sonic Bloom. Lying about were oddities that suggested Lee had an instinct for clowning, such as a cane with a bulbed bicycle horn attached. The audience was mainly middle-aged and white. There were also a few children, teenagers, and people of color scattered about the pews. Many of the men wore remarkably long beards and seemed quite serious. Many, like myself, held notebooks.

Lee came on stage and asked, 'Are you ready to have fun tonight?' He was a big man, with a Fu-Manchu moustache, light sideburns, and an intense look as he sized up his audience, trying to decide if he would have any hecklers or 'trouble'. He immediately asked the audience if he could remove his jacket, gained their assent and promised he would not take anything else off.

Lee seemed comfortable on stage, capable of both physical and verbal comedy; he has a droll voice with a wheedling quality and he enjoys playing to his audience, frequently asking rhetorical questions like, 'Does anyone remember Free Enterprise?' bringing shouts of 'Yep!' or 'Sure do!' He began by noting that he would be telling us what we did not know, and 'what it is we don't know in America will shock you'. He complained about 'Good Old Boy Politics' and corrupt Big Business. He informed the audience he had technology that could eradicate all forms of pollution in the United States. 'What level of pollution is O.K. for the United States?' he asked. 'None!' came the replies. He also said that at the end of the night he would make a job offer to everyone; at no cost to us we could earn more than our present salaries while working only part-time. He also let us know that his other 41 performances of the 2001 tour had been in hotel conference rooms – not churches. He had no connection with Promiseland; however, he announced, 'I am a Christian from the top of my head to the bottom of my toes. That's who I am.' He admitted that this did not necessarily give anyone credibility in this day and age, yet he wanted it noted. The inventions he would reveal were the Lord's work.

Like someone doing the 'Lord's work', he was attempting to convert audience members to a new world-view. Lee has been a salesman for many years and knows instinctively what American sales manuals long have been teaching apprentice salespeople and what evangelical pamphlets have been teaching leaders of revivals. A sale, like a religious conversion, is fraught with dangers. It requires a careful approach, an attention to setting, an intuitive reading of the audience, a presentation that blends logic and emotion, and a skillful 'closing'. The salesman and the evangelist must rely not only a simple display of logic, but create a heightened mood and emotional atmosphere. In his analysis of revivalism, *Lectures on Revivals of Religion* (1835), Charles Grandison Finney remarked, 'The state of the world is still such, and probably will be till the millennium is fully come, that religion must be mainly promoted by these excitements'.[14] If the evangelical preacher as confidence trickster has become an American archetype, the salesman who offers a revivalist show, like Lee, is yet another.

Like an evangelist cast among sinners, Lee had a difficult task before him. To convince his audience that the 'impossible' was not impossible, that 'free energy' could exist, and that they will soon have such a device on their lawn, requires a powerful conversion process. To these ends Lee generated wonders and delight. Technological demonstrations like those of Lee and wonder have long been linked. For the elites of the Middle Age and Renaissance, who amassed wonder cabinets, wonder was one of the ruling passions; they saw it as a faculty halfway between emotion and cognition, invaluable to the connoisseur for the speculations and vistas it opened. Bafflement, amazement, confusion, awe and delight might be mixed together when in the thrall of this passion. Once savored, a wonder – whether 'natural', 'technological', or a mixture of the two would prompt intellectual investigation.[15] Natural philosophers of the eighteenth and early-nineteenth century also often put on astounding displays to gain patronage.[16]

In addition to offering wonders that evoked miniature epistemological crises in audience members, Lee also relied on more worldly strategies to delight. He followed to the letter mainstream sales manual stratagems – to quote one from 1916:

> The sale is made, let it be whispered, to the child in the man… It is the child that dares, that ventures, and that loves the new and untried… To put analytical reason off her guard by pleasing with simple reason is the aim of the logical presentation. When the seller has accomplished this, he may address the child.[17]

Lee offers enough apparent technical knowledge to relax his audience, but appeals throughout, with humor, clowning, and spectacle, to the child in each of his spectators.

Early in his presentation, he held up a small pedestal, noting it was the sort that 'a toy elephant might dance on'. He set it down and spun a top on it. 'Let's see how long that keeps spinning.' This led to a monologue on how perpetual motion wasn't ridiculous if linked to a perpetual source, such as the motion of the Earth around the sun. As he put it, 'Everyone in this room is sitting on the biggest mass known' – laughter ensued – 'no I'm not insulting anyone – you're sitting on the Earth, which is moving 78,000 miles per hour. How does that make you feel? How long has it been moving? A long time. When will it stop? Not for a long time.' These thoughts led to a brief side-discussion of his company's 'dietary aids', which he depended upon to keep his weight down; he held up a spoon with a hole in it, again to much laughter.

He then went on to explain how he wanted to put a generator on each of our houses, as this 'was a dream God gave to me'. The machine would offer 100% of our heat, hot water, air-conditioning, and electricity. It would also put out 15 times more than the needed wattage. That was why our energy would be free. He would sell the surplus to the local power company to make his money and let us use the rest for free.

His first demonstration was designed as another game – he informed us that he could modify our cars to run on pickle juice. He then had his two assistants, one of whom wore a trucker's cap, the other a black tee-shirt bearing the portrait of Nikola Tesla, on the stage to help him run a small 'infernal combustion motor'. He was going to prove that we could run the engine on anything as part of his pitch for the environmentally friendly and economically pleasing formula of 80% water and 20% gasoline.

Acting like three conspiratorial clowns, he and his assistants began to produce samples of various household products, and Lee urged the audience to take sips or sniffs to authenticate them. Into a jar, they poured samples of Coca-Cola, water, 'Hot as Hell' hot sauce, crude oil, Aqua-Velva, sugar, salt, pickle juice, Frappuccino and urine, which he referred to as 'technician's juice'. This routine included many broad comedy moments, as when an assistant bravely tasted the hot sauce, and had a delayed reaction of horror. Lee then told us with his modified engine, no pollution would be emitted from the exhaust pipe, and, in fact, the exhaust would be 97% oxygen and perfectly safe to breathe. They attached the jar of fuel to the apparatus, and after many pulls on the starter, and a few engine starts and sputters, they got the engine running and Lee held a white handkerchief before the exhaust, showed it was still clean, then leaned down to breathe in the exhaust. Lee then told us his modified engine relied on a mysterious 'reactor rod'. Scientists had been 'astounded' by this rod, and nobody knew how it worked. Fiber optic photography showed that 'a blue lightning storm' was going on while it worked. He spoke of how these rods could be installed on a car, a complicated process of 'tuning' while having it face magnetic north, and making other seemingly magic adjustments. With such modified engines, we could save enormously on fuel bills by using a water/gasoline mixture. He also attempted to demonstrate how a lawn mower could 'run on its own exhaust', though he admitted that physicists would tell you this was 'impossible'. During this demonstration, as with the last, the lawnmower frequently stalled and Lee, the impatient showman, finally told his assistants, with some disgust, 'take it away'. Here Lee's acting out of exasperation gained the audience's trust despite the demonstration's failure.

Lee next demonstrated how to weld with 'water gas' as the fuel. The gas was not the mixture of hydrogen and oxygen one would expect from the electrolysis of water but a mysterious 'water gas' which does not explode but 'implodes', and had the structure of H-O-H rather than the H-H-O that he dubiously claimed was standard for water. Here he also added a new motif: the idea that organic nature has an anthropomorphic quality. Water gas had the remarkable homeopathic quality of adjusting its temperature to melt whatever substance you were working with. In this way it never burnt your hand. He said he discussed this with a scientist at Brigham Young University who said, 'atomic reactions must be involved for no conduction of heat to occur'. Water gas also left 'no slag' on steel when cut, left water streaks on surfaces it cut, and could burn through any substance on this planet, including diamonds. He and his assistants proceeded to cut various pieces of metal and discuss the costs of using the 'water gas' instead of acetylene. The cost for one of the welding units was approximately $1200 but Lee would also be happy to sell the bottled gas as well.

His following exhibit involved the concept, popular in the cold fusion and free energy community, that the transmutation of radioactive elements to inert elements was possible through cold fusion processes. He told us that the federal government was putting our lives at risk. He described an above ground nuclear waste storage facility in Richland, Washington, with brine circulating around spent rods to prevent spontaneous reactions, and how authorities were scrambling around to find salt mines to bury the waste in. This was all foolery, since Lee had 'a machine to neutralize all radioactive waste into inert materials. We know they know that', he added, because he had demonstrated the device for two unnamed US senators, one of whom responded favorably and was promptly voted out of office. Though scientists and the Department of Energy would disagree – 'anyone from the Department of Energy here tonight? No? I always invite them' – it was possible to 'transmutate' [sic] the nucleus of an atom. 'The alchemists were right.'

After demonstrating what background radiation sounded like with a Geiger counter, Lee had an assistant mix up a control sample and a solution of one gram of radioactive thorium along with 125 grams of water and an undisclosed amount of hydrochloric acid. These would be placed in his 'pure zirconium' cooker, with its electrodes, for 30 minutes. With a radioactive gauge they would test the sample before and after. Lee told us what to expect: a lowered radioactive count and traces of titanium and copper and other metals would be in the solution – proof of transmutation of the thorium. Though the most likely explanation would involve contaminated samples or electrodes, Lee insisted that this was out of the question because the cooker was 99.9% pure zirconium.

While the samples 'cooked', Lee spoke about the conspiracy of the power companies to rip off consumers with inefficient meters and appliances that drew more current than needed. It was all a result of the 'Good Ole Boy Routine', the short script of which runs, 'You lie, I'll swear to it'. He then extolled the virtue of his company's numerous products, starting with a power regulator that would make sure machinery only drew the amount of energy needed and demonstrated the device on a small generator hooked to an array of light bulbs.

These sales pitches for household products relied less on humor and instead played on the audience's desire for security. Earlier, he had made the audience uneasy about pollution, corporate conspiracies, and radioactive waste. Now he showed videos for a fire barrier spray and a fire shaker that put out kitchen fires that could otherwise swiftly spread through a home. He also revealed the 'Bandit' alarm system for homes or stores, which took three seconds to fill a room with thick fog, and 'Miracle Shield', which was an anti-graffiti liquid; a product that catered to the audience's fear of teen gang members, and an enzyme soil remover that 'cleans up the environment instead of polluting it'.

After these videos, Lee returned our attention to the zirconium cooker; his assistant offered precise measurements to confirm that the radioactivity had lowered. Lee then urged an audience member to bring a test-tube of the transformed solution to a university lab where trace amounts of newly-formed atoms of copper, titanium and other metals would be found. Lee then continued his theme of the insecurity of life in America, alluding to the terrorist attack on the World Trade Center in Manhattan that had taken place several weeks prior to his show. This was the one point in the lecture where his impeccable sense for what his audience would be willing to hear failed somewhat – a brief shudder seemed to greet the allusion. He soldiered on, though, and solemnly intoned that jet planes could use water as fuel. This had been demonstrated irrefutably. A 'hydrogen pulse separator' would turn the water to hydrogen fuel (apparently preferable, in this case, to 'water gas'). 'If a plane loaded with fuel tanks of water ran into a tower', he asked, 'what would happen? Far less damage.'

He then moved on to describe how he had been harassed in Kentucky and forced off the stage, and made a passionate stand about returning with federal marshals to claim his right to free speech. When the applause faded, he began his final pitch. It was over three hours into his performance, and as no hecklers had challenged him, he suspected, correctly, the docile crowd was now ready to accept his more absurd pronouncements. He told us that he believed he had found a perpetual energy source – and it was the magnet. 'I believe', he said, 'that energy flows into magnets.' Most scientists, he admitted, would disagree.

He offered us a few clues as to how his device might work. At the front of the stage he earlier had set up a series of small magnet-laden windmills. Spinning one caused the others to spin in a haphazard, chaotic way that Lee enjoyed; he gave personalities to these mills and their quirks, underlining his identification of the magnet as a trustworthy friend, a reliable source of unlimited power. Next he relied on a genuine demonstration of a scientific wonder that involved an unusual magnetic phenomenon known in the nineteenth century. He showed us a permanent magnet and a segment of wide copper pipe. He upended the pipe and set up a mirror so that a video camera could look down it. Then he had his assistant drop a magnet down the copper tube. The video screens showed it slowly falling, as it induced magnetic currents in the copper; it fell in what seemed slow motion. He then said that a stronger magnet would go even slower. We watched its slow, somewhat magical free-fall through the short length of tube on the video screen. 'My motor will use one hundred permanent magnets', he said.

He then said he was not demonstrating his free energy motor this tour because in 1999 he had demonstrated it to all comers. Using the magician's art of misdirection, he then switched the audience's attention from his miraculous but unseen 'permanent magnet motor' to the generator that it would be attached to on our lawns, the 'G-10'. The G-10 was brought out on stage, hooked to a heater and amid its thunder and fury, several spectators came down with devices to measure its efficiency. He assured us that the complete energy-producing unit would not make much noise on our lawn.

It was now close to 11.00 pm. Lee's audience had been listening to him for four hours. They were willing to take on trust Lee's miracle free-energy machine and to instead examine the efficiency of the G-10 generator. They apparently had faith in his 'permanent magnet motor' and interest in his other products, like the 'noiseless jackhammer' and the welding unit that used 'water gas'. All that was left was to sell products and dealerships. The incentive for takers would be personal wealth and a chance to help improve the environment. By moving our imaginations ahead to the day we would have the G-10 working for us, Lee had already psychologically closed the deal.

Some spectators might conclude that even if Lee was running a racket, he was a tireless front man who could help them sell products to others and so gain commissions.

4

I left Promiseland worn-down, able, almost, to believe in the miraculous. Lee seemed to me the embodiment of an American archetype, part salesman, part showman, part tinkerer, and part confidence trickster. Lee preyed on his audience's fears and insecurities – painting verbal pictures with video supplements of houses going up in flames, stores burglarized, jet planes exploding, terrorist attackers, and a variety of ecological disasters. He offered an 'alternative' – miracles that had some technical grounding, surrounded by clouds of magic and double-talk.

He gained his audience's trust by making religious appeals and by fanning their distrust of big government, big business, and big science. He championed instead a different science, seemingly like that of the cold fusioneers, one able to challenge established truths. Lee and his audience formed a small community of 'resistance' – a conservative one that projected an ideal world of ecological balance, small entrepreneurial business, and reliance on technology. He offered his audience not just 'free energy' but another form of 'power'. He was selling a democratic vision, one that gave each audience member the authority to reject scientific expertise and shape his or her own world-view. He offered a miracle gadget on the lawn, but, more importantly, a cosmos that was not grim and mechanistic but full of possibilities and promise. He also offered a vision of a social order in which the 'little guy' could once again be the basic unit of democracy.

Lee's 'resistance', however, was one made in the image of the dominant culture. His false claims placed him, the 'Director of Research', of a company presided over by Jesus Christ, on no higher moral ground than the scientists, big corporations, and politicians he assailed. Yet like public relations experts and advertising agencies, he knew how to employ both 'science' and 'wonders' to prove that things were not as simple as they seemed, and to evoke desire for an alternative to the norm, the no longer palatable 'Brand X' world that big business, big government, and big science had created. Like Francis Bacon before him, Lee was offering a 'Great Instauration', a restoration that linked the American Dream to the millennial Christian dream of the approaching reign of heaven on earth.

Bibliography

Čapek, Karel, *The Absolute at Large* (London: MacMillan, 1927).

Finney, Charles Grandison, 'What a Revival of Religion Is', in David A. Hollinger and C. Capper (eds.), *The American Intellectual Tradition* (2 vols.; New York: Oxford University Press, 1997), I, 194-203.

Daston, Lorraine, and Katharine Park, *Wonders and the Order of Nature, 1150–1750* (New York: Zone Books, 2001).

Greenblatt, Stephen, 'Resonance and Wonder', in Ivan Karp and Steven D. Lavine (eds.), *Exhibiting Cultures* (Washington, DC: Smithsonian Institution Press, 1991), 42-56.

Hovenkamp, Herbert, *Science and Religion in America, 1800–1860* (Philadelphia: University of Pennsylvania Press, 1978).

Huizenga, John, *Cold Fusion: The Scientific Fiasco of the Century* (Rochester, NY: University of Rochester Press, 1992).

Leichter, E., *Successful Selling* (New York and London: Funk & Wagnalls, 1916).

Moore, R. Laurence, *Selling God: American Religion in the Marketplace of Culture* (New York: Oxford University Press, 1994).

Nadis, Fred, *Wonder Shows: Performing Science, Magic, and Religion in America* (New Brunswick, NJ: Rutgers University Press, 2005).

Noble, David F., *The Religion of Technology: The Divinity of Man and the Spirit of Invention* (London: Penguin Books, 1999).

Ord-Hume, Arthur, W.J.G., *Perpetual Motion: The History of an Obsession* (New York: St Martin's Press, 1977).

Schaffer, Simon, 'Natural Philosophy and Public Spectacle in the Eighteenth Century', *History of Science* 21 (1983), 1-43.

— 'The Show That Never Ends: Perpetual Motion in the Early Eighteenth Century', *British Journal for the History of Science* 28 (1995), 157-89.

Simon, Bart, *Undead Science: Science Studies and the Afterlife of Cold Fusion* (New Brunswick: Rutgers University Press, 2002).

Notes

*   Substantial portions of this piece have been reprinted with permission from *Wonder Shows: Performing Science, Magic, and Religion in America*, by Fred Nadis (New Brunswick, NJ: Rutgers University Press, 2005).

1.   This description of Lee's show is based on the author's notes on Lee's 22 October, 2001 appearance at Promiseland in Austin, Texas.

2.   David F. Noble, *The Religion of Technology: The Divinity of Man and the Spirit of Invention* (London: Penguin Books, 1999). For Noble's discussion of Roger Bacon and medieval millennialism, see 21-34.

3.   Cited in Noble, *The Religion of Technology*, 51.

4.   One of the main flaws in Noble's argument is that he failed to consider whether some of the historical figures he ascribes millennial beliefs to – from Francis Bacon to Auguste Comte – might merely be employing religious language as a rhetorical strategy and not as a true expression of cherished beliefs.

5.   For a thorough discussion of the intertwining of science and religion in nineteenth-century American culture see Herbert Hovenkamp, *Science and Religion in America, 1800–1860* (Philadelphia: University of Pennsylvania Press, 1978).

6.   This home page also had contrasting advertisements for the 'Million Mom March' against handguns and one for 'Dangerous Books Online Bookstore', with a list that gives tips on how to open an offshore bank account, how to protect one's privacy, and travel internationally without a passport. Truth Radio homepage, 19 July, 2001. http://www.truthradio.com/

7.   Satirist and science fiction writer Karel Čapek mapped out the connection between free energy dreams and religion in his novel *The Absolute at Large* (London: MacMillan, 1927). In this tale, an inventor creates an atomic 'Karburator' that not only produces unlimited energy but religious ecstasy to those within its sphere of influence. The device creates not only religious frenzies but also economic and political havoc and an orgy of warfare and killing. The Karburator, finally, is banned, and small cells of cultists that still worship the few remaining, hidden Karburators are subjected to police raids.

8.   Simon Schaffer, 'The Show That Never Ends: Perpetual Motion in the Early Eighteenth Century', *British Journal for the History of Science* 28 (1995), 157-89.

9.   Perpetual motion scholar Arthur W.J.G. Ord-Hume argues that at least one such device 'of the second kind' was developed in the 1760s, when James Cox developed a clock that was automatically rewound by a device triggered by changes in barometric pressure. See Ord-Hume, *Perpetual Motion: The History of an Obsession* (New York: St Martin's Press, 1977), 11-24.

10.   Ord-Hume, *Perpetual Motion*, 139-50.

11.   Lee has run into trouble with the law in several states. One of his dealer's websites notes this trouble, but places a positive spin on it, as follows, 'In the states of Maine and Idaho, UCSA, BWT and ITEC have agreed with the Attorney Generals of those states that we will not ever promote, demonstrate or install proven or unproven Free Electricity generators or any device relating to electricity. *It is evident by the following, which is an exact quote from the agreement, that these states do not wish their citizens to have any device that produces free energy in their state either now or any time in the future*'. See http://www.ucsofa.com/announcement.htm. 19 September, 2003.

12.   John Huizenga, *Cold Fusion: The Scientific Fiasco of the Century* (Rochester, NY: University of Rochester Press, 1992), 23.

13.   For a recent sociological study of cold fusion, see Bart Simon, *Undead Science: Science Studies and the Afterlife of Cold Fusion* (New Brunswick, NJ: Rutgers University Press, 2002).

14.   Charles Grandison Finney, 'What a Revival of Religion Is', in David A. Hollinger and C. Capper (eds.), *The American Intellectual Tradition* (2 vols.; New York: Oxford

University Press, 1997), I, 194-203 (202). The connection between salesmanship and evangelism is thoroughly explored in R. Laurence Moore, *Selling God: American Religion in the Marketplace of Culture* (New York: Oxford University Press, 1994).

15. Stephen Greenblatt, 'Resonance and Wonder', in Ivan Karp and Steven D. Lavine (eds.), *Exhibiting Cultures* (Washington, DC: Smithsonian Institution Press, 1991), 42-56. For a thorough history of the cultural understanding of wonder see Lorraine Daston and Katharine Park, *Wonders and the Order of Nature, 1150–1750* (New York: Zone Books, 2001).

16. For a discussion of how eighteenth-century natural philosophers relied on performance and an evocation of the 'marvelous' to gain patronage for scientific research, see Simon Schaffer, 'Natural Philosophy and Public Spectacle in the Eighteenth Century', *History of Science* 21 (1983), 1-43.

17. E. Leichter, *Successful Selling* (New York and London: Funk & Wagnalls, 1916), 40.

Postcard II

Thomas MacKay

Here, the hills are long with homes and the myriad errands of land.
There are little vineyards and little mills for olives,
like the collective consciousness of specialty-store labels.
You would like the sun, a short-staying guest these days,
rounding the corner, spending the good hours,
visible on the road ahead for a little time after it leaves.

As one goes inside to chop vegetables or just to turn on the lights, the
    cathedral rings an hour
that is best heard here, in the distance, up among the
hills and houses and baying dogs; in the city, the churches stand in nar-
    row streets,
converse with the men on the corner, and smoke near red diamonds.
Foreign churches and foreign villagers: same wrinkles.

Yes, I left. Keep trying to end it.
I'm sorry. Keep trying to find some literary flourish.
But it ends and ends many times. I've closed a few books; I've boarded
    planes.
I've meditated on the centers of circles, tried to bed the mystic rose.
I've stared dumbly at the various facets of tombs,
I've pondered what whos should forgive what whoms.
Does it, can it rise into a cone of feeling, some storm-eye,
some crack and burst of the valve?

If it were all to finish tomorrow, if we were all caught up,
would we see one another at all? Could the words of our lives
be sluiced from the stew of meaning so that we could be, briefly,
two people? Maybe to ask how things are going. Share some inside joke.
Nice to think of the apocalypse as a big funeral,
bringing us together in that dark-suited way of seeing old friends.
But no, no history at the end I think, because there won't be irony,
no hermeneutic borders on the map: just oceans.

Right now you cannot escape the smell of small fires, of green and dead
    growth
burning rich and ritualized among the hills, among the cypresses shaped
    like
Pantheon pillars, among trees planted by Crusaders.
I've closed a few books, but I'm still living on some page or other. Still,
there is not always the time for museums, for annotation,
and every day my walk through the airs of history is a small, considered
    response,
or is no response at all.

I betrayed faith in as I measured it,
as I betrayed our seasons together, our book of roses;
there isn't apology for it, now; sorrow should be felt
as a sweet pass of smoke,
not forgotten, but breathed –

Part IV
Dis/tension

What happens when the end itself becomes a perpetual excitement, a kind of bankable celebrity? Is it ground down into the footpowder of the quotidian? Does the *pharmakon* of apocalypse become a coal tar panacea? Does the millennium get lost in the paste of albums and piles of newsclippings, a file less obsessively *x* than why?

It would be a mistake to ignore the tackier, more saccharine, or more homiletic forms of millennial accomplishment, particularly given the widespread appeal of sensational secular journalism, assessed here by Amelia Carr, and the series of Protestant *Left Behind* books studied by Tom Doyle. In Part IV, we contend with dis/tended time, which in Eurasian fictions has regularly been conditioned by a critical dystopianism, but which in American popular fictions has been rather disingenuous or preachy-keen. As Amelia Carr shows, the illustrated covers and stories in the *Weekly World News* and *Sun* feast upon prophecy, heedless of indigestion or bloat, with little point other than marvel, little meaning other than urgency. Tautology is hard at work in the tabloids, where the medium is nothing more nor less than (in a distilled but still spiritualist sense) the medium, revealing other worlds threaded through our own, familiarly strange and strangely hopeful. Apocalypse and millennium are datelines, their chronologies tissue-thin, their hells and heavens destinations for exotic vacations. And each week there will be more of the same, an old news. Or, as in contemporary Christian science fictions, evangel. Tom Doyle looks into these films and novels and discovers that, like the tabloids, they use science not as a Baconian means of access to natural laws or a Brunonian connector between microcosm and macrocosm but as taglines. The thrill of such films and novels is neither investigative nor speculative but eruptive: what you are reading or watching threatens to explode upon you, or within you, akin to the ambitions of neuropharmacists and pornographers. The tabloids are not evangelical or, ultimately, eschatological; their mission is to stay in business, never left behind, so they remove themselves from their own cachet of the immediate, dis/tending apocalypse and the millennium toward a portfolio of long-term investment that saps all tensions. Christian fictions of the end would seem utterly different...yet they too have been turned into cliff-hanging serials, like the enormously suggestively 'time, and times, and half a time' of Dan. 12.7 and Rev. 12.14, continually recalculated. It is, as poet Thomas MacKay writes,

> The grasping, bully wrong not of the end
> but of the end's shadow and shine.

H.S.

The End Is Still Near:
The Eternal Apocalypse of the Tabloids*

Amelia Carr

It is always the end of the world for the tabloids. In their bizarre and sensational pages, there has always been found place for reporting occult phenomena, miracles, acts of God, and fiery prophecies of the end of the world. 'Four Horsemen of the Apocalypse Photographed in Arizona' we read in a typical headline from December 1996, reminding us that the year, and perhaps everything else, was drawing to a close (fig. 1). But as the year 2000 approached, the amount of space devoted to end time subjects increased to the point that we were confronted by prophetic headlines every week at the supermarket checkout counter. Even those who never looked past the cover, and who wouldn't dream of buying the paper, were influenced by the heightened noise level of 150-point type screaming imminent doom. In 1998 and 1999, religious themes surrounding the end of the world grew to constitute the primary subject of a certain class of supermarket tabloid newspapers, in particular *Weekly World News* and *Sun*. Although the tabloids promoted a wide variety of end times scenarios and a series of ever-receding dates for the end of the world, there was a distinct focus on the possibilities for 1 January, 2000, as the climactic event.

The popular weekly newspapers made money hyping the change of the millennium, both creating and fulfilling the desire for excitement. As a large segment of our society's attention turned to New Year's Day 2000, supermarket tabloids may have also filled a unique journalistic function, acting as an intermediary between the general public, committed millennialist groups, and the fundamentalist press. But they succeeded by tapping into a deeply-rooted millennialist world-view of a distinct segment of our population who were curious about end time possibilities and willing to imagine various wild, even frightening scenarios.

When 1 January, 2000, passed without major incident, the tabloids cooled significantly in their end times coverage, but never entirely lost a taste for the headlines of doom that had always been part of their repertoire. In fact, in conjunction with major ownership changes, the tabloids marketing niche was radically refigured in 2001 with a significant focus on prophecy and prediction. *Sun*, in particular, continued to serve up a rich weekly mix of prophecy, from traditional religious exhortation to new age hopefulness. The tabloid vision of apocalypse is an open-ended narrative, never allowed to end so that it can be served up and savored again and again.

Figure 1. '*4 Horsemen of the Apocalypse Photographed in Arizona Just Days Ago!*' *Weekly World News* (17 December, 1996; 'American Media, Inc.' reprinted with permission).

After a brief orientation to the tabloid world, this paper will examine the themes prominent in end time coverage, particularly leading up to 1 January, 2000, but also in the reconfiguration of the tabloid market after November 1999. It is not an exhaustive study, although it is based on examination of over 200 issues from December 1996 through 2002, as the build-up to the war in Iraq engendered headlines about the new Armageddon.[1] Along the way and in conclusion, we will try to answer the questions that haunt any student of the tabloids: Who is the audience for tabloid end times reporting, and how does end times prophecy function in this milieu?

The term tabloid refers to the smaller, more convenient, half-broadsheet size of the newspaper, deriving from the idea of a small easy-to-swallow pill (or is it easy to chew, but hard to swallow?).[2] The history of the tabloids reaches back to the popular penny press of the nineteenth century and the 'yellow' journalism of the 1880s with its crusading populism and melodramatic repertory of romance and crime. By the 1920s, tabloids had become vehicles for sensational and gory pictures (utilizing straight photography as well as more creative imaging techniques) that compelled attention much like accidents along the side of the road. The tabloids were firmly established before World War II; for example, in 1937, 49 tabloids boasted a circulation of 3,525,000. But the format really took off after the war, with increased offerings of celebrity gossip, sensational crimes, and bizarre stories of human interest.[3]

Generoso Pope is credited with shaping the tabloid scene as it existed in the second half of the twentieth century. First, he made the decision to sell his newspapers in grocery stores, taking advantage of a newly-opening marketing niche. At the same time, he cleaned up his publications to be oriented toward a family audience. His decision to publish the *Enquirer* on a weekly basis shifted its focus away from breaking news and ever more directly toward human-interest stories and fringe phenomena of the bizarre and occult. In 1971, he moved the *Enquirer* out of New York City to Florida, where the major tabloids are headquartered today.[4]

In the heyday of the tabloids, the 1980s and early 1990s, the American supermarket tabloid scene was dominated by six publications that came to be controlled by two media corporations. In 1980, the *Enquirer* was joined by *Weekly World News*, founded by editor Generoso Pope to take advantage of his old one-color presses and to specialize on stories he termed 'creatively bizarre', 'outlandish' and 'kooky'. *Weekly World News* remains distinctive in its black-and-white newsprint format. After Pope's death in 1988, these two papers were acquired by MacFadden Holdings, which eventually added Rupert Murdoch's *Star* to their line-up. The least prestigious of this group, *Weekly World News*, once claimed a weekly circulation of nearly a million, but it had fallen to 350,000 by 2001.[5]

The centerpiece of Globe Communications was *The Globe* (founded in 1954 as *Midnight*, and then *Midnight Globe*). Owner Joe Azaria then acquired the *Examiner* and turned it into the *National Examiner*. In 1982, the company relocated in West Palm Beach, Florida, and in 1983 introduced *Sun* based on the success of *Weekly World News*. It was edited by John Vader, 'tabloidism's established "old master" in the art of blending fact and fiction'.[6] By the early 1990s, *Sun*'s circulation was nearly 600,000, but that number is down by at least a third in 2001.[7]

Within the two publishing empires, there was an attempt to stake out a separate sphere for each of the three papers that would minimize competition with other corporate holdings. Within a marketing niche, however, competition between publications was head-to-head and quite fierce. *Weekly World News* and *Sun* were often set against each other as rivals in the downscale market for human interest stories with a twist. These two papers rarely contain the celebrity gossip that evokes controversy and famous lawsuits against aggressive reporters and the *paparazzi*. They concentrate, rather, on unrecognizable 'little people' doing extraordinary things and/or experiencing unheard-of problems.[8] In form and content, their stories retain strong elements of orality and folklore.[9] These two are the 'wacky tabs', the pair devoted to the most bizarre, the camp and the frankly fictional. Of course, less affectionate adjectives have also been applied to them, like 'lowlife', 'sleazy' and worse. When people want to denigrate the credibility of the tabloids, *Weekly World News* and *Sun* are the publications most likely to be targeted for their frequent reports of Elvis sightings and alien abductions.

In the late 1990s, end-of-the-world stories appeared almost exclusively in *Weekly World News* and *Sun*. And these two had 'apocalypse on the brain', as one media commentator noted.[10] End times stories in the other tabloids were rare and invariably mild, even upbeat, such as when the *National Examiner* touted hopeful prophecies of cures for cancer for the year 2000.[11]

Who is the audience for these 'weeklies', as readers themselves refer to the supermarket tabloids?[12] Typical buyers are mostly white, predominantly female, and middle-aged or older, according to Elizabeth Bird, and tabloid writers picture their readers as middle-aged, low-to-middle income women.[13] However, it is also estimated that tabloid readership can be as much as five times greater than circulation numbers indicate, because of the tendency to pass the papers around, especially in families where it is the wife who does the weekly grocery shopping. In his recent history of the tabloids, *I Watched a Wild Hog Eat my Baby!*, Bill Sloan identified 'one major target audience [as] the subset of Americans who felt threatened or abandoned in an increasingly confounding world of high technology and low self-esteem: People who clung to simplistic, primitive, sometimes fanatical ideas about religion, politics, and society. People who were angry and confused at the uncontrollable changes taking place all around them. People who somehow managed to believe equally in space aliens and angels.'[14]

'Another group that could prove just as important to the new paper's success was made up of those who got their kicks from ridiculing the first group and its silly, backward notions', Sloan continues. *Weekly World News* is probably the more likely to attract the self-conscious and ironic reader, particularly well described by Bird in her study *For Enquiring Minds*.[15] These readers, usually more upper-income males, turn to the tabloids for pleasurable reading, therein finding escape, humor and parody of hard news. *Weekly World News* has a campus cult following and is carried in many college bookstores. The paper markets t-shirts, caps, and coffee mugs, directing its humorous running gags to those 'in' on the joke, with stories about Bat Boy and alien endorsements of presidential candidates (fig. 2).[16] *Weekly World News* is more likely to publish obviously faked photos, perhaps encouraging us to view its pages as primarily entertainment. Unlike *Sun*, *Weekly World News* caters to the wired generation with a website.[17]

Figure 2. *'Space Alien Backs Bush for President!'* *Weekly World News* (9 May, 2000; 'American Media, Inc.' reprinted with permission).

Despite their particular histories and styles, *Weekly World News* and *Sun* appeal to such similar audiences with roughly the same sorts of end times stories, reported in a similar sensational manner, that it makes sense to combine the two in this survey of continuing themes in tabloid coverage. But in reporting on religious and spiritual themes, clear differences between the two are evident. *Sun* appears to take itself more seriously. When *Sun* refers to itself in its own pages, it is usually in self-congratulation for previous reporting triumphs (even if these are not always deserved). Most of its end times stories carry bylines, with the same reporters contributing week after week. Even if these are pseudonyms for staff writers, as is likely the case,[18] the names establish a sense of professional authority and credibility. *Sun* is more likely to frame articles in theological terms, and especially promotes the Catholic prophetic tradition with an emphasis on Marian apparitions and papal pronouncements. *Sun* names a Religious Editor, marking the high priority that they give to this content in their pages. In the late 1990s, this position was held by Pat Roller, whose professional mission was to seek out compelling stories world-wide, his colorful writing adding corroborative detail to his quest for religious truth.

Weekly World News and *Sun* presented a wide range of coverage that might be broadly defined as 'apocalyptic' or 'prophetic' in content. At one end of the spectrum can be placed the many articles that predict what will happen to an individual, perhaps using numerology or astrology. Astrologers and clairvoyants such as Jeanne Dixon or Edgar Cayce might also be cited to predict events of national significance, so that fortune-telling blurs into prophecy. At the other end of the spectrum, there is exposition of Christian revelation, including dire predictions of the end of the world. Approaching 1 January, 2000, there was an increase in the sheer quantity of prophetic material of all types, as well as specific focus on apocalyptic and millennial subjects. Our survey reveals that the tabloids rely on a surprisingly eclectic array of prophetic authorities, representing a hodge-podge of Protestant, Catholic, and New Age beliefs.

The most-frequently cited source is certainly the Bible. Stories that show how prophecy is being fulfilled in our time are given special weight by the most authoritative religious text in our culture. A good example of how the Bible explains current events is seen in a *Weekly World News* story from 7 April , 1998: 'Bible Predicts El Nino Weather Holocaust' (fig. 3). El Niño is the name given to the disruption of the ocean-atmosphere system in the Tropical Pacific, and the Spanish term might be translated as meaning 'the boy'.[19] In this article, the current weather is said to be foretold by Zechariah 8.5: 'the streets of the city shall be full of boys and girls'. We are also warned that 'the girls', or La Niña, will be worse, and these storms are signs that the day of judgment approaches.

Tabloids have always covered weather disasters, but the burgeoning genre that David Plotz has labeled 'Weather Porn' is now given a fundamentalist twist.[20] Bad weather is one of the Last Signs, perhaps one of the Four Horsemen of the Apocalypse. In tabloid scenarios, the old complaint of our inability to forecast or control the weather takes on catastrophic proportions when even the National Weather Service cannot understand current events without recourse to revelation. While the headlines use scare tactics, the populist readership might not be surprised to find that religion can provide answers when science fails. In fact, they positively enjoy it when scientific authority is baffled.[21] Weird weather and world-wide devastation is comprehensible as part of God's plan.

Figure 3. *'Bible Predicts El Nino Weather Holocaust… And Warns the Worst Is Yet to Come!' Weekly World News* (7 April, 1998; 'American Media, Inc.' reprinted with permission).

'New Bible Mysteries' trumpets a *Sun* headline from 22 December, 1998. Although they do not cover breaking news, unlike journalists in general, the tabloids exploit the language of novelty, treating both scientific and religious material as a series of stunning breakthroughs. The word 'new' usually refers to a newly published interpretation of Christian prophecy, and both tabloids take pains to promote new books in the field. For the readership, a published book holds a special authority, and the papers often go so far as to publish a picture of the book and ways to purchase it. Sometimes the book itself makes the cover, as did the *Foreshocks of Antichrist* by William T. James, Grant Jeffrey, Chuck Missler et al., with the headline: 'Millennium 2000: The Beginning of the End?'[22] Many titles reviewed in the tabloids would be familiar to students of millennialism, such as: Billy Graham, *Approaching Hoofbeats: The Four Horsemen of the Apocalypse* (fig. 4), [23] Tim Lahaye and Jerry B. Jenkins, *Left Behind*,[24] Terry L. Cook, *The Mark of the New World Order: 666*,[25] and Thomas W. Petrisko, *The Fatima Prophecies*.[26]

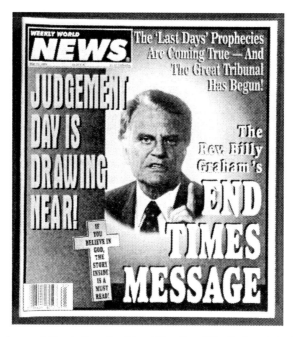

Figure 4. 'Judgement Day Is Drawing Near! The Rev. Billy Graham's End Times Message.' Weekly Word News (25 May, 1999; 'American Media, Inc.' reprinted with permission).

Thus, one important function of the tabloids is to review and popularize the products of the more specialized prophecy press. These titles are usually well-established bestsellers by the time they appear in their pages, but tabloids are the only papers in general circulation that pay any attention to this type of religious publication at all. The fact that the tabloids are often only repeating end time material published elsewhere means that, in some ways, even very speculative end time stories have a greater credibility than other items in the paper. Some readers will hear these ideas in other places, confirmed in church sermons and religious broadcast media. To put it another way, tabloids do not fabricate end times material in the same way that they might be composing the illustrations for Elvis sightings and alien landings.

However, this is not to say that the tabloids always present a high level of scholarship. They are loose about citation. Tabloids constantly cite biblical scholars and religious authorities from all over the world, whose existence is difficult to confirm. Tabloids indeed cultivate a wide array of experts in religious and occult fields. But in many cases, it was impossible to locate the titles mentioned, forcing the conclusion that the sources are either incredibly obscure, mistakenly reported, or just plain made up.[27] Insider reports on the tabloids such as that of Jim Hogshire would suggest that authorities quoted in articles often represent a clever amalgam of real and fictional people that is convincing to most readers.[28]

The tabloids give extensive coverage to Catholic prophecy belief, particularly the Marian apparitions at Lourdes and Fatima. They frequently publish predictions and wisdom from Catholic visionaries: medieval saints, popes living and dead, and near contemporaries Edith Stein and Mother Teresa. The tabloids claim or fabricate a vast quantity of information from the inner circles of the Vatican, sometimes extracted from the mythic Secret Vaults of the Popes, where sensitive material has supposedly accumulated for centuries. Significant space is also devoted to papal pronouncements on theological questions. For example, the 'shocking truth' that the Pope has revealed, according to the sensational *Sun* cover of 17 August, 1999, is that we must not think of heaven as a literal place, but as an abstract state of being in communion with God. That this idea might be unsettling to fundamentalist and literalist readers can be judged from the frequency with which articles locating heaven and hell appear in the tabloids. For example, a 1999 article from *Weekly World News* depicts the New Jerusalem literally arriving from outer space to fulfill the passage from Revelation 21.2, that the holy city will come down out of heaven from God.[29]

We are so accustomed to understanding prophecy culture as it is connected with evangelical Protestantism that this phenomenon bears exploration. While Catholic exegesis of the book of Revelation is the core of our western prophecy tradition, Paul Boyer could claim as recently as 1992 that 'Catholics do not as a rule...expend much energy on prophetic speculation'.[30] For one explanation of the tabloid obsession with Catholicism, perhaps we need look no farther than the history of ownership. Not averse to being known as the 'pope' in his own domain, Generoso Pope was a strong promoter of Italian-American interests, and his family's support dated back at least to 1928 when Generoso Sr acquired *Il Progresso Italo-Americano,* the nation's largest Italian-language newspaper.[31] Even after Pope's death in 1988, *Sun* continued to cater to its established readers who assumed that the pope would play a significant role in any end times scenario, and who had an avid interest in any gossip and speculation surrounding the Vatican.

However, since about 1995, Catholics themselves had been steadily turning to the year 2000, and this direction comes from the very top.[32] Within the Catholic church is a growing culture around Marian apparitions, and the tabloids have been quick to pick up on this new millenarian mode. John Paul II was a particular devotee of the Marian apparitions made at Fatima in 1917. Until recently, the famous third prophecy of Fatima had been read only by the twentieth-century popes, leading to rampant speculation on its content, rumored to give details on the appearance of the Antichrist. Is this the reason that the pope wanted the Jubilee of the year 2000 to be greater than any other, asks *Sun*? Even though the Vatican revealed the secret text on 13 May, 2000, *Sun* remained unconvinced that the full story had been told.[33] It boldly claimed in the 21 May, 2002, issue that priestly pederasty was mere pretense for a recent convocation of a Council of Bishops. The real purpose of the meeting was to hear the pope read the entire prophecy in secret. On 8 April, 2003, *Sun* published several 'as yet undisclosed revelations' from the third secret of Fatima, made available to them through 'sources close to the Vatican'.[34] And not content to let a fruitful source of speculation run dry, *Sun* revealed in the 3 May, 2004, issue that the Vatican is covering up the existence of a fourth secret of Fatima.[35] However, *Weekly World News* had already revealed the existence of a fifth Fatima prophecy on its 17 February, 1998, cover (fig. 5).

Other prophetic traditions are handled in the same way as Christian prophecy; tabloid coverage features recent publications, commented upon by an array of authorities, real and fictional.

Nostradamus may get more face time on tabloid covers than anyone, even Jesus (figs. 6, 8-12). Although early portraits of him are known from his published work, the tabloids have usually preferred to picture Nostradamus as a modern-day Rasputin, with long white hair, shaggy beard, and penetrating gaze. Michel de Nostradame actually lived (1503–1566), prophesied, and was taken seriously in his own time, particularly by the French court and Queen Catherine de Medici, the death of whose husband Henry II he predicted. Nostradamus published his predictions in a way that hid their obvious meanings, perhaps because his vision of the future was fragmentary and strange, perhaps due to threats from the Inquisition, and certainly in keeping with a philosophy that truth should only be revealed to the initiated. Providing endless fodder for interpretations both wild and reasonable are nearly 1,000 impenetrably arcane four-line verses known as 'quatrains', written in French, but heavily loaded with Latin, Greek, and other odd linguistic bits.[36] He spoke in a highly metaphoric and symbolic language designed to puzzle and conceal. A student of the skies, he frequently used astrological/astronomical indicators of time and place. As a final deterrent to easy understanding, Nostradamus deliberately mixed the order of his verses, so that the quatrains are in no discernible chronology.

Figure 5. 'Fifth Prophecy of Lourdes... Warns of a Cataclysmic Year 2000!'Weekly World News. 17 February, 1998. 'American Media, Inc.'Reprinted with permission.

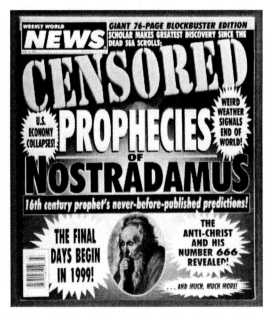

Figure 6. 'Censored Prophecies of Nostradamus.' Weekly World News (7 July, 1998; 'American Media, Inc.' reprinted with permission).

Figure 7. 'Virgin Mary's Most Devastating Vision about Future of the World. The Third Prophecy of Fatima.' Weekly World News. 25 August, 1998. 'American Media, Inc.' Reprinted with permission.

Figure 8. 'The Final Days/Nostradamas End Times Prophecies/Armageddon Year 2000 Computer Bug Will Turn Machine against Man!' Weekly World News (16 February, 1999; 'American Media, Inc.' reprinted with permission).

Figure 9. *'Famed Prophet Warns President: End of World Is Near.'* *Weekly World News* (28 September, 1999; 'American Media, Inc.' reprinted with permission).

Figure 10. *'Nostradamus Predictions for 1998/Exact Day the World Will End!'* *Weekly World News* (15 July, 1997; 'American Media, Inc.' reprinted with permission).

Figure 11. *'Nostradamus Predictions for 1999/Exact Day the World Will End!' Weekly World News* (24 November, 1998; 'American Media, Inc.' reprinted with permission).

Figure 12. *'Nostradamus Predictions for 2000/Exact Day the World Will End!' Weekly World News* (2 November, 1999; 'American Media, Inc.' reprinted with permission).

Nostradamus' vivid and difficult language is an interpreter's field day, and the tabloids are delighted to report the extravagant claims made by earnest students of the quatrains. The tabs also participate in the time-honored tradition of publishing 'newly-discovered' material from the sixteenth-century seer.[37] It is fairly easy to manufacture Nostradamus quatrains, for very few people are really familiar with all 942+ of them, especially in the original languages.[38] In most cases, very little need be done to tweak an existing prophecy into something more current and sensational. For example, by identifying the obscure location 'Insubria' as Florida and mistranslating the French, *Sun* can bring the dire message of C2 Q65 close to home: 'Great calamity through America, and in Florida the fire'.[39] Even though he continued his prophecies to the year 3797, Nostradamus could readily be invoked as a guide to the year 2000. In one rare example of specificity, Nostradamus predicted an asteroid in the seventh month of 1999.[40] He spoke specifically of the 'millennium', described a 'final battle' and foretold Antichrist-like leaders. Nostradamus becomes even more relevant to our concerns when we learn that his descendant is alive and serving as Clinton's on-staff prophet (fig. 10).[41] Thus, real and fake Nostradamus became a staple of tabloid end times prophecy in the late 1990s, and his emphasis on politics and nation-building through warfare added variety to the normal moralizing intonations of Biblical revelation.

Edgar Cayce is dubbed 'America's favorite prophet' by the tabloids, and the high level of coverage here must speak to readers for whom Cayce's legacy is very much alive only 50 years after his death in 1945. There is no lack of material, for over 14,000 readings dating from 1902-1944 have been preserved from the 'sleeping prophet', and more are currently being issued by the ARE (Association for Research and Enlightenment) founded in 1931 by the man himself. Cayce spoke on many subjects of direct relevance to Americans today, from predictions of the 'big one', an earthquake in California, to minute instructions on health and spiritual practice. Cayce is very much a prophet made to order for today's tabloids. The ARE defines its mission 'to research and explore transpersonal subjects such as holistic health, philosophy, dreams and dream interpretation, intuition, and contemporary spirituality', subjects dear to the weekly newspapers' aging readership in pursuit of insight for a better life.[42] Given so much authentic primary source material, it is difficult to verify the numerous tabloid citations from Cayce's predictions, again making it easy for the tabloids to skew their headlines and interpretations at will.

Both *Weekly World News* and *Sun* promote their own prophets. In the issue of 14 September, 1999, *Sun* unveiled its discovery, a young South American boy named Evaristo Pedrinho Monteiro whose abilities eerily parallel those in the movie *The Sixth Sense*. As Evaristo visits the important Marian shrines all over the world, he, too, is moved to prophecy. The article concludes: 'Evaristo indicated he had more startling new prophecies to make. *Sun* will be proud to bring them to you in the weeks ahead.'[43]

From time to time, both tabloids convene a panel of psychics and futurologists who dish up predictions for the times ahead. In the 15 July, 1997 issue, *Weekly World News* published the millennium predictions of a group they called 'the Nostradamus Fifteen'. *Sun* publishes a panel of ten psychics regularly.

It requires casting a wide net to find headlines week after week and, as a result of such pressures, tabloid coverage is extremely repetitive. Over the years, we recognize the same stock photos and formulaic phrases: new prophecies are always going to 'rock America', according to *Sun*.[44] And a successful formula does not need to be varied. The covers for issues featuring Nostradamus prophecies were identical in 1998, 1999, and 2000, even down to the sidebars featuring lucky lotto numbers and the headline advertising the 'exact date Jesus will return to earth' (figs. 10, 11 and 12). Despite the loud claims of novelty, the reality of tabloid coverage is a constant recycling of favorite themes.

But within a framework of consistency, there is a surprising variety. Tabloids have featured prophecies and predictions from Crazy Horse (fig. 13), Benjamin Franklin, Mother Teresa, the oracle of Delphi, Ronald Reagan, and the extra-terrestrial radio network. *Weekly World News'* article on Chief Crazy Horse featured his great-great-grandson, who claimed that his ancestor's ghost had chosen him 'to deliver his message from the Great Beyond'.[45] He warns us of world-ending catastrophes that turn out to be of our own making, for example ethnic hatred and global warming, such that they can be avoided if only the American government would cooperate. Both Reagan and Franklin offered up not so much prophecy, but genial speculation about what the future might bring. In these articles, the year 2000 sounds as if it was a distant future date evoked rhetorically, rather than a millennial vision. In the headlines of the tabloids, however, the words of our forefathers take on ominous weight. American political rhetoric has often been millennialist, and the tabloids continue the tradition of seeing the United States as fulfilling prophecy through actions that are central to the end times.

Figure 13. *'American Indian Prophecies Are Coming True!' Weekly World News* (2 March, 1999; 'American Media, Inc.' reprinted with permission).

Overall, the sources exploited by tabloid writers are incredibly eclectic. One week it's the Bible, the next week Nostradamus. If one of the main goals is to sell newspapers by piquing a wide range of interests at the checkout counter, then tabloids must be trying to attract a broad readership of Christians, Pagans, environmentalists and New-Agers. But the tabloids often go one step farther by claiming that there is little or no inconsistency between these various interpretive strains. The cover of *Weekly World News* for 18 November, 1997 proclaims that 'Leaders of EVERY major religion point to signs of the coming Apocalypse!' (fig. 14). To prove this agreement, tabloid covers often feature pairs of prophets. Edgar Cayce gives us the same message as the Virgin Mary at Lourdes,[46] Nostradamus and the Fatima prophecies agree,[47] or we might see Edgar Cayce paired with Mother Teresa.[48] The all-star line-up of prophets promoted in *Sun* of 2 February, 1999, included H.G. Wells, Billy Graham, Mother Teresa, and the Pope. In the 15 December, 1998, issue of *Sun*, headlines claimed to present a synthesis of more than 70 of the greatest prophets, all of whom agreed that 1 January, 2000 was the date of Christ's return.

Figure 14. *'Warning! World's Top 12 Bible Scholars All Agree… The End of the World Is Near!' Weekly World News* (18 November, 1997; 'American Media, Inc.' reprinted with permission).

How does such a synthesis work? On one level, it doesn't work. In any given list of ten psychics' predictions for the next year, many are downright contradictory. For critics of the tabloids, any single logical inconsistency discredits the entire publication; either we must take the entire paper as an entertaining joke, or label the readers as completely ignorant and credulous. But Bird's study indicates that readers, in fact, have a more discerning way of dealing with tabloid material.[49] Most people will believe some of what they read and dismiss other speculations on a story by story basis, usually in line with beliefs they have already developed. Very few readers believe everything published in the tabloid, or feel that they must. The process of reading a tabloid allows readers rather to test the limits of what they believe or not, thereby affirming their values.[50]

In fact, the tabloids must work hard to create a concordance between Catholic, Protestant and New Age thinkers. They achieve harmony by fabricating prophecies that buttress each other, but also by suppressing the differences. While it is safe to characterize the American tabloid audience as primarily Christian, other belief systems are casually accommodated.

Aliens exist cozily alongside angels in outer space. New age prophecies generally confirm the truth of the Christian message rather than question it. The anti-papal, anti-Semitic and isolationist worldview of evangelical sermons and books is simply not reported in the tabloids. Likewise, race issues rarely surface in tabloid writing. Blacks and other minorities are seldom pictured in the tabs, although *Sun* features the wisdom of Rev. Darminger from time to time.[51] But so also is the overt racism of many fundamentalists suppressed. In one interesting article, the writer even warns readers that 'the race card', as he puts it, will be played in the end times scenario, and suggests that such a strategy is satanic.[52]

An all-consuming level of religious commitment is usually not required, or even expected, of tabloid readers. Perhaps individual articles might seem to support the extremist postures of the prophecy culture, but overall, the tabloids address a centrist audience. Readers are advised to go to church and pray as ways to avoid the coming tribulation, but more sectarian dogma is not specified. This may indeed reflect the lukewarm piety of the tabloid writers themselves, a group of people that Bird found 'do not belong in the community of their readers' or share in their religious outlook.[53] But tabloid eclecticism seems designed to appeal to 'Middle America', however geographically widespread. These are the people who make up the surprising statistics such as the 62% who, in a 1983 Gallup poll, had 'no doubts' that Jesus would come to earth again, or the 52% who, in a 1997 *Newsweek* survey, believed that Jesus would return in the next millennium.[54] Taken altogether, the tabloids create an almost generic prophecy culture, eclectic and soft, like white bread. The tabloids synthesize diverse prophecies into a consistent message that includes all potential readers, suggesting a delicate interplay between the desire to shock and the need to sell papers.

The tabloids' synthetic end times vision only emerges when all of their prophetic coverage is examined as a single body. Individual articles are not ambivalent or vague, but quite specific in naming places and times that events will occur. The tabloids exhibit no trepidation whatever about naming exact dates for Christ's return to set into motion the events of the end of the world. In fact, 'Exact Date' or 'Exact Place of Christ's Return' is a often-featured headline on the covers. Needless to say, the dates have passed without incident (so far). The Armageddon comet did not strike in October of 1998, as predicted in *Weekly World News* of 25 August, 1998 (fig. 15). In July 1997, Nostradamus told us that Christ would appear briefly in December 1997, and then return permanently on 6 May, 2000 (fig. 10). In *Weekly World News* of 24 November, 1998, Nostradamus predicted that Christ would return on 25 December, 1999, although he will remain 'unknown to mankind' (fig. 11). In November 1999, Nostradamus said that Christ would appear on Easter Day in the year 2000 (fig. 12). The general formula is to name a date in the relatively near future, but then, as the date approaches, to ignore it, and name a date farther along. The end is always 'soon', but 'not yet'.

Figure 15. *'Censored! Armageddon Comet Speeding Toward Earth – & Could Strike In Ocotober!' Weekly World News* (25 August, 1998; American Media, Inc.' reprinted with permission).

In this context, it was completely in character for the tabloids to be caught up in the speculation surrounding 1 January, 2000.[55] In fact, tabloids were prime contributors to the hype surrounding that date. As early as 15 December, 1998, *Sun* reported that 70 religious leaders agreed that the second coming would be on that day. The cover of *Weekly World News* for 15 September, 1998, screamed 'January 1 2000: The Day the Earth Will Stand Still'. The first issue of *Weekly World News* for 1999 announced the 'beginning of the end' and subsequent issues continued the alert[56] (figs. 16 and 17). The 1999 issues of *Sun* reminded readers each week how many days were left in the countdown to the 'new millennium'. The tabloids dutifully capitalized on the widespread fundamentalist belief that the Y2K computer failure would be the trigger for the end times scenario worldwide. The tabloids also published articles on how to live through the catastrophes. A 'Bible's End Times Survival Guide' in *Sun* provided practical tips about stockpiling food and guaranteeing cash flow, following the advice of Christian evangelists Jerry Falwell and Pat Robertson[57] (fig. 18). Spiritual assistance might also be found, such as the 'Five Words to Save Your Soul, Guide You to Heaven – Guaranteed' in *Weekly World News*.[58]

Weekly World News kept the suspense building right up to the fateful day (keeping in mind that the publication date is the week ahead of when the paper appears on the newsstands). On 21 December, 1999, *Weekly World News* asked 'Is this the world's last Christmas?' Inside, a feature article warned: 'Do you think you can repent just before the End of the World?' Forget it! God is not fooled.[59] On 28 December, they repeated their prediction of a computer crash, and asked 'Is this the end?' On 4 January, 2000, *Weekly World News* suggested that the apocalyptic timeline had been triggered as the Devil was unchained. In fact, Satan was alive and well in Washington DC, hovering in storms over the nation's capitol, pictured on the menacing cover (fig. 19).

It was also in character for the tabloids to recover quickly when 1 January, 2000, proved uneventful. Following that tried-and-true principle of delaying apocalyptic gratification, *Sun* actually toned down its end-time coverage as the date approached. By 11 January, both tabloids were back to an earlier mode, with layouts and predictions that we have all seen so many times. Numerous articles in both tabloids had already suggested that the end times would actually commence on dates later in the year 2000, such as 1 July or Christmas. Other end time predictions were made for more distant years such as 2014 or 'before 2020'. On 18 April, 2000, *Weekly World News* predicted the next Great Depression, this one to come in March, recycling a headline that readers were accustomed to seeing about four times a year. On 2 May, 2000, *Sun* gave us predictions that, predictably, would rock us. An article inside told us how to be happier in the year 2000, although one suggestion they did not make was to stop reading the doomsday predictions of the tabloids. Nothing prophetic appeared in the next several issues.

Why do the tabloids continue to make concrete end-time predictions when time and again, those predictions fail? If there is one place to learn about 'millennial disappointment', it would be in the pages of the tabloid newspapers where, regularly, they predict an end to the world that never comes. But they never look back, and never seem to learn from their mistakes. People seem to want specificity, and will pay when firm information – names and dates – is offered. In fact, in the world of the tabloids, failure to predict accurately doesn't seem to be a mistake at all.

Figure 16. *'January 1, 1999. The Beginning of the End? Millennium Countdown Begins.'* *Weekly World News* (29 December, 1998; 'American Media, Inc.' reprinted with permission).

Figure 17. *'1999. Are We On the Eve of Destruction?' Weekly World News* (2 February, 1999; 'American Media, Inc.' reprinted with permission).

Figure 18. *'Bible's End Times Survival Guide.'* *Sun* (16 March, 1999; 'American Media, Inc.' reprinted with permission).

Figure 19. *'Face of Satan Seen Over U.S. Capitol!'* *Weekly World News* (4 January, 2000; 'American Media, Inc.' reprinted with permission).

Stephen O'Leary, among others, has argued that apocalyptic discourse invokes the topos of time in order to seek closure.[60] Naming a specific place and date for the end fulfills a natural desire for formal completion, a desire perhaps so compelling that the good sense and reasonable doubts of predictor and audience are overcome. The acceptance of an end time forces readers over a 'threshold of unrecuperability', such that simply entertaining the idea of specificity begins the end time process that the discourse only predicts. In this understanding, identifying that the end is coming on a specific date is a key element of an apocalyptic world-view, one that creates and sustains the sense of urgency. And yet, tabloid apocalyptic rhetoric provides anything but closure. True, individual items may specify a date and demand commitment to an interpretation. Yet overall – and sometimes even within a single article or issue – the tabloids resist completion of an end time narrative. The tabloids seek openings, not closings.

Tabloid readers might simply be happy when the dire predictions of doom do not come true. Some prophets themselves dread their own disastrous conclusions and want to be mistaken. A book by Stefan Paulus on the Nostradamus quatrain predicting an asteroid in the seventh month of 1999 was featured in *Weekly World News* of 7 July, 1998. Paulus begins thus: 'This book is fervently dedicated to the hope that it is wrong. May the events envisioned never occur, and the devastation it foresees never come to pass.'[61] In the same vein, readers may have earnestly desired the prediction to be wrong, and were therefore relieved when the asteroid did not strike.

Boyer suggests that this current wave of the evangelical movement is so busy with its newly-developed social and political conscience that they are actually pretty cheerful about prophecy belief. As he says, '...when things are going well, reports of "signs and wonders" are taken as evidence that a great move of God is underway'.[62] Prophets envision possible, but not pre-determined, futures. Tabloid coverage that boldly exposes the presence of demons in the world encourages readers to think in literal terms about spiritual warfare. If the end of the world doesn't come, it can be taken as evidence that Christians are winning the battle against Satan. It may be in this spirit that tabloids regularly publish advice about how to prevent the apocalypse.[63] And sometimes, religious leaders are quoted in their pre-millennialist visions for an era of peace, such as a Lutheran minister's 'New Hope for the Year 2000'[64] or Billy Graham's 'Message of Hope' distilled from his autobiography *Just As I Am*.[65]

Because tabloids are often only reporting on predictions of other authors, perhaps they really do not need to feel guilt or responsibility when prophecy fails. *Weekly World News* has always billed itself as a compilation of articles 'drawn from different sources, including the world press and our foreign correspondents'. Their heavy reliance on revenue from sales, and their dependence on attracting the weekly impulse purchase, makes tabloids particularly responsive to the moods and desires of their readers. In effect, each tabloid issue is simply stating, 'This is the crazy stuff that folks are talking about this week'. The tabloids posit nearly incredible scenarios, and readers respond by wondering 'What if that were true?' In her study, Bird found that articles did become the occasion for discussion and debate, usually confirming the values of the reader, but always testing the boundaries.[66] In this context, the stakes really aren't very high when any given prediction fails. The readers have not really been asked to believe, or to cross a threshold of unrecuperability, but simply to try on an idea. Articles that name an exact date might prove to be wrong, but their specificity is not a demand for commitment, only an indexical marker that the content is important. The end times could be upon us, so think about these things now, we are prodded. A specific end time scenario serves as a *momento mori*, requiring us to confirm our ultimate concerns on a weekly basis.

The tabloids consistently refuse any narrative strategy that eliminates possibilities. To tease out the riddle of the end of the world is not, as fundamentalists might claim, to narrowly settle on a single reading of a single text (i.e., the Bible), but to assemble diverse pieces of a puzzle whose imagery and dimensions are as yet unknown. Tabloids share the same critical underlying assumption of apocalyptic thinking that O'Leary found fundamental to William Miller's rules for Biblical interpretation: there is but a single divine truth such that all contradictions must eventually be reconciled in the fullness of time.[67] For the moment, we gaze through the glass darkly, but even bizarre and unusual events will ultimately be understood in a clarifying light. It then follows logically that it is dangerous to eliminate any possible conclusion too soon, or to discount information that seems anomalous on the surface.

In their apocalyptic discourse that resists closure, the tabloids don't claim that they have a single answer, but, instead, insist that the full story has not been revealed. The Vatican has yet to make full disclosure from its secret vaults, for example. The United States government is usually an ally in the end times scenario, but other stories suggest that the government withholds information and manipulates popular opinion. In the meantime, insight is potentially available from many sources, and the significance of any one clue will only be revealed in time. Readers value tabloids for the information that they provide, from herbal cures to eschatological truths. And tabloid journalists depict themselves in a constant struggle to uncover that information, to reveal 'The Forbidden Prophecies You Weren't Meant To Know'[68] and to liberate information that others have wanted to censor (figs. 6 and 15). An eclectic array of prophets, from Crazy Horse to St John, are deliberately evoked as sources of knowledge. The tabloid appetite for imperfect prophecy is fed by the suspicion and hope that all of the small meaningless pieces might eventually add up to something that is true and insightful.

Constant predictions of end-time catastrophe thus stimulate the curiosity of readers while providing them insider information to prepare for the unexpected. These same readers acquire a sense of relief when the worst does not happen, and can congratulate themselves for not having believed the prophecies in the first place. However, the very nature of tabloid coverage blunts the prophetic weapons of fundamentalist religion. If publicity is given to the prophecy press, so too do the tabloids implicitly advertise the failures. History shows us that community can be built on failed prediction, but to the extent that tabloids treat prophecy in broad and burlesque strokes, we are not encouraged to treat the subject with dignity. Rather, it is apocalypse in the comic mode, ever deferred, always subject to the choices of fallible humans.[69]

If we follow the line of cultural analysis suggested by Jodi Dean in *Aliens in America*, we recognize that the tabloids thus provide a site of resistance to religious and secular authorities, or to anyone who claims to understand how the world works.[70] The generally 'down-market' audience of the tabloids consists of people more vulnerable to the dark side of capitalistic success, less able to manipulate the system to their own advantage, and thus more subtle in their negotiations with failure. Their world view is echoed in the tabloids, which some observers have likened to a repository of popular, oral tradition. The tabloids present a world uncontrolled and uncontrollable, in which weird events are commonplace, and individuals are always subject to unforeseen highs and lows of fortune. For tabloid readers, the world is not a rational place. Despite sincere efforts, government and religious authorities cannot consistently explain what is happening in the world or predict outcomes. Awareness of the ever-present possibility of total upheaval is epitomized in one *Weekly World News* headline: 'Your most treasured beliefs are wrong!'[71]

Given the tabloids' preference for eschatological flirtation over consummation and for openings over closings, the extent to which they embraced 1 January, 2000, as a climactic moment is all the more remarkable. In their understanding of this date as the moment of millennial change, the tabloids were reflecting a widespread consensus. In identifying the Y2K computer bug as a trigger, they were only following the leads of a group of computer experts who found many high-profile media outlets.[72] *Weekly World News* and *Sun* picked up scattered signals and amplified them into a resounding crescendo, always framing the potential for catastrophe or enlightenment in apocalyptic terms. With headlines that insinuated themselves into the minds of a far greater number than ever bought the papers, the tabloids revived and kept alive the old hopes and fears surrounding that date. Yet ultimately, their coverage must be seen as a barometer of public mood. The tabloids could only exploit the date because anxieties about 1 January, 2000, were strongly felt at many other levels of society.

In the uneventful period following 1 January, 2000, it would seem to be business as usual for the tabloids. With a sigh of relief and perhaps a chuckle, popular attention was no longer transfixed by the millennial possibilities of 2000, and end times coverage fell back to its pre-Y2K level and style. But in fact, the tabloid business had been drastically transformed. Changes in the kinds of prophetic headlines that greeted customers in the checkout line every week were not only influenced by a post-millennial depression, but also by a reconfiguration of the market.

By November 1999, the six major tabloids that had been owned by two media corporations came into the hands of a single owner: American Media, Inc. The new CEO was David Pecker, who immediately announced plans for change. Although he wanted to keep all six tabloids, he felt that circulation numbers were falling because they overlapped too much with each other. He planned to give each paper a different focus. *Sun* would concentrate on stories of the paranormal and the supernatural, cultivating a more mature readership, with health-orientated and religious articles. *Weekly World News* would be 'all fictional' and 'very, very funny'. Pecker wanted to pitch the tabloids 'up market' to compete with *People* magazine, and 'to appeal to advertisers and the masses of people who are under-served with accurate celebrity information'. To gain credibility, in *The Wall Street Journal*, Pecker offered $50,000 'from his own pocket' to be donated to charity 'if any potential advertiser can find an alien, U.F.O. or a picture of Elvis' in *The Enquirer*. Observers were quick to point out that he did not make the same promise about his new acquisition *Weekly World News*, which continued to publish such stories.[73]

Over the course of the next year, *Sun* got a face lift under the direction of Mike Irish, former managing editor, with long experience on the more upscale tabloids the *Examiner* and the *Enquirer*. Critically dependent upon weekly impulse sales for survival, the tabloid tweaked its formula constantly to find the right mixture for success at the supermarket. Slogans and features were tested, disappeared or were retained, according to reader response. The paper had long carried a disclaimer: '*Sun* stories seek to entertain and are about the fantastic, bizarre and paranormal. The reader should suspend belief for the sake of enjoyment.' This mission is even more explicit in the 'All New *Sun* Unexplained Mysteries & Marvels', for which the editor promised to scour the world for amazing people, mysterious places, and bizarre happenings.[74]

Features now routinely appeared in installments, in order to turn 'lookers' at the check-out into 'buyers' committed to keeping up week by week. A four-part book bonus, 'four dazzling pages to save', was a serial publication of a dictionary of the paranormal, *Out of This World: Aliens to Zombies*. In the issue of 4 April, 2000, former Religion Editor Pat Roller now appears as an intrepid Tabloid Correspondent, an energetic mixture of Fox Muldur and Ernest Hemingway. His talent was formerly dedicated to uncovering millennium secrets; now he will 'travel the world far and wide in search of the most exciting, unusual and strangest stories ever set in print'. These are invariably two-part narratives, so that if readers are hooked by Part One, they must come back next week for Part Two. On 18 July, 2000, a Sizzling Double Issue again announced a 'new' *Sun*, whose contents probably reflected the results of a reader survey conducted in the Spring.[75] Among other things, readers 'pleaded for a bigger-than-ever *Sun*... 76-pages of everything from eerie ghost encounters to sizzling swim fashions...the hottest medical breakthroughs to truly startling prophecies and stunning horoscopes.'

Prophecy was a definite ingredient in the 'new' *Sun*, but only a small one. Apparently, readers wanted to hear about Jesus' return on a regular basis, but they refused to be nourished on a steady diet of catastrophic predictions; that moment had passed. The issue of 3 April, 2001 was a good example of the new recipe. As they often do, *Sun* invoked a panel of psychics, although now the predictions seemed more than ever concerned with celebrity futures. This issue also published 'Project Black Book', the government's secret files on UFO's. *Sun* is trying to grab the old X-files audience here, but with a sly wink to *Men in Black*, the 1997 film that charmed audiences when Tommy Lee Jones picked up a tabloid, the only trustworthy source for real news about real aliens. It is also worth noting that in July 2001, the tabloids went mainstream when the Sci-Fi channel aired a series about a tabloid newsroom called *The Chronicle*.[76]

Finally, with the issue of 31 July, 2001, *Sun* hit on the winning formula that was successful enough to be repeated monthly ever since. This special double issue included an entire pull-out section, *Prophecy* magazine, that dealt with 'tomorrow' in a strange mixture of prediction, prophecy, and futurology.[77] Always featured is some sort of cutting edge engineering and science, such as 'How NASA Has Transformed Our Lives'[78] or 'Welcome to Mars'.[79] This celebration of technology in general and computers in particular is a full 180-degree turn from the demonization of modern life in the tabloids' reactionary Y2K coverage. Equally prominent are future style trends, particularly in hair, clothing, and home furnishings. *Sun*'s downright anti-apocalyptic attitude toward the future is reflected in its ever-changing slogans. In the issue of 26 June, 2001, it was 'Your Health, Your Life, Your Future'; on 31 July through August, 'Health, Hope, Happiness'. There are many, many articles predicting the future. Horoscopes are a mainstay, but *Prophecy* magazine always features one or more with some sort of twist, such as a horoscope coordinated to mythic animals, gemstones, pets, and so on. As it turns out, there can never be too many horoscopes in a tabloid; one issue contained five, four is routine.

In regular rotation, 'America's Best-Loved Weekly' continued to feature the familiar, eclectic array of the best-loved prophets: Edgar Cayce, Nostradamus, and Old Testament patriarchs. The dramatic stories with religious millennial content, like Vatican statues crying blood, are reserved for the main part of the magazine and the cover.[80] But even when these prophets make dire predictions, the new *Sun* delivers an upbeat message. Our guide through *Prophecy* magazine is Psychic Sarah, reflecting the New Age optimism of most of this material. After all, how bad can the future be if we're going to be licking delicious super-suckers in the year 2100, as featured on the 25 June, 2002, *Prophecy* magazine cover touting 'Super foods of the future'?

Overall, in the 20 months after 1 January, 2000, the tabloids spoke to us in a gentler voice, reconfigured for success in a different market. *Weekly World News* delivered minimal end-time content, while *Sun* perfected an attitude of prophecy as an avenue to self-improvement, supplementing catastrophic end times warnings with predictions to assist its 'mature readership' in making better choices in vitamin supplements, home furnishings, and lottery numbers.

One of the reasons that the tabloids did not fall prey to 'millennial disappointment' is that, typically, something else came along to fill the void. The events of 11 September, 2001, renewed the sense of impending doom that fuels and legitimizes end time fears, and the tabloids stepped up their doomsday headlines in response. The reaction was slightly delayed. Perhaps future issues were planned far enough in advance that it took a few weeks to get a response in press. Perhaps, in the new hierarchy of American Media, Inc., it seemed more appropriate to give 9/11 coverage to other tabloids. It may be that the events were so shocking that the staff were not sure how to react. Perhaps, even, the relatively upbeat tone of the new *Sun* was a kind of contribution to the cause of keeping America on an even keel. In any event, the 18 September issue of *Sun* is a lightweight entry from Nostradamus on horoscopes, and even the 2 October issue featured dire warnings from Edgar Cayce, but nothing specific to 9/11.

In the 9 October issue, *Sun* revealed that, in fact, they had predicted the 11 September catastrophe long ago in their own pages. In a feature article they cited five earlier issues that alluded to the events, for example, a Native American prophecy that spoke of a house falling from the sky.[81] Out of the many column-inches of prophecy published in *Sun*, this is not a terribly impressive showing, and yet many readers might have been impressed nonetheless. At this time, *Sun* also revamped its cover to be more patriotic. An American flag provided a backdrop to the magazine's title in the corner of the cover, which also sported new slogans: first 'God Bless America' (16 October) and later, 'United We Stand'. By the end of the year, we were back to 'America's Best-Loved Weekly', but the flag remains an element of the cover to the present day.

More important, the unexpected 9/11 attack confirmed a need for prophecy, or for anything that could help readers understand what had happened, and what would happen next. By October 2001, prophecies of disaster were being discussed in the mainstream press. A feature on Nostradamus appeared in the more upscale tabloid the *National Examiner*, citing well-known authority John Hogue.[82] Although the *National Examiner* may have been over-confident in predicting that America would win the war on terrorism by Spring, it refrained from publishing 'recently discovered newly made-up' Nostradamus quatrains, as *Sun* would do over the next months.[83] A heightened national awareness of this prophet may have encouraged *Sun* finally to get rid of the bearded, robed fellow who had served as Nostradamus on their covers for years, replacing him, if not consistently, with a contemporary portrait of the master.[84]

The tabloids were themselves at the center of post-9/11 terrorist activity. On 5 October, 2001, the first death from anthrax was a *Sun* photo editor, Robert Stevens.[85] No definitive explanation of why Stevens was targeted has ever emerged, but the attack suggests that the tabloids were seen to be as prominent in shaping public opinion as other targets Senate Majority Leader Tom Daschle and Tom Brokaw. At that time, the American Media buildings in Boca Raton were evacuated and employees moved to other quarters. The tabloid staff took pride in not missing a beat in their relentless weekly publishing schedule, but they were forced to abandon work in progress, to say nothing of the contents of their desks and libraries, in the move to new quarters. Only in late August, 2002, did the FBI even enter the building to investigate[86] and the building was eventually sold at a loss to a developer who would undertake the burden of decontamination.[87]

In 2002, as worldwide events escalated toward war, the tabloids did not hesitate to frame the conflict in apocalyptic terms. When the United States government could identify an Axis of Evil, it was not difficult to believe *Sun* headlines like 'Armageddon Has Begun'[88] or 'Apocalypse Now'.[89] In 2003, *Sun* featured revelations of doom nearly every week, and even *Weekly World News* provided the occasional bizarre revelation, despite the potential overlap in material from its sister publication. Every month or so, *Sun* published an edition of *Prophecy* magazine, eagerly anticipating future progress and prosperity.

The tabloids are nothing if not patriotic, yet their end time rhetoric could still provide a subtle resistance to a conservative vision of a holy war in response to terrorism. The tabloids routinely accuse both government and church of withholding pertinent information about the future. On 22 October, 2002, in the same week that Bush was asking the United States to declare war, *Sun* ran a story about Nostradamus' vision of World War III. His predictions, they state, make it clear that no soldier will survive this Armageddon. In a list of what readers should do to save themselves, any draft-age person is advised to seek conscientious objector status. This point of view had been heard before, and in fact, replayed an earlier story from 2 April, 2002. But in October 2002, the tabloid was providing the loudest anti-war sentiment in the country.

It is not clear to observers whether the present tabloid market can be maintained, especially under a single management. Tabloid Valley, the area in Florida where tabloid newspaper production is centered, has not fully recovered from the terrorism of anthrax. Circulation has steadily decreased from its high point in the early 1980s. But if the past is any indication, failure will only be interpreted as a new market challenge. The tabloids will always try to feed the appetite for knowledge about the future with headlines that are loud, cautionary, and apocalyptic. But the tabloid visions of apocalypse never really seek commitment or closure. Thereby, in an odd way, they actually convey a sense of hope. The end of the world is near, but information that might help you survive only costs a few dollars, and the prediction is probably wrong, anyway.

Bibliography

Bird, S. Elizabeth, *For Enquiring Minds* (Knoxville: University of Tennessee Press, 1992).

Boyer, Paul, *When Time Shall Be No More: Prophecy Belief in Modern American Culture* (Cambridge: Harvard University Press, 1992).

Dean, Jodi, *Aliens in America* (Ithaca, NY: Cornell University Press, 1998).

Hogshire, Jim, *Grossed-out Surgeon Vomits inside Patient!: An Insider's Look at Supermarket Tabloids* (Venice, CA: Feral House, 1997).

Howe, Ellic, *Astrology and Psychological Warfare during World War II* (London: Rider, rev. and condensed edn, 1972).

Lunsford, Darcie, 'Taming the Tabloids', *American Journalism Review* 22 (September 2000): 52.

O'Leary, Stephen, 'A Dramatic Theory of Apocalyptic Rhetoric', *Quarterly Journal of Speech* 79 (November 1993), 385-426.

— *Arguing the Apocalypse: A Theory of Millennial Rhetoric* (New York: Oxford University Press, 1994).

Paulus, Stefan, *Nostradamus 1999: Who Will Survive?* (St Paul, MN: Llwellyn Publications, 1997).

Poulson, Kevin, 'The Y2K Solution: Run for your Life', *Wired* 6.08 (August, 1998), 122-25, 164-67.

Radford, Benjamin, 'Bogus Nostradamus Prophecies Circulate following Terrorism', *Skeptical Inquirer* 25.6 (November-December, 2001), 8.

Sloan, Bill, *I Watched a Wild Hog Eat my Baby: A Colorful History of Tabloids and their Cultural Impact* (Amherst, NY: Prometheus Books, 2001).

Thompson, Damian, *The End of Time: Faith and Fear in the Shadow of the Millennium* (Hanover, NH: University Press of New England, 1996).

Todeschi, Kevin J., 'Edgar Cayce's ESP: Who He Was, What He Said, and How It Came True' (Virginia Beach, VA: ARE Publishing, 1971).

Ulrich's Periodicals Directory (New Providence, NJ: R.R. Bowker, 2003).

URLs

http://news.com.com/2100-1023-832201.html

http://search.rja-ads.com/pdfs/wn-print.pdf

http://slate.msn.com/id/1833/

http://slate.msn.com/id/35486/

http://www.edgarcayce.org/

http://www.religious tolerance.org/chr_poll3.htm.

http://www.salon.com/media/col/elde/1999/11/23/media/index1.html

http://www.scifi.com/chronicle/

http://www.vatican.va/roman_curia/congregations/cfaith/documents/rc_con_cfaith_doc_20000626_messagefatima_en.html

http://www.weeklyworldnews.com/

http://www.wikipedia.org/wiki/2001_anthrax_attack

Notes

* Earlier versions of this paper were read at Center for Millennial Studies conferences in 1999 and 2002. I would like to thank Paul Achter and the volume editors for their insightful comments, and Dean Linda DeMeritt of Allegheny College for financial assistance in publishing the illustrations.

1. For example, in *Sun*, 20 August, 2002, cover headlines read 'Apocalypse Now! 7 Signs End Of the World Is Here'.

2. The standard broadsheet size varies somewhat between 12-13.5" x 21-21.5", with the standard tabloid size 10" x 11.625-13.5" or even 10" x 15". Tabloids have also experimented with trimming their publications to a slightly smaller size, approaching the dimensions of a magazine.

3. S. Elizabeth Bird, *For Enquiring Minds* (Knoxville: University of Tennessee Press, 1992), especially 7-38 for the history of the tabloids.

4. However, *Star* moved its headquarters to New York City in 2003, perhaps signaling another sea change in the tabloid market.

5. Bill Sloan, *I Watched a Wild Hog Eat my Baby: A Colorful History of Tabloids and their Cultural Impact* (Amherst, NY: Prometheus Books, 2001), 219. Circulation numbers for WWN are difficult to come by. Sloan's figure is confirmed by *Ulrich's Periodicals Directory* (New Providence, NJ: R.R. Bowker, 2003). Paul Festa cites a circulation of 306,000 in March 2000, but a figure of 254,000 a year later, in 'Tabloid to readers: Log off and cough up', *CNET News.com*, 7 February, 2002, online at http://news.com.com/2100-1023-832201.html. However, in a document listing the paper's advertising rates, *Weekly World News* listed a circulation of 441,000 weekly and estimated a readership of over 2,000,000. See 'Weekly World News 2004 Classified Advertising Rates' secure online ordering form at http://search.rja-ads.com/pdfs/wn-print.pdf.

6. Sloan, *I Watched a Wild Hog Eat my Baby*, 62-64.

7. Sloan, *I Watched a Wild Hog Eat my Baby*, 219. *Sun*'s circulation figures are not included in *Ulrich's Periodicals Directory*.

8. Sloan, *I Watched a Wild Hog Eat my Baby*, 176.

9. Bird, *For Enquiring Minds*, 43.

10. Sean Elder, 'The Tabloids That Ate their Competition', Salon.com. 23 November 1999. Online: http://www.salon.com/media/col/elde/1999/11/23/media/index1.html

11. *National Examiner*, 21 September, 1999.

12. According to Bird, *For Enquiring Minds*, 114, most readers do not typically use the term 'tabloid'.

13. Bird, *For Enquiring Minds*, 113.

14. Sloan, *I Watched a Wild Hog Eat my Baby*, 172.

15. Bird, *For Enquiring Minds*, 116-19.

16. *Weekly World News*, 9 May, 2000.

17. http://www.weeklyworldnews.com/

18. Bird, *For Enquiring Minds*, 169.

19. The name El Niño, or 'the little one' is claimed to have been given by Spanish fishermen off the coast of South America who noticed the phenomenon of warm

waters around the time of Christmas. El Niña, refers to a corresponding situation when the waters are colder than usual.

20. David Plotz, 'Mother Nature. Why you can't trust Mom'. Slate. Posted Friday, 24 September, 1999. Online: http://slate.msn.com/id/35486/ and David Plotz, 'El Niño. Perfect weather for a conspiracy'. Slate. Posted 28 September, 1997. Online: http://slate.msn.com/id/1833/.

21. Bird, *For Enquiring Minds*, 127.

22. (Harvest House Publisher, 1997), reviewed in *Weekly World News*, 8 December, 1998.

23. (Originally published 1983, paperback edition Morrow/Avon Word Publishing, 1985; reissued since), reviewed in *Weekly World News*, 30 December, 1997.

24. (Tyndale House Publishing, 1995), reviewed in *Sun*, 15 December, 1998.

25. (Whitaker House, 1996), reviewed in *Weekly World News*, 14 September, 1999.

26. (St Andrew's Productions, 1998), reviewed in *Sun*, 5 January, 1999; *Weekly World News*, 20 April, 1999.

27. See Bird, *For Enquiring Minds*, 98-101 for a discussion of tabloid credibility, citing studies by Greenwell and Thorn that also reported tremendous difficulty in verifying sources.

28. Jim Hogshire, *Grossed-out Surgeon Vomits inside Patient!: An Insider's Look at Supermarket Tabloids* (Venice, CA: Feral House, 1997).

29. 'Astronomers Say Holy City of New Jerusalem Is Headed Toward Earth!', *Weekly World News*, 16 March, 1999, 20.

30. Paul Boyer, When *Time Shall Be No More: Prophecy Belief in Modern American Culture* (Cambridge: Harvard University Press, 1992), 8.

31. Hogshire, *Grossed-out Surgeon Vomits inside Patient!*, 31.

32. Damian Thompson, *The End of Time: Faith and Fear in the Shadow of the Millennium* (Hanover, NH: University Press of New England, 1996), esp. 167-90.

33. The history and text of the 'third secret of Fatima' is described on the Vatican website. The text was revealed 13 May, 2000: http://www.vatican.va/roman_curia/congregations/cfaith/documents/rc_con_cfaith_doc_20000626_messagefatima_en.html

34. Beth Gimmel, 'Last Days Have Begun', *Sun*, 8 April, 2003, 37.

35. 'America's Fatima', *Prophecy* section, *Sun*, 3 May, 2004, 36-38.

36. These texts are gathered into groups of 100, known as Centuries. 353 original texts were published as *Centuries* in 1555 and a complete edition of the quatrains appeared in 1568, after Nostradamus' death. All together, his writings consist of 10 centuries (with Century 7 containing only 42 verses), extra prophetic verses, medical treatises, and some correspondence, notably the Preface written to his son César explaining his life's work and a letter to King Henry II.

37. For example, new texts were published in *Weekly World News* on 15 July, 1997 and 26 May, 1998, while *Sun*, announced 17 'newly-discovered quatrains' on 24 March, 1998.

38. For an account of activities during World War II, when Germans dropped fake prophecies of doom on the Allies, and the British returned the favor in a leaflet campaign over Germany, see Ellic Howe, *Astrology and Psychological Warfare during World War II* (London: Rider, rev. and condensed edn, 1972).

39. *Sun*, 28 July, 1998, reporting on C2 Q65.

40. C10 Q72. *Weekly World News*, 7 July, 1998.

41. *Weekly World News*, 28 September, 1999.

42. Kevin J. Todeschi, 'Edgar Cayce's ESP: Who He Was, What He Said, and How It Came True' (Virginia Beach, VA: ARE Publishing, 1971). Online at the ARE website 6 October, 2003. http://www.edgarcayce.org/

43. *Sun*, 14 September, 1999: 20-21. No further predictions from Evaristo Monteiro ever appeared.

44. See, for example, *Sun*, covers of 7 July, 1998, and 14 September, 1999.

45. *Weekly World News*, 2 March, 1999: 38-39.

46. *Sun*, 9 November, 1999.

47. *Sun*, 29 September, 1999.

48. *Sun*, 8 September, 1998.

49. Bird, esp. 107-37.

50. It's useful to keep in mind that a great many articles in the tabloids cover more mundane subjects, covering alternative health, advice to the lovelorn, financial tips, etc. and do not always require suspension of disbelief.

51. George Sanford, 'Destroy Satan's Evil Influence on Your Life', *Weekly World News* 27 October, 1998: 6.

52. *Sun*, 27 October, 1998: 20-21.

53. Bird, *For Enquiring Minds*, 194.

54. See the religious poll statistics summarized by the Ontario Consultants on Religious Tolerance, 'Religious Beliefs of Americans' online: http://www.religious tolerance.org/chr_poll3.htm.

55. When the time came, *Sun* certainly promoted 1 January, 2001, as the beginning of the end, although not much apocalyptic fervor was roused by the date that scientists called the end of the millennium. The cover of 19 December, 2000 read 'New Star of Bethlehem Heralds Jesus' Rebirth in 2001', while the next week 26 December, 2000 *Sun* cover proclaimed 'Last Days Begin on January 1'.

56. *Weekly World News*, 29 December, 1998.

57. *Sun*, 16 March, 1999.

58. *Weekly World News*, 24 August, 1999. The five words were Surrender, Humility, Equality, Love, and Forgiveness.

59. George Sanford, 'Do You Think You Can Repent just before the End of the World?' *Weekly World News*, 21 December, 1999, 7.

60. Stephen O'Leary, *Arguing the Apocalypse: A Theory of Millennial Rhetoric* (New York: Oxford University Press, 1994), 80.

61. Stefan Paulus, *Nostradamus 1999: Who Will Survive?* (St Paul, MN: Llwellyn Publications, 1997).

62. Thompson, *The End of Time*, 163.

63. *Sun*, 22 July, 1997; 22 July, 1998.

64. *Weekly World News* 19 January, 1999: 24-25.

65. 'Dr Billy Graham's Message', *Weekly World News*, 25 May, 1999: 8-9.

66. Bird, *For Enquiring Minds*, 121-22.

67. O'Leary, *Arguing the Apocalypse*, 117.

68. *Sun*, 30 March, 1999.

69. Stephen O'Leary, 'A Dramatic Theory of Apocalyptic Rhetoric', *Quarterly Journal of Speech* 79 (November 1993), 385-426.

70. Jodi Dean, *Aliens in America* (Ithaca, NY: Cornell University Press, 1998), esp. ch. 5, 'The Familiarity of Strangeness'.

71. *Weekly World News*, 18 December, 2001, 37.

72. For example, Kevin Poulson, 'The Y2K Solution: Run for your Life', *Wired* 6.08 (August, 1998), 122-25, 164-67. The cover advertised the story with the blurb, 'Millennium Bugout: If you knew what the experts know, you'd be buying guns, too'.

73. Sloan, *I Watched a Wild Hog Eat my Baby*, 221-22; Darcie Lunsford, 'Taming the Tabloids', *American Journalism Review* 22 (September 2000), 52.

74. *Sun*, 21 March, 2000. Editorial. This title was retained through April and May.

75. 'Your chance to be a *Sun* editor – Without Leaving Home', *Sun*, 22 May, 2002.

76. See the program's official website: http://www.scifi.com/chronicle/

77. The magazine itself is variously titled, the first issue being *Tomorrow: Prophecy & Prediction*.

78. *Sun*, 31 July, 2001.

79. *Sun*, 29 January, 2002.

80. In the 31 July, 2001 issue of *Sun*, the cover headlined 'Vatican Statues Weep Blood', while inside, *Prophecy* magazine called 'Tomorrow, Magazine of Prophecy & Prediction' set a very different tone with the headline 'Atlantis Rising from the Deep'.

81. *Sun*, 19 June, 2001.

82. *National Examiner*, 9 October, 2001, a secondary headline proclaimed 'Nostradamus: American Will Win by Spring!' while the main story promised to explain 'Laura Bush: George's Secret Strength'.

83. See also Benjamin Radford, 'Bogus Nostradamus Prophecies Circulate Following Terrorism', *Skeptical Inquirer* 25.6 (November-December, 2001), 8.

84. A portrait featuring Nostradamus as a sixteenth-century scholar appeared on the *Sun* cover of 22 October, 2002.

85. Amanda Riddle, 'Florida man dies after contracting rare form of anthrax', The Associated Press State & Local Wire (Lantana, Florida), 5 October, 2001. See also Wikipedia, '2001 Anthrax Attack'. Online: http://www.wikipedia.org/wiki/2001_anthrax_attack.

86. Jill Barton, 'FBI to renew search for anthrax at Boca media building', The Associated Press State & Local Wire (Boca Raton, Florida), 26 August, 2002. Barton continued to cover this story for the Associated Press until the FBI left the building on 11 September, having confiscated a great deal of material, but never admitting whether or not the original letter to American Media Inc. had been located.

87. 'Anthrax building sold for $40,000', The Associated Press State & Local Wire (Boca Raton, Florida), 17 April, 2003.

88. *Sun*, 30 April, 2002.

89. *Sun*, 20 August, 2002.

Christian Apocalyptic Fiction, Science Fiction and Technology

Tom Doyle

Premillennialist Christian apocalyptic fiction is hotter than burning brimstone. The leaders of this newly popular genre, the 12 *Left Behind* books, have sold over 62 million copies.[1] Such books follow the outlines of the modern premillennialist 'end times' biblical interpretation first popularized by Hal Lindsey in *The Late Great Planet Earth* in 1970.[2] This end times speculation has benefited from the recent anxieties regarding Y2K and 9/11, and many other examples of the genre have sprung up contemporaneously with the *Left Behind* books, including novels by Lindsey (*Blood Moon*) and Pat Robertson (*The End of the Age*).

Bookstores or web sites often identify such works as 'Christian science fiction'. Does Christian apocalyptic fiction belong on the science fiction shelves, or are there important distinctions between these genres? The Christian apocalyptic genre is generally poorly written, but that doesn't mean much; as Theodore Sturgeon told us, 90% of science fiction as well as everything else is crap.[3] The authors of Christian apocalyptic fiction have a strong and definite religious viewpoint, but again, so do many science fiction authors. What else distinguishes these genres?

To address this question, it is helpful to draw some distinctions between the more familiar genres of science fiction and the techno-thriller. Science fiction is the self-understood literature of new ideas and things, in particular new scientific ideas and new technologies.[4] Change is a central part of science fiction.[5] When we think of science fiction, we often think of the future.

Not so with the contemporary techno-thriller or political thriller. The thriller is ideologically conservative in the literal sense – no new ideas or fundamental changes are needed for its events to occur. The thriller's gadgetry is at the cutting edge of technology, but does not require fundamental new discoveries. The techno-thriller is usually set in the proximate future tense – it could be happening right now.

The thriller is also ideologically conservative in the more general sense – its politics are old and generally right wing. Science fiction, however, can be politically subversive and challenging even when it is conservative to the point of fascism, as old ideas may become new in the novel contexts postulated by science fiction. The contrast also may be viewed in terms of redemption versus emancipation: the thriller is about saving the world as we know it, in contrast to much of science fiction, which is about liberating a new world.[6]

The protagonists of the techno-thriller are typically intelligence agents, journalists or government workers caught in an unfolding global mystery or plot. These protagonists are seldom truly ordinary, but they would not normally be considered suited to the job of uncovering the plot and saving the world. Although the settings of the thriller have changed somewhat in the post-Cold War world, the favorites are still Russia, the Middle East and Washington. Science fiction, on the other hand, offers a much wider range of possible protagonists and settings.

These distinctions between science fiction and the techno-thriller provide a framework for analyzing the plot of the Christian apocalyptic novel. It is quite fair for me to generalize about *the* plot. Because this genre follows with few exceptions a particular set of interpretations of biblical prophecy, the plots of the various books are often quite similar.

First, Jesus Christ returns in secret to instantaneously take faithful Christians away to Heaven in the Rapture, with nonbelievers 'left behind' to face the evil days to come. Second, the Antichrist arises, usually connected to the European Community which constitutes a 'second Roman Empire'. He makes a treaty with Israel, which initiates the seven-year countdown to the visible Second Coming of Jesus Christ known as the Tribulation. The Antichrist is not recognized by the world as evil; instead, he is hailed for bringing peace. An assassin kills the Antichrist with a head wound, but the Antichrist is resurrected, and obtains world hegemony for three and a half years. The Antichrist persecutes believers and requires everyone to bear his mark (the proverbial '666') in order to buy or sell anything.

The Middle East is central to the scenario. Usually Russia, as the biblical 'Gog', attempts the destruction of Israel and the conquest of the Middle East, but its forces are destroyed in a nuclear strike or some similar disaster. The armies of the Antichrist battle against the kings of the East (an East Asian bloc) at Armageddon, and the battle threatens to consume the world until the Second Coming cuts it off.

Throughout the Tribulation, the judgments described in the biblical Book of Revelation afflict the earth and humankind. Much has been made in apocalyptic circles of the resemblance of the judgments to ecological disasters, asteroid strikes, new diseases and the latest weaponry, so the novels often modernize the judgments so that they appear to be 'history written in advance'.[7]

Given these plot parameters, it is not surprising that the most common and successful variety of Christian apocalyptic fiction has been in the form of the straight techno-thriller. Most Christian apocalyptic novels owe very little to science fiction; reviewers lump them with Clancy rather than with Clarke.[8] The apocalyptic protagonists are often talented journalists, computer people or military/government/intelligence personnel. The plots focus on political developments in the standard theaters of the techno-thriller: Russia, the Middle East and the Washington corridors of power. The main protagonists must uncover the underlying biblical conflict to save the world, though unlike the political thriller this means religious salvation, as the world is physically doomed. The technological gadgetry that pervades such books is at the cutting edge of current capability, but does not require fundamental new discoveries.

Almost all of the technology in the *Left Behind* books, for instance, was available at the time of publication, except for the subcutaneous computer chip 'mark of the Beast'[9] (now within our ability, and which is a staple of the genre) and a miraculous formula that allows the deserts to bloom.[10] This food formula is the linchpin of the Antichrist's rise to global domination, but there is no speculation in the *Left Behind* series on just what the nature of such a formula might be, giving it rather the aspect of fantasy than hard science fiction.

The central element for most Christian apocalyptic fiction is that the apocalypse, like the techno-thriller, could happen today. This is not contradicted by the fact that some of these books are set a generation or more in the future. The date is often chosen more for reasons of prophecy than reasons of speculation: authors are more often concerned about predicting the end of the world too soon than actually imagining the world more than a decade hence. For example, the Christian apocalyptic *Omega Trilogy* imagines a world in 2050 that really has changed very little in technological terms (but quite a lot in some religious ways).

Furthermore, Christian apocalyptic fiction often characterizes science-fictional tropes, such as the ideas of extraterrestrials and the triumph of science, as beliefs that may lead to damnation. A frequent Christian apocalyptic plot device is to have the general public erroneously believe that the Rapture was caused by extraterrestrials in UFOs, thus condemning the contemporary obsession with the science-fiction-inspired belief in alien visitors.[11]

In the last few years, however, some authors have made interesting efforts to make their Christian apocalyptic stories appear more like science fiction, both in their handling of scientific elements in particular and new ideas (if only new religious ideas for premillennialist Christians) in general. This mixture of Christian apocalyptic fiction and science fiction owes as much to C.S. Lewis and his space trilogy as to Hal Lindsey. Examples of this mixture are *The Omega Trilogy*[12] by the Morris family, *The Fire of Heaven Trilogy* by Bill Myers, *The Christ Clone Trilogy* by James BeauSeigneur, *Seal of Gaia* by Marlin Maddoux, *Nephilim* by L.A. Marzulli, the *Rift in Time* books by Michael Phillips and, perhaps, the unique *We All Fall Down* by Brian Caldwell. But even these works retain fundamental differences from science fiction in their treatment of science and technology.

For purposes of this comparison, the term science fiction refers to a genre of literary works. Much of film and television (and the serial books based on such film and television) that goes by the name 'science fiction' is not considered as such by professional science fiction authors. Science fiction is also to be treated as a distinct genre from fantasy (such as Tolkien's *Lord of the Rings*) in which things occur regularly in contravention of known science.

Science fiction starts with the general acceptance, for good or ill, of the modern scientific world-view. This does not mean that every book within the genre approves of every use of technology whatever its moral or practical consequence. The genre may consider religious or spiritual matters seriously or even favorably. For example, Orson Scott Card, one of the masters of the genre, regularly includes aspects of his Latter-day Saint beliefs and values in his works. The moral struggle between humankind's subjective and spiritual beliefs and the demands of scientific and technological knowledge and change is at the core of many great works of science fiction. But this struggle takes place within the boundaries of scientific facts, known or speculated.

In contrast, Christian apocalyptic fiction does not accept significant portions of the modern scientific world-view. Instead, it often uses specific scientific ideas for its religious ends in a manner that most scientists would regard as unscientific. Sometimes, this is just a question of technical details.[13] For example, in the *Fire of Heaven Trilogy*, changes to blood cell DNA are inexplicably supposed to rapidly change mental behavior.[14] What probably happened is that the author used as his model procedures to treat genetic disorders affecting the blood or immune system. But the more interesting tactic is the reinterpretation of scientific ideas to support the religious ones. For instance, the *Fire of Heaven Trilogy* consistently interprets string theory as allowing for the existence of spiritual dimensions in the style of *Flatworld*.[15] The *Rift in Time* series bends the scientific ideas of human evolution, plate tectonics and the Second Law of Thermodynamics to boot, all to suit its anti-evolution argument.[16]

There is throughout these works a consistent portrayal of anecdote and subjective experience as being at least equivalent to, and often more important than, the scientific methods of measurable observation and replicable experiment. Such a portrayal is used both to elevate the spiritual arguments and to punch holes in the scientific ones. Convoluted explanations of human biology and natural history that conform to a spiritual world-view are accepted despite the availability of simpler alternatives that better conform to Occam's razor.

Christian apocalyptic fiction is able to readily reinterpret scientific ideas for religious ends because it frequently divorces specific technology and ideas from their broader implications within scientific reasoning or their likely social effects. For example, these fictional works will obsess over the details of genetic engineering or cloning procedures. Such procedures clearly allow for humans to create new species and alter humanity itself, and one reason that the end must be coming soon is our potential to misuse such power. These works would never acknowledge that a new species could arise without human or divine intervention, and the author of the *Rift in Time* series even conjectures that no floral species has truly gone extinct.[17] Yet, from a scientific perspective, the same understanding of genetics and DNA that allowed humans to develop genetic engineering also supports, along with the other evidence, a theory of natural evolution in which new species arise and old ones become extinct.

As for the practical implications of genetic engineering, Christian apocalyptic fiction assumes that there are not going to be any within the time allotted. Genetic engineering is used only for individual freakish experiments (cloning Jesus or Hitler, creating human/animal or human/demon hybrids). It is not described as potentially curing diseases or altering humans in any positive fashion.

By way of contrast, a good science fiction author is expected to consider the broader implications of any new or postulated scientific developments, both in terms of scientific theory and social effects. For example, it is often not enough to narrowly speculate that if the hero invents the automobile, he can capture the horse-riding villains. Traffic jams and drive-in movies will follow. If the science fiction author does not consider such implications, she will suffer criticism within the genre for inadequate and unrealistic 'world building'.

Christian apocalyptic fiction frequently borrows some recognized plot devices of science fiction – cloning, advanced computers, asteroids and other astronomical cataclysms, biological weapons, advanced conventional weaponry and so forth. However, even in the more science fiction-like works, these sci-fi devices are often just props, existing without any

scientific explanation, literal *deus ex machinae* to help move the apocalyptic story along. They are not speculative ideas integral to the story,
which means they are not being used in a science fiction fashion.[18]
Though these technological innovations or cosmic phenomena may be
partially instrumental in the apocalyptic destruction of most of humankind, they remain merely God's instruments, interchangeable with more
miraculous manifestations of wrath. Sometimes there is a more complete
conflation of technology and magic, as if Clarke's Third Law ('any sufficiently advanced technology is indistinguishable from magic') were being
turned on its head.[19] In *Seal of Gaia*, for example, a supercomputer is
super because it's possessed by the devil.

   Christian apocalyptic fiction also addresses some of the same themes
as science fiction, including encounters with aliens, the uses of genetic
engineering technology and the growth of environmental concerns. However, Christian apocalyptic fiction's response is consistently negative
towards these themes and their underlying science, particularly where
they appear to threaten the Christian idea of human identity. Science
fiction, on the other hand, may be found on both sides of these themes
(aliens may be good or bad), and is generally respectful of any scientific
principles involved (alien life forms could evolve naturally, they are not
necessarily demons in disguise).

   In addressing genetic engineering, Christian apocalyptic fiction is concerned with hybridization: scientifically mediated interbreeding or inter-
mingling of the alien or supernatural and the human. That Christian
apocalyptic fiction is hostile to such hybrids is not surprising, given the
genre's general insistence on purity and rejection of the impure as
damnable.

   For example, two series, the *Fire of Heaven Trilogy* and the *Christ
Clone Trilogy*, focus on the evil that results when scientists attempt to
place the genetic code of Jesus in a modern human. In the *Christ Clone
Trilogy*, the source for Jesus' putative DNA is the Shroud of Turin.[20] The
fact that carbon dating has given a medieval age for the Shroud is, in a
fashion typical of the genre, supernaturally finessed – the Shroud was kept
in a mystical stasis chamber until the Crusades and did not age. In the *Fire
of Heaven Trilogy*, the DNA source is a wax-encased portion of the Crown
of Thorns.[21] In both instances, the Antichrist is the result. As the hero of
the *Christ Clone Trilogy* warns, 'it's one thing to do lab research or grow
cells in a petri dish, but you just can't go around cloning people, especially if the guy you want to clone might just be the son of God!'[22]

   In Van Kampen's *The Fourth Reich*, a clone of Hitler powered by
Hitler's reanimated soul and demonic forces becomes the Antichrist. In

the book *Nephilim*, the fallen angels imitate extraterrestrials in order to crossbreed with humans. The results are the Nephilim of the title: Goliath-like monstrosities 'fearsome to behold, horrible and commanding. Human and yet not human. From this earth but not entirely of this earth.'[23]

There is an exception to this fear of the hybrid: the empathic hero of *The Omega Trilogy* is an artificially incubated human with some reptilian genes. This hybrid seems to have a powerful spiritual empathy with both animals and humans.[24] But this hero is literally a miraculous exception. In general, when genetic engineering or cloning appear in these books, the resulting hybrid creations mean trouble. However, these same books are quick to point out that we can, with God's help, triumph over our DNA, even when it's been tainted. As the protagonist of the first volume of the *Fire of Heaven Trilogy* says, 'I'm more than just some kid's chemistry set... I've got to be'.[25]

On a related front, Christian apocalyptic authors, like science fiction authors, are interested in aliens. But again, they don't like them. Although C.S. Lewis could fit other worlds with sentient beings into his Christian beliefs, this is not the case for premillennialist Christian apocalyptic fiction. In such works, extraterrestrials are usually just a hoax – but if they exist, they are actually fallen angels. In *Nephilim*, the demons look just like the alien greys.[26] In *We All Fall Down*, the demon aliens (called the Celestine Prophets) give a long speech to explain away the Rapture in terms of alien intervention, but the apocalyptically savvy protagonist just laughs at the devil's obviousness. 'Nice try, cocksucker. Next time why don't you just try offering me the fucking apple.'[27]

Connected to this fear of the alien is a general silence regarding the human space program. Because these novels are so heavily grounded in Earth-bound biblical prophecies, their authors have a vested interest in keeping the action on Earth. A future including an altered, expanded humanity on other worlds would mean that the end of this planet would not necessarily correspond to the end of humankind. Novels based on fundamentalist biblical interpretation are not yet ready to concede such a possible future (as even C.S. Lewis would not).[28]

Two exceptions to the silence regarding human space travel support the idea that space travel creates difficulties for Christian apocalyptic fiction. In *The Fourth Reich*, Van Kampen takes the time to describe how God launches a piece of lava into orbit for the specific purpose of destroying the space shuttle, making it clear that nobody can escape. In *The Illuminati*, the author notes humankind's failure to get to Mars,[29] again as if to emphasize that an Earth-wide apocalypse is an apocalypse for all humanity.

Christian apocalyptic fiction, like science fiction, addresses the implications of ecology and evolution, but with an idiosyncratic, negative critique. Evolution is the obvious *bête noire* of much of fundamentalist Christianity due to its contradiction of the literal interpretation of the Genesis creation story. Consistently in these novels, the propagation of the theory of evolutionary biology in the modern era is the result of a deliberate plot by the forces of evil. The *Rift in Time* series, with its paleoanthropologist-archaeologist hero, states this view of evolution the most strongly.[30] It counters evolutionary theory with its own scenario of God playing jigsaw games with the continents after the Fall of Man.[31]

Science fiction has proved a useful genre for the exploration of environmental concerns. Christian apocalyptic fiction, on the other hand, has surprisingly often expressed an anti-environmentalist point of view. These works typically view environmentalism as one of the ideologies which advance the new world order of the Antichrist, and conflate environmentalism with a kind of nature worship or idolatry. This anti-environmentalism is most strong in *The Omega Trilogy* and *Seal of Gaia*. In *The Omega Trilogy*, humans have been herded into overcrowded cities, supposedly in order to allow vast tracts of land to return to nature but actually to make it easier for their evil masters to control them.[32] In *Seal of Gaia*, the forces of evil are designing new plagues to wipe out a large percent of the human population so that nature can recover. The counter-ideology is ironically expressed in *The Omega Trilogy* by a character viewing a map of the new ecological preserves. 'I guess it's a matter of who you think is a waste of time and space. If you think animals and plants and air are more important than people, then I guess you don't think the space is wasted.'[33]

Science fiction, of course, also has a profound pessimistic tradition, dating back at least to Mary Shelley's out-of-control monster, and in Christian apocalyptic fiction we often see the classic sci-fi theme of science out of control. One scenario in particular stands out. Prior to the year 2000, there were novels in which the apocalypse begins due to the repercussions of the Y2K computer bug. For example, Jeffrey and Hunt's *Flee the Darkness* identifies the Y2K problem as a tool for the Antichrist to control the information age. The more cautious *Omega Trilogy*, set in 2050 but with its first volume published in 1999, uses an electricity-eating bacillus in the place of the Y2K bug,[34] but the covert use of the Y2K model is obvious.

Christian apocalyptic fiction also directly engages the notion of human transcendence through technological progress. The idea that people can perfect themselves and move beyond the human condition through cutting-edge scientific endeavors has become pervasive, as described by David Noble.[35] Sometimes, Christian works argue against such transcendence by showing the limitations of technological efforts against the divine plan: for example, in the *Christ Clone Trilogy*, humans cannot stop the asteroids of God's judgment despite their best efforts. Sometimes, the argument is that truly ultimate solutions to human problems are not achievable through technology or any merely human endeavor, as in the *Left Behind* books, where technology that could feed the world is predestined to become a tool of the Antichrist. And finally, sometimes these works directly confront the most radical efforts to transcend the human condition through technology, such as the efforts to create computer consciousness or genetically engineer better humans, by imagining their ultimate results as abominations.

As is evident from these books, premillennialist Christians are seemingly as fond of modern gadgetry, particularly communications technology, as any other group in our society. But for the Christians in these novels, religious transcendence has already been achieved in the most technologically primitive of conditions (that is, the early Christian church) and may be achieved today merely by being 'born again'. Within this world, physical transcendence or ultimate spiritual transcendence is not to be achieved prior to the end. The idea of transcendence through technology smacks of the worship of the 'god of forces',[36] and it is this religion of technology that is viewed explicitly as a competitor. The fictional Antichrist typically offers a spiritual transcendence inextricably linked to a material transcendence supported by new technologies. The *Rift in Time* books go so far as to assert that the technological emergence of Europe was largely a Satanic plot,[37] and the book *Nephilim* has a similar demonic origin for much of our technology.[38]

It would be interesting if Christian apocalyptic fiction confronted scientific hubris and the science-based moral dilemmas in the world as it is, where the relationship between faith and science is at best uncertain. But instead, Christian apocalyptic fiction is more concerned with creating a world where faith can beat science in a clear-cut, factual fashion. For example, in the *Rift in Time* series, the discovery of Noah's ark confirms the Genesis account, and puts evolutionary biologists in the position of defending a now atavistic version of natural history. But this confrontation about Noah's Ark, like the confrontations in other like novels, relies on the fictional discovery as its fundamental premise. Little attempt is made to confront science in a way that would even by analogy translate effectively into our (apparently) Ark-less world.

Science fiction, however, must confront the science's full power to successfully consider its moral implications, not just its scope now, but its projected scope in the future. Some of the best science fiction stories are full-fledged philosophical thought experiments, and their conclusions are the more powerful because they are applicable by analogy to our present world absent the speculated change.

One exceptional book in the Christian apocalyptic fiction genre, both in its treatment of science and its literary quality, is Brian Caldwell's *We All Fall Down*. Its protagonist is a man who is very familiar with many apocalyptic scenarios. Caught up in the Christian end times, he tries to use his learning to advantage without submitting to God. Compared with other genre works, *We All Fall Down* is unflinching in its psychological and descriptive realism. And although this book uses little science, that science is presented with relative sophistication – the book has an interesting discussion of chaos theory and makes the effort to account for a four-billion-year-old earth and a six-thousand-year religious history.[39] Most importantly, its moral conclusions are powerfully resonant in the present world even absent the threat of an imminent end. Perhaps science fiction fans would *want* a work like this on the science fiction shelves.

Several Christian apocalyptic films have been produced since 1998, exceeding the pioneering *Thief in the Night* films in production values and theatrical box office.[40] The most interesting films from a science fiction perspective are productions of the Lalonde brothers' company, Cloud Ten Pictures. Cloud Ten has produced a loosely tied series beginning with the film *Apocalypse* and continuing with the films *Revelation*, *Tribulation* and *Judgment*.[41] In these films, the entire world is given virtual reality headsets. When a person puts one on, he or she enters a world without physical limitations in which the Antichrist offers the person his or her heart's desire in exchange for renouncing God. The people who renounce are often physically handicapped in some fashion and are healed by the Antichrist. If the person refuses to renounce, they are executed in cyberspace, and through supernatural means that execution occurs in real space as well.

This use of virtual reality technology in these films combines several of the themes discussed above. The distrust of human-machine symbiosis is a variation on the fear of hybridization. The combination of demonic miracles with technology is the conflation of science and magic. The evil use of virtual reality represents an implicit criticism of those who seek transcendence, including transcendence of particular physical limitations, through computers. Most importantly, it appears that one could leave out this *Matrix*-inspired prop with very little change to the plot – it is not a scientifically speculative idea integral to the story. The virtual reality machines in these movies just provide a more cinematic, visual setting for interior spiritual choice.

In sum, a general distinction between the Christian apocalyptic fiction and science fiction genres is that science fiction generally accepts the modern scientific world-view and that Christian apocalyptic fiction rejects significant portions of that world-view, even when using scientific props and themes. As the protagonist of *Rift in Time* puts it, the Christian apocalyptic response to the challenge of science is that 'Isn't *everything* a matter of faith in the end? ...What about the faith we scientists put in our own science? Science takes just as many leaps across the void of unprovability as do Christians.'[42] Though a Christian apocalyptic work and a science fiction novel may share science-based concerns, they will diverge in their responses to those concerns. Christian apocalyptic fiction consistently responds to even seemingly scientific problems with the antithetical non-rational principles of biblical authority, prophetic interpretation and fundamentalist ideas of human identity. Science fiction is more likely to respond to a science-based moral dilemma by depicting a more balanced struggle for a solution that accepts the scientific world-view and the pre-eminence of science within a certain sphere but also allows room for a subjective, humanist perspective.

Bibliography

Selected Christian Apocalyptic Fiction:

BeauSeigneur, James (*The Christ Clone Trilogy*) [Note: Although the Warner Books data is shown for reference the books were all practically self-published in 1997-98]:
—*In His Image*, 1997 (New York: Warner Books, 2003).
—*Birth of an Age*, 1997 (New York: Warner Books, 2003).
—*Acts of God* (New York: Warner Books, 2004; [Rockville, MD: SelectiveHouse, 1998]).
Burkett, Larry, *The Illuminati* (Nashville: Thomas Nelson Publishers, 1991).
Caldwell, Brian, *We All Fall Down* (Haverford, PA: Infinity Publishing, 2000).
Dolan, David, *The End of Days* (Grand Rapids: Fleming H. Revell, 1995).
Jeffrey, Grant R., and Angela Hunt, *Flee the Darkness* (Nashville: Word Publishing, 1998).
Jones, Robert R., *Covenant with the Beast* (Oklahoma City: Hearthstone Publishing, 1997).
LaHaye, Tim, and Jerry B. Jenkins (*The Left Behind Series*):
—*Left Behind* (Wheaton, IL: Tyndale House Publishers, 1995).
—*Tribulation Force* (Wheaton, IL: Tyndale House Publishers, 1996).
—*Nicolae* (Wheaton, IL: Tyndale House Publishers, 1997).
—*Soul Harvest* (Wheaton, IL: Tyndale House Publishers, 1998).
—*Apollyon* (Wheaton, IL: Tyndale House Publishers, 1999).
—*Assassins* (Wheaton, IL: Tyndale House Publishers, 1999).

—*The Indwelling* (Wheaton, IL: Tyndale House Publishers, 2000).

—*The Mark* (Wheaton, IL: Tyndale House Publishers, 2000).

—*Desecration* (Wheaton, IL: Tyndale House Publishers, 2001).

—*The Remnant* (Wheaton, IL: Tyndale House Publishers, 2002).

—*Armageddon* (Wheaton, IL: Tyndale House Publishers, 2003).

—*Glorious Appearing* (Wheaton, IL: Tyndale House Publishers, 2004).

[Note: A separate children's series of *Left Behind* books has also been published.]

Lalonde, Peter, and Paul Lalonde, *Apocalypse* (Niagara Falls, NY: This Week in Bible Prophecy, 1998).

Lindsey, Hal, *Blood Moon* (Palos Verdes, CA: Western Front Publishing, 1996).

Maddoux, Marlin, *Seal of Gaia* (Nashville: Word Publishing, 1998).

Mahan, Walter L., *The Unveiling of End-Time Events* (Nashville: Winston-Derek Publishers, 1993).

Marzulli, L.A., *Nephilim* (Grand Rapids: Zondervan Press, 1999).

Meier, Paul (*The Millennium Trilogy*)

—*The Third Millennium* (Nashville: Thomas Nelson Publishers, 1993).

Meier, Paul, with Robert L. Wise

—*The Fourth Millennium* (Nashville: Thomas Nelson Publishers, 1996).

—*Beyond the Millennium* (Nashville: Thomas Nelson Publishers, 1998).

Morris, Gilbert, Lynn Morris and Alan Morris (*The Omega Trilogy*) [Incomplete, only two volumes released]:

—*The Beginning of Sorrows* (Nashville: Thomas Nelson Publishers, 1999).

—*Fallen Stars, Bitter Waters* (Nashville: Thomas Nelson Publishers, 2000).

Myers, Bill, *Fire of Heaven Trilogy* (Grand Rapids: Zondervan Press, 2001). Originally published as:

—*Blood of Heaven* (Grand Rapids: Zondervan Press, 1996).

—*Threshold* (Grand Rapids: Zondervan Press, 1997).

—*Fire of Heaven* (Grand Rapids: Zondervan Press, 1999).

O'Brien, Michael D., *Eclipse of the Sun* (San Francisco: Ignatius Press, 1998).

Phillips, Michael (*The Rift in Time Series*)

—*Rift in Time* (Wheaton, IL: Tyndale House Publishers, 1997).

—*Hidden in Time* (Wheaton, IL: Tyndale House Publishers, 2000).

Robertson, Pat, *The End of the Age* (Nashville: Word Publishing, 1995).

Van Kampen, Robert. *The Fourth Reich* (Grand Rapids: Baker Book House, 1997).

Walker, Ken, and Val Walker, *Escape from Armageddon* (Glen Waverly, Victoria, Australia: Good News Australia, 1997).

Zinn, Jay, *The Unveiling* (Mukilteo, Washington: WinePress Publishing, 1997).

Films

The Apocalypse Series

Apocalypse (Dir. Peter Gerretsen with Leigh Lewis and Richard Nester; Cloud Ten Pictures, 1998).

Revelation (Dir. Andre Van Heerden with Jeff Fahey and Nick Mancuso; Cloud Ten Pictures, 1999).

Tribulation (Dir. Andre Van Heerden with Gary Busey and Howie Mandel; Cloud Ten Pictures, 2000).

Judgment (Dir. Andre Van Heerden with Corbin Bernsen and Mr. T; Cloud Ten Pictures, 2001).

Left Behind (Dir. Victor Sarin with Kirk Cameron and Brad Johnson; Cloud Ten Pictures, 2000).
Left Behind II (Dir. Bill Corcoran with Kirk Cameron and Brad Johnson; Cloud Ten Pictures, 2002).
The Omega Code (Dir. Rob Marcarelli with Michael York and Casper Van Dien; TBN Films, 1999).
The Omega Code II (Dir. Paul J. Lombardi and Brian Trenchard-Smith with Michael York and Michael Biehn; TBN Films, 2001).

Related Works

Balmer, Randall, *Mine Eyes Have Seen the Glory* (New York: Oxford University Press, 1989).
Bova, Ben, *The Craft of Writing Science Fiction That Sells* (Cincinnati: Writer's Digest Books, 1994).
Doyle, Thomas M., 'Competing Fictions: The Uses of Christian Apocalyptic Imagery in Contemporary Popular Fictional Works. Part One: Premillennialist Apocalyptic Fictions', *Journal for Millennial Studies* (Winter 2001), at http://www.mille.org/publications/winter2001/winter2001.html
Dozois, Gardner, et al., *Analog* and *Asimov's Science Fiction: Writing Science Fiction and Fantasy* (New York: Davis Publications, 1991).
Gates, David, 'The Pop Prophets', in *Newsweek*, 24 May, 2004, 44-50.
Goldberg, Michelle, 'Fundamentally Unsound', in *Salon.com* 29 July, 2002 at http://www.salon.com/books/feature/2002/07/29/left_behind
Kreuziger, Frederick A., *Apocalypse and Science Fiction: A Dialectic of Religious and Secular Soteriologies* (Chico, CA: Scholars Press, 1982).
—*The Religion of Science Fiction* (Bowling Green: Bowling Green State University Popular Press, 1986).
Lindsey, Hal, *The Late Great Planet Earth* (Grand Rapids: Zondervan Press, 1970).
Noble, David F., *The Religion of Technology* (New York: Penguin Books, 1997).
Sagan, Carl, *The Demon-Haunted World* (New York: Random House, 1995).
Scithers, George H., Darrell Schweitzer and John M. Ford, *On Writing Science Fiction* (Philadelphia: Owlswick Press, 1981).

See also http://www.jargon.net/jargonfile/s/SturgeonsLaw.html

Notes

1. David Gates, 'The Pop Prophets', *Newsweek*, 24 May, 2004, 44-50 (46).
2. For a discussion of premillennialist apocalyptic fiction generally, see Doyle, 'Competing Fictions: The Uses of Christian Apocalyptic Imagery in Contemporary Popular Fictional Works. Part One: Premillennialist Apocalyptic Fictions', *Journal for Millennial Studies* (Winter 2001), at (http://www.mille.org/publications/winter2001/winter2001.html).
3. Sturgeon's Law as originally stated was that 'Sure, 90% of science fiction is crud. That's because 90% of everything is crud.' But nearly everyone changes 'crud' to 'crap' when quoting his Law. http://www.jargon.net/jargonfile/s/SturgeonsLaw.html.
4. 'Science fiction is a literature of ideas – and new ones at that'. George Scithers, et al., *On Writing Science Fiction* (Philadelphia: Owlswick Press, 1981), 7. 'That is

science fiction's special advantage and its special challenge: going beyond the boundaries of the here-and-now to test the human spirit in new and ever-more-powerful ways'. Bova, *The Craft of Writing Science Fiction That Sells*, 9.

5.   'Science fiction deals, or should deal, with *change*'. Gardner Dozois, 'Living the Future: You Are What You Eat', in Gardner Dozois, et al., *Analog, Writing Science Fiction and Fantasy*, 12-27 (16).

6.   For a discussion of the dynamic between redemption and emancipation in science fiction, see Frederick A. Kreuziger, *Apocalypse and Science Fiction: A Dialectic of Religious and Secular Soteriologies* (Chico, CA: Scholars Press, 1982).

7.   Tim LaHaye and Jerry B. Jenkins, *Left Behind* (Wheaton, IL: Tyndale House Publishers, 1995), 214. (Biblical prophecy is 'history written in advance'.)

8.   For example, Michelle Goldberg, 'Fundamentally Unsound', in *Salon.com* 29 July, 2002 at http://www.salon.com/ books/feature/ 2002/07/29/left_behind (the *Left Behind* series is a 'Tom Clancy-meets-Revelation saga').

9.   Tim LaHaye and Jerry B. Jenkins, *The Mark* (Wheaton, IL: Tyndale House Publishers, 2000), 86.

10.   LaHaye and Jenkins, *Left Behind*, 8.

11.   The idea of flying saucers appears to have originated in 1945 within the pages of a science fiction magazine, *Amazing Stories*. Carl Sagan, *The Demon-Haunted World* (New York: Random House, 1995), 72.

12.   The third volume, *Seven Golden Vials*, will not be published.

13.   One noted editor has the following rule for science fiction stories: 'Whatever science the story uses is *plausible* in the light of known science'. Stanley Schmidt, 'Good Writing is Not Enough', in Gardner Dozois, et al., *Analog, Writing Science Fiction and Fantasy*, 91-104 (93).

14.   Bill Myers, *Fire of Heaven Trilogy* (Grand Rapids: Zondervan Press, 2001), 39.

15.   Myers, *Fire of Heaven Trilogy*, 337-38.

16.   Michael Phillips, *Rift in Time* (Wheaton, IL: Tyndale House Publishers, 1997), 74-75, 95.

17.   Phillips, *Rift in Time*, 477.

18.   Science fiction has been defined as fiction in which 'At least one speculative idea is *integral* to the story'. Schmidt, 'Good Writing is Not Enough', 93.

19.   'Arthur C. Clarke', in *The Concise Oxford Dictionary of Quotations* (Oxford: Oxford University Press, 4th edn, 2001).

20.   James BeauSeigneur, *In His Image* (New York: Warner Books, 2003), 52-53.

21.   Myers, *Fire of Heaven Trilogy*, 26.

22.   BeauSeigneur, *In His Image*, 43.

23.   L.A. Marzulli, *Nephilim* (Grand Rapids: Zondervan Press, 1999), 411.

24.   Gilbert Morris, et al., *The Beginning of Sorrows* (Nashville: Thomas Nelson Publishers, 1999), 7-14.

25.   Myers, *Fire of Heaven Trilogy*, 164.

26.   Marzulli, *Nephilim*, 381.

27.   Brian Caldwell, *We All Fall Down* (Haverford, PA: Infinity Publishing, 2000), 92.

28.   Although interpretations differ on whether this world is ultimately renewed or replaced by God, humankind remains centered on just one world in all premillennialist Christian apocalyptic fiction.

29. Larry Burkett, *The Illuminati* (Nashville: Thomas Nelson Publishers, 1991), 43.

30. Phillips, *Rift in Time*, 174, 193.

31. Phillips, *Rift in Time*, 346-49.

32. Morris, et al., *Beginning of Sorrows*, 93.

33. Morris, et al., *Beginning of Sorrows*, 56.

34. Morris, et al., *Beginning of Sorrows*, 226-28.

35. David F. Noble, *The Religion of Technology, The Religion of Technology* (New York: Penguin Books, 1997), 206-207 (summary regarding transcendence).

36. Daniel 11.38.

37. Michael Phillips, *Hidden in Time* (Wheaton, IL: Tyndale House Publishers, 2000), 325.

38. Marzulli, *Nephilim*,110.

39. Caldwell, *We All Fall Down*, 98, 111.

40. The *Thief in the Night* films were exclusively disseminated among believers in explicitly proselytizing contexts to help scare the audience into the 'altar call'. Randall Balmer, *Mine Eyes Have Seen the Glory* (New York: Oxford University Press, 1989), 62. As such, they differ in kind from later works mass-marketed for entertainment. For example, the second *Left Behind* film's copyright warning explicitly bars unauthorized church viewings and their equivalents.

41. Cloud Ten also produced the *Left Behind* films. Another company, TBN Films, produced *The Omega Code* films, in which the Bible becomes an acrostic of prophecy.

42. Phillips, *Rift in Time*, 68-69.

Unto
(Rose Window, Ste-Chapelle, Paris)

Thomas MacKay

Smiling the logos-smile, sword in the mouth, owed reverence as the fierc-
est calamity, he comes, and the world unclasps into stray petals around
him.

Poppy red, the glass here is framed against thick
arms of stone; each flicker of a scene stands
as a shimmering piece that meets its puzzle like an astronaut meets space.

The supplicant and his tree see the sword-tongued Christ
in an island torn precisely from the landscape
so as to be designed to fit there. A mosaic place
for all things, the vertigo of metonymy.
Maybe the figure is not praying but reeling, giddy in an
orgasm of absent mindedness: where did he put his life?
Where are his symbols and prayers,
his home, his family?

Can he understand the last tree shading him? It is a monster now,
singular, uncorroborated by forests or natural histories. Could he return
home
and find any comfort in old soft clothes? They are
hard now, strange and forceful in their indifference.
The pattern of a tea cup against sudden blinding light in the window:
sick painted thumb.
The grasping, bully wrong not of the end
but of the end's shadow and shine.

What is the prayer at the fused centre of convention?

In one sound, round and bronze like the sex of a trumpet,
such a soul will bend and break itself,
not in a prayer but an act of escaping surrender.

Part V
Tense

tasis: a stretching, not *stasis*, standing, though stasis by equilibrium of opposing forces...

Cameron's game, like poetry, suggests that revelations, apocalyptic, individualistic, and otherwise, are best found not in the quest for truth but rather at the interstices of thought and words. As Cameron once said, it is the tendons of society that need attending to, the betwixt and between where new imaginings arise from ideas that collide. As MacKay writes,

> I move too much to know where to sit, and
> I sit too long to know if I should move –

Always in motion, the millennial moment slips between words and worlds, stretching across boundaries and definitions as it stands between opposing forces, a tension between the implied and the perceived, where meaning is created in the middle.

C.G.

Y2KO to Y2OK*

Charles Cameron

The other day, I found out the name for someone who does what I do. I'm a 'forensic theologian'. Stephen Grey introduced the term in 'Follow the Mullahs', an article in the *Atlantic Monthly* for November 2004. It refers to someone who analyzes the religious content of intelligence data:

> The analyst is engaged in a new and increasingly important aspect of the fight against terrorism—one that might be called forensic theology. Authenticating terrorist documents is just one of its uses. It can also help identify perpetrators, and targets for surveillance, sometimes far more effectively than conventional intelligence practices. Its greatest potential, however, may be strategic: with theologians at the center of the battle, forensic theology may help us pinpoint the groups that present the greatest threat.

I have been monitoring 'open source intelligence' for indicators of apocalyptic activity as an associate with the Center for Millennial Studies for a decade or so, and during the year 1999 rollover, I was Senior Analyst with The Arlington Institute and Principal Researcher with the CMS, tracking both sacred and secular indicators with a special view to the potential social impact of the date change.

I am also the designer of a family of thinking tools known collectively as the HipBone Games. These games derive from my interest in the Glass Bead Game as described in Hermann Hesse's *Das Glasperlenspiel* (1943), for which he was awarded the Nobel Prize in Literature in 1946.

The essence of Hesse's Game is the juxtaposition of ideas (which may be textual, numerical, musical, or visual) as if they were themes in a fugue:

> A Game, for example, might start from a given astronomical configuration, or from the actual theme of a Bach fugue, or from a sentence out of Leibniz or the Upanishads, and from this theme, depending on the intentions and talents of the player, it could either further explore and elaborate the initial motif or else enrich its expressiveness by allusions to kindred concepts.

Playable derivatives of Hesse's Game, then, will be games *sui generis*, playful in a sense closer to that in which one plays an organ than to that in which one plays football, perhaps. Analytic games such as the one presented here, also have kinship with such 'serious' game genres as wargames

and the 'game theoretic' games used in modeling conflict and coopera-
tion, Prisoner's Dilemma and the like. The entire enterprise, indeed, might
come under the aegis of Ficino's motto, *Studiossime ludere*, to play most
assiduously.

The HipBone Games are 'played' by graphically 'mapping' relevant
concepts onto a board, using the analogies (both parallelisms and oppositions) between them to provide the connective tissue in which the pith of
the game resides. What follows, then, is the *score* of a piece in what I have
termed the 'virtual music of ideas'. The piece has already been played, in
the sense that I built up this polyphony of quotes and anecdotes during
my years of research into Y2K and related matters. It can be played again,
in the reader's mind, by first reading the series of 'moves' or 'beads' and
then visualizing them in juxtaposition as indicated by their respective
positions and linkages on the various small boards and final board found
in the figures of this text.

The first part of this mental replay, reading the text, will allow the
reader to glimpse the diversity of issues swirling around the simple change
of a date via a list of representative quotes and anecdotes—conveying
something of the complexity of the event, and of its human qualities. But
that is no more than to read a list, an index: the essence of the game is
found when these quotes and anecdotes are held in the mind in tension,
in counterpoint. It is John Hamre's 'cold sweat' (Move 7) at the thought of
how difficult the Y2K transition might be which gives context for the Dalai
Lama's comment that the rollover is 'nothing special' – a calm which must
have been sorely tried by his knowledge that his colleague the Karmapa
Lama was engaged in a dangerous escape from Tibet across the Himala-
yas at the time...

Lines on the board connecting different moves are intended to correspond to associative and analogical linkages between the moves themselves. It may help to consider the moves as pebbles thrown into a pond,
or stones in a zen sand-garden: what is significant here is not so much the
individual stones as the ripples between them...

In developing and deploying these games in a millennial context, I was
heartened to find Hesse's own keen discussion of apocalypticism in his
novel, where he discusses the work of Swabian Pietist theologian Johann
Albrecht Bengel (1687–1752), who 'devoted years of study to the Revelation of St. John' and devised a 'system...for interpreting its prophecies'.
Joseph Knecht, the future Master of the Game, comments,

> what Bengel lacked, and unconsciously longed for, was the Glass Bead
> Game. You see, I consider him among the secret forerunners and ancestors
> of our Game.

and also:

> if Bengel had possessed a system similar to that offered by our Game, he probably would have been spared all the misguided effort involved in his calculation of the prophetic numbers and his annunciation of the Antichrist and the Millennial Kingdom...

I was also delighted to be able to trace conceptual mapping—the visual representation of ideas and their connections—all the way back to the apocalyptic diagrams of Joachim of Fiore, some eight centuries ago, as studied by Marjorie Reeves and Beatrice Hirsch-Reich, *The Figurae of Joachim of Fiore* (Oxford: Clarendon Press, 1972).

The game I present here, then, is an analytic game, using HipBone 'moves' and 'links' to offer two dozen of the more interesting quotes, facts and anecdotes I ran across during the Y2K period, not in the course of a reasoned argument but as 'stars' in 'constellation'. It makes no claim to provide a definition of Y2K, or to touch on all the important details of that extraordinary, world-girdling event and non-event. It is polyphonic, speaking with many voices and setting them in counterpoint to one another rather than arguing with one or against another. It is a free-spirited, non-authoritative collage, or perhaps a pointillist rendition, capturing my own personal sense of the ideas in play and the tensions between them. It is a work of contemplation. It is a record of events and thoughts. It is a game.

I invite you to build your own architecture out of the analogical connections between these ideas, like arches rising from the game-board as from an architect's blueprint. Hold the whole in your mind's eye, and you will perhaps glimpse something of the welter of significant details in search of a central meaning that was Y2K.

Each move consists of a move title, the move content (a text, quote, anecdote), and a diagram with suggested links to one or more other moves. I shall briefly hint at the links in the text between moves, leaving much to the reader's imagination. I shall also post a more detailed hypertext version of the game at http://www.beadgaming.com/CMSY2K.html—with more links between ideas, a more complex version of the board, and further commentary.

Enjoy. We begin with move 1...

Move 1: On the threshold

> Its bow in one year, its stern in another, the U.S.S. Topeka marked the new millennium 400 feet beneath the international date line in the Pacific Ocean. The Pearl Harbor-based Navy submarine straddled the line, meaning that at midnight, one end was in 2000 while the other was still in

1999… The 360-foot-long sub, which was 2,100 miles from Honolulu, Hawaii, straddled the equator at the same time, meaning it was in both the Northern and Southern hemispheres. Some of the 130 crew members were in winter in the north, while others were in summer in the south. Many took small water samples to keep as mementos, the Navy said. 'Words can't describe the feeling', said Lt. Michael Bratton of Little Rock, Arkansas. 'It's better than Times Square…' Patton said the Topeka's position was not just a publicity stunt. He says that positioning the sub along the date line submerged demonstrated the Navy's confidence that it's ready to handle the Y2K computer bug… 'Topeka was probably one of the safest places to be for Y2K', he said.

Straddling Two Years: One Sub
Auckland, New Zealand
31 December, 1999, Associated Press
http://www.cbsnews.com/stories/1999/12/31/archive/main144846.shtml

USS Topeka is a vessel worth roughly $1billion, and its presence where the equator meets the deadline at midnight as one millennium rolled over into another was no mistake, but a PR decision which reflected the ritual bonding principle known to anthropologists as liminality. Y2K occurring at the end and beginning of millennia, centuries, decades, years, months and even days, stands on the threshold between them. Liminal or threshold situations have the potential to stir deep, archetypal feelings in the human psyche, as our next move illustrates:

Move 2: Eyes sewn shut

Concord, New Hampshire (AP)—A prison inmate sewed his eyes and lips shut with dental floss because he feared the new year, officials said. New Hampshire State Prison guards found the inmate, who was serving time for cocaine possession, covered in baby powder and clutching a Bible on Friday night, said Mark Wefers, chief of internal investigations at the prison. 'The inmate told corrections officers he was in fear of the new year', Wefers said.

Prison inmate fearing millennium sews eyes, lips shut
2 January, 2000
http://cnn.com/2000/US/01/02/eyes.sewed.shut.ap/index.html

The inmate in question may well have conceived the idea of sewing his eyes shut after viewing the pilot episode of *Millennium*, Chris Carter's follow-up to the *X-Files*, which featured a serial killer who buried one victim up to his neck, after sewing his eyes and mouth shut—and this would be the content of our third move. *Humankind*, as T.S. Eliot famously said, *cannot bear too much reality*.

Move 3: Carter's Millennium

> Stalking the gay cruising scene for his next victim, the killer is lost in a
> warped world of hallucinations, surrounded by passers-by with eyes and
> mouths gruesomely sewn shut. Alerted by sudden insight, Frank leads the
> cops to their most horrifying discovery: a man buried alive, his eyes and
> mouth sewn shut, his fingertips roughly amputated.
>
> Millennium website, pilot show, Chris Carter for Fox TV
> http://www.foxworld.com/millnium/epi100.htm

The psychic impact of looking towards the new millennium runs strong
and deep, whether we see it portrayed in the entertainment media, in a
prisoner's stylized attempt at denial, or in the actions of a ship's captain in
the US Navy.

Our board thus far:

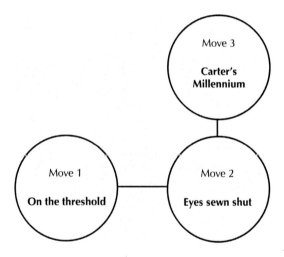

We now have a feel for the intensity of the psychic event: let's take a
look at the breadth of the thing:

Move 4: The whole enchilada

> As you'll notice, we call our project the Year 2000 International Security
> Dimension Project – not the Y2K International Security Dimension Pro-
> ject. Why? It's our firm contention that DoD should view the Millennial
> Date Change Event as comprising a constellation of simultaneously
> unfolding elements, of which Y2K is clearly the most important. Our draft
> list of globally significant pieces to this puzzle would begin as follows:

- Year 2000 computer problem (e.g., software and embedded chips) in and of itself
- Y2K—the global remediation effort and all that it entails
- Y2K as a global education process regarding the pervasiveness of 'all this invisible technology'
- Y2K as a global crisis management challenge and economic threat
- Global economy just coming off a period of significant widespread turmoil (e.g., the Asian Financial Crisis of 1997 and its subsequent spread to Russia and Brazil), resulting in significant reform efforts by many of the affected countries
- Millennial Event in its largely secular form, i.e., the 'world's largest party ever'
- Millennial Event in its religious form, i.e., celebrating the onset of the Third Millennium since Christ's birth
- Millennial Event in its sociopolitical form, i.e., marking a milestone period in the planet's history during which political leaders, as well as ordinary citizens, engage in extraordinary debate regarding the status quo and what should logically follow
- Millennial Event in its extremist form, i.e., the strong assumption by some in society that the event will usher in profound and cataclysmic global change, typically associated with apocalyptic visions involving a deity or supernatural force
- Tendency of humans to seek grand unifying theories for periods of human history that involve above-average levels of complexity, and utilize those theories as guides for self-perceived 'strategic' action.

Year 2000 International Security Dimension Project Report
Dr Thomas P.M. Barnett, US Naval War College
http://www.nwc.navy.mil/y2k/y2krep1.html

That's the bigger picture as it faced me in my first month with The Arlington Institute, when I attended a session of Dr Barnett's 'gaming' Project at the Naval War College. It is teaching interconnectedness, the theme that unites E.M. Forster with Donald Rumsfeld and Gregory Bateson with A.-L. Barabasi.

Move 5: Increasingly interconnected

If you learn something at this website about what Y2K may yet teach us about the nature of such potential system crises as we become increasingly interconnected and interdependent in a global, information-driven New Economy, then great, for in that case we've provided you the same service we set out to provide to US Government decision makers—namely, opening up their thinking to the full range of possible dynamics, outcomes, and legacies connected to Y2K and the Millennium Date Change Event.

If, however, you insist on leaving here full of fear and anguish (e.g., the military obvious [sic] knows more than it's telling us!), then you miss the entire point of this exercise, which we basically liken to checking your blindspot before switching lanes while driving.

Year 2000 International Security Dimension Project
Dr Thomas P.M. Barnett, US Naval War College
http://www.nwc.navy.mil/y2k/y2krep1.html

Y2K faced us with the intricate weave of the world…a weave that crosses over, not merely between the electric grid and transportation, or just-in-time logistics and military force projection, but across the Cartesian divide between mind and body, perception and reality…

Move 6: Lightning

Y2K is like a lightning bolt: when it strikes and lights up the sky, we will see the contours of our social systems.

Don Beck, National Values Center/The Spiral Dynamics Group, Denton, TX, private communication

The lightning struck and failed to strike, a team from the Mitre Corporation produced a voluminous report on what the material and social connectivity of the world boded in case of significant Y2K computer failures, we got our first major glimpse of the world weave, and very little of what we saw took place in the event. The possibilities were indeed disturbing.
    How serious might it be?

Move 7: Cold sweat

Deputy Defense Secretary John Hamre, the Pentagon's Y2K point man, has acknowledged the difficulty of predicting the impact of the problem on such a vast network. 'Probably one out of five days I wake up in a cold sweat, thinking Y2K is going to be much bigger than we thought', Hamre testified before Congress. 'The other four days I think maybe we really are on top of it. Everything is so interconnected, it's very hard to know with any precision that we've got it fixed.'

James Kitfield , Y2K Clock Is Ticking
Government Executive Magazine, August 1999
http://www.govexec.com/features/99top/08a99s15.htm

And that brings us to our second stopping point, with a sense of what was facing us, how varied the strands were, what they portended in terms of our understanding of the world around us, and how serious it might turn out to be…

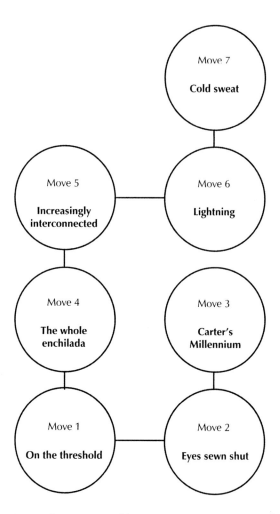

But then again, perhaps it wouldn't prove so serious at all. The Dalai Lama didn't seem flustered…

Move 8: Nothing special

> Many people seem to be excited about the new millennium, but the new millennium in itself will be nothing special. As we enter into the new millennium things will be the same; there will be nothing unusual. However, if we really want the next millennium to be happier, more peaceful and more harmonious for humankind we will have to make the effort to make it so. This is in our hands, but especially in the hands of the younger generation.

We have had many experiences during this century—constructive as well as extremely destructive ones. We must learn from these experiences. We need to approach the next millennium more holistically, with more openness and farsightedness.

His Holiness the Dalai Lama, 1 January, 2000
http://hhdl.dharmakara.net/HHDL2000.html

If anything, the world of Tibetan lamas must have been worried and excited by a very different event taking place as the year 1999 rolled over into 2000: the escape of the young Karmapa, one of the most senior Tibetan lamas, across the roof of the world…

Move 9: Karmapa's escape

On December 28, 1999, under the cover of a dark night, my senior attendant and I escaped from my monastery in Tibet and fled to India to seek refuge… On December 28, around 10:30 at night, my attendant and I slowly climbed down from my room and jumped onto the roof of the Protector Mahakala's shrine room. From this building, we leapt to the ground where a jeep was waiting nearby with Lama Tsultrim and a driver… Driving day and night, we stopped only to change drivers. By taking back roads through the hills and valleys, we evaded check posts and two army camps. Through the power of my prayers to the Buddha and through his compassion, we were not discovered and arrived in Mustang, Nepal, on the morning of December 30, 1999. Continuing the journey on foot and horseback, we crossed over several passes and finally reached Manang as I had planned… Once in Manang, a close friend of Lama Tsewang Tashi helped us hire a helicopter. We landed in a place of Nepal known as Nagarkot and then went by car to Rauxal. From there, we traveled by train to Lucknow and continued with a rented car to Delhi, arriving at last in Dharamsala early on the morning of January 5, 2000.

Press Statement, HH the 17th Karmapa Lama, 27 April, 2001
http://www.kagyuoffice.org/karmapa.reference.officialreleases.010427State ment.html

Other religions had other timelines, and part of the fascination of the event had to do with the fact that both Hinduism and Judaism had groups who considered the years immediately surrounding *our* millennial rollover as religiously significant in terms of their own calendars.

Move 10: Kala Jnana

> Sri Krishna thus announced His arrival in each age at the nadir of Dharma
> (righteousness) with the aim of protecting the virtuous and destroying the
> evil-doers. In accordance with His promise, He has now re-incarnated as
> the the [*sic*] lord of Chaturdasha Bhuvanas (14 worlds) as announced by
> the Divya Maha Kala Jnana written by Jagad Guru Srimad Virat Potaluru
> Veera Brahmendra Maha Swami, who lived in Kandi Mallayya Palli of
> modern Andhra Pradesh, India, about 1000 years ago. The Kala Jnana (lit-
> erally, Knowledge of Time) describes the events which will occur before
> the arrival of Kali Purusha (Kalki Avatara) Sree Sree Sree Veera Bhoga
> Vasantaraya Maha Swami by the year Kali 5101 (1999 CE).

> Kala Jnana Home Page
> http://web.archive.org/web/19990203033325/http://www.wp.com/
> KalaJnana/

And…

Move 11: Mikvah

> What made Y2K such a source of concern for the believing Jew was two
> ominous predictions from centuries ago regarding the year of Y2K:

> 240 years before the Seventh Millennium, the Lower Waters will rise up
> and cover the entire world, and only Israel will remain, which will float on
> the surface of the water like Noah's ark. They will approach the Garden of
> Eden, the place from which the Four Rivers emanate…' (Rokayach—'Gali
> Razyah', twelfth century)

> The amount [of undrawn water] necessary for a mikvah [to be kosher] is
> [a volume equal to the displacement of] 5,760 eggs. The secret regarding
> this is that, at the end of the year 5760 from creation, the verse, 'I [God]
> will remove the impure spirit from the land' (Zechariah 13.2) will be
> fulfilled, as well as the verse, 'I will give peace in the land, and you will lie
> down, and no one will make you tremble; and I will remove the evil beasts
> from the land..'. (Leviticus 26.6); that is, the forces of spiritual impurity, as
> is mentioned in the Zohar. (Avraham Azulai—'Chesed L'Avraham' Nahar
> 59, B'Sod Mikvah, 88)

> Rabbi Pinchas Winston, Current Events and Kabbalah
> http://www.aish.com/spirituality/kabbala101/Current_Events_and_Kabbalah_
> -_Part_1.asp

Islam had a more complex response to the millennial date:

Move 12: Islamic apocalyptic

The year 2000 is a Christian date that should have no apocalyptic significance for Muslims, and especially not Islamists; it corresponds to the years 1422-23 in the Muslim calendar. Nonetheless, many Muslims believe it is a significant date for Jews (for whom in actuality it is meaningless), and have therefore ascribed to it a demonic significance as the date when Jews intend to rebuild the Temple—which they assume means pulling down the Dome of the Rock and Al-Aqsa Mosque.

How have Muslims come to attach the year 2000 to such momentous events? Da'ud points to a speech by Dan Shomron, a former Israeli chief of the general staff, who told the graduates of an Israeli war college that 'in the year 2000 we will see the growth of a new leadership'. Da'ud assumes this to be a reference to the dajjal, 'since he is their messiah and their king, whom they are expecting in the year 2000 to build them the Temple'.

David Cook, 'Muslim Fears of the Year 2000'
Middle East Quarterly (1998), 5.2.
http://www.meforum.org/article/397

And to return to the western perspective, still bearing religious influence in mind, Christians had been thinking about this sort of thing for a thousand years...

Move 13: Year 1000

Dum saeculum transit finis mundi appropinquat... [As the saeculum (century?) passes, the end of the world approaches.]

Cartulaire de Saint-Jouin-de-Marnes, 964 CE
The Apocalyptic Dossier: 967-1033
http://www.mille.org/scholarship/1000/1000-dos.html

The single most striking pair of religious documents I ran across in my monitoring of the entire rollover period both came from unexpected sources. First, the FBI issued a report on potential extremist Christian responses to the millennium, including commentary on the terminology and imagery of the book of Revelation:

Move 14: Megiddo report

Domestic terrorist groups who place religious significance on the millennium believe the federal government will act as an arm of Satan in the final battle. By extension, the FBI is viewed as acting on Satan's behalf.

The philosophy behind targeting the federal government or entities perceived to be associated with it is succinctly described by Kerry Noble, a former right-wing extremist. He says the right-wing 'envision[s] a dark and gloomy endtime scenario, where some Antichrist makes war against Christians'. The House of Yahweh, a Texas-based religious group whose leaders are former members of the tax-protesting Posse Comitatus, is typical: Hawkins (the leader) has interpreted biblical scripture that the Israeli Peace Accord signed on October 13, 1993, has started a 7-year period of tribulation which will end on October 14, 2000, with the return of the Yeshua (the Messiah). He also has interpreted that the FBI will be the downfall of the House of Yahweh and that the Waco Branch David-ian raids in 1993 were a warning to The House of Yahweh from the federal government, which he terms 'the beast'.

Project Megiddo, FBI Report, October 1999.
http://permanent.access.gpo.gov/lps3578/www.fbi.gov/library/megiddo/megiddo.pdf

And then the American Banking Association issued, of all things, a sermon.

Move 15: Mammon's sermon

ABA has developed this generic 'Y2K sermon' for bankers to share with members of the clergy as a way to calm people's concerns over the Jan. 1 date change. A sermon is a very personal means of communication. This one cannot possibly cover all religions or speaking styles, nor is it in-tended to. However, by sharing this sermon with a minister, priest or rabbi, you can generate interest in the Y2K topic and enlist their help in calming peoples' fears and concerns.

Thinking about Y2K: Moses, Orson Welles and Bill Gates
Sermon published by American Bankers Association, August 1999.
http://www.reclaimingwalther.org/articles/-400/jmc00065.htm

The New Testament describes apocalyptic times in terms of wars and rumors of wars, and the approach of Y2K made the banking industry somewhat concerned about bank runs and rumors of bank runs—con-cerned enough to issue that somewhat unlikely sermon, but what fasci-nating me was the generalized formula—*x and rumors of x*—with its implication that the distinction between perception and reality, mind and world, can evaporate in time of apocalyptic sensibility.

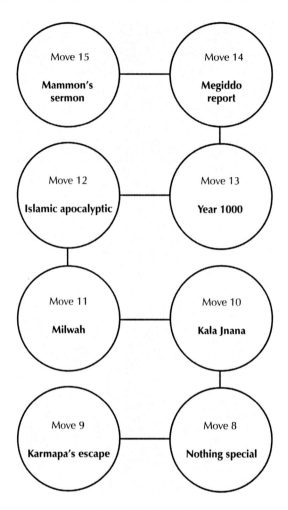

Let's turn to the 'event' itself, and begin with the worst case scenario:

Move 16: Y2KO

'Y2 KO!' refers to the Worst Case Scenario, meaning Y2K is big and bad and we're far more vulnerable than we realized. We are collectively 'knocked to the mat', with the real uncertainty being, do we get back up before the 'referee' finishes his 'count?' Or do we lie there prostrate, dazed and confused? Of course, at some point we do get up, and how humanity emerges on the far side of this crisis is largely determined by the nature of the 'knockout'. Is Y2K merely a 'TKO', meaning a 'knockout' attributed solely to 'technical' failures? Or is Y2K a genuine 'whupping' where all our systems (political, economic, social, and network) fail us miserably? In other words, are we merely embarrassed and so continue on as before? Or are we truly humbled and thus serious changes result?

Thomas Barnett, Year 2000 International Security Dimension Project Report
http://www.geocities.com/ResearchTriangle/Thinktank/6926/NWCY2000
Report.pdf

I seem to recall Y2KO was my own contribution to Dr Barnett's scenario planning workshop. Breakdown of the electrical grid? Failure of transportation systems? Pockets of famine? Militia uprisings and a hundred Wacos? Russian missiles launched by computer error? It is as difficult to spell out in detail what a cluster of Y2K failures and their ripple-through impact on life as we know it might have been, so let us just say that the acronym TEOTWAWKI – for 'the end of the world as we know it' was a popular phrase at the time.

There were early warning signals...

Move 17: Year 2000

In January of 1970, mortgage officers found something amusing. They would calculate the monthly payments of a thirty (30) year mortgage and the computer returned an error. The ending date of the thirty year mortgage, January 00, is an invalid date. This was probably the first known instance of Y2K showing itself up. In short, banks have known of Y2K for almost thirty (30) years now.

Y2K: Fact or Fiction
http://star2.abcm.com/~thrill/y2k.htm

Which didn't help a whole lot...

Move 18: Fixing the problem

When D.O.D. lobbying kept that appeal from reaching the Oval Office, Bemer recruited the presidential science advisor, Edward E. David, to plead the case in person. Nixon listened, then asked for help fixing his TV set.

Robert Sam Anson, The Y2K Nightmare, *Vanity Fair*, January 1999
http://www.bobbemer.com/anson.htm

There were various attempts to peer into the crystal ball and scry the future by means of games—another distinction getting blurred is that between games and realities. There was an Arlington Institute role playing game at the Center for Strategic and International Studies:

Move 19: TAI game

> In addition to primary roles that people will play, a handful of players will
> be asked to adopt a secondary trait such as 'conspiracy theorist', or 'quietly
> concerned about the environment'. We added this element to the game
> because people are complex decision-makers, guided by more than one
> set of values, goals, and beliefs. The head of the Boy Scout troop could also
> be obsessed with his large stock portfolio; the fire chief could be a religious
> fundamentalist anxiously expecting the new millennium.
>
> Be bold and innovative with your interpretation of the roles.
>
> Countdown to Y2K: A Game of Perception, The Arlington Institute, 1999
> http://www.arlingtoninstitute.org

with which it is instructive to compare Steve Jackson's GURPS role playing
supplement for Y2K, published for the entertainment role playing market:

Move 20: GURPS game

> Millennial Magic
>
> Even if the computers weather 2000 without a hitch, our preoccupation
> with the millennium could be strong enough to invoke Cabbalistic power
> all by itself. As we approach and live through year 2000, those who use the
> Gregorian calendar will be thinking about the date. Billions of souls world-
> wide focused on one number could work some powerful magic, and if the
> dominant emotion is millennial apprehension, it might not be good magic…
>
> What all this implies is up to the GM… Y2K could be the year that the
> Illuminati take their rightful place as the Overlords of Humanity… Do
> Jewish, Islamic, or Christian factions have big plans for the Holy City? Will
> Israel be recognized as a world power? Tying it all together, perhaps the
> Illuminati will be behind events in the Middle East that will ultimately lead
> to escalating war and Armageddon (p. 120). Given the current political
> situation in the real world, this doesn't seem so far-fetched…
>
> GURPS Y2K: The Countdown to Armageddon, Steve Jackson Games
> http://www.amazon.com/exec/obidos/tg/detail/-/1556344066/

There were attempts to head off the worst of the worst, with their own
internal Y2K problems:

Move 21: Nuclear cooperation

> The Center will consist of two Russian officers sitting alongside a US mili-
> tary officer and a senior US civilian officer, who will be in voice communi-
> cation with the US early warning command center, NORAD, inside nearby

Cheyenne Mountain. Plans call for the Center to operate from December 27 to January 6. Russian facilities will be linked to the Center by voice networks.

However, the United States and Russia have since identified Y2K problems that would prevent the full operation of all but one of the existing seven direct communications links, or 'hotlines', that guarantee immediate communications between US and Russian leaders.

Y2K and Nuclear Arsenals: A Final Report
Michael Kraig, British American Security Information Council,
http://www.basicint.org/pubs/Research/1999-Y2Kpart4.htm#Russian

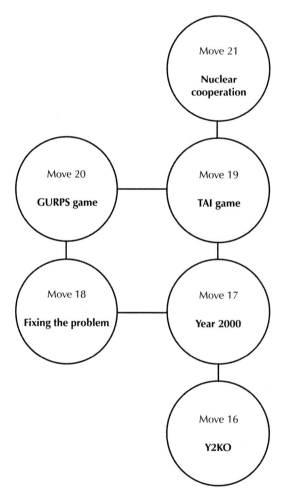

And in the event, there was a resounding non-event.

Move 22: Y2OK

> Slot machines in Delaware, customs offices in Gambia, and some temporary blindness for Uncle Sam's spy satellites. Such is the awful, actual toll of the Y2K bug. The feds likely got their money's worth with the $8 billion spent on Y2K readiness. For the private sector, the tens of billions spent on new software should pay off in productivity gains later.

> Y2OK – only minor glitches in Y2K readiness but upgraded software should lead to productivity gains
> Jeff A. Taylor, Reason magazine, March 2000

This was, after all, a man-made apocalypse, and we are not always the most ruthlessly efficient of species:

Move 23: Man-made Apocalypse

> No single issue more exquisitely expresses the irony of post-modern culture: all the elements of an apocalyptic prophecy without a deity, the man-made Apocalypse at the end of the man-made millennium.

> Richard Landes, Owls and Roosters: Y2K and Millennium's End
> http://www.mille.org/people/rlpages/Y2K-CLTR.html

But then we have the 'there but for the grace of God go I' factor. The truth is that at least two events that had been scheduled for the rollover happily failed to take place at that time—if they had, the dawn of the year 2000 would have felt very different.

Move 24: Ten Commandments

> Kanungu, Uganda, April 2 – The police say he appears to be the only survivor, and today Peter Ahimbisibwe, 17, said members of a doomsday cult in Uganda began to rise at church services after January 1 and to ask cult leaders a difficult question.

> Where will we live, Mr Ahimbisibwe said they asked, now that we have sold our property and the world has not ended, as the cult had predicted?

> 'The people who sold their property would inquire one by one', Mr Ahimbisibwe said. 'Whoever would inquire, they would disappear.'

> Mr Ahimbisibwe allowed himself to be interviewed for only a few minutes and did so reluctantly just before a large prayer service here today in memory of the 924 cult members whose bodies have been discovered in recent days. After the service, he refused to talk further unless reporters paid him.

Uganda Survivor Tells of Questions When World Didn't End
Ian Fisher, New York Times, 3 April, 2000
http://www.cesnur.org/testi/uganda_022.htm

I was briefly interviewed on MSNBC about an hour before the rollover was complete in Washington, and drank champagne shortly thereafter to celebrate a successful transition. There would surely have been some mixed feelings if the rollover had been accompanied by the Jonestown-like immolation of 400 members of the Movement for the Restoration of the Ten Commandments of God (and related deaths of hundred more) in Uganda, an event which was delayed by divine providence until a less media-intensive date in April of 2000.

And there would have been intense mourning rather than celebration if Ressam had made it to LA…

Move 25: 9/11 in 1999

In December 1999, Ahmed Ressam was arrested at the US-Canadian border with a carload of explosives. Ressam is an Algerian who was living in Canada and he was convicted of plotting a millennium-eve attack on Los Angeles International Airport.

Armed Islamic group, MIPT Terrorism Knowledge Base
http://www.tkb.org/Group.jsp?groupID=27

The real implication of all this is that the 'Y2K event'—the signal disruption which would change our world and bring into focus the tenuousness of all those interconnections—didn't *not* happen, it was postponed, and we know by another acronym:

Move 26: 1999 at 9/11

Y2K is…a new type of crisis that leaves us particularly uncomfortable with its lack of a clearly identifiable 'enemy' or 'threat' with associated motivations.

Our bottom line (paraphrasing Rick in Casablanca): We'll always have Y2K…

Except of course, now we call it '9/11'.

Thomas Barnett, section from The Pentagon's New Map MS deleted during editing
http://www.thomaspmbarnett.com/delscenes/scene16.htm

That's it, that's my personal version of the many faces of Y2K.

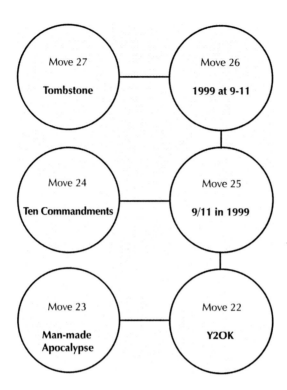

I want to leave you now with an image which isn't about computers, but represents an analogous 1999/2000 date-change problem, and is in its own way darkly humorous…

Move 27: Tombstone

Enough of the Year 2000 computer bug. Now comes the Year 2000 buga-boo: expired tombstones.

The dawning of the new millennium might be a bit inconvenient, not to mention costly, for those forward-thinking people who long ago inscribed their gravestones with expected death dates of 19– .

'I spend a lot of time in cemeteries, and believe me, there are hundreds of thousands' of such tombstones, declares Clyde Chamberlin, 69, who's spending his retirement publishing a newsletter, Solitude in Stone, filled with pictures of unusual gravestones.

Y2K—Presents a Grave Problem for Many Tombstones
Maria Puente, *USA Today*, March 1999
http://www.rense.com/ufo3/y2kprobfmany.htm

Here's the complete game board.

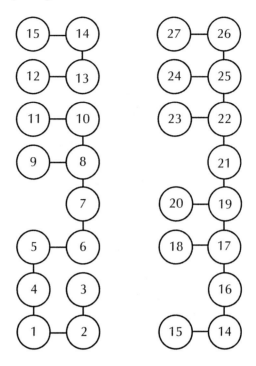

For the more detailed version of this game with commentary, please go to http://www.beadgaming.com/CMSY2K.html.

Until next time…

Note

*   Websites cited were operative as of their respective dates of collection, but may not be operative by time of publication of this volume. In some cases, webpages that are no longer available at their original URLs may be located via the 'wayback machine' at http://www.archive.org/web/web.php.

Cloister

Thomas MacKay

A monk moves quietly, that the leaves not turn and stare—God
is in them, wells as deep as cold columns are high,
up-arched—he could fall in them, into the sprawl,
the circuit of petals more full than a wine of every sky

—don't open your eyes O God, do not wake and burn and
write me into your book—
unready, I move too much to know where to sit, and
I sit too long to know if I should move—

His cell lies behind the tall dark of walls, shaped by the sky
as radiance shapes the sure brows of saints; enclosed,
the gardens rustle with a wind from the mountains, and the monk
stops, terrified.

A lantern has been left lit, and around it,
white roses sit awake and eager;
they eat the light and grin it outwards again
and he cannot move out from their eyes!

Respite

Thomas MacKay

Can we rest here? Where the gray land splits
gently, without some optical lesson.

I have bread made for me, somewhere,
and my feet are hot with the walking.

While chewing, I am able to think, think that
it scares but we still move long into the night

sure of the small drinking sounds of the river, or
of the cold against the coat, or—

Or: even the idea of surety can flee, figurative,
and sweet; might I turn from my small words, and see the crisis,

the inability to love or to revenge past solitude? Might I see
the nattering of dying and treat it like children's voices

playing outside the window I can hardly see? Or
will it always be this fantasy, this final piece of alone:

alone, yes, but in a room of screaming colour,
of tall, tall torrents—

Part VI
Ex/tension

Come to the final physical pages of this volume, we take up the end of the world as a particular physical geography. As much as the millennial is accomplished through time, it has as well its favorite places, which are at once ex/tensions and projections. Ex/tensions: land's ends that nearly everywhere are extended offshore by legends of sunken cities or ghostly remnants of perfected civilizations audible or visible at certain sweeps of tide; pyramids and space needles that intimate at destinies miles higher or galaxies away. Projections: of cultural space, unbidden or latent energies. Here in Part VI, Michelle Dent tackles Seattle's ageing Space Needle, built for the Century 21 World's Fair in 1962 and desperately in need of another world of tomorrow once the twenty-first century had dawned despite Y2K the Computer Fix and Election 2000 the Rigged Victory. Dent investigates a scheme to move the Space Needle, which she understands as an apocalyptic scheme, for like other more explosive apocalypses it would have obliterated a landmark, excised a memory site, eliminated a locality of hopefulness in the name of statewide rejuvenation. How strikingly similar this apocalypse to that feared in the 1999 Battle in Seattle against the globalizing practices of the World Trade Organization, whose policies (said thousands of protesters who came to Seattle from around the world) were displacing or distancing people from their sacred places and destroying homelands or homeland security in the name of global capitalism…and how very complementary to the hegemony of Microsoft in Redmond just outside Seattle, whose digital billionaires ex/(press)alt the no-place of a monopolized virtuality. Apocalypse then as anticipated absence, removal with no Rapture.

Obversely, there is Jerusalem, a sacred center to three religions that is also, by virtue of its contested tombs and perimeters, its ruins and museums, its politically volatile Temple on the Mount, its overlook of the Dead Sea, and its proximity to the plain of Megiddo, an *ultima thule*, a place on the edge of wild(er)ness, a place beyond which can lie only Hell, the Millennium, or the great Vanishing: ex/tension as the *ex* of a once-and-future greatness, as the *x* of the unknown, as the site of humanity's exit. Anchor of the antique and locus of final judgment, Jerusalem is generating station to the antenna of the Space Needle. As Hillel Schwartz might argue in his essay on Jerusalem, the city represents not so much millennial accomplishment as a millennial project, a New Jerusalem stretched across millennia, in which are concentrated all the tensions touched upon throughout this work. 'I want a current of other places', writes Thomas MacKay, as if in summary, 'I want/this little finale of place, the world the sum of air and light…' and always, as with everything millennial, a little more.

H.S.

The Space Needle Hits the Road:
The Portability of Home, Landmark, and Memorial

Michelle Dent

Homesickness

Like most people within contemporary global culture who are separated from kith and kin by the dreams, necessities, and vagaries of working toward a better life, my mother and I share a long distance relationship that is mediated by the technological proxies of the Information Age. Through daily e-mail exchanges, intermittent cell-phone updates, and the more customary tradition of Sunday evening phone calls, we stitch together a discursive cloth that redefines our previously held understanding of this thing called home. This is good: for without the interconnectivity of web and wire, we would be caught in the intergenerational disappointment and guilt of a mother's steady stream of weekly letters against the slower trickle of her daughter's quarterly responses.

At the same time, I am also aware that we are piecing together a record of artifact (a time capsule) that captures the poignancy and tedium of everyday life in contemporary global culture. While at its most basic our correspondence is a means of creating intimacy in the face of a deadening geographical void, it is also a means of documenting and archiving the emergence of newly imagined cultural spaces that extend far beyond the realm of our own family's domain. This new space that we have built is a place in which countless others increasingly find themselves, and it is located at the interstices of travel, dislocation, memory, loss, hope, and malaise. In our particular case, it is the circuit we have come to travel between the temperate rainforests that give topographical definition to the Emerald City, and the granite bedrock out of which the gritty caverns of Gotham have been carved.

In all of this, my mother has frequently been obliged to learn what those of us who are academically inclined *do*. To her credit, she has at times traipsed alongside me through research sessions at assorted libraries, festivals, civic events, and museums, and in this sense she has also unwittingly and sometimes involuntarily (and even surprisingly) taken on the role of the dependable and intuitive research assistant. Not yet altogether certain which particular pieces of regional news (or news trivia) are of interest to me, she mentioned in passing during a phone conversation in the fall of 2002 that she had heard something strange about the Space Needle, something that maybe I'd want to know about.

'What is it?' I asked.

'Well', she said, 'I heard on TV the other day that some guy had bought the Space Needle? and now he's planning on having it moved to Eastern Washington?'

I filtered the information slowly: 'They sold the Space Needle?' *I suppose it could have been sold, perhaps as part of a corporate merger or something.*

'But, did you say some *guy* bought it?' *Did she mean some 'guy', like notable Northwest billionaires Bill Gates and Paul Allen of Microsoft, Howard Schultz of Starbucks, or Jeff Besos of Amazon.com?*

'And he's moving it to Eastern Washington?' *He's moving the most recognizable icon from the center of downtown Seattle's panoramic landscape to the desolate, open-spaced hinterland on the other side of the volcanic spine of the Cascade Mountains?*

Preposterous. Compelling. Impossible. Why?

'Mom, wait a second, what are you talking about? Are you *sure*? Where did you hear this?'

'Well', she said, 'I think I heard it on the news, but, no, I'm not sure. It was really strange; but that's what they said, so I thought you'd want to know.'

The story—cleverly packaged to encourage rumor and speculation—was a savvy three-part advertising campaign launched by the Washington State Lottery Commission's 'Mega-Millions' jackpot game in which participants had the opportunity to win upwards of $300,000,000. Expertly co-opting the format of the breaking-news story that has become so profoundly internalized within the collective psyche of postmodern subjectivity, the ads are a unique portal for examining the millenarian, and even apocalyptic impulses built into the city of Seattle's history and its landscape.

Equally important, the ads call attention to the personal impact these apocalyptic impulses have as we increasingly move between a global/local fault-line that forces us to redefine our most private associations of home and family life. In other words, the ads underscore the process whereby the iconography of regional specificity—the *lieux de mémoire*—becomes uprooted from the actual sediment and landscape that previously factored into our sense of where we belong. Pierre Nora captures this process when he writes that '[we] feel a visceral attachment to that which made us what we are, yet at the same time we feel historically estranged from this legacy, which we must now coolly assess. These *lieux* have washed up from a sea of memory in which we no longer dwell: they are partly official and institutional, partly affective and sentimental.'[1] It is for this reason that I am compelled to write from the hybridized voice of memoirist and scholar, lingering here before moving deeper into this cultural biography of one of the Pacific Northwest's most iconic landmarks.

On the one hand, when I see the Space Needle pop up on the nightly news, I do not merely think of a host of other iconic landmarks such as the Pike Place Market, Mount Rainier, the Boeing Fields, or the Mariners. I do not merely think of Nordstrom, Starbucks, Microsoft, or even the WTO protests of 1999, and I do not merely think of the geographical distance that separates me from those I love. Instead, a time-released memory unfolds in my head, one with my mother and I first arriving in Seattle in the early 1980s; our brand new Toyota Tercel packed to the roof with two cats, a hamster named Lady Diana, and the remnants of a past life whose trail now extended from Seattle to California and Ohio. Not having a clue of how to begin to define our sense of home within the foreign streets and neighborhoods of this northwestern city, we found ourselves lost—anxiously circling round and round the magnetic base of the city's most accessible landmark.

Exhausted finally, we bit the bullet, parked the car, and paid the exorbitant sum to lunch at the top of the 605-foot Needle's revolving restaurant. From this vantage, the panorama of our new city's grammar slowly began to lock into place. Undoubtedly, the feeling of being able to take some sort of control of the skyline by being at the center of the revolving restaurant would have been a factor in architect John Graham Jr's original design. In this regard, to be physically taken up within the landmark—to be taken to the eye of the needle—becomes an object lesson in personal sovereignty and civic duty. Invariably, it is an occasion for dreams of grandeur.

Yet on the other hand, when I look at the Lottery Commission's ads, I am confronted in new ways by a malaise reminding me that we take for granted the stability of the spatial relations that connect our sense of home to the landscape of our beloved cities. Of course this is something that we have likely always done, but within the context of a post 9/11 world it is something we have been forced to consider with new eyes, suddenly reminded of the disorienting impact of standing face to face with the uncanny. To entertain the transformation of landmarks from a state of fixity to one of ephemerality and portability leaves us with a newly-indiscernible cityscape, one that reflects the mobility and mutability of making a home within a global landscape that is increasingly haunted by terror and unrest.

Figure 1. 'High–in-the-Sky Century 21.' December 1961 water color by staff artist Parker McAllister anticipating the completion of the Seattle Monorail and the Space Needle. Both were built in time for the opening of Century 21, the 1962 Seattle World's Fair. (Image appears courtesy of The Seattle Times).

The World-of-Tomorrow

Constructed in 1962 as the crown jewel of the Century 21 World's Fair, the Space Needle was designed as a giddy and celebratory landmark of a Cold War sensibility that was thought to be so ahead of its time it could only be recognized in terms of the twenty-first-century science fiction associated with Space Age technology. Yet, if the original goals of the 1962 Century 21 World's Fair were to move the city into the World-of-Tomorrow, to put Seattle on business and tourist maps once and for all, and to encourage young families to plant homeowners' roots in the Pacific Northwest, the irony is that these goals would be accomplished by becoming a key player in a global network that pays little mind to regional specificity. On its way to becoming the local powerhouse of high-technology dreamed of by mid-century boosters, the concept of regionalism consistently gave way to the socioeconomic and neoliberal imperatives of free trade and globalization.

Figure 2. *Century 21 Exposition fairgrounds featuring the Space Needle. Downtown Seattle and Mount Rainier can be seen in the background.* (Image appears courtesy of Manuscripts, Special Collections, University Archives, University of Washington Libraries, UW23053z).

In a sense, in the final years of the overblown buildup to the twenty-first century, the Pacific Northwest seemed swept up in a new Gilded Age that had supra-geographical consequences. In *Seattle and the Demons of Ambition*, Seattle writer Fred Moody ruefully captures the local sense of technological messianism that began to gather steam throughout the 1990s. In this hyperbolic transformation, the former economic and cultural periphery of the US believed itself to be poised not only to take over the center of the country's commerce and technology; but rather, it believed itself to be on the threshold of 'taking over the universe [while] …trumpeting the planet's entrance into the "Information Age" '.[2] The nostalgic idea of Seattle as a humble one-company town headed-up by Boeing Aircraft seemed only a dim blip on the radar screen of local history.

Yet, by the time the twenty-first century and its Millennium 2000 Big Brother were literally bearing down upon the world at large, the city of Seattle found itself not altogether at the threshold of utopic bliss anticipated by Century 21 fair planners (though certainly there had been plenty of irrational exuberance along the way), but at the precipice of a storm that was only just beginning to announce itself as *the* new millennial landscape. The under-anticipated threats of anti-globalization protest and Al-Qaeda terrorism that irrupted in Seattle in November and December 1999 set off panicked alarms in which American faith in technological innovation, national sovereignty, and national security were tested, and continue to be tested to this day.

The prognosticators had gotten it only partially right: Seattle would indeed be at the center of the world stage as the new century approached; not as the glittering jewel in enlightened urban planning, but as the volcanic font of a world of discontent. Which is to say, if 9/11 came as the second shoe dropping on what we had previously only imagined in terms of a looming Y2K disaster, then the 1999 Countdown in Seattle (including the 'Battle in Seattle' and the 'Millennium Bomb Plot') can be said to have been the first shoe dropping—a rehearsal of things to come.[3] Taking an even broader millennial stride, I also want to argue that the utopically conceived Century 21 World's Fair (1962) functions as both an anchor and a rehearsal to the chaotic Millennium 2000 events that began with the Battle in Seattle and only provisionally ended in September 2001. For the relationships implied in these transhistoric pairings remind us that the utopianism of World's Fairs is always to some degree in conversation with an overwrought doppelganger—a dystopic narrative of city planning gone awry. By looking at the relationships contained within the history that is loosely circumscribed by the Space Age technology of the Cold War on the one hand and the Digital Revolution of the 1990s on the other, we can come to a fuller understanding of the dialectical process by which these relationships unfold and gather meaning.[4]

The Lottery Commission's ads are a wily and funny tip of the hat to this complex chain of events. They represent this social landscape with a near perfect blend of chutzpah and self awareness, and in so doing they create a playfully mordant commentary. In essence, they enact a satirical counterpart to the austere practices referred to by James E. Young in his discussion of holocaust memorials that function as countermemorials: 'brazen, painfully self-conscious memorial spaces conceived to challenge the very premises of their being'.[5] Indeed, the Space Needle ads are a commentary that spoofs not only the booster's premise of the future implied in World-of-Tomorrow landmarks, but they underscore the particularized myths that have since become associated with the landscape upon which the city of Seattle has been built. They are a cheerful yet peculiar salute welcoming us, once again, to the new twenty-first century.

'A New Home for the Space Needle'

The series of ads opens at the base of the Space Needle, where a young female reporter named Kristin Mackay tells us that 'we're live here at the Seattle Center where officials have just announced that the Space Needle has been sold and will be moved to Moses Lake'. We can see that as a consequence of the sale, the city's most prominent tourist destination is now marked off as a construction zone. In the background, the crew of workers is going about the business of uprooting the landmark, while tourists and pedestrians walk by as if en route to whatever other landmarks might still be open to the public. The reporter tells us that the Space Needle's new owner is Steve, 'an area man' from Moses Lake who has just won the Mega-millions lottery, where the winnings are so large 'you could even buy the Space Needle'.

Figure 3. *'The Space Needle has been sold!' From the 2002 Washington State Lottery television ad campaign that spoofed the disappearance of the Space Needle from downtown Seattle. Here the Space Needle begins its journey across Interstate 90.* (Photo appears courtesy of the Washington State Lottery and Publicis USA. The Space Needle is a registered trademark of the Space Needle Corporation and is used with permission.)

Within the frame of the construction zone a smaller window opens up featuring a stark black-and-white insert of the futuristic tower as it sits within the local skyline; the Needle can best be described as sci-fi kitsch: a cross between a 1950s flying saucer and a gigantic souvenir pepper grinder. Next, the scene telescopes out to a longer color-shot of the Space Needle; recently repainted in classic 'galaxy gold' for the fortieth anniversary of the 1962 Seattle World's fair. Against this image of the Space Needle dressed up in what is, in fact, its pedestrian-orange birthday suit, we see Steve accepting his winnings from the lottery commission.

Figure 4. *The Space Needle settles into its new digs in Moses Lake, located in Eastern Washington.* (Photo appears courtesy of the Washington State Lottery and Publicis USA. The The Space Needle is a registered trademark of the Space Needle Corporation and is used with permission.)

Mackay—the Washington State Lottery public relations Account Supervisor *qua* actor *qua* reporter—informs us of the logistics of the purchase; that Steve intends to transport the landmark from Seattle to Moses Lake on a 'crawler'—'which', she tells us with a proverbial wink, 'is usually reserved for moving *something else* space-related'. In the next image, we see a crawler loaded down with a massive space-shuttle rocket bundled with fuel missiles and booster rockets, reminding us that the Space Needle has deep synecdochic roots connecting it—and the entire Pacific Northwest—to the military industrial complex. Indeed, the US defense industry kept the local economy reaching for prosperity—albeit through boom and bust—and, it kept the rest of the country power-housing its way to the head of the arms race for a large part of the twentieth century. Gesturing toward this history, the first ad ends with the reporter's final comment on the impact of Steve's windfall: 'a new *home* for the Space Needle, a new *game* for Washington!'

The second ad of the series opens onto the desolate landscape of Moses Lake in rural Eastern Washington where Mackay interviews Steve in front of his modest little house while a construction crew works in the background. As Mackay asks about the details of the move, we see the

Space Needle loaded up on the crawler, which is hauling the landmark eastward on the I-90 highway; one of the region's most heavily trafficked arteries, now completely free of all other vehicles. When Mackay asks Steve 'Just how much did you win?' he tells her 'Enough to shut down I-90'.

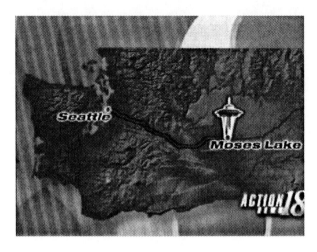

Figure 5. *Map of the Space Needle's journey from Seattle to Moses Lake.* (Photo appears courtesy of the Washington State Lottery and Publicis USA. The The Space Needle is a registered trademark of the Space Needle Corporation and is used with permission.)

Figure 6. *Downtown Seattle, former site of the Space Needle.* (Photo appears courtesy of the Washington State Lottery and Publicis USA. The The Space Needle is a registered trademark of the Space Needle Corporation and is used with permission.)

Figure 7. *Downtown Seattle with a ghostly sketch of where the Space Needle once stood.* (Photo appears courtesy of the Washington State Lottery and Publicis USA. The The Space Needle is a registered trademark of the Space Needle Corporation and is used with permission.)

Meanwhile, back in downtown Seattle, according to the third and final ad, the foggy gray skyline is unrecognizable without its iconic landmark. To help us get our bearings, the television engineers trace a dotted line recalling the shape of the Needle in its former location at the Seattle Center. The scene cuts once again to the Space Needle, relocated behind Steve's little house on the empty banks of Moses Lake and Mackay asks the new owner if he has any advice for Seattleites who are dismayed at the loss of their favorite landmark. 'I'd say, come visit the Steve Needle!' he happily exclaims of the far-fetched good fortune that has made him the proud new owner of a tourist destination that no one will ever visit.

At the Crossroads of Topophilia and the Uncanny

In his quietly whimsical yet philosophical introduction to *The Poetics of Space*, Gaston Bachelard ruminates over how our memory is informed by the objects and space that we associate with house and home. In his concern for the ways in which the 'poetic image is an emergence from language', and the way it is 'always a little above the language of signification',[6] he moves toward a geo-philosophical methodology that can help us to think through the ways in which a contemporary cityscape like the Seattle skyline is shot through with the historical remembering and forgetting we associate with the regional specificity of landmarks, civic space, and the places we call home. Bachelard muses that history is animated by the psychic movement of particular objects in relationship to the space that surrounds them. The images that we glean from our encounter with the materiality of the world do not so much contain history within them as set off reverberations within surrounding spaces in which 'the distant past resounds with echoes'.[7] In thinking about our deep-seated nostalgia for images that refer back to our primary understandings of house and home and of space and place in relationship to the iconic status of landmarks, the Space Needle's role in Seattle's landscape is not only in the way it has operated as 'an echo of the past', but it also increasingly marks the dialectical movement between icon and space. This kind of movement confounds our understanding of fixity and landscape as our image of the Space Needle fluctuates between the categories of landmark, monument, and memorial. No longer simply identified as the insouciant tourist destination *par excellence*, we parody newly emerging mourning rituals in anticipation of its absence. Beloved landmarks and monuments transform before our very eyes into sites of loss and memorialization, the remains of the downtown skyline haunted by the dotted-line drawing showing us where the Needle once stood. The idea of the Space Needle being sold and moved to a new locale disrupts and deterritorializes what Nora describes as the second-order process associated with commemorations that aim to fix fading images of home and region within the viewfinder of stable landmarks.[8] In disrupting the *lieux de mémoire*, the ads thus also destabilize the sorts of imagined communities that bind us to a sense of regional and national identity.[9] When the beloved landmarks that we associate with home pick up and move seemingly at random, we enter into a new place of apocalyptic dread. Topo*philia,* described by Yi-Fu Tuan as 'the fondness for place because it is familiar, because it is home, and incarnates the past...' morphs from within the charged contours of our imaginations such that our regard for the landscape becomes increasingly inflected by a growing sense of topo*phobia*.[10] 'Meet me at the Needle', the old theme song from the 1962 fair beckons, but when none of our old landmarks remain stationary, how will we ever know where to find each other?[11]

For Bachelard, our relationship to images of house and home is described through a similar notion of our 'topophilia' for 'felicitous space', where the work at hand is to 'determine the value of the sorts of space that may be grasped, that may be defended against adverse forces, the space we love'. He continues by saying that for 'diverse reasons, and with the differences entailed by poetic shadings, this is eulogized space'.[12] In a sense, Bachelard is articulating every millenarian's relationship to the euphoria associated with utopic narratives of time that stands still. But in the case of imagining the Seattle landscape without its most iconic landmark, the sense of topophilia, the love of home, is disrupted by the very apocalyptic gesture of absence that Bachelard so curiously skirts within the prose of his philosophical inquiry. When he does mention this sort of 'adversity', it appears all the more sudden, as an unintended irruption within his own idyll. If the felicitous space is that which comes into being through the power of imagination as it moves between and beyond the grasp of language, the horror and abjection associated with the apocalyptic side of this mental process is lightly sidestepped. He confesses that,

> Hostile space is hardly mentioned in these pages. The space of hatred and combat can only be studied in the context of the impassioned subject matter and apocalyptic images. For the present, we shall consider the images that attract. And with regard to images, it soon becomes clear that to attract and to repulse do not give contrary experiences.[13]

If writers like Bachelard and Tuan help us to think about the whimsy and primacy of spatial relationships as they combine with the force of imagination and myth in reminding us of our roots, it's also hard not to think of Freud's discussion of dreams, jokes, and the uncanny in trying to read the various levels of meaning contained within the more sinister humor of the Lottery Commission's ads. For Freud, the concept of the uncanny can be etymologically traced to the German *heimlich* and *unheimlich*, loosely translated in English as the experience of feeling at 'home' and 'not home', or the feeling of being liminally caught up between the familiar and the strange. Written in the apocalyptic aftermath of World War I, Freud tells us that the 'subject of the uncanny is…undoubtedly related to what is frightening—to what arouses dread and horror',[14] and he reminds us that repression is the act that sets the experience of the uncanny in motion. But, he is also careful to point out that what gives the uncanny its strength—and what makes the differentiation between the terms *heimlich* and *unheimlich* nearly impossible—is the porous boundary separating the familiar from the strange; the way each is contained within the other.[15] In other words, 'the uncanny is that class of the frightening which leads back to what is known of old and long familiar'.[16] On first glance the story of the Space Needle being bought by Steve and relocated to the town of Moses Lake is nothing more than a playful spoof on a beloved cultural icon—there is nothing overtly frightening or dread-inducing about it. Yet, by suspending our willingness to disbelieve, we are left with an absurd and apocalyptic scene that is predicated on the cultural and technological history of the Pacific Northwest, both of which are as deeply coded in meaning as the most carefully disguised dream-work of our unconscious minds.

Decoding the Past

The 1962 Seattle World's Fair began, like most fairs, as an event created by city boosters to draw tourists, new residents, and new industries to the region. With the rise of suburbanization and car culture at mid-century, there was a growing concern that Seattle's downtown business center, like many urban centers throughout the rest of the country, had become increasingly debilitated. Coupled with this was a concern that Seattle needed to diversify beyond its status of being a one-company town in-debted to Boeing and the aerospace industry's biggest customer—the US Government. Even though the fair was originally conceived by prominent downtown businessmen as an event that would lend a stronger degree of regional specificity and economic diversity to Seattle and the Pacific North-west, the theme of the fair ultimately became much more global and futuristic in its aspirations. In refashioning itself from the more provincial concept of a 'Festival of the West', to a World-of-Tomorrow Fair, writer Don Duncan tells us that 'Seattle launched itself into the 21st Century – 38 years early'.[17]

In his book *Magic Lands: Western Cityscapes and American Culture After 1940*, John Findlay clarifies the seeming shift in local expectations about the fair when he writes that:

> the message of the international exposition was hardly incompatible with either the average resident's sense of the metropolitan area or the world view of the Urban West after World War II. Space and science impinged far more closely upon the personal interests of fairgoers than did the concerns of downtown businessmen.[18]

In fact, the Emerald City—also known as Jet City—had been well aware since at least the Boeing boom years of World War II that the success of the local economy lived and died on external demands for the high technology that required the combined natural resources and labor pools of the entire region, not just the downtown corridor. Findlay goes on to tell us that:

> Even before the federal government had seized upon the fair to promote its work in science and space, the proximity of airplane factories and naval facilities suggested to publicists that the fair might commemorate the 'jet age' and modern shipping. Regional hydroelectric plants provided another distinctive technology worthy of display, and the Hanford nuclear complex in Eastern Washington recommended an exhibit on atomic energy, and

perhaps even an operating reactor on the fairgrounds. If the fair succeeded in attracting industry to the region, organizers hoped that the new companies would be high-tech.[19]

Not only does Findlay show us the bizarre and quirky optimism of fair planners (imagine an Expo with an operating reactor!), but he also traces the shifting awareness of the original boosters from a basic concern with improving the downtown shopping district to a more accurate picture of the actual governmental and science agendas that were competing to fuel the local economy. These forces came from the entire Pacific Northwest including places like Moses Lake in the east and the Hanford nuclear facility to the south, where the key to the region's industrial and manufacturing strength lay in harnessing the energy potential of the Columbia River Basin through public works projects such as the Grand Coulee Dam. That the Washington State Lottery Commission's 2002 ad campaign would have the character of Steve relocate the Space Needle to Moses Lake— the home of the Larson Air force base until 1966 and what in recent years has become a designated 'foreign trade zone'—speaks to this earlier history as much as it speaks to post 9/11 anxieties about the fragility and ephemerality of elements of city life that we had heretofore held as constant and unchanging.

Much has been made of the repressive yet antiseptically good-natured confidence that American postwar consumerism brought to the draconian agenda of the Cold War. Findlay puts this idea into conversation with Century 21:

> The Washington state theme of the exposition, life in the twenty-first century, like the fair's built environment, attracted attention because it envisioned tomorrow's world, yet was premised upon the continuation of those mid-twentieth-century trends – rising levels of affluence, growing mastery of the environment, soaring faith in science and technology – that evoked optimism as well as a sense of order during the postwar years.[20]

Never mind the fact that the urban streets of America were approaching a threshold of unprecedented crisis from a longstanding set of social ills that could only be challenged by the collective emergence of the Civil Rights Movement, the anti-war movement, environmental activism, and a new theory of urban planning put forth by scholars like Jane Jacobs in the *Death and Life of Great American Cities*. For that matter, never mind the threat of nuclear annihilation.

Expositions like Century 21 instructed fairgoers on how to effectively merge naïve and optimistic faith in the power of science and technology to solve all social ills—and this was nowhere more true than with respect to the apocalyptic implications of nuclear warfare, urban race riots, and environmental catastrophe that loomed ominously on the horizon. Seattle residents seemingly had everything to gain in accepting with blinders this missionary zeal for science and technology, and everything to lose in taking stock of their own certain destruction at being in the center of a target that included the Hanford Nuclear facility, Boeing, and a host of military bases buttressing the United States Armed Forces.[21]

In a sense, the arrival of Century 21 and the Space Needle in 1962 *did* put Seattle on the map once and for all as the rain-soaked capital of youthful pluck and technological zeal. Nestled between the imposing snow-topped grandeur of Mount Rainier to the south and Puget Sound and the Olympic Mountains to the west, the Space Needle added to the expansiveness of this western panorama a testimonial flourish of city residents' and newcomers' goals of dreaming their way into the future. But it would be a mistake to say that this alone was the moment that set the city and the region on its course to becoming the center of the new Gilded Age of the 1990s. For Seattle's first big splash onto national consciousness had come in its role in that earlier gold rush when it had functioned as a gateway to floods of prospectors making their way to Alaska and the Yukon on the promise of quick and unprecedented riches.

The commemorative event of that earlier benchmark in irrational exuberance came in the form of the 1909 Alaska-Yukon-Pacific Exposition (AYP), whose fairgrounds would gradually morph into the blueprint of campus-life at the University of Washington. In his opening day speech at the AYP, railroad magnate James J. Hill proclaimed:

> If the star of empire in history has moved westward, it followed rather than led those bold spirits by which empires are made and upheld. This exposition may be regarded as the laying of the last rail, the driving of the last spike, in unity of mind and purpose between the Pacific coast and the country east of the mountains.[22]

Seen as the industrial capitalist's ruthless and enthusiastic rally for the riches contained within the prospects of a globalizing world economy, Hill's confident boast was that visitors would 'carry away with them along with recollections of new possibilities of wealth, new methods, new markets and new trading peoples, a fund of new ideas and old ones recast in a larger mold'.[23] In *All the World's a Fair*, Robert Rydell emphasizes that the sort of utopic expositions 'reared in Portland and Seattle focused national attention on the possibilities for economic growth through the development of trans-Pacific markets'.[24] It should come as no surprise then that the far corner of the country has continued to expand and build upon this self-fashioned claim to global and technological hegemony.

By the late 1990s and the peak of the tech-industry bubble, James Hill would have surely relished from the grave the fact that Seattle was home to the two richest men in the world—Bill Gates and Paul Allen—and that it boasted more millionaires per capita than anywhere else in the country. The effects of this wealth—where for a time it seemed just about any-body working within earshot of Microsoft or Amazon or Starbucks had the chance to cash in on a bonanza of stock options—have been seen all throughout the economy and to the dismay of many, they have been writ-ten on the landscape of the city itself. If the Space Needle has been, and continues to be, the beloved cultural icon and monument by which Seat-tleites gauge their driving time and distance from work to home, the pro-liferation of new self-made monuments by philanthropists like Paul Allen —in the form of new sports arenas and museums like the Experience Music Project—have been incorporated into the skyline with a greater sense of civic debate and scorn.

The likelihood of average citizens, like Steve from the Lottery Commis-sion's Mega Millions ad campaign, ever having the opportunity of cashing in on the new economy have been about as great as picking the winning number in the weekly lottery drawing. Steve's populist decision to move the Space Needle to his little piece of land on the banks of desolate Moses Lake resonates less with the mindset of a robber baron and more with the topophilia and nostalgia that comes with longing for the landscape of the past. At the same time though, it is also a reflection of a kind of topophobia that is concerned with safeguarding beloved cultural icons from hostile and apocalyptic forces that we associate with the future.

Projecting the Sovereign Landscape

In 1966 11-year-old Bill Gates won a dinner at the Space Needle restau-rant through a contest offered by his church pastor Reverend Dale Turner. The rules of the contest required participants to memorize chapters 5, 6 and 7 of the Gospel of Matthew, better known as the Sermon on the Mount. The young Gates recited the sermon flawlessly, later explaining to his astonished pastor: 'I can do anything I put my mind to'.[25] In *Hard Drive: Bill Gates and the Making of the Microsoft Empire*, writers James Wallace and Jim Erickson document what would otherwise seem a folk-loric story of Gates' own experience of being ushered up into the eye of the Needle:

> At dinner that night, 'Trey' Gates feasted his eyes on the region where he would later make his mark. To the northeast was the University of Wash-ington and the nearby residential district of Laurelhurst, where the Gates

family lived, along the shores of Lake Washington. To the south, the Seattle waterfront jutted into the Sound, with its ships, piers, seafood restaurants, and curiosity shops. To the southeast rose the skyscrapers of the city, with 14,410-foot Mt. Rainier looming like a sentinel in the distance. To the east, against the backdrop of the Cascade Mountain range on the horizon, were the suburbs of Bellevue and Redmond, where 13 years later Gates would build his computer software empire.[26]

Wallace and Erickson go on to tell us that when 'Reverend Turner took his 32 disciples to the plush, revolving restaurant on top of the Space Needle...' that 'Gates looked out on the city, the suburbs, the mountains, and the waters of the Sound, [and] he was oblivious to his destiny slowly revolving around him'.[27] Although the definitive profile on Gates' experience of the 1962 Century 21 World's Fair remains to be written, this biographical morsel unabashedly correlates the young brainiac's 1966 trip to the Space Needle as part of the creative ur-engine that helped catapult him to a messianic dream of conquering the world through technology and commerce.

But the point here is not so much to posit a direct correlation between Gates' youthful enthrallment with science and technology and his unparalleled sovereignty in changing the technological and socioeconomic landscape at regional, national and global levels, although that certainly seems obvious enough. Rather, it is to mark the fact that the digital revolution has long and deep roots connecting it not only to the Space Age technology of mid-century, but to the millenarian aspect of world's fairs, especially the future oriented world-of-tomorrow fairs as they were deployed as forecasters of what the future would bring. While Century 21's predictive accuracy successfully anticipated the growth of the high-tech industry, it could not have known then what we know now. At mid-century, technology was still imagined in the astronomically large terms of NASA rocket launches, atomic bombs, B-52 fighter planes, and plum 707 commercial jets. Big Science could not have fully anticipated the value that we have come to place on the power of the infinitesimally shrinking microchip, and the immense power and social control contained within it. Indeed, Michel de Certeau's 'voyeur-god' haunts this page—for writer and reader alike.[28] The Gatesian technological force animating my desktop is the same we are all now so dependent upon in articulating the minute (and private) details of our everyday lives.

In *The Production of Space*, Henri Lefebvre cautions against trusting the state to benignly choreograph the grid-work of urban planning. Woven into an argument that also cautions against the political nihilism of discourse-analysis as a philosophical method, Lefebvre believes that both risk the kinds of paralysis that encourage fascism and the dissolution of civil society. Instead, he argues for an engagement with space that interrogates the 'illusion of transparency [that] goes hand in hand with a view of space as innocent, as free of traps or secret places',[29] and his concern is that we not fall sway to 'fetishization of space in the service of the state'.[30] In so doing, he asks that we attend to the fact that 'everyday life and its functions are coextensive with, and utterly transformed by, a theatricality as sophisticated as it is unsought, a sort of involuntary *mise-en-scene*'.[31] Space is not only laden with historical meaning, with lingering traces of the past; it is also a living archive constituted by an ensemble of social practices intent on wresting control of the codes that determine the imagined communities contained within our landscapes.[32] Lefebvre sums this up himself when he writes:

> What we are concerned with, then, is the long *history of space*, even though space is neither a 'subject' nor an 'object' but rather a social reality – that is to say, a set of relations and forms. This history is to be distinguished from an inventory of things *in space* (or what has recently been called material culture or civilization), as also from ideas and discourse *about space*. It must account for both representational spaces and representations of space, but above all for their interrelationships and their links with social practice.[33]

In this sense, the Lottery Commission's ads function as a trigger, one that allows us to begin to tease out the consequential ways that the power and ideology of the past remain in dialogue with the present; not only do they recount the 'long history of space', they enact it. But it is not just the ads that enact this long history; the landscape itself is actively engaged in the telling, the contesting, and the rewriting of this history.

At the height of their usefulness, World's Fairs enacted 'representations of space', which Lefebvre defines as 'the space of scientists, planners, urbanists, technocratic subdividers and social engineers'—they were, in effect, the blueprints of dominant space.[34] As such, fairs were launches for emerging social practices that involved carving up space in order to put new technologies at the service of the city's dominant cultural and economic voices and their vision of civic life. Yet, even though fairs were invested in determining the outcome of civic and urban space, the fairgrounds themselves were nevertheless designed with their own obsolescence in mind. In this regard, they were constructed as temporary and virtual realities (bookmarks, if you will) of what the future held in store.[35]

Nonetheless, in spite of their ephemerality (the sites were usually demolished shortly after the fairs closed), certain buildings and landmarks were strategically retained as permanent monuments. World's Fairs, then, operated not only as predictors of the future, they were built to archive and commemorate particular versions of the past. Left behind, the Space Needle continues to effect the Seattle landscape by creating a 'monumental space', one that Lefebvre would argue offers 'each member of a society an image of that membership, an image of his or her social visage'.[36] In this regard, the 'monument thus effected a "consensus", and this in the strongest sense of the term, rendering it practical and concrete. The element of repression in it and the element of exaltation could scarcely be disentangled; or perhaps it would be more accurate to say the repressive element was metamorphosed into exaltation.'[37] Within monumental space a kind of memorial narrative gets constructed, which Geoffrey H. Hartman describes in 'Public Memory and its Discontents' as a kind of 'anti-memory' that limits 'the subversive or heterogeneous facts' in order to create a national consensus based on a heroic and homogenized past.[38]

In the case of Century 21, much of the fairgrounds were self-consciously preserved as the Seattle Center, the city's civic center, which has housed not only the Space Needle's restaurant and observation deck, but also the Seattle Super Sonics, the Opera House, the Bagley Wright Theatre, the Seattle Science Center, and most recently, Paul Allen's Experience Music Project. It has also thrived as the site for local festivals including the annual Folk-Life festival, the Bite of Seattle, and Bumbershoot—the city's big end-of-summer blow out party. In these common spaces of public life, residents are tacitly instructed in the proper methods of understanding the landscape. It is in our movement through these shared spaces that we rehearse the appropriate ways to act out our local sense of self and belonging. In this sense, we must also keep in mind the physical impact civil planning has on shaping the habits of everyday life; habits that our bodies absorb under the faith and reason associated with Gramscian notions of common sense.

Who Owns This Landmark?

On 21 April, 1999, the Space Needle was named an official City of Seattle Landmark. In granting it this special status, the Landmarks Preservation Board wrote, 'The Space Needle marks a point in the history of the City of Seattle and represents American aspirations towards technological prowess. [It] embodies in its form and construction the era's belief in commerce, technology and progress'.[39] That summer, Mike Myers released his second Austin Powers film, *The Spy Who Shagged Me*, a kooky and kinky story about the struggle between good and evil and the perils of time traveling between the 1990s and the 1960s. Twenty minutes into the film, fans caught their first glimpse of the dangerously dysfunctional and nerdy Dr Evil perched inside his contemporary headquarters atop the Space Needle. Through product placement and a corporate wink at a kind of self-parody and dream condensation, the Space Needle had been converted into a floating Starbucks-in-the-sky. In November 1999, several months after Starbucks' and Meyer's wickedly funny and prescient nod at the ways in which Pacific Northwest corporate culture was shaping both the local and the global landscape, the Space Needle found itself in the middle of a media tug-of-war between the free-trade and fair-trade ideologies that were craftily exploiting it to broadcast their competing political platforms as far and wide as their satellites and high speed connections would take them.

Figure 8. *See details following Figure 9.*

From Sunday, 28 November through Friday, 3 December, 1999, the city of Seattle was torn asunder by the violent crackdowns of the naïve and under-prepared Seattle Police Department as it tried to contain a massively well organized direct action protest against the World Trade Organization. Robin Blackburn of the *New Left Review* comments that '[the] twentieth century ended with a stunning debacle for free-trade capitalism in Seattle, once a renowned centre of syndicalist militancy, now HQ to corporations which hold the world in thrall'.[40] It goes without saying that this 'stunning debacle' was not at all in the same league as the triumphal booster's fantasy that had opened the 1962 World's Fair and that had claimed that Seattle had 'launched itself into the 21st Century—38 years early'. Call it the doppelganger effect, or the return of the repressed, this dystopic unfolding of the twenty-first century was uncannily juxtaposed on top of its utopic predecessor.

Figure 9. *When did the Space Needle become a Starbucks? A clever visual pun on globalization as well as shifting cultural and consumer trends in the Pacific Northwest from the 1999 film 'Austin Powers: The Spy Who Shagged Me', copyright MCMXCIX, New Line Productions, Inc. All rights reserved.* (Photos appear courtesy of New Line Productions, Inc. and Starbucks. The Space Needle is a registered trademark of the Space Needle Corporation and is used with permission.)

Tuning in to the news emerging from the Pacific Northwest, the world was astonished, and in many quarters heartened, to see the WTO's 'Millennial Summit' dramatically transforming into the 'Battle in Seattle'. Archly characterized by organizers and protesters alike as 'The Battle of the Century', the site of the former World's Fair quickly emerged as the nexus of a new genre of protest on the one hand, and the opening gambit of a newly emerging domestic security economy on the other. The conflagration of this new genre of protest alongside the first brutal act of this new domestic security economy can be seen retrospectively as a precursor to that which has ensued on the heels of 9/11 and the passage of the Patriot Act.[41] In essence, the Battle in Seattle marks a pivot-point in the shift away from the exuberance of the dot com landscape to the malaise associated with the new social landscape of economic downtown, political terror, and domestic security.

There on our television screens was the Space Needle, outfitted in cameo appearances ripe for transmitting its image far and wide. Carefully framed by media-savvy banners that were marked 'WTO' and 'Democracy' and were pointed in opposite (and by implication, contradictory) directions, NGOs like the Ruckus Society used the Space Needle to tell an alternative story of the impact of technology on the city and the world. This particular visual statement—of the mutually exclusive relationship between free-trade and democracy—operated as a clever pun on giving directions to visitors upon first arriving at the city's most recognizable tourist destination.

But also on our TV screens, our front pages, and our computer desktops were images of cops in Darth Vader-gear, aiming tear gas and rubber bullets at the festively clad protesters who were beaten into submission while chanting 'the whole world is watching'. The shock of seeing these brightly costumed participants, inspired by Bread and Puppet theatricality, brutally attacked by a newly imposed police state came as an immediate confirmation that all was not well within the steamrolling engine of free-trade and globalization that had been trumpeted by the cheerleaders of GATT, NAFTA, and the WTO throughout President Clinton's administration and the boom years of the 1990s.

Of course the shock of watching these events unfold from afar had a completely different impact than watching them unfold in your own front yard. Listening over long distance phone wires to my mother describing the crush of protesters being bullied past her front door on 10th Avenue East in the Capitol Hill neighborhood just east of what eventually became the barricaded downtown corridor drove this point home. The fact that neighborhood residents making their way home from work had been randomly caught up in the police brutality, and the fact that the sound of concussion grenades and helicopters had filled the air well into the night would be cause for uproar and on-going city council investigations and block-watches in the weeks, months, and years that would follow.

Throughout the week-long demonstrations, the history of various generations of urban planning was constantly contested and re-mapped by both the mobilization and the state-sponsored crack down as each fought to regain control of the streets. At stake here was nothing short of taking control of the history and ideologies contained within an urban landscape that had been franchised to a global market. Protesters assembled and moved between strategic points swinging from the Space Needle on the northern-most edge of the city to the downtown corridor itself, which included the heart of the shopping district and the Washington State Convention Center—the main venue of the WTO meetings. The degree to which the protests moved across the very landscape on which the earlier World's Fair boosters had laid their claims exemplifies the kind of 'representational space' that Lefebvre describes as 'directly *lived* through its associated images and symbols…the space of "inhabitants" and "users" '… the space 'which the imagination seeks to change and appropriate. It overlays physical space, making symbolic use of its objects.'[42]

This Battle in Seattle, then, was also very much a battle *for* Seattle: it became a contest for reclaiming the ability to define the heart and soul of the city and its landscape. In became, in short, a battle for and over monumental space, which included the right to redefine the processes of building a consensus that enables residents and citizens to locate themselves within that same landscape. Lefebvre tells us that to

> the degree that there are traces of violence and death, negativity and aggressiveness in social practice, the monumental work erases them and replaces them with a tranquil power and certitude which can encompass violence and terror. Thus the mortal 'moment' (or component) of the sign is temporarily abolished in monumental space.[43]

At this particular 'moment', the violence and contestation emerging from beneath the seeming tranquility and certitude of the Seattle landscape were laid bare for the whole world to see the telling of an alternative history. On the eve of Y2K and the Battle in Seattle, it seemed for a time that the revolution would, in fact, be televised after all.

In *Globalization from Below: The Power of Solidarity*, authors Jeremy Brecher, Tim Costello, and Brendan Smith cite a 13 December, 1999 issue of *Newsweek* that claimed '[one] of the most important lessons of Seattle is that there are now two visions of globalization to offer, one led by commerce, one by social activism'.[44] The success of the Battle in Seattle was not just about the local population reclaiming their city and its image from corporate branding and the excesses of the new Gilded Age, it was also about the cultural debut of a newly emerging form of social activism at the global level. A shot-in-the-arm to increasingly moribund theories of social protest and revolution, the Battle in Seattle was a huge stride toward revitalizing the fervor of the Left. In so doing, it revealed a fresh face of organizational zeal that could conceivably be identified under the banner of the Newly Apocalyptic Left.

The unique thing about the nuts-and-bolts of this newer brand of social activism was the way it worked with the grain of globalization, rather than against it. Using the same digital, cellular, and satellite technologies as those inside the conference rooms of the Washington State Convention Center, the protesters assembled a critical mass that included participants from all over the world. Unlike 'globalization from above', Brecher, et al., qualify that 'globalization from below', is not a single vision, 'but rather a complex process in which many elements are converging, sometimes to form a new unity, at other times to jostle along side by side in the same direction'.[45] This form of globalization takes the concept of networking within structures that are rhizomatic rather than those that are hierarchical as a core principal. In Seattle, it was deployed most successfully through on-the-ground and consensus-driven management as well as the tactical deployment of 'NGO swarms'. The protest began with intensive emailing, faxing, and local networking, and ended with 'not only conventional NGOs, but also local social movements, foundations, the media, churches, trade unions, consumer organizations, intellectuals, [and] parts of regional and international governmental organizations' descending upon the city.[46] The Battle in Seattle set off a flare for all-the-world to see that the promise of globalization was more limited than guarantees along the way had seduced us into believing. The tide was beginning to turn in ways that we could not yet conceive, but felt in our bones nonetheless.

Along the road to the events that lead to the protests against the WTO, globalization had been characterized as inevitable and without alternatives. But, as a consequence of the Battle in Seattle, we watched our vague anxieties about a Y2K crisis transform into a concrete and tangible reality, where the observation that 'the new global regime is highly vulnerable', quickly became understatement.[47] Echoing Marx and Engel's claim in the Communist Manifesto that 'the bourgeoisie, therefore, produces above all, [...] its own gravediggers', the fear that our technological accomplishment would be used against us unfolded in a logic that made perfect sense, even though it still knocked the wind out of us just the same. To make matters worse, this was, after all, only the first shoe falling. Where and when would the dreaded second shoe land?

While the idea that the Battle in Seattle taught us that there were now two visions of globalization, one corporate-driven, and the other socially-driven, is compelling and based on concrete evidence, it is still, nevertheless, only partially true. What also emerged in Seattle was a third, terror-driven vision of globalization. During the Battle in Seattle, this vision was realized through the disbandment of civil liberties of both the city's own citizens and the tens of thousands of visitors who had only a few days earlier been optimistically welcomed by the Mayor as a merry band of progressive tourists. The slope from tourist to terrorist was fast and steep: once the police started to turn on protestors it quickly became clear that the big guns in DC had been scheming up new strategies for managing civil disobedience far in advance of the small group of anarchists intent on smashing windows at McDonalds and Starbucks. Distinguishing between civil disobedience, civil disturbance, and domestic security suddenly seemed a quaint relic of the past.

The advance of this new domestic security imperative quickly found its counterpart in the threat of Islamic terrorism. Two weeks following the protests and the failed WTO summit, Seattle was rocked again, this time by Ahmed Ressam, an alleged terrorist and presumed cohort of Osama bin Laden, caught at the US/Canadian border for attempting to smuggle explosives into Washington State. While it was much later revealed that Ressam had been intent on making the Los Angeles International Airport his target, the word that spread like wildfire in Seattle was that he had been on his way to the Space Needle. This notion was fueled in part by the shock of the violence brought on by the protest and by the fact that the holiday shopping season had been derailed by the riots downtown. Coming on the heels of all this chaos, the city was thus easily spooked by the idea of its millennium celebration at the Space Needle being the target of international terrorism. Both events quickly became conflated into a Y2K panic over the more violent possibilities of the turning of the century and millennium, and by 30 December the Seattle police commissioner had resigned over criticism of his role in the police brutality directed against WTO protesters. Within nearly the same breath, the city's New Year's Eve celebration scheduled at the Seattle Center was cancelled do to the perception that terrorists were out to destroy the Space Needle.

The End Is Near!

At its simplest, the social unrest and the threat and fear of terrorism that occurred in Seattle at the end of 1999 provide a counternarrative of disappointment to the utopic narratives associated with the official Millennium 2000 Countdown celebrations specifically, and the history of world's fairs more generally. The rupture that occurred in Seattle in 1999 was born out of the Y2K anxiety concerning technological failure and global terrorism; a product of late capitalism, high technology, and the digital revolution. The events of 1962 and 2000, as well as those of 2001 and beyond are deeply interpenetrating for the way that they tap into issues of urban and global development and contests for unfettered economic growth. An urban palimpsest, the crises in Seattle at the end of 1999 were written on top of the geographical landscape of the former world's fair, and each event bears the legacy of the other within its opposing vision of the future.

On the morning of 11 September, the complete failure of technology in Manhattan surged throughout the nervous system of the entire country and world. Finding no connection through my cell phone or the in-house phones of the language school where I was teaching conversational English to Japanese businessmen, I exited onto 5th Avenue where the violent landscape we had anticipated at the millennial countdown now seemed to be unfolding. I walked over to a payphone, placed a collect call to my mom, informed her of the news, and assured her that I would immediately begin the long walk home from 42nd Street to Amsterdam and 130th. Central Park and its open space felt like the safest place that day; my only concern standing there at that payphone was getting past the inventory of monuments that lay along the route: Grand Central, St Patrick's Cathedral, Rockefeller Center, and The Plaza Hotel.

The Washington Lottery Commission's trace marks of where the Space Needle formerly stood remind us of both the soul-stealing sense that high-tech wealth has had on the Pacific Northwest, and the dread brought home by the twin towers coming down in New York. In that sense then, the ads are not only a parodic commentary (one that could not have been made any sooner than its fall 2002 release), they are a rehearsal of the need for emergency preparedness associated with earthquakes, terrorism, threats of nuclear attack, and technological catastrophe that the region has increasingly been obliged to anticipate. At the moment one sees the image of the Seattle skyline with only the trace of its former landmark and monument we realize that the Space Needle—in its spectral absence—has now become the site of its own memorial. We realize, as Pierre Nora has suggested elsewhere, 'that some *lieux de mémoire* are portable'.[48] That the Space Needle will be the first monument threatened when the next round of twenty-first century violence is unleashed in Seattle almost seems a foregone conclusion, because that has already happened countless times within the collective imagination of the region.

If this image of the absent Space Needle suggests that maybe we should begin to plan for its eventuality, it also suggests something else about how Northwesterners distinguish themselves from their Eastern counterparts. Unlike the twin towers, anchored as they were to Lower Manhattan, Wall Street, and the financial district, the idea of the Space Needle hitting the road on its way to Steve's place in Eastern Washington speaks of a quirky brand of cyber-folksiness not likely to be found anywhere else. For that matter, it is a folksiness that would be considered nothing short of bad taste anywhere else, say, east of Cleveland. Therein lays the pluck of the Space Needle. Like the sudden fickleness of long-time Seattle industries (notably Boeing) that have recently moved out of the region due to the combined effect of a weakened post-bubble economy and intransigent traffic problems, the Space Needle too, just may be a landmark ready to pick up and go—to franchise and syndicate itself, to protect and shelter itself—to hit the road, once and for all.

Bibliography

Anderson, Benedict, *Imagined Communities* (London and New York: Verso, 1983).

Bachelard, Gaston, *The Poetics of Space* (trans. Maria Jolas; New York: The Orion Press, 1964).

Brecher, Jeremy, Tim Costello and Brendan Smith, *Globalization from Below: The Power of Solidarity* (Cambridge, MA: South End Press, 2000).

de Certeau, Michel, *The Practice of Everyday Life* (Berkeley, CA: University of California Press, 1984).

Duncan, Don, *Meet Me at the Center: The Story of Seattle Center from the Beginnings to the 1962 Seattle World's Fair to the 21st Century* (Seattle: Seattle Center Foundation, 1992).

Findlay, John M., *Magic Lands: Western Cityscapes and American Culture after 1940* (Berkeley, CA: University of California Press, 1992).

Freud, Sigmund, 'The "Uncanny"', *The Standard Edition of the Complete Psychological Works of Sigmund Freud* (London: Hogarth [Chatto & Windus], 1955).

Greenhalgh, Paul, *Ephemeral Vistas: The Expositions Universelles, Great Exhibitions and World's Fairs, 1851–1939* (Manchester: Manchester University Press, 1988).

Hartman, Geoffrey H., 'Public Memory and its Discontents', in *idem, The Longest Shadow: In the Aftermath of the Holocaust* (Bloomington, IN: Indiana University Press, 1996).

—'Like Niobe All Tears: Reflections on Memorials and 9/11', Paper sponsored by the Center for Religion and Media, presented at New York University (3 October, 2003).

Lefebvre, Henri, *The Production of Space* (Oxford, UK and Cambridge, USA: Basil Blackwell, 1991).

Marx, Karl, *The Marx-Engels Reader* (ed. Robert Tucker; New York and London: Norton, 2nd edn, 1978).

Moody, Fred, *Seattle and the Demons of Ambition: A Love Story* (New York: St Martin's Press, 2003).

Nora, Pierre, et al., *Realms of Memory: Rethinking the French Past*, I (ed. Lawrence D. Kritzman; trans. Arthur Goldhammer; 3 vols.; New York: Columbia University Press, 1996).

Rydell, Robert W., *All the World's a Fair* (Chicago: The University of Chicago Press, 1984).

Tuan, Yi-Fu, *Topophilia: A Study of Environmental Perception, Attitudes, and Values* (New York: Columbia University Press, 1990 [1974]).

Wallace, James, and Jim Erickson, *Hard Drive: Bill Gates and the Making of the Microsoft Empire* (New York: John Wiley & Sons, 1992).

Young, James E., *The Texture of Memory: Holocaust Memorials and Meaning* (New Haven, CT, and London: Yale University Press, 1993).

Notes

1.   Pierre Nora, *et al.*, *Realms of Memory: Rethinking the French Past* (ed. Lawrence D. Kritzman; trans. Arthur Goldhammer; 3 vols.; New York: Columbia University Press, 1996), I, 7. For Nora *lieux de mémoire* 'are fundamentally vestiges, the ultimate embodiments of a commemorative consciousness that survives in a history which, having renounced memory, cries for it. The notion has emerged because society has banished ritual', 6. While Nora writes within the context of a loss of tradition in French regionalism, the idea is useful for interpreting the shift of consciousness that has accompanied the changes in which Seattle has been transformed from it own kind of folksy regionalism to a behemoth of corporate globalization.

2.   Fred Moody, *Seattle and the Demons of Ambition: A Love Story* (New York: St Martin's Press, 2003), 119.

3.   In a presentation titled 'The New Domestic Security Economy' given as part of New York University's 'Scholars Lecture Series' (16/10/03), economist Marc Leiberman also invokes this metaphor of the gap between a first shoe and second shoe falling. However, he does so within a slightly different context to what I am talking about here. In his analysis of what he describes as a new domestic security economy, he describes the post 9/11 recession that lingers with us today as the first shoe to what might happen in the event of another major terror attack. Were that to occur, local, national, and global economies would experience a plummet in terms of standard of living, and this plummet would take years to recover from. This may at first seem self evident, but the point Leiberman is making is that although since 9/11 we have experienced a deepening of the recession that began in March 2000, the economy has been relatively resilient in its ability to change gears and absorb the shocks of the downturn. His argument is that this has provided us with something of a rehearsal for the real acts of economic distress that would occur in the event of say a dirty bomb or the deployment of other kinds of weapons of mass destruction.

4.   Geoffrey H. Hartman, Project Director of the Fortunoff Video Archive for Holocaust Testimonies and Sterling Professor of English and Comparative Literature at Yale University, recently presented a paper in which he commented that the issue of dates and temporal data hover between punctuating and being punctuated by the temporal field. Dates have a branding effect that disrupts the casual passing of time. 'Like Niobe All Tears: Reflections on Memorials and 9/11', sponsored by the Center for Religion and Media at New York University (3 October, 2003). I am arguing that something similar happens in the juxtaposition of temporal moments that I am working with here.

5.   James E. Young, *The Texture of Memory: Holocaust Memorials and Meaning* (New Haven, CT, and London: Yale University Press, 1993), 27.

6.   Gaston Bachelard, *The Poetics of Space* (trans. Maria Jolas; New York: The Orion Press, 1964), xxiii.

7.   Bachelard, *The Poetics of Space*, xii.

8.   Nora, *et al.*, *Realms of Memory*, 6.

9.   See Benedict Anderson, *Imagined Communities* (London and New York: Verso, 1983).

10. Yi-Fu Tuan, *Topophilia: A Study of Environmental Perception, Attitudes, and Values* (New York: Columbia University Press, 1990 [1974]), 247.

11. In *Topophilia*, his 1974 groundbreaking study of geography and space, Yi-Fu Tuan writes that in 'great metropolises, no man can know well more than a small fragment of the total urban scene; nor is it necessary for him to have a mental map or imagery of the entire city in order to prosper in his corner of the world. Yet the city dweller seems to have a psychological need to possess an image of the total environment in order to place his own environment.' Further in the passage, he continues by saying that '[on] the high level of abstraction, the immense complexity of a city may be encapsulated in the name itself such as Rome, or to a monument (Eiffel Tower), or to a silhouette such as the famous skyline of New York, or to a slogan or nickname such as The Queen City of the West' (192). The Space Needle fulfills just this sort of function within the Seattle skyline, were it to disappear we would lose our internal compass, which is what many New Yorkers experienced in the aftermath of losing the twin towers.

12. Bachelard, *The Poetics of Space*, xxxi.

13. Bachelard, *The Poetics of Space*, xxxii.

14. Sigmund Freud, 'The "Uncanny"', in *The Standard Edition of the Complete Psychological Works of Sigmund Freud* (London: Hogarth [Chatto & Windus], 1955), 228.

15. Freud addresses the confusion over terminology when he writes:

> What interests us most…is to find that among its different shades of meaning the word 'heimlich' exhibits one which is identical with its opposite, 'unheimlich'. What is heimlich thus comes to be unheimlich. In general we are reminded that the word 'heimlich' is not unambiguous, belongs to two sets of ideas, which, without being contradictory, are yet very different: on the one hand it means what is familiar and agreeable, and on the other, what is concealed and kept out of sight. 'Unheimlich' is customarily used, we are told, as the contrary only of the first signification of 'heimlich', and not of the second. Sanders tells us nothing concerning a possible genetic connection between these two meanings of heimlich. On the other hand, we notice that Schelling says something which throws quite a new light on the concept of the unheimlich, for which we were certainly not prepared. According to him, everything is unheimlich that ought to have remained secret and hidden but has come to light (233-34).

16. Freud, 'The "Uncanny"', 229.

17. Don Duncan, *Meet Me at the Center: The Story of Seattle Center from the Beginnings to the 1962 Seattle World's Fair to the 21st Century* (Seattle: Seattle Center Foundation, 1992), 54.

18. John M. Findlay, *Magic Lands: Western Cityscapes and American Culture after 1940* (Berkeley, CA: University of California Press, 1992), 229.

19. Findlay, *Magic Lands*, 229.

20. Findlay, *Magic Lands*, 249.

21. See Moody, *Seattle and the Demon's of Ambition*. Moody argues that throughout the course of local history, mainstream Seattleites have repeatedly allowed themselves to be swept away by the hype of boosterism. He describes two kinds of Seattleites: the first are those belonging to 'Greater Seattle'—the ones eager to jump

on the booster's bandwagon, and the second are those belonging to 'Lesser Seattle'—those who have historically chosen to live in Seattle not out of a sense of ambition, but rather because of an underachieving desire to drop out of the so-called rat race, to live simply, and to enjoy the leisure associated with the mountains and waterways that make up the local landscape. He has been criticized for his reductionist characterization of local culture, but he does nevertheless make a valid observation about the pervasiveness of certain cultural attitudes and stereotypes in which residents internalized a utopic belief about the value of living in the Northwest.

22. Quoted in Robert W. Rydell, *All the World's a Fair* (Chicago: The University of Chicago Press, 1984), 185.

23. Quoted in Rydell, *All the World's a Fair*, 185.

24. Rydell, *All the World's a Fair*, 185.

25. James Wallace and Jim Erickson, *Hard Drive: Bill Gates and the Making of the Microsoft Empire* (New York: John Wiley & Sons, 1992), 8

26. Wallace and Erickson, *Hard Drive*, 8.

27. Wallace and Erickson, *Hard Drive*, 7.

28. Michel de Certeau, *The Practice of Everyday Life* (Berkeley, CA: University of California Press, 1984).

29. Henri Lefebvre, *The Production of Space* (Oxford, UK and Cambridge, USA: Basil Blackwell, 1991), 28.

30. Lefebvre, *The Production of Space*, 21.

31. Lefebvre, *The Production of Space*, 74.

32. In *The Grundisse*, we can see the influence Marx has on Lefebvre's characterization of the relationship between production and history. Marx writes: 'Bourgeois society is the most developed and the most complex historic organization of production. The categories which express its relations, the comprehension of its structure, thereby also allows insights into the structure and the relations of production of all the vanished social formations out of whose ruins and elements it built itself up, whose partly still unconquered remants are carried along within it, whose mere nuances have developed explicit significance within it' (241). *The Marx-Engels Reader* (ed. Robert Tucker; New York and London: Norton, 2nd edn, 1978).

33. Lefebvre, *The Production of Space*, 116.

34. Lefebvre, *The Production of Space*, 38.

35. By today's standards this earlier form of information technology could be measured in terms similar to the impact that the Internet has had in reorganizing our lives. On the subject of the ephemerality and built-in obsolescence of the fairs, see Paul Greenhalgh's *Ephemeral Vistas: The Expositions Universelles, Great Exhibitions and World's Fairs, 1851–1939* (Manchester: Manchester University Press, 1988).

36. Lefebvre, *The Production of Space*, 220.

37. Lefebvre, *The Production of Space*.

38. Geoffrey H. Hartman, 'Public Memory and its Discontents' is a chapter taken from Hartman's book *The Longest Shadow: In the Aftermath of the Holocaust* (Bloomington: Indiana University Press, 1996), 104.

39. See http://www.historylink.org/output.cfm?file_id=1443

40. Blackburn here refers to the November–March 1909 boycott (nearly 90 years to the date of the WTO protests) by hundreds of 'Wobblies' from the International

Workers of the World, who came by trainloads to the city of Spokane in Eastern Washington in order to protest about the unfair labor practices of the day, 1.

41. Marc Leiberman gives definition to the parameters of this new domestic security economy when he argues that from the late 1980s through the late 1990s three major economic adjustments factored into the boom economy. The first adjustment revolved around the end of the Cold War and the consequent drop in defense spending, which resulted in an increase in transfer of payments, and an increase in productivity as a consequence of a reduction of the budget deficit. The second major adjustment came with the tech-industry revolution and the increases it also brought in terms of gross domestic product (GDP), access to resources, standard of living, and overall productivity. And the third adjustment came with the expansion of international trade due to the intensive lobbying efforts by organizations such as the WTO, NAFTA, etc., which reduced trade barriers and paved the way for tremendous economic gains, even though they also created massive problems in terms of the equitable distribution of wealth and fair access to resources. Leiberman's final point is that we are currently somewhere in the beginning or the middle of a fourth economic adjustment, which is the post 9/11 reallocation of resources to national defense and domestic security. This fourth adjustment, where the reversal of gains from international trade at the demands of increased security checks and monitors with respect trade and goods, works to reverse all of the gains experienced in the other three adjustments. 'The New Domestic Security Economy' given as part of New York University's 'Scholars Lecture Series' (16/10/03).

42. Lefebvre, *The Production of Space*, 39.

43. Lefebvre, *The Production of Space*, 222.

44. Jeremy Brecher, Tim Costello and Brendan Smith, *Globalization from Below: The Power of Solidarity* (Cambridge, MA: South End Press, 2000), 61.

45. Brecher, et al., *Globalization from Below*, 62.

46. Brecher, et al., *Globalization from Below*, 83.

47. Brecher, et al., *Globalization from Below*, 9.

48. Nora, *Realms of Memory*, 18. Nora writes that the quintessential example of a portable monument is located within Judaism's relationship to the Torah. Of course, the Space Needle ads are trivial by comparison, but it is relevant to consider both as part of a similar kind of logic precisely because it situates the tragedy of the holocaust against the spoofing irony of the Washington Lottery's ads and the deeper fear of annihilation contained within that humor.

Ultima Thule – The City at the End of the World:
Jerusalem in Modern Christian Apocalyptic

Hillel Schwartz

> Ultima Thule! Utmost Isle!
> Here in thy harbors for a while
> We lower our sails; a while we rest
> From the unending, endless quest.
>> Henry Wadsworth Longfellow, *Ultima Thule* (1880)

My chosen subject—or has it chosen me?—is Ultima Thule, the Farthest Point, 'limit of any journey', a place at once final and frontier. Such a subject, in such a place as Jerusalem, may inspire a terrible illusion of self-importance, an illusion that local psychiatrists call the 'Jerusalem Syndrome'.[1]

But one Emily Hiestand is the more important figure here.

At the end of July, 1990, Emily Hiestand traveled with her mother to the Orkneys, a group of islands off the NW coast of Scotland just south and east of the Faroes—and of Iceland, which appeared as Ultima Thule on many a medieval map and was still Ultima Thule to British adventurer Sir Richard Burton as late as 1875. In a meditative essay, 'South of the Ultima Thule', Hiestand describes her 'transatlantic crossing by air' from New York to Glasgow as itself 'a chamber of eschatological thought': strapped into a world with its own recirculating air, its own overhead light, its own fictions of departure and arrival, she is being transported from the New World at one end of the ocean to an Ancestral World at the other end, along a polar trajectory.[2] She and her mother are headed for the land of her mother's Presbyterian faith. Once on the ground and driving north out of Glasgow, she finds the fields 'a radiant green, the lochs clean; outside the rare cities the air is an edenic vapor'. But, just as she reaches Findhorn, that magical community of sprites, spiritualists, and giant sprouts, she hears over the Edenic vapors that an Iraqi army has invaded Kuwait. Thenceforward, her journey to the farthest points south of Ultima Thule will be bound to the Mediterranean and that twentieth-century place and phrase, the 'Middle East'.

Arrived in the Orkneys—67 bleak islands eroded by hard wind and cold rain and enshrouded in coastal fog—Hiestand finds that the people too blend in, civil but dour, as unprepossessing as they are unimpressed by the anxious grandeur of other, younger societies. Crossing from island to island, she is struck by two kinds of neolithic ruins laid bare 'under the largest sky I have ever seen'. First, great circles of standing stones in open fields; second, chambered tombs beneath massive mounds.

These are the oldest such ruins in Europe; the stones were raised, the chambered tombs hollowed out just before or just as neolithic culture began to turn away from goddesses toward gods, during the third millennium BCE. Tribes had made their way up from the Mediterranean to the Orkneys a millennium before, when the North Atlantic climate was nearly tropical; kindred tribes left the earliest, Chalcolithic, evidences of human settlement in Urshamen, or Urusalm. While the rest of Europe and the 'Middle East' fell before the onslaught of Indo-Europeans with horses, bows and arrows, and a thunderously male sky god, the Orkney people were burying their dead in mazy tunnels and arranging 17-foot-high, 4-foot-thick slabs of stone in 100-foot-wide circles for rituals of regeneration or rites of astronomical calculation. For millennia, Orkney couples would be married within the circles of Stenness or Brodgar—stone rings, writes Hiestand, that 'are flung-open public forms, filled with light'.

She herself ventures into the chambered tomb at Maeshowe through a narrow flagstoned passageway to a central room, cut as square as the Qa'aba or, it is said, the Holy of Holies. The walls of Maeshowe run wild with neolithic images of dragon, walrus, and serpent, and with runes of a much later date—among them, a rune from 1151 CE, memorial of crusaders leaving for the Holy Land, for Jerusalem. Emerging from the tomb of Maeshowe is, she writes, 'like coming out of a matinee movie: you rub your eyes in the too-bright light'.

We are still in the dark about the why and wherefore of these 'stone sermons' south of the Ultima Thule, but, writes Hiestand, 'We do not have to decide between astronomy and ritual to know that the stones—already old when the Neolithics plucked them from the earth—vibrate with the slowest breath in nature and bring us intimately in touch with planet time. They call us to consider that time itself, born again each moment, is also tall and worn.' This Land's End, these almost northernmost islands built up of Old Red Sandstone, lead Hiestand from a First Place and a Last Place to the sense of a First Time and Last Time. And at every turn, through the faint static of what will become the Gulf War, she is led back from Ultima Thule to Jerusalem. 'In the late-twentieth century', she writes, 'we are the same species as the Neolithic builders, and we know that we are capable of Mardi Gras, test tubes, Mount Palomar, and *wailing walls*, and of growing reflective under the stars.'

The Norse or Vikings who took over these Neolithic sites, marking their runes on standing stones and the walls of tombs under Orkney cairns, moved on toward what the classical and medieval world, pagan or Christian, knew most often as the Ultima Thule, Iceland, a place 'six days' sail North of Britain and near the Frozen Sea'.[3] True, the Vikings momentarily went beyond this last stop, venturing to Greenland and Vinland, but memories of such places were as short as the North Atlantic climate was favorable; after the arctic ice tightened once again around northernmost North America, late in the thirteenth century, Iceland was, for every intent and purpose, the last stop, Ultima Thule.

'Thule'—from the Phoenician *tzul*, darkness? the Hebrew *tzalul*, obscurity? the Arabic *Tul*, afar off? the Greek *telos*, end or goal?[4]

For St Brendan, *Thule* or *Tila* had been neither end nor goal nor darkness but flame and smoke. Drawn by an angelic vision of a land across the sea where the saintly might live joyfully and forever, Brendan set sail in the sixth century with 17 comrades in a curragh 'ribbed and sided with oak-tanned ox-hide strips' but in mid-voyage was blown toward a 'large and high mountain in the ocean…with misty clouds above it, and a great smoke issuing from its summit… Then they saw the peak of the mountain unclouded and shooting up flames into the sky which it drew back again to itself so that the mountain was a burning pyre.'[5]

Brendan in legend journeyed redemptively beyond this *Tila*, which at least in its fearsome isolation appealed as undisturbed refuge to Irish Christian monks who settled there in 793 CE, when Iceland was green enough to sustain the prayers of shepherd anchorites and well enough forested to sustain the shipbuilding and woodbeam-houses of Viking *landnámsmenn* who arrived about a century later.

By the year 999, these Norse 'landtakers' had established a society of perhaps 40,000, all of whom, in that year or the year 1000, at the behest of an evangelical King of Norway, Olaf Trygvesson (who was holding some Icelandic merchants hostage), embraced Latin Christianity. The conversion, like other national conversions in the Baltic, was rather a sly accommodation to the cross and creed of Latin Christendom than a retreat from the oak and oaths of Scandinavia, but it did prompt the end of slavery in Iceland and confirm a process of political mediation that had begun in 930 CE with the founding of the Allthing, the first semi-democratic parliament in the West (other, possibly, than one in the Faeroe Islands north of the Orkneys—Faeroe not a Semitic term but Old Norse for sheep).[6]

By the mid-thirteenth century, however, Icelandic feuding had produced such violent internecine struggles, and the worsening weather had cornered farmers and fishermen in such poverty, that Iceland lost its sovereignty to a distant Denmark. Late medieval accounts of Iceland were of a desolate, savage land, full of horrible sounds such as those reported in the Brendan legends—'the noise of bellows blowing like thunder'.

That thunder was ice cracking, glaciers calving, volcanoes rumbling. Iceland, which lies athwart the Mid-Atlantic ridge, owes its existence as one of the youngest landmasses in the world to continuous eruptions of magma from the depths of our planet.

What does all this have to do with Christian apocalyptic? The horrible sounds were understood by medieval Catholics and early modern Protestants to be the shrieks and groans of sinners in Hell. 'Soldiers of Christ', St Brendan had urged his men, 'be strong in faith unfeigned and in the armor of the Spirit, for we are now on the confines of Hell.' Beneath the sulfurous pall that hung over Hekla, most visibly relentless of Icelandic volcanoes—erupting five times between 1104 and 1300, and twelve times after—lay an opening into Hell. Christian eschato-geographers knew nothing of the North American and Eurasian continental plates that meet exactly on the fissured plain of Thingvellir where the Icelandic parliament met, but they knew that one could glimpse Hell from the Hekla of Ultima Thule.[7]

'There is in Iceland', wrote the son-in-law of Melanchthon, the sixteenth-century theologian whose Lutheranism the Icelanders too would adopt via devoutly mournful Danes, 'There is in Iceland, Mount Hekla, being of as dreadful a depth as Hell itself which resoundeth with lamentable and miserable yellings… The common people of that country are verily persuaded that there is a descent down into Hell by this gulfe; and therefore when any battles are fought elsewhere, in whatsoever part of the whole world, or any bloody slaughters are committed, they have learned by long experience, what horrible tumults, what monstrous screeches are heard around this mountain.' Geopolitically and mythopoetically, Land's End and Life's End, the far wall of the Norse Middle Garden and the never-so-far-off war of Christian Armageddon, coincided.

There were equally prevalent stories, noted in classical sources, that put Vulcan's furnace under Italy's Mount Vesuvius, which Christian mythographers knew as another likely opening into Hell. Yet another and similar geofiction brings us screaming back to Jerusalem. For even as the Jebusite, Canaanite and Jewish 'Place of the Covenant of Peace' was known to medieval Christians as the site of the first stone by which heavens and waters were separated and site of the dust from which the Lord scraped Adam, Jerusalem was also supposed to be the site of Adam's grave, of the

Crucifixion and, looking out over the valley of Jehoshaphat, the Last Judgment. Indeed, it was said that from certain crevices in this valley one could hear—Christian or Muslim—the cries of the damned. In 1047 the traveler Nasir-i Khusraw visited Jehoshaphat on the eastern side of Jerusalem—already confused with the biblical valley of human sacrifice and filth, Ge Hinnom or Gehenna, on the western side—where 'The common people state that when you stand at the brink of the valley you may hear the cries of those in Hell'.[8]

So a set of subterranean eschatological circuits connects the cartographic and geological Ultima Thule of Iceland with a cartomantic and cosmological Jerusalem, a place as Last as it is First, as conclusive as it is originary. These circuits were not shorted by modernity. From the sixteenth through to the late-nineteenth century, Iceland was devastated by volcanic eruptions, erosion of scant topsoil from deforested overgrazed land, recurrent famine, and Danish depredations, until Iceland was regarded for all practical purposes as being at the End of the World, where was heard 'neither the sound of the churn nor the shout of the shepherd', and Icelanders themselves seemed a people at the end of their rope. Yet when Sir Richard Burton in 1875 completed his two-volume account of a tour of Iceland, he chose as epigraph to his *Ultima Thule; or, A Summer in Iceland* the following:

> Not among nymphs and sirens, founts and flowers,
>   Not in voluptuous herbage in the shade;
> But on the toilsome steep where valour towers
>   Alone, O Prince, our supreme good is laid.

This is an English translation of a stanza from Torquato Tasso's sixteenth-century epic poem, *Godfrey of Bulloigne, or, The Recoverie of Jerusalem*, the stanza itself an encouragement toward the Crusader King's recovery of Jerusalem from the clutches of Islam in 1099.[9]

The Iceland-Jerusalem connection was no afterthought; Burton prefaced his Iceland volumes with these words: 'The subject is, to some extent, like Greece and Palestine, of the sensational type'. Each of us, he explained to fellow Victorians, each of us has imagined our own Iceland as we have imagined our own Athens, our own Jerusalem. Travellers with 'Iceland on the brain' had there exclaimed at scenes of 'thrilling horror', 'majestic grandeur' and 'heavenly beauty' that Burton, with the unjaundiced eye of a veteran adventurer, found meagre, just as Nasir-i Khusraw, with his cosmopolitan ear, heard no cries splitting through the cracks of Jehoshaphat/Gehenna, or what Muslims call *al-Sahira*, the 'dry-as-dust plain'.[10]

   While Iceland over the centuries had become ever more remote and subject thus to ever more hyperbolic fantasies, Jerusalem had receded from the center of the world and from the center of world maps. Christian pilgrims had perforce to invoke fantasies—personal, biblical, or, like Tasso's, historical—so as not to be disappointed in the actual place. From the sixteenth through to the late-nineteenth century, as an Ottoman *sanjuk*, a second-class outpost, Jerusalem was a desolate vision for the relatively rare pilgrim. If Columbus the Cristoferens or Christ-bearer had been looking West to find the East so that he could demonstrate the proximity of Earth's landmasses and thus the real likelihood of bringing the Evangel to China and the Indies in the short time before the end (around, he thought, 1666 CE), he died willing what little remained of his wealth to the restoration of the Church of the Holy Sepulchre, a dirty place of cavilling Christian communities who kept watch over an increasingly indefinable glory. The very structure of the Church was about to collapse in 1555, and despite a restoration that year at the suffrance of Sultan Suleiman, the rest of Jerusalem—especially Roman Catholic and Jewish areas—suffered from casual neglect and calculated nuisance.[11]

   When René Chateaubriand visited Jerusalem in 1806, the city was in no way comparable to the Renaissance and Baroque splendors of Rome, however that city may have been embarrassed by Napoleon's troops, and in no way comparable to the still glowing splendors of Constantinople. Jerusalem hardly resembled that holy city depicted in the Book of Tobit as quoted at length by Christiaan van Adrichen in his 1595 guide to Jerusalem:

> O Jerusalem the holy City... Blessed are they which have been sorrowful for all thy scourges. For they shall rejoice for thee, when they shall see all thy glory...for JERUSALEM shall be built up with Saphires & Emeralds, and thy walls with precious stones, and thy towers & thy bulwarks with pure gold. And the streets of JERUSALEM shall be paved with Beryl and Carbuncle and stones of Ophir. And all her streets shall say, Hallelujah![12]

To Chateaubriand, her streets said nothing at all:

> one asks oneself if these are not the scattered monuments of a cemetery in the midst of a desert. When you enter the city you find no consolation for the sadness of its exterior. You wander in the tiny unpaved streets which rise and descend over the uneven terrain and you walk amidst clouds of dust and over slippery gravel... There is no one on the streets, no one at the gates of the city.[13]

Surely this was Ultima Thule, a last resting (if unrestful) place, and it was only through fantasy—biblical, historical—that Chateaubriand could make of Jerusalem anything other than a burial ground:

> I stood there, my eyes fixed on Jerusalem, measuring the height of its walls, recalling all the memories of history from Abraham to Godfry of Bouillon, reflecting how the entire world was changed by the mission of the Son of Man, and seeking in vain the Temple, on which 'not a stone rests upon a stone'. If I were to live a thousand years, never would I forget this wilderness which still seems to breathe with the grandeur of Jehovah and the terrors of death.

Nikolai Gogol, seeking refreshment of his dead soul in Jerusalem in 1848, found himself parched instead. 'Not only were my prayers unable to rise up to heaven', he wrote to Count Tolstoy; 'I could not even tear them loose from my breast. Never before had I felt so keenly my insensitivity, and how dry and hard I was, like a block of wood.'[14]

Jerusalem was a dull, drear terminus for Christian visitors of all stripes: the romantic Gallican Alphonse de Lamartine, the Catholic Flaubert, longing for a sentimental education, and the always-Protestant always-prickly Herman Melville. Lamartine, touring the Levant in 1832, arrived in Jerusalem on a November day when he could hear and see women moaning over the dead, but apart from that he saw nothing, heard nothing: 'no one came out of the city, no one entered; the same desolation, the same silence…as we should have expected before the entombed gates of Pompeii… A complete eternal silence reigns.'[15] Flaubert in 1850 found Jerusalem 'a charnel house encased in walls', and the French consul in Jerusalem 'a human ruin, in a city of ruins, who believed in nothing and hated everything, except the dead'.[16]

Herman Melville, New Englander but hardly Puritan enough to fall head over heels for arid rock, stood before the gates of Jerusalem and shrank before a '*Village of Lepers* – houses facing the wall – Zion. Their park, a dung-heap. – They sit by the gates asking alms, – then whine – avoidance of them & horror.' He was struck by the '*Ghostliness of the names* – Jehosophat – Hinon &c'. In Jehosophat, Melville saw Jewish gravestones everywhere, 'So thick, a warren of the dead – so old, the Hebrew inscriptions can hardly be distinguished from the wrinkles formed by Time… The grave stones project *out* from the side-hill, as if already in act of resurrection.' Christian Jerusalem was no livelier; the Church of the Holy Sepulchre was 'overhung by the lofty & ruinous dome whose fallen plastering reveals the meagre skeleton of beams & laths…a sort of plague-stricken splendor reigns in the painted & mildewed walls around'. At Christ's tomb, 'Wedged & half-dazzled, you stare for a moment on the ineloquence of the bedizened slab, and glad to come out, wipe your brow glad to escape as from the heat & jam of a show-box. All is glitter & nothing is gold.'[17]

Deriving *Zion* from the Hebrew *ziya*, parched desert, Amos Elon observes in *Jerusalem: City of Mirrors*: 'at most times, people in Jerusalem must have felt themselves not at the world's center but at its end'. Even after Thomas Cook, a Baptist lay preacher, launched his Eastern Tours in 1869, capitalizing upon some 2000 Holy Land travel books issued in the nineteenth century;[18] and even after thousands of Russian peasants made the pilgrimage to Jerusalem on foot at the instance of czars and metropolitans eager to reconstitute the connection between a first Jerusalem in the Holy Land and a second, third, or New Jerusalem in Moscow;[19] and even as the Holy Land itself was excavated and exalted by pious archeologists and Anglo-American Zionists,[20] the rhetoric may have been, as Czar Alexander II said, that 'Jerusalem is the center of the world and our mission must be there', but the experience of Jerusalem was as an End. The German Templers, British Israelites, American colonists under the apocalyptic tutelage of Horatio Spafford, all were moved toward Jerusalem as a place of the Endtimes and an Ultima Thule, much as Jews, Muslims and Christians alike had been moved for centuries to specify that their last remains, ash or corpse, be sent to Jerusalem to be interred close to the valley where redemption must take place and where it seemed reasonable that those whose bones lay closest to the narrow valley would have first best places in New Jerusalem amidst the crowds and hallelujah chaos of a truly jumping Jehoshaphat.[21]

The English writer G.K. Chesterton, in a 1920 work entitled *The New Jerusalem* and emphatically anti-hallelujah, nonetheless starts by noting that he began his trip to the holy city at a time 'when people were talking about some menace of the end of the world, not apocalyptic but astronomical'. He appears to take such a meteoric End lightly, but then writes of his home town of Beaconsfield with 'its own domestic day of judgment'; the four corners of Beaconsfield are called 'ends' after the four nearest towns, and Chesterton is taken with 'London End'—'the very name of it was like a vision of some vain thing at once ultimate and infinite. The very title of London End sounds like the other end of nowhere, or (what is worse) of everywhere.' London itself is a mess, and so is the West; feeling himself and his civilization at 'loose ends', Chesterton goes to Jerusalem to 'get hold of the right end of it [of civilization? history?], and especially the other end of it'. He enters Jerusalem under the shield of the Red Cross—guest in an ambulance—as aware of the symbolism of such an entry as was Kaiser Wilhelm II in 1899, entering all in white on a white horse, and as in 1917 was Edmund Allenby, who knew that his name in Arabic could be read as 'Allah en nebi', prophet of the Lord, and who dismounted and entered on foot while being filmed for a 13-minute newsreel, *General Allenby's Entry into Jerusalem*, the most successful newsreel of World War I.[22]

Once within the walls of the holy city, arrived at the 'right end' of things, does Chesterton the critic of Victorian pessimism and industrial capitalism, writer of detective fictions and comic allegories, feel centered? No, he feels as if 'in a prison and on a precipice'. In Jerusalem 'All the sights are glimpses; and things far can be visible and things near invisible'. He pursues this metaphor toward a philosophy of sightseeing in which one comes to see exactly what one has in mind—but then (and I mean to make as much of this here as he does in his book)—then Chesterton is overwhelmed by a vision in white. It begins to snow. The snow continues, day and night, a persistent, driven snow, unlike any in the historical record, or so he believes. 'Nothing', he writes a dozen pages farther on, 'nothing has been so wholly missed in our modern religious ideals as the ideal of tenacity', a tenacity he finds in the Jerusalem snow and, under that, in the white stone of Jerusalem, this ruinous, precipitous, OLD place at the right end of things, in a headdress of snow.[23]

Chesterton says nothing about Iceland or Ultima Thule, but he has read his Burton and knows very well where he is. He is not at the center of things or of spirit. In two years, back in Beaconsfield, he will convert to Roman Catholicism[24] and, perhaps, enter his New Jerusalem, but the place he entered by Red Cross ambulance was the End. For modern Western Christians, Jerusalem until 1919 or 1967 could only be the Ultima Thule:

1. It was no longer at the center of Christian maps.
2. It was not a major center of Christian population.
3. It was not a commanding center of Western Christian ceremony, either at the Church of the Holy Sepulchre or at the Protestant Garden tomb[25] located outside the city walls late in the nineteenth century.
4. It was not a center of Western Christian church offices.
5. It was not yet a center of Western political maneuvering, although such may have been in the mind of the evangelical American Admiral, Alfred T. Mahan, writing his *Retrospect and Prospect*, and declaring in 1902, 'the Middle East, if I may adopt a term which I have not seen, will some day need its Malta, as well as its Gibraltar'.[26]
6. It was not a center of Western Christian culture. Most restoration campaigns had foundered in denominational squabbling.

And it was not, I would be willing to argue, a center for the renewal of Western Christian faith. Those Europeans or Americans who went to Jerusalem after 1500 went with their faith intact; once there, they struggled to keep their faith. Rarely did they claim to return transformed. Mark Twain's Innocents Abroad in 1910 had some Protestant doubts about the relics they were towed past, but were much more dubious of a short column rising from the middle of the marble pavement of the Greek Chapel in the Church of the Holy Sepulchre, a column marking 'the exact *centre of the earth'*, and capable of changing position as the center of the world changed due to convulsions during which 'whole ranges of mountains, probably – have flown off into space, thus lessening the diameter of the earth, and changing the exact locality of its centre by a point or two'.[27]

In only one sense, Jerusalem WAS a center—a center of Christian burial, and so a Last Place, an Ultima Thule. The British military engineer Charles Warren, excavating Jerusalem for the Palestine Exploration Fund in the 1870s, was surprised by the familiarity of visiting Americans with the topography of the country; 'they accounted for it by telling me that their clergy made a point of explaining and describing it from the pulpit frequently'. Why? In part because, for both Jews and Christians, burial in Jerusalem would save them the 'long underground journey on the great day' of resurrection.[28] In so far as Jerusalem is a Place-In-Waiting for resurrection, it is also part of the Last Times. But how does its being a Last Place affect the Last Times, or vice versa?

Much has been written by historians of religion about sacred centers; much has been theorized in general by sociologists concerned with centers and peripheries, by social and structural anthropologists weaving their way between the focal and the liminal.[29] And long have been the debates about the nature of frontiers, especially at the ends of centuries when one seems about to cross a threshold,[30] but the number of theoretical studies of Last Places is vanishing small, especially with regard to questions of Last Things or End Times.[31]

Before I make some gestures toward a theory of Last Places, I need to distinguish Ultima Thule from Antipodes. The Ultima Thule is by definition the farthest place for us all; it is an absolute, and without bias, for in a positional sense it is neutral. Ultima Thule may be the last familiar setting, the last recognizable foothold, or the last known outpost; whether this delights or disturbs you is a personal matter. On the other hand the Antipodes is the farthest place from you, or me, or from her over there; it is relative and it is oppositional: what happens at the Antipodes, where people walk on their heads and worship the mud, is a polar reverse of what happens here. In eschatological terms, the Ultima Thule is one form or another of apocalypse as revelation; the Antipodes is one form or another of apocalypse as cataclysm, for it insists upon the antinomian and/or the impossibly pure and perfect, and either way those are the makings for human disaster. An Ultima Thule can slide toward the Antipodes when seen as the last pure place, unadulterated, untouched, and hence in need of the most vehement protection (Münster, seventeenth-century Old Believer camps in Russia), or when seen as the last frontier of the noble outlaw or survivalist, hence in need of the most vicious defense.[32]

Now onto some pairs of confluence between Last Place and Last Time, with brief allusion to relevant episodes in modern Christian apocalyptic that put Jerusalem at that confluence.

1. *Last Place as the Lost Place, vanished under layers of debris/Last Time as the elusive time, always at hand though difficult to decipher.*

I think here of biblical archeology driven by the apocalyptic need to know the exact dimensions of the First and Second Temples so that a Third Temple can be designed in advance of the Second Coming. This need, I suspect, drove Charles George Gordon to take a measuring rod to Jerusalem in 1883, during a sabbatical between his famous marshalling of British forces against Taiping millenarians led by a man who styled himself Tien Wang, Heavenly King, and his defense of Khartoum against Islamic millenarians following their Mahdi into battle. It was this need that drove the Christadelphians I met in the 1970s to build exquisite three-dimensional models of what the Third Temple most certainly must be like when Jesus comes, very soon. And it is this need that drives American evangelical Protestants to support the Temple Institute of Rabbi Yisrael Ariel, hoping to hasten the [second] advent of the Messiah by making all necessary surveys and plans for rebuilding the Temple.[33]

2. *Last Place as the secret place, the last place one would look/Last Time as the time when secrets are revealed or common truths at last respected.*

I think here of a 1750 magical tract, *La véritable magie noire, ou le secret des secrets: manuscrit trouvé à Jerusalem dans le sépulcre de Salomon*, in which the secrets of the world revealed to Solomon and told to his son Rehoboam and thenceforward hidden lest they fall into the wrong hands are at last revealed in the form of astromancy, conjuration, magical chants, and runes, now that an enlightened world is ripe for salvation.[34] This magical millenarianism was shared by two enlightened Swedes, August Nordenskjöld, a mineralogist and alchemist, and Carl Bernhard Wadström, mineralogist, and anti-slavery activist, when in 1789 they published a *Plan for a Free Community*, a Swedenborgian New Jerusalem to be planted in Sierra Leone. For Emanuel Swedenborg's followers, it was clear that people had looked in all the wrong places for the New, the true, Jerusalem; they had been looking toward the Judean hills or some celestial ever-after when Jerusalem was always in plain sight: it lay within. Once everyone found the holy city in the last place that anyone would think to look, the world would be transformed. So thought Nordenskjöld, unofficial royal alchemist to Gustave III; so thought Wadström, editing the *New Jerusalem Magazine* in London; and so thought Edward Beaman almost a century after the Sierra Leone scheme had been aborted and amidst many an American Swedenborgian New Jerusalem. Wrote Beaman in 1881, 'As with Moses when he came to the "Mountain of God, to Horeb", so with the loving, rational, regenerated humanity of this New Jerusalem age, as it rises to its spiritual mountain state; not only the "bush will burn with fire", but every tree, every plant, every hill and mountain and valley, every landscape, every flowing stream, every raindrop, every pebble even, "will burn" with the presence of God as the very Spirit of Truth, will glow with living fire, and yet will not be "consumed" '.[35] I think also recently of Tom Robbins' 1990 novel, *Skinny Legs and All*, in which the artist Boomer Petway is invited to install his work, *Ministry of Covert Operations*, in a Jerusalem gallery; he is dubious, for to him Jerusalem 'was founded in Sunday school and developed on the six o'clock news', and was 'not a place anyone actually visited', but his friend Ultima thinks it will be good for his career.[36]

3. Last Place as the last remaining place, where survivors gather/Last Time as a perpetually last chance.
    I think here of Rua Kenana Hepetipa (baptized Hephzibah), who in 1907 gathered together members of the devastated Tuhoe and Whakatohea tribes to build a Maori City of Redemption at the foot of the sacred mountain Maungapohatu. They called themselves *Iharaira*, Israelites, and *morehu*, the remnant, in fulfillment of the 1885 prophecy of the founder of Ringatu faith that his successor would restore the land confiscated by white settlers and make that land (the richest and most fertile) once again fruitful. Rua's own house, in this community of 500, was a double-gabled house of sawn timber called New Jerusalem; the meetinghouse, modeled upon a color lithograph of the Dome of the Rock and impressively circular, was called *Hiona*, Zion. The city was to thrive because it would be the terminus of a railroad line; Maori chieftains had been persuaded by Rua to grant large tracts of land to the British in return for promises of the building of a road and a railroad line 18 miles up from the last junction.

When this did not happen, Maungapohatu the City broke up, in 1914, then was reconstituted in September of 1915, Rua boasting, 'I am able to destroy the Temple of God, and rebuild it, in three days'. With the new temple came a new covenant and British arrest. Rua returned from prison in 1918 to find himself competing with a Presbyterian mission, but in 1926, when the Presbyterians left, he and a faithful remnant once more rebuilt Maungapohatu,which lasted into the 1930s only to succumb to high infant mortality rates, potato crop failures, and British passive aggression toward a Maori version of a modern, if not new, Jerusalem.[37]

4. *Last Place as the most unreachable place, on the edge of the known world/Last Time as the hardest test or stretch of faith, on the edge of a new world.*
   I think here of the lines from Seneca's tragedy, *Medea,*

> There will come an era in the following years
> During which Ocean will loose the chains
> Of things, when Tethys will reveal new worlds,
> And Thule not be a limit to the lands.

These are the lines that Columbus wrote into his *Libro de la profeciás* and which became such a stumbling block, Columbus refusing for years to acknowledge that new continents stood in the way of an imminent redemption. These are the lines that Washington Irving put as epigraph to his *History of the Life and Voyages of Christopher Columbus,* from which Edgar Allan Poe would draw the first stanza of his 1844 'Dream-Land',

> By a route obscure and lonely,
> Haunted by ill angels only,
> Where an Eidolon, named NIGHT,
> On a black throne reigns upright,
> I have reached these lands but newly
> From an ultimate dim Thule—
> From a wild weird clime that lieth, sublime,
> Out of SPACE—out of TIME.[38]

I think here also of that other 'Dream-Land' in a remote part of Northeast Brazil, Canudos, built by followers of Antonio Conselheiro, who expected the end of the world in 1900 and urged in the meantime a frontier New Jerusalem. Pounded to the ground by Brazilian artillery, Canudos disappeared into legend but resurfaced recently with Revd Sun Yung Moon, who has ratified himself as successor to Jesus Christ and in 1994 began purchasing a two-million-acre tract in the Brazilian jungle along 300 miles of the border with Paraguay, for a 'New Hope Ranch' whose community of 200 souls is meant to demonstrate the Moonish millennial wisdom of a new way of life, under an archway reading, 'Welcome to the Garden of Eden'.[39]

5. *Last Place as Treasurehold, the Full Place, beyond which one need not look/Last Time as Fullness, the Completion of Time, beyond which one need not go.*

I think here of Zion City, founded by John Alexander Dowie in 1899. Dowie began as a down-at-the-heels healer in Australia, moved to the States, built up a national following and a team of business investors. His ministry of healing became prophetic, his ambitions theocratic and corporate. Dowie's headquarters were in Chicago's Imperial Hotel, renamed Zion, and then on 6,500 acres on the shores of Lake Michigan north of Chicago, in a place still called Zion. If the City was a utopia, it was the kind of utopia imagined by sociologists and benevolent industrialists in the late-nineteenth century, a Peaceable Kingdom of workers and bosses, carpenters and investors. The Temple site at Zion was consecrated in the summer of the centurial year, 1900. 'Inside of five years', said Dowie, 'you will see a city of twenty-thousand inhabitants here, and in twenty years there will be two hundred thousand people.' One may be surprised that he did not estimate 144,000 people, a more conventional figure for the number of elect, from the Book of Revelation, but Dowie had no use for such limits; he was an expansionist, and Zion City was all about the in-dwelling spirit of capitalism, its fullness of place. Paradoxically, the gradual decline of the City as a millennial enterprise was due in good measure to Dowie's rejection of the fullness of capitalist time; Dowie learned to rely upon capitalist wealth, but he shunned those instruments of interest and credit by which industrialists and financiers consolidated their fortunes. Only he the prophet must be in charge of the fullness of time.[40]

6. *Last Place as universal Mausoleum: A final resting place/Last Time as Millennium: A final rest.*

I think here of a recent poem by Jean Nordhaus, 'From a Window in Jerusalem',[41] in which

> I watch the cold city
> revive and think of
> my own dead. Even before we put
> them in the earth, the bones
> began to crumble in their bodies.
> Now they walk my feet
> over stony hills…

It seems to me that, with regard to Jerusalem, a longing for rest can be apocalyptic without being catastrophic, for it may simply be a longing—a Viking, Icelandic longing—for the end to a feud. Ultima Thule may be a place in which or from which one seeks not resurrection but reconciliation. I think in this context of American astronaut Thomas Stafford choosing Psalm 122 as text for his Sunday sermon in orbit in 1969.[42] He could not see Jerusalem from the Ultima Thule of space, but still he celebrated its symbolic reunification:

> Our feet shall stand within thy gates, O Jerusalem.

Jerusalem is builded as a city that is compact together; or, in the more exuberant translation from the *Jerusalem Bible*,

> And now our feet are standing
> in your gateways, Jerusalem.
> Jerusalem restored! The city
> one united whole!

Seventh, for the 7 Gates of Jerusalem, and of course last,

7. Last Place as Land's End: The place beyond which, nothing more is to be found—the vanishing point/Last Time as History's End: The time beyond which, nothing more is to be done—the asymptote.

I think here of a recent exhibition at Baltimore's Museum of Visionary Art, 'The End is Near!'[43] Previously on exhibit as part of the permanent collection of the works of self-taught and often obsessive artists has had been a 1974 drawing by Peter Minchell, 'Economic Downfall of the Earth', where the year 2000 is marked 'Nihil', nothing, or the end of everything. Among the paintings and drawings of the 56 featured artists, fantastical Jerusalems erupted, exploded, and rose crystalline from exorbitant ashes—as they always do, appearing on far horizons wherever one comes, by carragh or collage, to Land's End in the Christian West. But these Jerusalems came in company with fantastical cosmogonies that appear whenever one arrives at what appears to be the end of history. Born too young to fly a plane in World War I and too old to be a pilot in World War II, Leslie Payne— black, poor, uneducated, uninstructed in the technology of flight—began building planes of his own. They had no innards, no engines, but they were lifesize and they sized his life as 'Airplane Blayne', who in flight suit and goggles recorded his imaginary flights in a log book of 'The Four Winds of Heaven', complete with photographs, maps, drawings, postcards and descriptions of his journeys. Truly he flew beyond the Ultima Thule and truly he made time his own.

'In Ultima Thule', writes the poet Timothy Russell,[44]

The lithe dancer up on her toes
could be another Pandora bringing a small gift,
and there is the oldest man in the world, hatless,
carrying his fishing pole on his shoulder
the same way he has for a thousand years.

Bibliography

Adrichem, Christiaan van, *A Briefe Description of Hierusalem & of the Suburbs Thereof, As It Florished in the Time of Christ* (London: Thomas Wight, 1595).

Ajami, Fouad, 'Rediscovering Jerusalem', *U.S. News & World Report* (8 March, 1993), 74.

Ambjörnsson, Ronny, trans. J. Heyun, ' "La Republic de Dieu": une utopie suédoise de 1789', *Annales historiques de la Révolution française* 277 (1989), 244-73.

American Visionary Art Museum, *The End Is Near! Visions of Apocalypse Millennium and Utopia* (Los Angeles: Dilettante, 1998).

Bagge, Sverre, *Society and Politics in Snorri Sturluson's 'Heimskringla'* (Berkeley, CA: University of California, 1991).

Barthélemy, Dominique, 'L'intégration de l'espace et du temps dans la nouvelle Jérusalem', in Daniel Marguerat and Jean Zumstein (eds.), *La Mémoire et le temps* (Geneva: Labor et Fides, 1991), 179-92.

Batalov, A.L., and T.N. Viatchanina, 'The Moral Significance and Interpretation of the Image of Jerusalem in Russian Architecture of the Sixteenth and Seventeenth Centuries', *Arkhiteckturnoe Nasledstvo* 36 (1988), 22-42.

Beaman, Edmund A., *Swedenborg and the New Age; or 'The Holy City of New Jerusalem'* (New York: AMS, 1971 [1881]).

Benvenisti, Meron, *City of Stone: The Hidden History of Jerusalem* (Berkeley, CA: University of California, 1996).

Billington, Ray Allen, *The Genesis of the Frontier Thesis* (San Marino, CA: Huntington Library, 1971).

Binney, Judith, 'Maungapohatu Revisited; or, How the Government Underdeveloped a Maori Community', *Journal of the Polynesian Society* 92.3 (1983), 353-92.

Blowers, Paul M., ' "Living in a Land of Prophets": James T. Barclay and an Early Disciples of Christ Mission to Jews in the Holy Land', *Church History* 62.4 (1993), 494-513.

Brennan, Joseph P., 'Jerusalem – A Christian Perspective', in John M. Oesterreicher and Anne Sinai (eds.), *Jerusalem* (New York: Day, 1974), 226-30.

Burton, Richard Francis, *Ultima Thule; or, A Summer in Iceland*, I (London: Nimmo, 1875).

Byock, Jesse L., *Medieval Iceland: Society, Sagas, and Power* (Berkeley, CA: University of California, 1988).

Chateaubriand, François August René; G. Moulinier and A. Outrey (eds.), *Journal de Jérusalem: notes inédites* (Paris: Belin, 1950).

Chernoff, Richard Z., 'God's City', *U.S. News & World Report* (18 December, 1995), 62ff.

Chesterton, G.K., *The New Jerusalem* (London: Hodder & Stoughton, [1920]).

Colón, Cristóbal; Consuelo Varela (ed.), *Textos y documentos completos* (Madrid: Alianza Editorial, 2nd edn, 1984).

Cook, Philip L., *Zion City, Illinois: Twentieth Century Utopia* (Syracuse, NY: Syracuse University, 1996).

Elon, Amos, *Jerusalem: City of Mirrors* (Boston: Little, Brown, 1989).

Flaubert, Gustave, *Notes de voyage*, in *Oeuvres complètes* (Paris: Conard, 1910–54), XIX, 147.

Friedland, Roger, and Richard D. Hecht, 'The Politics of Sacred Space: Jerusalem's Temple Mount/al-haram al-sharif', in Jamie Scott and Paul Simpson-Housley (eds.), *Sacred Spaces and Profane Places: Essays in the Geographics of Judaism, Christianity and Islam* (Westport: Greenwood, 1991), 21-62.

—'The Politics of Time and Space in Jerusalem: Interest, Symbol and Power', in Sabrina P. Ramet and Donald W. Treadgold (eds.), *Render unto Caesar: The Religious Sphere in World Politics* (Washington, DC: American University, 1995), 373-424.

Gamini, Gabriella, 'Brazilians turn heat on Moonies' swamp heaven', London (Sunday) *Times* (18 August, 2002); consulted 3 July, 2003 on the internet at http://www.rickross.com/reference/unif/unif180.html.

Goldsmith, Steven, *Unbuilding Jerusalem: Apocalypse and Romantic Representation* (Ithaca, NY: Cornell, 1993).

Gorenberg, Gershom, *The End of Days: Fundamentalism and the Struggle for the Temple Mount* (New York: Free Press, 2000).

Grindea, M., (ed.), *The Images of Jerusalem: A Literary Chronicle of Three Thousand Years* (Rochester: University of Rochester, 1968).

Hiestand, Emily, 'South of the Ultima Thule', *Georgia Review* 46.2 (Summer 1992), 289-343.

Hoornaert, Eduardo, *Os anjos de Canudos: uma revisão histórica* (Petrópolis: Editora Vozes, 2nd edn, 1997).

Horne, Alexander, *King Solomon's Temple in the Masonic Tradition* (London: Bayliss, 1972).

Iroe-Grego, Mage, *La veritable magie noire, ou, le secret des secrets: manuscrit trouvé à Jerusalem dans le sepulcre de Salomon* (Rome: Garcia, 1750).

Klatzker, David, 'American Catholic Travelers to the Holy Land, 1861–1929', *Catholic Historical Review* 74.1 (1988), 55-74.

Kochav, Sarah, 'The Search for a Protestant Holy Sepulchre: The Garden Tomb in Nineteenth-Century Jerusalem', *Journal of Ecclesiastical History* 46.2 (1995), 278-301.

Larner, John, 'The Certainty of Columbus', *History* 73 (1988), 19-21.

Lee, Rebecca, 'The Jerusalem Syndrome', *Atlantic Monthly* 275 (May 1995), 24ff.

Levine, Robert M., *Vale of Tears: Revisiting the Canudos Massacre in Northeastern Brazil, 1893–1897* (Berkeley, CA: University of California Press, 1992).

Lippy, Charles H., *The Christadelphians in North America* (Lewiston, NY: Mellen, 1989).

Llosa, Mario Vargas, *The War of the End of the World* (trans. Helen R. Lane; New York: Farrar Straus Giroux, 1984).

Magnusson, Magnus, *Iceland Saga* (London: Bodley Head, 1987).

Mahan, Alfred T., *Retrospect and Prospect* (Boston: Little, Brown, 1902).

McKernan, Luke, ' "The Supreme Moment of the War": General Allenby's Entry into Jerusalem', *Historical Journal of Film, Radio and Television* 13.2 (1993), 169-81.

Melville, Herman; Howard C. Horsford (ed.), *Journal of a Visit to Europe and the Levant, October 11, 1856–May 6, 1857* (Princeton, NJ: Princeton University Press, 1955).

Meyers, Mary Ann, *A New World Jerusalem: The Swedenborgian Experience in Community Construction* (Westport, CT: Greenwood, 1983).

Nordhaus, Jean, 'From a Window in Jerusalem', *Poetry* 163 (October 1993), 33.

Peters, F.E., *Jerusalem: The Holy City in the Eyes of Chroniclers, Visitors, Pilgrims and Prophets from the Days of Abraham to the Beginnings of Modern Times* (Princeton, NJ: Princeton University, 1985).

Pieterse, Jan Nederveen, 'The History of a Metaphor: Christian Zionism and the Politics of Apocalypse', *Archives de sciences sociales des religions* 75 (July–September 1991), 75-103

Richardson, Ethel Florence Lindesay ['Henry Handel'], *Ultima Thule* (London: W. Heinemann, 1929).

Robbins, Tom, *Skinny Legs and All* (New York: Bantam, 1990), 205.

Röder-Bolton, Gerlinde, 'Conrad, Goethe, and the King of Ultima-Thule', *Conradiana* 24.1 (1992), 41-45.

Ronnick, Michele V., 'Seneca's "Medea" and Ultima Thule in Poe's "Dream-Land" ', *Poe Studies – Dark Romanticism* 27.1-2 (1994), 40-42.

Ross, J.M., 'The Spelling of Jerusalem in Acts', *New Testament Studies* 38.3 (1992), 474-76.

Rozen, Minna, and Eliezer Witztum, 'The Dark Mirror of the Soul: Dreams of a Jewish Physician in Jerusalem at the End of the Seventeenth Century', *Revue des études juives* 151.1-2 (1992), 5-42.

Russell, Timothy, 'In Ultima Thule', *Poetry* 163.3 (1993), 138.

Scherman, Katharine, *Daughter of Fire: A Portrait of Iceland* (Boston: Little, Brown, 1976).

Schoon, Simon, 'Christian Attitudes toward Israel and Jerusalem', in David Burrell and Yehezkel Landau (eds.), *Voices from Jerusalem* (New York: Paulist Press, 1992), 91-106.

Schütz, Christiane, *Preussen in Jerusalem (1800–1861)* (Berlin: Mann, 1988).

Sharif, Regina, *Non-Jewish Zionism: Its Roots in Western History* (London: Zed, 1983).

Shepherd, Naomi, *The Zealous Intruders: The Western Rediscovery of Palestine* (San Francisco: Harper & Row, 1987).

Shils, Edward, 'Center and Periphery: An Idea and its Career, 1935–1987', in Liah Greenfeld and Michel Martin (eds.), *Center: Ideas and Institutions* (Chicago: University of Chicago Press, 1988), 250-75ff.

Silberman, Neil A., *Digging for God and Country: Exploration, Archeology, and the Secret Struggle for the Holy Land, 1799–1917* (New York: Knopf, 1982).

Smith, Jonathan Z., *To Take Place: Toward Theory in Ritual* (Chicago: University of Chicago Press, 1987).

Solovyov, Vladimir, *War, Progress, and the End of History* (trans. A. Bakshy and Thomas R. Beyer, Jr; Hudson, NY: Lindisfarne, 1990 [1900]).

Suriano, Francesco, *Treatise on the Holy Land* (trans. T. Bellorini and E. Hoade; Jerusalem: Franciscan Press, 1949 [1516]).

Sweet, Leonard I., 'Christopher Columbus and the Millennial Vision of the New World', *Catholic Historical Review* 72 (1986), 369-82.

Tasso, Torquato, *Godfrey of Bulloigne; or, The Recoverie of Jerusalem* (trans. Edward Fairefax; London: Jaggard and Lownes, 1600).

Troyat, Henri, *Divided Soul: The Life of Gogol* (trans. N. Amphoux; Garden City, NY: Doubleday, 1973).

Turner, Victor, *Dramas, Fields, and Metaphors* (Ithaca, NY: Cornell, 1974).

Twain, Mark, *The Innocents Abroad* (London: Ward Lock, 1910 [1872]).

Wallerstein, Immanuel, *The End of the World as We Know I: Social Science for the Twenty-First Century* (Minneapolis, MN: University of Minnesota Press, 1999).

Wardi, Charles, (ed.), *Christian News from Jerusalem* 20 (June 1969), 22.

Warren, Charles, *Underground Jerusalem* (London: Bentley, 1876).

Watts, Pauline M., 'Prophecy and Discovery: On the Spiritual Origins of Christopher Columbus's "Enterprise of the Indies" ', *American Historical Review* 90 (1985), 73-102.

Wilson, Bryan R., *Sects and Society: A Sociological Study of the Elim Tabernacle, Christian Science, and Christadelphians* (Berkeley, CA: University of California, 1961).

Wright, Stephen K., *The Vengeance of Our Lord: Medieval Dramatizations of the Destruction of Jerusalem* (Toronto: Pontifical Institute of Medieval Studies, 1989).

Yiftachel, Oren, and Avinoam Meir (eds.), *Ethnic Frontiers and Peripheries: Landscapes of Development and Inequality in Israel* (Boulder: Westview, 1996).

Notes

1.   Rebecca Lee, 'The Jerusalem Syndrome', *Atlantic Monthly* 275 (May 1995), 24ff. An earlier historical form is hypothesized by Minna Rozen and Eliezer Witztum, 'The Dark Mirror of the Soul: Dreams of a Jewish Physician in Jerusalem at the End of the Seventeenth Century', *Revue des études juives* 151.1-2 (1992), 5-42.

2.   Emily Hiestand, 'South of the Ultima Thule', *Georgia Review* 46.2 (Summer 1992), 289-343, quotes at 292, 298, 320, 323, 324 and 325.

3.   This is the Greek geographer and historian Strabo, as quoted in Richard Francis Burton, *Ultima Thule; or, A Summer in Iceland* (London: Nimmo, 1875), I, 3.

4.   Burton, *Ultima Thule*, 31ff. for derivations.

5.   Katharine Scherman, *Daughter of Fire: A Portrait of Iceland* (Boston: Little, Brown, 1976), 71.

6.   See Sverre Bagge, *Society and Politics in Snorri Sturluson's 'Heimskringla'* (Berkeley, CA: University of California, 1991); Jesse L. Byock, *Medieval Iceland: Society, Sagas, and Power* (Berkeley, CA: University of California, 1988).

7.   For this and next paragraph, see Scherman, *Daughter of Fire*, 70-72 on the Brendan legends, 136-39 on son-in-law Kaspar Peucer, citing his *De Dimensione Terrae* (1550). Cf. Magnus Magnusson, *Iceland Saga* (London: Bodley Head, 1987), 3, a map of Iceland made in 1585 showing Mount Hekla erupting, labeled, 'Hekla, cursed with eternal fires and snow, vomits rocks with a hideous sound'.

8.   F.E. Peters, *Jerusalem: The Holy City in the Eyes of Chroniclers, Visitors, Pilgrims and Prophets from the Days of Abraham to the Beginnings of Modern Times* (Princeton, NJ: Princeton University, 1985), 456. Cf. M. Grindea (ed.), *The Images of Jerusalem: A Literary Chronicle of Three Thousand Years* (Rochester: University of Rochester, 1968).

9.   Torquato Tasso, *Godfrey of Bulloigne; or, The Recoverie of Jerusalem* (trans. Edward Fairefax; London: Jaggard and Lownes, 1600), Book 17, stanza 61.

10.   Magnusson, *Iceland Saga*, 141 (sound of the churn); Burton, *Ultima Thule*, I, epigraph, ix; Peters, *Jerusalem*, 456.

11.   On the prophetic role Columbus imagined for himself with particular regard for Jerusalem, see Cristóbal Colón; Consuelo Varela (ed.), *Textos y documentos completos* (Madrid: Alianza Editorial, 2nd edn, 1984), 279-91 for his 'Libro de las Profecías'; Pauline M. Watts, 'Prophecy and Discovery: On the Spiritual Origins of Christopher Columbus's "Enterprise of the Indies"', *American Historical Review* 90 (1985), 73-102; Leonard I. Sweet, 'Christopher Columbus and the Millennial Vision of the New World', *Catholic Historical Review* 72 (1986), 369-82; John Larner, 'The Certainty of Columbus', *History* 73 (1988), 19-21; Peters, *Jerusalem*, 503-504.

12.   Christiaan van Adrichem, *A Briefe Description of Hierusalem & of the Suburbs Thereof, As It Florished in the Time of Christ* (London: Thomas Wight, 1595), preface. Van Adrichem's spelling was not idiosyncratic; he was aligning himself with the vision

of the city as developed by Matthew, Mark, and John, who used the Greek form of the name, 'Hierosolyma'; Luke shared a more 'Jewish' vision and used the Hebrew form, 'J/Yerousalem' (modern Hebrew: Yerushalaim). See J.M. Ross, 'The Spelling of Jerusalem in *Acts*', *New Testament Studies* 38.3 (1992), 474-76. More broadly, see Revd Joseph P. Brennan, 'Jerusalem – A Christian Perspective', in Msgr. John M. Oesterreicher and Anne Sinai (eds.), *Jerusalem* (New York: Day, 1974), 226-30.

13. Peters, *Jerusalem*, 563; François August René Chateaubriand; G. Moulinier and A. Outrey (eds.), *Journal de Jérusalem: notes inédites* (Paris: Belin, 1950), 140.

14. Henri Troyat, *Divided Soul: The Life of Gogol* (trans. N. Amphoux; Garden City, NY: Doubleday, 1973), 372-73.

15. Amos Elon, *Jerusalem: City of Mirrors* (Boston: Little, Brown, 1989), 137.

16. Elon, *Jerusalem*, 140, for Lamartine; Gustave Flaubert, *Notes de voyage*, in *Oeuvres complètes* (Paris: Conard, 1910–54), XIX, 147.

17. Herman Melville; ed. Howard C. Horsford (ed.), *Journal of a Visit to Europe and the Levant, October 11, 1856–May 6, 1857* (Princeton, NJ: Princeton University Press, 1955), 140-61, quotes at 140, 144, 148-49. This aesthetic mood and mode of description was not new; indeed, it belonged to quite an august tradition; see Stephen K. Wright, *The Vengeance of Our Lord: Medieval Dramatizations of the Destruction of Jerusalem* (Toronto: Pontifical Institute of Medieval Studies, 1989).

18. Elon, *Jerusalem*, 14, 22, 141.

19. See A.L. Batalov and T.N. Viatchanina, 'The Moral Significance and Interpretation of the Image of Jerusalem in Russian Architecture of the Sixteenth and Seventeenth Centuries', *Arkhiteckturnoe Nasledstvo* 36 (1988), 22-42. The Russian Christian apocalypticist Vladimir Solovyov predicted that the imperial capital would be transferred from Rome to Jerusalem in the late-twentieth century, and all cults would be unified at the Temple Mount by the antichrist Apollonius, who claims to be the last savior and judge of the Universe: *War, Progress, and the End of History* (trans. A. Bakshy and Thomas R. Beyer, Jr; Hudson, NY: Lindisfarne, 1990 [1900]), 176-80.

20. See Neil A. Silberman, *Digging for God and Country: Exploration, Archeology, and the Secret Struggle for the Holy Land, 1799–1917* (New York: Knopf, 1982); Regina Sharif, *Non-Jewish Zionism: Its Roots in Western History* (London: Zed, 1983); Paul M. Blowers, ' "Living in a Land of Prophets": James T. Barclay and an Early Disciples of Christ Mission to Jews in the Holy Land', *Church History* 62.4 (1993), 494-513.

21. Naomi Shepherd, *The Zealous Intruders: The Western Rediscovery of Palestine* (San Francisco: Harper & Row, 1987); Fouad Ajami, 'Rediscovering Jerusalem', *U.S. News & World Report* (8 March 1993), 74, on Alexander II; Richard Z. Chernoff, 'God's City', *U.S. News & World Report* (18 December, 1995), 62ff. On German architecture for Jerusalem, see also Christiane Schütz, *Preussen in Jerusalem (1800–1861)* (Berlin: Mann, 1988).

22. G.K. Chesterton, *The New Jerusalem* (London: Hodder & Stoughton, [1920]), 4-7; Luke McKernan, ' "The Supreme Moment of the War": General Allenby's Entry into Jerusalem', *Historical Journal of Film, Radio and Television* 13.2 (1993), 169-81.

23. Chesterton, *New Jerusalem*, 60, 73.

24. See in this context David Klatzker, 'American Catholic Travelers to the Holy Land, 1861–1929', *Catholic Historical Review* 74.1 (1988), 55-74, noting Pope Leo XIII's 'unusual interest in the Holy Land'.

25. Sarah Kochav, 'The search for a Protestant Holy Sepulchre: The Garden Tomb in Nineteenth-Century Jerusalem', *Journal of Ecclesiastical History* 46.2 (1995), 278-301.

26. *Oxford English Dictionary* (1971), Supplement, 45, *sive* 'Middle', citing Alfred T. Mahan, *Retrospect and Prospect* (Boston: Little, Brown, 1902), 237.

27. Mark Twain, *The Innocents Abroad* (London: Ward Lock, 1910 [1872]), 565. Cartographically as well as spiritually and ritually, Jerusalem has often been placed at the center, no more emphatically than in Francesco Suriano's *Treatise on the Holy Land* (trans. T. Bellorini and E. Hoade; Jerusalem: Franciscan Press, 1949 [1516]), where Suriano argues, 100, that Jerusalem is the Middle of the World, 3,200 miles distant from the extreme East, 3,300 miles from the extreme West of Gibraltar, 3,100 from the end of Asia, 3,200 from the end of Ethiopia, and 3,200 from the end of Europe, Norway. Establishing a center by reference to its ends, of course, is simply the obverse of the Land's End motif.

28. Charles Warren, *Underground Jerusalem* (London: Bentley, 1876), 93, 256.

29. See Edward Shils, 'Center and Periphery: An Idea and its Career, 1935–1987', in Liah Greenfeld and Michel Martin (eds.), *Center: Ideas and Institutions* (Chicago: University of Chicago Press, 1988), 250-75ff.; Victor Turner, *Dramas, Fields, and Metaphors* (Ithaca, NY: Cornell, 1974), 231-70 et *passim* on liminality.

30. Frederick Jackon Turner's highly influential theory about the end of the American frontier was proposed in the 1890s, for which see Ray Allen Billington, *The Genesis of the Frontier Thesis* (San Marino, CA: Huntington Library, 1971). Immanuel Wallerstein's equally influential geopolitical theory about centers and peripheries within a shifting 'world-system' came to a head in 1999 with his *The End of the World as We Know It: Social Science for the Twenty-First Century* (Minneapolis, MN: University of Minnesota Press, 1999). Most apt to cite with regard to Jerusalem might be Oren Yiftachel and Avinoam Meir (eds.), *Ethnic Frontiers and Peripheries: Landscapes of Development and Inequality in Israel* (Boulder: Westview, 1996).

31. Notable exceptions: Roger Friedland and Richard D. Hecht, 'The Politics of Sacred Space: Jerusalem's Temple Mount/al-haram al-sharif', Jamie Scott and Paul Simpson-Housley (eds.), *Sacred Spaces and Profane Places: Essays in the Geographics of Judaism, Christianity and Islam* (Westport: Greenwood, 1991), 21-62; idem, 'The Politics of Time and Space in Jerusalem: Interest, Symbol and Power', in Sabrina P. Ramet and Donald W. Treadgold (eds.), *Render unto Caesar: The Religious Sphere in World Politics* (Washington, DC: American University, 1995), 373-424; Jonathan Z. Smith, *To Take Place: Toward Theory in Ritual* (Chicago: University of Chicago Press, 1987); Dominique Barthélemy, 'L'intégration de l'espace et du temps dans la nouvelle Jérusalem', in Daniel Marguerat and Jean Zumstein (eds.), *La Mémoire et le temps* (Geneva: Labor + Fides, 1991), 179-92. See Steven Goldsmith, *Unbuilding Jerusalem: Apocalypse and Romantic Representation* (Ithaca, NY: Cornell, 1993) for a literary pass.

32. Nonetheless, a neat convergence of Ultima Thule and the Antipodes (understood, post-1800, as the 'down under' of Australia) may be found in Ethel Florence Lindesay ['Henry Handel'] Richardson's *Ultima Thule* (London: W. Heinemann, 1929), the final novel in her trilogy, *The Fortunes of Richard Mahony*, in which the hero, financially ruined, finds himself at many ultimate ends in the Australian countryside.

33. Meron Benvenisti, *City of Stone: The Hidden History of Jerusalem* (Berkeley, CA: University of California, 1996), 72; Elon, *Jerusalem*, 12,106, 110-11, 223 and 147-48 on Gordon; Bryan R. Wilson, *Sects and Society: A Sociological Study of the Elim Tabernacle, Christian Science, and Christadelphians* (Berkeley, CA: University of California, 1961); Charles H. Lippy, *The Christadelphians in North America* (Lewiston, NY: Mellen, 1989). Masonry also had a well-cemented tradition of modeling the Temple; see Alexander Horne, *King Solomon's Temple in the Masonic Tradition* (London: Bayliss, 1972), esp. 54-56. For divergent perspectives on evangelical Zionism and its relationship to Jerusalem, see Jan Nederveen Pieterse, 'The History of a Metaphor: Christian Zionism and the Politics of Apocalypse', *Archives de sciences sociales des religions* 75 (July-September 1991), 75-103; Simon Schoon, 'Christian Attitudes toward Israel and Jerusalem', in David Burrell and Yehezkel Landau (eds.), *Voices from Jerusalem* (New York: Paulist Press, 1992), 91-106; Gershom Gorenberg, *The End of Days: Fundamentalism and the Struggle for the Temple Mount* (New York: Free Press, 2000).

34. Mage Iroe-Grego, *La veritable magie noire, ou, le secret des secrets: manuscrit trouvé à Jerusalem dans le sepulcre de Salomon* (Rome: Garcia, 1750).

35. Ronny Ambjörnsson, trans. J. Heyun, ' "La Republic de Dieu": une utopie suédoise de 1789', *Annales historiques de la Révolution française* 277 (1989), 244-73; Edmund A. Beaman, *Swedenborg and the New Age; or, The Holy City of New Jerusalem* (New York: AMS, 1971 [1881]), 181; Mary Ann Meyers, *A New World Jerusalem: The Swedenborgian Experience in Community Construction* (Westport, CT: Greenwood, 1983).

36. Tom Robbins, *Skinny Legs and All* (New York: Bantam, 1990), 205.

37. Judith Binney, 'Maungapohatu Revisited; or, How the Government Underdeveloped a Maori Community,' *Journal of the Polynesian Society* 92.3 (1983), 353-92.

38. Michele V. Ronnick, 'Seneca's "Medea" and Ultima Thule in Poe's "Dream-Land" ', *Poe Studies—Dark Romanticism* 27.1-2 (1994), 40-42. Another recurrent literary motif is assessed by Gerlinde Röder-Bolton, 'Conrad, Goethe, and the King of Ultima-Thule', *Conradiana* 24.1 (1992), 41-45.

39. See Eduardo Hoornaert, *Os anjos de Canudos: uma revisão histórica* (Petrópolis: Editora Vozes, 2nd edn, 1997); Robert M. Levine, *Vale of Tears: Revisiting the Canudos Massacre in Northeastern Brazil, 1893–1897* (Berkeley, CA: University of California Press, 1992), and, fictionalized, Mario Vargas Llosa, *The War of the End of the World* (trans. Helen R. Lane; New York: Farrar Straus Giroux, 1984). For the Unification Church's 'New Hope Ranch' on 2 million acres in northern Brazil, see Gabriella Gamini, 'Brazilians turn heat on Moonies' swamp heaven', London (Sunday) *Times* (18 August, 2002), consulted 3 July, 2003 at http://www.rickross.com/reference/unif/unif180.html.

40. Philip L. Cook, *Zion City, Illinois: Twentieth Century Utopia* (Syracuse, NY: Syracuse University, 1996).

41. Jean Nordhaus, 'From a Window in Jerusalem', *Poetry* 163 (October 1993), 33.

42. Charles Wardi (ed.), *Christian News from Jerusalem* 20 (June 1969), 22 (published by the Israeli Ministry of Religious Affairs, Jerusalem).

43. American Visionary Art Museum, *The End Is Near! Visions of Apocalypse Millennium and Utopia* (Los Angeles: Dilettante, 1998).

44. Timothy Russell, 'In Ultima Thule', *Poetry* 163.3 (1993), 138.

International Radio

Thomas MacKay

For R

So late, so early, this is in between hours. I'm leaving,
wrenching myself from a gargoyle of sleep, swollen-eyed.
The summered husk of the city is simple and remembers night
enough to still have the streetlights on. My clothes are wooden on my skin.

We're done, we're all we needed to do. The radio's loud
and filled with news of German importance.
The taxi dispatcher dispatches.

This mantle of the Traveler isn't so comfortable, but it is a steeling rule.
An ascesis as stiff as the Tarot, my movements are spare,
and my silences, I'd like to think,
arch and flower cathedrally. I want the world a clockwork
that produces rivulets of the unclocked, the unzoned,
I want the watch over memories and movements of world rituals, maybe
    to read
my own flower of departure.

Unevent the time? This strange summer hour is a released grip on my arm
and it is a broken calendar. Our last season was my wrecked gray February,
your grieving April earlier. I may want to pass out of months into a room
    of omens
but my goodbye city makes me wait for my cab, my plane ticket
makes me wait for the sky, and I'm left with the terminal
that just wishes it could be monastic.

All the doubt of reverie. The city you leave
advertises itself as visitable; wide bright kiosk wall of hotels pictures, beds,
appointed lamps and views. Dreamed dreams won't fill the space.

I left the radio running; I want a current of other places, I want
this little finale of place, the world the sum of air and light
beneath shuddering metal wings.
I want strange names to catch me like dust.

Glossary

art of memory: in extant texts, first described by Cicero; a technique for improving 'natural' memory by envisioning data as vivid images; the art of memory was cultivated from antiquity to the late Renaissance and, in the acts of magicians and mind-readers, well beyond.

apocalypse: usually based on Biblical prophecy, the final showdown between the forces of good and evil that will result in the end of history and usually the ushering in of the millennium; also, from the Greek and more neutrally, to unveil or reveal.

carnivalesque: from literary theory, a celebration of the grotesque marked by inversions of dominant and marginal voices, upper and lower body, high and low culture; a temporary space in which subversive opinions may be aired and acted out.

cosmos [also, *kosmos*]: ancient Greek word meaning order, ornament, world-order and universe; in later Greek, *cosmos* is a synonym for *oikoumene*, the known or inhabited world.

Daniel, book of: from the Hebrew scriptures, a central prophetic text describing the apocalypse, characterized by a radical dualism between the forces of good and evil and the use of allegory and fantastic imagery to refer to historical personages and eras.

disappointment, millennial: a period following an expected end of days when believers grapple with the loss or delay of their expected reward, whether personal redemption or collective transformation; often associated with 'cognitive dissonance,' a social-psychological term referring to the process by which believers handle growing discrepancies between their anticipations and actual events, so as to protect their overall set of expectations from collapse.

dystopia: an imagined or perceived place characterized by suffering, angst, or terror; generally used as the antonym to utopia.

end time: in apocalyptic or millennial rhetoric, the period immediately before the final coming of the apocalypse, an epoch usually characterized by tumult and confusion; also, sometimes used to refer to the end of chronological or calendar time that the apocalypse is expected to declare, in which humanity will no longer experience the ravages or reversals of time.

epistemology: the study of the nature and foundations of knowledge

eschatology: a doctrine or theology that is concerned with the end of the world or the 'last things' (the *eschaton*)

Hegelian dialectical time: an early-nineteenth-century philosophical concept that refers to an objective, continuous, progressive notion of time that is worked out by means of thesis, antithesis, and synthesis—in other words, through a series of historical movements and counter-movements, whether intellectual, political, economic, or religious.

liminality: from anthropological studies of rites of passage, the state of being 'betwixt and between', such as adolescence; a threshold beyond which conventional values no longer operate at full strength or a period during which the usual structured order of society or of time is disrupted, either by ritual fiat or extraordinary circumstance (natural catastrophe, sudden invasion).

millennium: technically, the thousand-year reign of Jesus on earth predicted in the book of Revelation, from the Latin for 1000 (*mille*); more commonly, the (usually future) state of perfection that will be inaugurated by the final days or endtime.

mnemotechnics: a strategy , plan, or system to aid the process of memory.

New Jerusalem: from the book of Revelation, the coming state of perfection that is literally or metaphorically an instantiation of a city of the faithful, beyond time and free of all suffering; the fulfillment of prophecy in the reaching of a Promised Land.

Nephilim: a race of giants referred to at Gen. 6.1-4 who, according to some Christian commentators, were the children of demon fathers and mortal mothers.

Occam's razor: the principle that, for any explanation or logical argument, no more assumptions should be made than are absolutely necessary.

pharmakon: from ancient Greek, a word that means both remedy and poison

predestination: a theological doctrine, elaborated by John Calvin (1509–1564), which claims that the salvation of the few (the faithful) has been no less predetermined by God than the damnation of the many (the sinners), and that no human behavior can influence or alter this divine determination.

pseudoscience: an umbrella term for any number of quasi-religious, fraudulent, or irreproducible claims made in the name of science; as-yet-unproven items of belief that are put forward as matters of fact.

Neoplatonism: philosophical or mystical developments of Plato's ideas, especially those that posit an ascending ladder of knowledge or a spiritual hierarchy in the experience of the divine, ranging from the strictly material to a (usually secret) apprehension of the ineffable.

Nietzschean genealogical time: a late-nineteenth-century philosophic construct that refers to a non-linear, discontinuous, and interruptive notion of time; opposed to or disjoint from Hegelian dialectical time.

rapture: in Christian apocalypticism, the moment of ecstatic transport at the end of times when the saved will be lifted bodily to heaven or into a celestial New Jerusalem.

soteriology: doctrine about, or study of notions about, salvation

transference: in Freudian thought, the unconscious projection of desire or emotions respecting one person onto a stand-in such as the analyst; the psychological displacement of feelings from their original or rightful target onto a substitute.

Tribulation or Great Tribulation: seven-year period prior to the visible Second Coming (*parousia*) of Christ during which the judgments described in the book of Revelation afflict the earth and humankind, except for those already saved.

utopia: from Thomas More's 1516 Greek pun on 'good place' (*eutopos*) and 'nowhere' *(outopos)*: a perfected space in which the conditions of living are optimal or even perfect; frequently used with reference to this-worldly experimental communities or theories of social engineering as well as to the post-apocalyptic existence of the redeemed in a millennial state.

Index

Printed in the United Kingdom
by Lightning Source UK Ltd.
119509UK00001B/101